EFFECTIVE WASHINGTON REPRESENTATION

EFFECTIVE WASHINGTON REPRESENTATION

edited by
Stanley J. Marcuss

Law & Business, Inc.
Harcourt Brace Jovanovich, Publishers

Printed in the United States of America

Library of Congress Cataloging in Publication Data
Main entry under title:
Effective Washington representation.
1. Administrative procedure — United States.
2. Representation in administrative proceedings — United
States. 3. Administrative agencies — United States.
4. Legislative bodies — United States. 5. Industry and
state — United States. I. Marcuss, Stanley J.
KF5402.E35 1983 342.73'066 83-5387
ISBN 0-15-004287-6 347.30266

*To Rosemary, Elena and Aidan
and all my other colleagues, associates
and friends whose learning and insights
are reflected in this book.*

ACKNOWLEDGMENTS

I wish to acknowledge first and foremost the publishers of this book who insisted that it could be done. Thereafter, acknowledgments are due to the contributors and to my former superiors and colleagues in Congress and the executive branch for insights conveyed under their tutelage, although tutors they surely did not intend to be. Finally, credit is due to my partners for their indulgence, to Elise O'Shaughnessy for the sensitivity to language that she displayed in reviewing portions of the manuscript, to Peter Halle for similar assistance, to Glen Gerstell for general perspective, to Mary Mazzocco for a sharp eye for details, to Judy High for organizing the final product and to countless others who in ways big and small made this book happen. All share whatever credit accrues; none share the blame.

Stanley J. Marcuss
Editor

INTRODUCTION

STANLEY J. MARCUSS

Effective Washington representation, to paraphrase Justice Brandeis, is not an exact science. It is an elusive concept; hard to define in the abstract, but you know it when you see it.

This book does not attempt to define effective Washington representation in the abstract. Instead, it is a practical guide to the principles and procedures that are fundamental to effectiveness in Washington. In it, individuals with broad experience in Washington as well as in law, business and academic life share their perceptions of how Washington works and what it takes to get things accomplished.

How particular interests are pursued in Washington is central to the way the government deals with the conflicting demands of its citizens. It determines whose voices will be heard and why, and which goals will be pursued and why. The subject is important to corporations and individuals alike, and to those who advise them. They need to know whether and how to seek help from Washington. And students of government and the citizenry as a whole need to understand how Washington decides who will be heard and why. For out of those decisions emerge the shape and character of the country.

This book does not attempt to bare hidden secrets or expose a magic formula for getting things done in Washington. For there is no magic formula. It is not a question of secrets but rather of understanding principles and procedures. What the book does is provide a framework for the reader to deal with his problems and to understand how others deal with their problems in the Washington environment.

Being effective in Washington requires an intimate understanding of an intricate web of personal and institutional relationships, relationships that are in a constant state of flux. The actors include members of Congress, their staff, executive branch officials and their staff, law firms, lobbyists, consultants, research groups, the general press, the specialized press and many others. They are part of a complex array of continually shifting concerns and issues, with new alliances, coalitions and priorities established virtually every day.

Issues, personalities and institutions in Washington are constantly changing. So no one approach is adequate in all circumstances. Indeed, worse than being inadequate, one approach can be disastrous if used in the wrong setting. That is why effectiveness in Washington depends critically on how one thinks about the problem, what questions one asks, how well one understands the forces at work and how well one understands the dimensions of an issue and the constellation of interests that affect the outcome.

Too often there is a tendency to think of an issue as involving one agency alone or as an issue that is exclusively within the purview of the Executive Branch. However, the agency that has official responsibility is itself likely to be under pressure from other agencies, Congress, the press and private and public interests; it is seldom free to act in accordance with its own view of the matter.

Most important matters involve multiple issues and interests, and the boundaries are often obscure. For example, a decision on whether to permit high technology exports to the Soviet Union involves national security concerns and the defense establishment, to be sure, but it also involves U.S. foreign policy, U.S. export performance, relationships with U.S. allies and a variety of other domestic and international factors.

As a consequence, it is folly to assume that approval of an export license by the Commerce Department, the nominal licensing agency, is the only approval required. Concurrence must often be obtained from the State Department, the National Security Council, the Department of Energy, the Treasury Department and White House political advisors as well. At a minimum, it is important that they have no objection or at least none upon which they are prepared to act. Moreover, it is important to make sure that key members of Congress and their staff have no objection even though they may have no formal jurisdiction over the matter.

In addition, even though an agency may officially approve a transaction, individuals within the bureaucracy may have objections that they are prepared to voice in an effort to reverse an agency decision. This may take the form of leaks to the press or Congress. So there is seldom any such thing as a final decision in the executive branch. One must be vigilant to the possibility of decisions becoming unravelled, sometimes long after they have been made and resources have been committed in reliance on them. That is why it is so important to build the broadest possible consensus around a proposed course of action. The more support a decision has, the harder it is to undo it.

Being effective in Washington requires an understanding of all the dimensions of an issue as well as an understanding of the public and private interests at stake. It also requires an understanding of when to oppose those interests; when to enlist them on one's side; when to ignore them; and how to build coalitions, some of which may include adversaries on one occasion and allies on another.

Many people inside and outside Washington make mistakes in representing their interests or those of their clients because they do not understand the environment. They do not understand how Washington will analyze an issue and the forces that affect its resolution. As a consequence, a realistic assessment of the chances of success or failure is virtually impossible, and decisions about strategy and tactics are made in the dark. The most common failure is not so much a failure to have adequate information about the problem itself, although inadequate information can be fatal; it is more often a failure to conceptualize the problem; a failure to identify the interests that could have an impact on it; and a failure to devise solutions that inventively match private needs and public goals.

What this book does is identify techniques for dealing with the forces at work. It provides yardsticks for measuring the resources that are required for success. For those who are familiar with Washington and for those who are not, the book provides the tools for developing an individual checklist of things to consider when assessing a Washington problem and deciding what to do about it.

The book deals with several basic situations. In Chapter 1, David Acheson, a practicing Washington lawyer and former law enforcement official with vast experience in Washington, outlines the principles involved in seeking help from an agency that has considerable freedom in choosing both its goals and its methods. Examples are efforts to secure a license, grant, or loan when no private party objects. These principles apply to such things as requests for export licenses, Export-Import Bank loans or guarantees, Department of Housing and Urban Development grants or loans, Internal Revenue Service rulings on tax questions, Justice Department antitrust rulings, Securities and Exchange Commission rulings on proposed courses of action and certain kinds of broadcast licenses.

After describing how situations involving discretionary agency action differ from more restricted proceedings, Mr. Acheson describes how to make a presentation to an agency, learn the identity of those who will participate in the decision, uncover sources of relevant information, discover the agency's basic point of view, create or avoid creating a record of contacts made with the agency, choosing the proper advocate and protecting confidential information from disclosure to the public.

In Chapter 2, Edward Grenier, a Washington lawyer and leading expert on administrative law, describes how formal agency proceedings differ from those described in Chapter 1 and the different roles they play. These typically include situations where someone seeks to secure a license or to defend an alleged violation of the law where the agency must act in strict accordance with legally specified criteria. These proceedings may be contested or uncontested. They may involve the making of rules that apply to the general public or rules that apply to a specific company or individual. They may involve such diverse agencies as the Federal Energy Regulatory Commission on energy matters, the Federal Trade Commission on antitrust matters and the Food and Drug Administration on matters pertaining to the safety and effectiveness of medicines.

Mr. Grenier describes the importance of understanding how such proceedings can be affected by Congress, the courts, the President and the Office of Management and Budget. He identifies the rules that govern how to decide whether to participate in a proceeding, how to conduct oneself at such proceedings and the rules of thumb for planning and executing a strategy. Finally, he describes how to snatch victory from the jaws of defeat when all else fails and the agency rules against you.

In Chapter 3, John Shenefield, a Washington lawyer and former Associate Attorney General with wide experience in antitrust and other law enforcement matters, deals with the sensitive matter of seeking advice from a government agency about the legality of past or proposed action when the law is unclear or where the agency has a significant degree of discretion in deciding whether to prosecute. This is an especially sensitive area because there is always a risk of disclosing matters that might trigger an investigation. Mr. Shenefield explains those perils and how to assess the risks. He then provides useful guidance on how to prepare for meetings with law enforcement officials, how to frame the issues and how to predict and influence the outcome. He illustrates how these general principles apply in practice in seeking antitrust advice from the Justice Department under its Business Review Procedure.

In Chapter 4, James McIntyre, a former director of the Office of Management and Budget and now a practicing lawyer, explains the important role that OMB plays in decisions made in Washington. OMB is often overlooked by the Washington representative, but it is a mistake to do so since OMB often intervenes when agencies have disputes and is generally responsible for ensuring that agency actions are consistent with the President's overall policies.

In Chapter 5, I set forth some of the basic principles involved in dealing with the White House. It is always tempting to think of the White House as the key power center in Washington. Sometimes it is; sometimes it is not, for its freedom of action can be significantly restricted by other forces such as Congress, the media and the law. Working with the White House requires an understanding of its inner dynamics, the interests of those who occupy it and why a matter deserves White House attention.

This chapter identifies the key questions to consider in determining whether and how to seek White House assistance. Many of these apply to dealings with other agencies as well. This chapter also outlines a number of concrete ways to identify which individuals in the White House should be approached, who should make the contact, what to do during and in advance of White House meetings and what to do when the meeting is over.

The risks in dealing with the White House are high, for there is seldom a higher court of appeal. But so too are the possible rewards, and no one can be an effective Washington representative unless he is prepared to deal with the White House when the need and opportunity arise.

The book next turns to the workings of Congress, one of the most difficult institutions in Washington to understand. Yet it is often a key part of the solution to any Washington problem.

In Chapter 6, Robert Russell, who has had extensive experience on Capitol Hill as a member of the Senate staff and who is a respected political scientist and student of international finance, describes the inner workings of Congress. He tells how Congress can be a potent and dangerous force because of its power to affect lives and fortunes. He details its intricate relationships with the executive branch and the interest groups that often besiege it. He outlines the many roles Congress plays, from overseeing the executive branch to conducting investigations, intervening in executive branch decisions and passing legislation. Finally, Mr. Russell provides practical advice on getting to know the players and the rules of the game, as he details step-by-step the intricate process of making a bill become law, from the introduction of a bill, to hearings, to final passage. Especially useful is his treatment of such specialized topics as the passage of authorizations and appropriations bills and the often baffling Congressional budget process.

Next the book turns to Washington as viewed from the eyes of the corporate representative, the person who must bring order out of the chaotic picture that Washington often conveys to corporate headquarters back home. Fruzsina Harsanyi is responsible for government affairs in the Washington office of a major U.S. manufacturing company. She has had extensive experience in both business and government.

In Chapter 7 she identifies the reasons why business and government often seem to be at loggerheads and attacks some of the illusions that each has about the other. She describes how the representation of business interests in Washington has evolved over the years to its present demanding professionalism and provides valuable insights into the structure and role of a company's Washington office. She provides practical advice on how to identify issues, how to be sure that corporate management is informed about emerging problems and how to get government to see an issue from the corporation's perspective.

Finally, in Chapter 8, Elliot Richardson reminds us of the need to take the larger view. Too often, he says, corporations assume a hostile environment in Washington and resist to the bitter end efforts to deal with emerging problems on the public agenda. Drawing on long experience as the head of many major departments in Washington, including Commerce, Health, Education and Welfare, Justice and Defense, Mr. Richardson, now in private law practice, makes an earnest plea for corporate planners to look to the horizon, to help shape the environment in which public debate occurs and to help mold solutions that serve both public and private interests. In short, strategic planning.

The failure to engage in strategic planning has brought about needless and costly confrontation between business and government, with business, as well as the public, the loser. Past controversies on environmental protection, worker safety and toxic substances might have been resolved with fewer burdens on business and greater benefits for the public if business had engaged in strategic planning. In many ways strategic planning is what this book is all about, and Mr. Richardson provides keen insights into how to make strategic planning work.

For some, being effective in Washington smacks of influence-peddling. Some think it is a question of knowing the right people and making sure they are friendly and cooperative. Back-scratching is the order of the day, they say, and scandals involving pay-offs of political figures and conflicts of interest among present and former government employees lend an aura of truth to that perception. But the perception is false.

While some things in Washington are achieved through pay-offs or cultivated friendships of convenience, most things are achieved through the hard and conscientious work of those government employees whose job it is to make the thousands of decisions made every day in carrying out the public's business.

Washington is a cauldron into which is stirred an enormous variety of demands, many of which conflict with each other. Public servants of all color and stripe must sort out those demands and make their decisions on the basis of the best information available. That information relates not only to the immediate matter at hand, but also to the broader ramifications of the decisions they make.

A government official must understand the environment in which he acts. Only then can he fulfill his obligation to carry out the public's business. He must know who will be affected and how. He must know which interests coincide and which diverge. He must understand how decisions relating to private interests mesh with his perception of the public interest. He must know whether his decision is within or beyond the discretion accorded by law. He must understand that his decisions may be challenged and reviewed. He must assess the degree of support or opposition he will receive from the media, his colleagues, other parts of the bureaucracy and those who may be harmed by his decisions. Ultimately, his decisions must be compatible with his perception of his basic responsibilities.

In such an environment, effectiveness is not always measured by immediate success. For no matter how effective one is, decisions, on occasion, will be adverse, for God and the government often say "no," no matter how earnest the prayer.

But the government, at least, has little chance to say "yes" unless the right approach is made. The right approach in Washington requires an understanding of the pressures placed on decision-makers; it requires dealing with those pressures in a way that makes those who must decide willing to take action consonant with one's own interests.

Private and public interests coincide as often as they conflict. But if they are perceived as conflicting, the chances of success are vastly reduced. Finding the points of common interest, minimizing perceptions of conflict, mobilizing support and deflecting opposition is what effective Washington representation is all about.

Stanley J. Marcuss
January 1983

CONTENTS

Chapter 1

DISCRETIONARY AGENCY ACTIONS

DAVID C. ACHESON*

WHY DEAL WITH DISCRETIONARY AGENCY ACTION?

Why, one may ask, does this chapter treat discretionary agency action as a distinct subject? Other ways of cross-sectioning the subject matter of this book might well distribute the material of this chapter across a variety of other subjects, substantive and procedural, so why this particular way?

This is, of course, tantamount to asking what we mean by "discretionary agency action" and whether it is in fact a distinct subject, abutting and nonencroaching upon adjudications, formal rule-making, and other subjects given distinct treatment by other chapters. These are fair questions and call for straight—if not simple—answers.

The authors seek to present the subject of effective Washington representation in a fashion that will address particularly predictable concerns of practitioners and corporate house counsel. Regulatory matters in which the agency possesses broad discretionary authority either in the substantive standards or in the procedures it may apply, or in both, comprise a predictable concern of the advocate in Wash-

---

*David C. Acheson is a senior Washington partner of Drinker Biddle & Reath. He has been a Washington lawyer since 1948. In addition to practicing law, he has served as U.S. Attorney for the District of Columbia, Special Assistant (for Enforcement) to the Secretary of the Treasury, and Senior Vice President and General Counsel of Communications Satellite Corporation.

ington representation. In such matters the agency has a high degree of freedom to determine policy goals and the means of reaching those goals, a relatively wide and complex field of choice in making its decisions, so far as nature and available resources allow. This fact is likely to bring about policy controversies, political pressures, and attentive Congressional oversight that agencies do not have to contend with in matters arising under narrow criteria. Discretionary authority will imply relatively wide differences of opinion among the senior agency staff and among the members of a multiheaded or collegial commission. One may also expect considerable controversy in the affected private sector and in the media. There will be wider play, compared with a jurisdiction of narrow discretion, for the resources of advocacy. There will be a richer mix of available arguments. There will be, inevitably, a commensurate attraction that such work will hold for advocates of mettle and ability.

These characteristics mark discretionary agency action as a distinct playing field for the advocate and therefore as an appropriate subject for treatment from a distinct perspective. This does not mean that this subject does not overlap others in this volume. Taxonomy establishes starting points, not dispositive arrangements of life.

WHAT IS MEANT BY DISCRETIONARY AGENCY ACTION?

Or, what is not meant? For present purposes, we may think of it as the relative absence of detailed or exacting constraints and the presence of a relatively wide latitude of choice, within legal limits. Certainly we do not mean to define agency discretion as judgment that is wholly unguided, since that case does not exist in real life. Nor is some degree of discretion ever wholly absent in regulatory matters, since no standard is wholly mechanical or self-executing.

For practical purposes, all agency action is subject to legislative constraints of some kind. In our system regulatory agencies (independent or executive) apply legislative criteria, however broad, under a legislative charter.

Putting aside the powers granted directly to the President by Article II of the Constitution,[1] some of which he has delegated to the executive departments, most of the substantive matters coming before the agencies and departments derive from, and must be decided under, an act of Congress. The missions of the agencies are defined by Congress; the agencies, to a greater or lesser extent, are left to fill in the details and make the mission work. This is what we mean when we say that agencies exercise delegated legislative power. Their missions lie within the areas of legislation given to Congress by Article I of the Constitution,[2] but Congress has not legislated in fine enough detail to govern each regulated transaction. In these interstices Congress has authorized the agencies to enact regulations, the second tier of legislation, as it were. We deal in this chapter with matters in which Congress has left the standards for regulatory action to be defined by the agencies under relatively broad legislative mandates.

So conceived, the frame of this chapter cuts across actions that are commonly described as informal rule-making and actions commonly viewed as licensing. In the former situation would be included the formulation of a regulation by an agency in which the participation of the public is limited, extending at the most to the submission of written comments on a proposed rule published in the *Federal Register* or to comments submitted in response to a notice which does not specify the text of a proposed rule. Some of what appears in this chapter would also apply to formal rule-making, i.e., the promulgation of rules after a full evidentiary hearing, cross examination, and findings of fact upon a public record, since (if the record is complete) the substantive standards that the agency may adopt can be drawn from the same breadth of choice as in informal rule-making. But because the constraints of the actual record very often limit the discretion of the agency to something less than a full range of the possible policy judgments, and because the procedural aspects of formal rule-making are so preoccupying and distinct, formal rule-making will be left to Chapter 2. The licensing category would include agency actions in response to applications by a party for an agency's leave to take private party action that is forbidden by statute or regulation without agency authorization.

Licensing situations can be of several varieties. One variety is actions requiring very simple procedures and basically consisting of a consultative process. An illustration might be an application to the Department of Commerce for an export license. Typically, this situation involves an application submitted by an applicant party in a nonadversary posture, granted by the agency without eliciting public comment, characterized by a process of query and response between the agency and the applicant. An application for a national bank charter is a roughly parallel form of licensing.

A different situation is one in which competing interests are very likely to be touched by the application, such as an application to the Federal Communications Commission (FCC) for a broadcast license or an application to the FCC for construction of communications common carrier facilities, in which public notice and opportunity for comment are required. Such proceedings very often become adversary, for example, where an applicant applies for a license to construct and operate a television station on a frequency that will cause interference with one or more existing stations. In such a case the governing procedure would be considerably more elaborate and formal than in the nonadversary situation.

A third situation arises where an application is submitted for which the agency has not yet framed a regulatory policy, such as an application for a license to construct and operate communications satellite facilities for direct to-the-home broadcasting. In such a case, the matter becomes a rule-making with licensing consequences, the fate of the license application being dependent upon the nature of the regulatory policy adopted by the FCC. While the nature of the license proceedings may differ widely among these three licensing situations (and these are only three among many possible examples), a common feature is the very broad discretion of the agency to frame and apply the substantive standards against which the outcome of the application will be determined.

No observer of recent history could approach representation before the agencies with the view that broad agency discretion, delegated by Congress, is an ephemeral phenomenon. A growing tendency has been noted toward what has been called ". . . the abdication by Congress of substantive policy making in favor of broad delegation of what may essentially be the power to make new laws and not merely to administer them. . . ."[3] Whether this is or is not a desirable trend, it is clear enough that advocates in regulatory matters will find themselves dealing, for years to come, with agency matters in which agency discretion assumes a quasilegislative dimension.[4]

Very broad delegation by Congress to an agency, while it is unlikely in today's world to lead a reviewing court to find an unconstitutional abdication of legislative authority, is likely to lead a court to make an exacting search for various constraints upon the agency's discretion.[5] Courts have characterized such constraints as the permissible "range of choices," and have asked whether the agency "properly construed" its authority and whether the agency decision was based upon "a consideration of the relevant factors." The advocate, therefore, should keep his[6] mind open to the opportunity to press upon the agency considerations that he thinks the agency ought to take into account as "relevant factors," similar to those which reviewing courts have identified as mandatory factors of record for related agency actions.[7]

In order to focus on the problems facing the advocate in discretionary agency actions, it may be useful to refer to concrete examples. In what follows, frequent reference will be made to one executive agency, the Department of Commerce, and one independent agency, the FCC. Both will involve very broad reaches of substantive discretion. The Commerce Department examples involve regulatory action of marked procedural informality; FCC examples involve more formal licensing or rule-making procedures. Some background information is given here, in order to give meaning to our frequently used examples.

The Export Administration Act[8] confers on the President something approaching untrammeled discretion to control exports of "any goods or technology" from the United States, pursuant to legislative policies (a) to restrict the export of goods and technology which would make a significant contribution to the military potential of another country to the detriment of national security, and (b) to further the foreign policy of the United States. The President may, in accordance with this statute, prohibit or curtail the export of any goods or technology. This authority appears in Section 5 of the Act, dealing with national security controls and, with modification not material to our purpose, in Section 6 dealing with foreign policy controls.[9] In each of the two sections it is provided that the authority shall be exercised by the Secretary of Commerce in consultation with the Secretary of Defense (Section 5) or State (Section 6), and such other departments and agencies as the Secretary considers appropriate, and shall be implemented by means of export licenses issued by the Secretary of Commerce. Criteria which the President shall "consider" are enumerated under national security controls and foreign policy controls, but the President's authority is not otherwise circumscribed.

The Secretary has promulgated voluminous regulations under the Act and its predecessor legislation. The approach is to itemize categories of commodities, by country of destination, that require a validated export license, commodities not so itemized being licensed under a General License.[10] The itemization is accomplished by a detailed Commodity Control List and a Munitions List.[11] Technical data are barred from export unless covered by one or more of the general licenses provided in the regulations.[12] Controls imposed by the Munitions List are administered by the Secretary of State.

In passing upon export license applications, the Office of Export Administration (OEA) considers a variety of factors drawn from the application, its own store of information, and information received from, and the views of, the consulted agencies. These factors include the likelihood that the export, or a component thereof, could provide technology or a capability that could make a significant contribution to a foreign military potential that would be detrimental to national security; the degree to which the design or capability of the item is available from non-United States sources; the likelihood that the export could be modified to provide a contribution to a military capability; whether the technology is more advanced, or has a substantially greater capability, than is necessary for the intended end use; whether the export is being supplied pursuant to an international obligation of the United States. These are merely illustrative of a wide spectrum of factors considered by OEA and the consulted agencies. The discretion exercised by the Department of Commerce and the consulted agencies is heavily reinforced by the broad constitutional authority of the President in the area of foreign policy and by the concentration in the executive branch, among the branches of government, of the chief competence to make sophisticated judgments regarding military weapons systems.

As mentioned earlier, the procedure used for passing on export license applications is very informal. There is no public notice. There may well be opportunities for explanation by the applicant (usually in writing or confirmed in writing) and for modification of the application in order to remedy deficiencies or to meet objections. The degree of give-and-take and the mode of achieving it are entirely discretionary with OEA. No hearing is mandated by statute or regulation. The consultation between OEA and the sister agencies takes place both at scheduled meetings and informally, not on the record and often not in the presence of the applicant. Both in substantive and procedural discretion, the actions of OEA with respect to export controls are near the high limit of discretionary flexibility, perhaps exceeding that of Henry II dispensing personal justice under the Royal Oak. King Henry, after all, usually had the applicant before him.

A sense of the broad substantive reach of discretionary agency action may be suggested by another illustration, this time from the FCC, an independent agency. The FCC is authorized by the Federal Communications Act of 1934 (as amended) to grant certificates for the service facilities of communications common carriers, in the following terms:

> (a) No carrier shall undertake the construction of a new line or of an extension of any line, or shall acquire or operate any line, or extension thereof, or shall engage in transmission over or by means of such additional or extended line, unless and until there shall first have been obtained from the Commission a certificate that the present or future public convenience and necessity require or will require the construction, or operation, or construction and operation, of such additional or extended line:. . . .
>
> (c) The Commission shall have power to issue such certificate as applied for, or to refuse to issue it, or to issue it for a portion or portions of a line, or extension thereof, or discontinuance, reduction, or impairment of service, described in the application, or for the partial exercise only of such right or privilege, and may attach to the issuance of the certificate such terms and conditions as in its judgment the public convenience and necessity may require.[13]

Reams have been written on what the "public convenience and necessity" includes, or should include, in this context. The standard is one that is largely left to the FCC, not merely to apply, but to define. A similar standard appears with a modestly altered formulation in Section 309 of the Communications Act[14] regarding the licensing of broadcast facilities, as well as in subsection 201(c)(9) of the Communications Satellite Act regarding the authorization by the FCC of satellite communications facilities ". . . required by the public interest, convenience and necessity."[15] Procedural requirements aside (and they are quite exacting), the FCC enjoys a substantive latitude comparable to that associated with legislation, in applying the "public interest" standard to a given set of facts. No statutory definition of "public interest" appears. In defining this standard and applying it to a given set of facts, the FCC is making a delegated legislative judgment, i.e., making a judgment that Congress chose to pass to the FCC rather than make itself. Congress does not attempt, in the brevity of human life, to write a statutory subsection for each factual situation that may arise.

The dimension of discretion involved in determining the public interest can be broadened exponentially in matters as to which policy is not yet established, perhaps not yet even addressed, by the agency. In the ordinary case, where, for example, the Bell System proposes to augment interstate long lines facilities on an existing route, the FCC's discretion normally will play across the span of service requirements and economics according to conventional criteria. For instance, what is the load on existing facilities? Are there inconvenient delays in completing calls? What incremental costs will be added to the toll rate structure? Is it cost-effective? Policy criteria having been settled, the decision of the agency will turn upon answers to factual questions such as these.

Very much broader is the discretion involved where the application requires a new policy framework, as, for example, where Microwave Communications, Inc. (MCI) came in with an application for a specialized carrier route to serve traffic between two Bell System service points, Chicago and St. Louis.[16] Up to that time, the Bell System not only provided local telephone service for the two city areas, but also provided the chief toll and leased-line service between those areas. The MCI application proposed that MCI be allowed to compete for the leased-line service, thus diluting a virtual Bell System monopoly on that route and threatening to establish a principle fraught with weighty implications for other heavy traffic routes on the Bell System. The Bell System, of course, vigorously opposed MCI's application, as did other carriers providing other services to that area. Thus, the licensing application became an adversary rule-making proceeding in which a new underlying policy had to be considered—in that case, a question of common carrier competition versus retention of the "chosen instrument" philosophy. In the outcome of the MCI case, the policy-making discretion of the FCC was exercised, on a major legislative scale, in a decision that the public interest called for establishing competition on that interstate route.

Of even broader policy dimension is the question currently before the FCC of whether to license a new broadcast technology in the form of direct communications satellite transmission to home rooftop antennas. Initially before the FCC in the form of an application for a narrowly specialized "pay television" system proposed by a subsidiary of the Communications Satellite Corporation, direct broadcast proposals now involve additional applicants and consequences that have major structural implications for the broadcast industry and the role of the media in American life. These potential consequences—admittedly far off, but more weighty than many matters hotly debated by the Congress—are to be decided by the FCC applying the "public interest" standard, though it is hardly to be doubted that Congressional views on the matter will find their way from Capitol Hill to the FCC.[17]

Most discretionary agency actions are not on such a grand legislative scale. In many cases, narrow agency rulings occur under formal rules issued by an agency derived from its legislative mandate, that is, under standards made not by Congress but by the agency itself. An example of this is the authority of the Securities and Exchange Commission (SEC) under Section 17(d) of the Investment Company Act[18] to prescribe rules and regulations for permissible joint and several participations in transactions by investment companies and their affiliated persons. Rather than define permissible transactions, the SEC in Rule 17d-1 requires that, with certain specific exceptions, application be made for an exemptive order. The standard stated in Rule 17d-1 for granting such orders is whether the proposed transaction "is consistent with the provisions, policies and purposes of the Act and the extent to which [the proposed] participation is on a basis different from or less advantageous than that of other participants."

Still another kind of discretionary action is what could be called interpretive, which would include releases, policy statements, or *ad hoc* rulings on particular matters, and "no action" advice. For example, the 1933 Securities Act inartfully applies to securities transactions between any foreign country and any state,[19] with the result that, if a telephone call to the United States is made from a foreign country in aid of the transaction, the Act arguably applies. However, based on a 1964 SEC statement[20] and a few "no-action" letters, there is no doubt that genuinely foreign offerings are exempt from the 1933 Act's registration requirements.

In a great many other areas under the securities laws, "no-action" letters form an existing body of observed law forged on a largely discretionary basis. A "no-action" letter is written advice from the agency that, in the precise circumstances detailed by the request of the party seeking such a letter, the agency will not take enforcement action against the party. The "no-action" letter procedure in many agencies has an interesting two-way operation. It offers the Washington practitioner the opportunity to ascertain and influence an agency's conduct in applying existing statutes and rules to new sets of facts. It also offers the agency an opportunity to ascertain and influence the conduct of businessmen in cases in which the agency's authority has never been tested. To some degree, the no-action procedure gives the agency the opportunity to extend its theory of the law to cases which no rule making has yet reached and to place restraints upon the conduct of compliant (or risk-avoiding) parties without an established legal basis for doing so. No judicial review is possible, since the action of the affected party, should he choose not to challenge the agency's advice, is voluntary. Hence, the advocate must make a trade-off calculation if he asks for a no-action letter. He may be able to learn the agency's view toward his client's transaction, but the agency position may go beyond the guidelines of the cases or the formal rules. In matters involving possibly protracted and expensive litigation, the prospect of adverse agency action—an injunction suit, a cease-and-desist proceeding, or even criminal action—may well be enough to kill the intended transaction. This is usually exactly what the agency seeks to achieve. An example of that in the antitrust area is the "business review letter," the Justice Department's version, through its Antitrust Division, of the no-action procedure. Still, many—perhaps most—businessmen would rather have access to these means of evaluating risk than to be left to guess what the agency will do.

There is no need to develop at further length illustrative examples of discretionary agency action. The purpose here is to suggest the range of situations. Obviously, any agency action retains some residue of discretion, since not every factual case is provided for by the letter of the law, and each will be different from the next, by whatever hair's breadth. Nevertheless, we may contrast with "discretionary" agency actions those agency determinations governed by well-developed, detailed criteria, such as the decision of a federal bank examiner in determining whether a loan, as a claimed asset of a bank, should be unclassified or given a classification as "substandard," "doubtful," or "loss." The criteria for this determination have been refined and are inculcated in bank examiners by training precisely to avoid individual policy making that could lead to disparate treatment of like situations in a decentralized organization.

THE CHALLENGE AND THE OPPORTUNITY FOR THE ADVOCATE IN AGENCY DISCRETION

As discussed above, the significance of broad agency discretion in a given matter is that policy making of a quasilegislative nature will be or can be made by an agency. To the imaginative advocate, this presents an inviting and potentially rewarding opportunity. For precisely the reason that it presents such an opportunity to different advocates, promoting quite different objectives, discretionary agency action will present challenges commensurate with the opportunities.

In the informal rule-making process, the opportunity to the advocate lies in the expansive scope for constructing an appeal to agency discretion, for designing and supporting a new policy initiative he will press upon the agency, in expounding the consistency of the result he seeks with policies already adopted, and in the workmanship of marshalling the facts and arguments to buttress the case.

The advocate will seek to identify and invoke the established policy objectives; to touch the known predispositions and fixations of his forum and its individual members and staff; to draw upon supporting history and economic data; and to neutralize, so far as possible, the legal, factual, institutional, and business arguments adduced by those with adverse interests. If the advocate seeks a new policy initiative, he will emphasize dissatisfaction with the existing rules, drawing upon the best of the literature portraying that sector of regulation as mired in policies that have outlived their purpose. He will hold out to the agency the temptation of unleashing, by forward-looking rule-making, forces of the market or of technology which can realize great benefits to the citizenry.

To illustrate, proponents of direct broadcast satellite systems emphasize several points: the capability of a new technology to offer an enlargement of householder choice of program materials; a very great potential saving in transmission cost; the desirability of permitting risk-takers to go forward in testing new ideas in the market place; the desirability of freeing the market from dependence upon the established broadcast networks with all the familiar associations of objectionable programs and advertising.

These arguments are aimed to touch well-known attitudes that have been voiced from time to time by congressional leaders and members of the FCC. The arguments gain strength from a permeating, but unspecific, attitude in both quarters favoring a degree of deregulation in the communications industry. Proponents of direct broadcast systems also seek to allay the apprehensions of the established broadcast industry by foreseeing an industry structure in which direct broadcast satellites and conventional stations may coexist, the latter distributing program materials of a local nature and interest that do not lend themselves to truly national distribution. Proponents wish to calm any anxiety that direct broadcast satellites may threaten potential damage to the role and revenue base of the networks and the conventional broadcast industry. There is also advantage, in all probability, in seeking to persuade the FCC staff that direct satellite broadcast will not alter the institutional premises of the regulators so profoundly that the familiar jurisdictional lines of the Common Carrier and the Broadcast bureaus within the FCC will require significant rearrangement or suffer losses of authorized staff positions.

In short, the advocate's opportunity is that of advocacy on an expansive scale, in which he will seek to convey to the agency the most compelling blend of research, business and regulatory history, public policy, economic promise, and parochial advantage. If he is successful, the advocate may durably stamp some corner of the regulated sector as his own creation and make a bit of business history.

It is apparent that the same factors that expand the advocate's opportunity also work to sharpen the challenges that beset him. The size of the business stakes, a deviation from regulatory history, fear of the unknown confronting agency habit and jurisdiction, and, generally, the roiling of the status quo in Congress and elsewhere in government—in short, all the issues that offer broad scope to a proponent of new policy initiatives will equally multiply his obstacles and adversaries. Arithmetic increments in the quantum of controversy tend to produce exponential increments in the number and passion of the voices of special pleading.

Naturally, advocates will not always be pressing fresh policy departures upon federal agencies. The role of defending the status quo will be played at least as frequently. The tools for advocacy of this kind are, not surprisingly, the converse of those that are employed in the cause of innovation. A fundamental law of gravity works in favor of the status quo advocate, arising from the fact that no selection of new policies need be made in order to stand pat. All that is necessary is a failure to select among the alternate policies open to the innovator. In addition, many respectable reasons can be advanced to encourage the postponement or avoidance (often synonymous terms) of choice. Have pending studies been completed? Is it not necessary to develop additional data? Is the proposed innovation going to cost agency jobs or create a loss or confusion of agency jurisdiction? Will there be a loss of or encroachment upon agency "turf"? Is the proposed innovation too far ahead of the views of the agency's congressional oversight committee or subcommittee?

It does not require electrifying innovation of policy, or a great quantum of controversy, to introduce delay and to throw dust in the air. A multiplicity of parties will often have that effect. Illustrating, once more, from the broadcast satellite arena, the advocate for a license applicant will have to take account of the views of the following players, at a minimum, not counting other applicants and participants of record and FCC principals and staff:

1. *The National Telecommunications and Information Administration (NTIA) in the Department of Commerce* (the reincarnation of the old Office of Telecommunications Policy in the Office of the President): NTIA can make submissions to the action agency, but usually acts as a coordinator in sifting

executive agency positions for the Secretary of Commerce, the Office of Management and the Budget, and the communications subcommittees of either house of Congress. While not often a major actor in its own right, NTIA can be a sleeper to the unwary. Its views can surface anywhere.

2. *The Antitrust Division of the Department of Justice:* The Antitrust Division often appears formally in agency proceedings. It also submits statements of views in informal agency rule-making. The Antitrust Division would be expected to take an interest in any agency matter that might have an important effect upon competition or market structure in a major industry sector, particularly a sector that commands the visibility and political clout that the electronic media command.

3. *Communications Subcommittees of the Congress:* These are the Communications Subcommittee of the Senate Committee on Commerce, Science and Transportation and the Telecommunications, Consumer Protection and Finance Subcommittee of the House Committee on Energy and Commerce. These subcommittees have strong lines running to the FCC through the long-standing delegation of legislative power to the FCC, through the political sensitivity of the FCC's work and through the frequent migration of committee staff to appointment on the Commission or FCC senior staff. Moreover, the Congressional committees and their members have flexible and effective ways of communicating their aims to the FCC, through committee reports, oral statements and interrogation at hearings, speeches, press releases, interviews, legislative proposals, visits among the staff, and other means too numerous to exhaust. Since Congress is the source both of the FCC's jurisdiction and its funds, the FCC ear cocked at the committees is very sensitively tuned, a fact that the resourceful advocate can put to good account. Further mention will be made of this point later in this chapter.

4. *The Office of Technology Assessment (OTA):* An analytical support agency serving the United States Congress and organized as an agency of that branch of government. It explores legislative issues associated with a high technology

society and can become engaged in study of a particular matter by direction of its Technology Assessment Board (consisting of 12 House and Senate members). It has not traditionally played an advocate's role but rather an evaluative one.

5. *Aerospace and electronics contractors:* In every major application for satellite systems there will be contractors who lost out in the bidding for prime responsibility for building spacecraft and subsystems. These contractors may be expected to continue to wage war for their specific versions of hardware and system design and to carry the selling effort to the FCC and to its congressional constituency. Nor will this effort be lacking in zeal and determination, since each protagonist will have millions or scores of millions of dollars at stake and can deploy a sophisticated Washington sales effort.
6. *The media:* Principally the broadcast networks and major station owners, at least some of which will have easy access to the congressional subcommittees and to the FCC.

This identification of parties in interest is far from complete. These and lesser players are certain to communicate their interests and views, either in comments of record before the agency or in informal expressions or briefing memoranda to FCC personnel or to one or more of the other players who may be thought to have superior channels to the FCC. Not all their footprints will be visible and not all their visits or representations will be ascertainable, much less subject to effective rebuttal. One or more of these constituencies may seek legislation in order to preempt a favored, or to overturn a disfavored, disposition of the matter. The advocate will be preoccupied with his main effort directed to the agency, but he cannot neglect his intelligence, his effort to find out who is selling what line to whom and, as in warfare, protection of his flank and interdiction of air attack while maintaining his own offensive.

In matters of other kinds before other agencies, naturally the list of players will be different from this example. But the central point is that the advocacy process is likely not to be a mere bilateral affair limited to the interaction of the advocate with the forum agency. It may well be a multilateral affair in which the shape of the action taken by the agency will be affected by the views of a number of advocates, public and private. In such cases it can develop that the advocate's best chance to achieve the optimum result lies in moderating his proposal to form a plurality view with other agencies and advocates. By sacrificing some of his preferred blueprint, he may add to the probability of achieving the next best solution. However, it is tactically important not to proffer the sacrifice until the moment when it appears that other players are also ready to concede something in exchange for terms that they, too, believe will add to the probability of their next best solution. Concessions prematurely proffered never buy much, often nothing. They are likely to communicate lack of confidence and encourage a "ganging up" on the party first exhibiting weakness.

In depicting the wide reach and quasilegislative scope of informal rule-making in the preceding FCC example, we have admittedly chosen an illustration going beyond the advocate's every day experience. Most discretionary agency action in which advocates are involved will occur in the context of more settled policy, of narrower substantive scope, more slender stakes, and milder controversy. In such matters the advocate will focus on helpful facts and interpretive arguments rather than on revising policy goals of the agency.

By way of example, we can revert to the export license context, specifically to an application to export computer hardware and software to the Peoples Republic of China for use in analyzing offshore soundings for petroleum exploration. A major question scrutinized by OEA will be whether the speed and capability of the hardware and the flexibility of use of the software will make the package adaptable to military uses (such as antisubmarine warfare) so as to make a "significant contribution to the military potential" of the PRC.[21] In such an examination the matter will be governed by factual questions revolving around the criteria considered by OEA and the consulted agencies.

For example, are the performance specifications more capable and advanced than the intended use requires? Is the package susceptible (without stretching facts to fantasy) to adaptation for a military use? If so, does such a use represent a significant contribution to military potential? Is it possible to secure reliable assurance against re-export or leakage of the technology? If the specifications were degraded to provide greater margin against possible military diversion, would it impair the intended use? What is the degree of availability of comparable technology from non-United States sources?

The advocate must see that these and related questions are answered by the application and supporting materials, if he is not to risk refusal of the application or encounter long delay while he researches from his client's resources the answers to these and follow-up inquiries. In some cases he will want to have explored with his client in advance some acceptable fall-back level of performance specifications against the chance he may be forced to that exigency. The advocate and his client's engineers and salesmen must be able to put themselves, so to speak, inside the heads of the OEA staff and the agencies consulted by OEA, anticipate the questions, emphasize the helpful facts, and be ready to help OEA and its consulted agencies (in this case chiefly the Department of Defense) solve the problems that they see as their own.

It follows that the Chinese contracting agency, in our example, must be apprised of foreseeable problems and must have provided all necessary information on the circumstances of use. (This is often sticky, because such an inquiry may be seen as an affront to Chinese sovereignty.) The importing agency must sometimes be forced to think in advance about acceptable modifications in the performance specifications, so that such a necessity does not come as a last-minute, unexpected crisis in the application process. To this extent, it is often prudent that the contract, while it must be firm before an export license application can be made, not be cast in concrete in every detail. To accomplish all this without conveying an unsettling message to the importing customer agency, and without signaling premature concessions to OEA, requires some delicacy of judgment and precision in communications, made the more difficult by language obstacles, by distance, and by the importer's unfamiliarity with the nuances of the process.

WHAT THE ADVOCATE NEEDS TO KNOW

One of those solemn clichés that Washington "insiders" hold dear asserts that knowledge is power. The proposition is stated far too absolutely to be correct much of the time, but it is nevertheless true that lack of knowledge is vulnerability. In dealing with discretionary agency action, the advocate must know the agency stage set and cast surrounding the role which he himself is to play. In addition to knowing his clients' case, he must know the forum. This involves a dimension of knowledge far greater than knowing the decisional history of a federal judge. It involves something similar to knowing the stage set and cast of legislative action, in which multiple personalities, political history, and policy trade-offs interact to frame the problem.

LEGAL FRAMEWORK

Lawyers, of course, or advocates of any kind, would be expected to know the statutes and agency regulations that govern the matter at hand. Nevertheless, advocates sometimes get well into exploration of the matter by office visits and telephone calls to agency personnel before taking the time to absorb the statutory and regulatory materials. This is often the result of a "chicken-or-egg" calculation. The common instinct is to pick up the telephone and explore basic information about the posture of the matter, about what the agency is doing or what it thinks it is doing. But there is a point at which basic exploration becomes two-way communication and begins to convey impressions to agency personnel. Such communication should never be allowed to convey uncertainty on the part of the advocate about what *he* is doing, or thinks he is doing. For this reason, though it seems trite to say so, it is better to look up the basic law and regulations before one has attempted much exploration at the agency, then talk at length with agency personnel without running the risk of communicating uncertainty. One would always go back to the legal material to run down the finer points that emerge from completion of the exploration stage.

Given the huge volume of regulations that appear in the *Federal Register*,[22] the advocate should suspect that there may be new regulations or amendments in the pipeline. An inquiry to that effect should be a standard step in exploring the posture of the matter. Moreover, he will want to know whether there are internal guidelines to the staff[23] on how to apply the published regulations;

these may place a helpful or unhelpful gloss upon those regulations. Agency rules of practice and procedure would normally be published in the *Code of Federal Regulations,* but in any case will be available in the agency's office of public information or in the general counsel's office.

In matters other than formal rule-making or adversary matters in which the rules governing *ex parte* communications apply, it will be appropriate for the advocate to find out all he can about how agency staff view the matter, what the range of possible actions might be, and what the criteria are that would cause the advisory or decision-making personnel to lean one or another way. In the writer's experience, agency legal staff often are willing to dispense such information to a fellow professional in the interest of having the matter proceed in a businesslike and professional manner without misunderstandings on either side. Often the agency's general counsel's office is organized in a way that permanently assigns a lawyer to each major functional division within the agency, a mode that gives the agency lawyer a close and current familiarity with matters of the kind engaging the advocate at the moment.

At this point a word would be useful about the substantial body of written information that is available to the public about agency policies, areas of concentration, and proposed actions. Proposed rules of agencies appear in the *Federal Register*, published daily by the Government Printing Office. The *Federal Register* can be purchased on subscription and can be picked up in advance of the nominal publication date and well prior to the normal mailing delivery.

Numerous commercial sources and newsletters are available in every field of regulatory practice—environmental, labor, securities, bank regulation, international trade, taxation, and all the rest. Several of the agencies publish their own bulletins showing amendments and interpretations of the regulations; these may be purchased from the Government Printing Office (e.g., OEA publishes Export Administration Bulletins). The FCC, among other agencies, publishes its official reports of Commission actions, which are indexed and chronologically released like the advance sheets of judicial reporters. A conversation with an agency librarian or a knowledgeable law firm librarian will usually suffice to winnow the essential from the nonessential and enable the stranger to a field of regulatory activity to ascertain the useful range of published resources.

The major regulatory agencies maintain their own reference libraries where their published regulations and decisions can be found, as well as periodicals and commentary in that sector of activity. However, as indicators of wind direction, so to speak, these materials may well lag behind intended changes of course. Such changes should be probed in conversations with agency staff. The trade press should be scoured for hints of change. The commercial reporting services, by contrast, usually do not purport to anticipate developments that are brewing in particular agencies.

Structure and Personnel

In discretionary agency matters, it is vital to identify the principal personnel who will decide the matter and those who will advise those who will decide. It is also vital to learn the mechanism of decision making in the particular agency.

As a start, one must ascertain the organization and functional relationships of advisory staff, as a means of identifying where the advice is coming from. The functional divisions of many, perhaps most, agencies have organization charts that can be had on request at the originating office or at the Office of Public Information. These charts often show quite a bit of detail about the organization of particular divisions, as well as of the entire agency. There are also commercial directories that are important working tools for the agency practitioner. Some of these directories are very detailed and comprehensive. The writer urges subscription to commercial directory services that distribute revised pages and changes between major editions, as a means of obtaining maximum currency. (To avoid "plugola," no proprietary names are mentioned, but any librarian can identify them.)

It is more difficult, but equally important, to have a sense of the relative weight of advisory personnel. At a so-called collegial agency, such as the FCC, the possibilities can be quite complex. The pertinent bureau chief will draw upon his staff for recommendations or for materials supporting one or more points of view. The thrust toward a preferred resolution may commence with such material. The bureau chief himself may have a strong predisposition. From the bureau chief a recommendation will go to the Commission. The advocate will want to become sufficiently familiar with the institutional process to judge who on the staff is likely to write the memorandum of decision. Each of the commissioners may well have a predisposition on the matter; some of these predispositions may be known or ascertainable from prior actions or public statements. Rarely is a commissioner's mind a *tabula rasa*. Each of the commissioners has a legal assistant and, in some cases, an engineering assistant, who may have the opportunity to test ideas in discussion with his chief and to prepare draft language. The legal assistants also may interact in informal discussion with each other, as do the commissioners. Laterally introduced views may come from the General Counsel's office and from the Office of Science and Technology. Certain matters may be decided by the bureau chief under a delegation of authority from the Commission. It is, naturally, vital to know when a bureau chief—or any staff official—is in charge of the matter rather than acting in an advisory capacity. Normally, the public notice will disclose that fact.

The Commission members, at least the more senior of them, will probably have left a written indication of their views on related prior matters in reported decisions of the Commission. Where a commissioner has previously been an academic or a published writer, there will be a body of writing that provides certain clues to intellectual leaning. The staff, however, normally cannot be read in this fashion. Their respective leanings or conditioning can only be sensed by acquaintance and personal discussion. This will require the advocate to invest considerable effort and time over a sustained period if he wishes to develop a confident sense of the way the agency staff are likely to think. Indeed, this is a major reason militating toward the specialization of Washington practitioners. There is not enough time to exhaust this type of learning process with respect to the senior staff of all the major agencies, nor are clients usually willing to pay for the learning time that would have to be invested among many agencies.

It does not require a multiheaded commission to present complex staff relationships or crosscurrents in the decision-making process. Consider the export license function of the Office of Export Administration in the Department of Commerce. While OEA has the license authority, in cases involving advanced technology exports (commodities or data), the OEA staff will consult with other agencies likely to be concerned—the State and Defense Departments, the CIA, the Energy Department, and other agencies that have a responsibility in technical and scientific matters. These consultations, involving, as they often do, analyses and comparisons requiring classified information, take place behind doors that are closed to the applicant and to other private parties. The advocate's opportunity to find out what criteria are applied and to register his own views directly to the consulted agencies must depend upon his establishing his own lines of communication to the key personnel who participate in the consultation process for the collateral agencies. At its best, such reconnaissance will not provide a full opportunity to elicit all the problems in the minds of those personnel or a full opportunity for rebuttal. But over time a prudent advocate will seek to create and strengthen the impression that his representations and his discretion can be relied on, the essential precondition for two-way communication of a satisfactory character.

This last point should be emphasized, for it has far wider application than the context of this illustration. It is that an advocate's effectiveness in representing his client before the agencies depends upon, more than any other factor, his demonstrated reliability in his facts and his undertakings. In representations no fact should be stretched; in execution no undertaking should be trimmed. This is more than a matter of personal integrity, though that is primary. It is also a matter of sagacity in building long-term professional relationships.

The advocate should not vouch for facts supplied by clients, if he is queasy about them. He should shake the facts down to see if any loose pieces fly off. He should not make any undertaking that the client may be unwilling to honor. The worst damage that the client or the advocate can inflict on their case is to fail to live up to a commitment made to the agency, and the occasion may arise when the client needs to be told this. The client must always be aware that the critical factor in regulatory treatment is likely to be the agency's confidence that the client and his advocate can be trusted. In this relationship any tendency to be slick or cute or to mislead the agency carries a backfire potential of fatal dimensions. Moreover, this discipline must be adhered to even if the advocate senses that he is not able to extend the same trust to the agency. It can cause difficult client relations if the client does not understand that reliability is a discipline incumbent on him even if the agency personnel do not always reciprocate.

Ex Parte Restrictions

The process of educating agency personnel in the advocate's point of view and of eliciting their own points of departure will be radically constrained in proceedings or actions in which rules governing *ex parte* communications come into play. Such proceedings are commonly called restricted proceedings. Typically, these are adversary proceedings, i.e., proceedings in which there are, or probably will be, mutually exclusive applications or formal oppositions or adversary pleadings of one or more parties against one or more other parties. Some agencies have quite detailed *ex parte* rules which reach even beyond adversary proceedings to other categories of restricted proceedings.

Ex parte rules govern *ex parte* communications and representations, i.e., communications directed to decision-making personnel and their advisors and not served on parties to the proceeding. The object, of course, is to preserve fairness in the proceeding by closing the side doors to advocacy and putting all representations on the record. Since the normal instinct of the advocate is to press argument upon any willing ear, it is most important that the advocate know when this instinct can and cannot be given free play. Sanctions and penalties for infraction of *ex parte* rules can be quite serious, extending to disqualification from the proceeding, dismissal of the offending party's claim, and professional discipline.

The agencies vary widely in the presence or absence of *ex parte* rules, in the degree of their sophistication and detail, and in the comprehensiveness of their reach. The advocate cannot afford to be guided merely by the seeming common sense of the matter. He must know the particular agency's rules that are applicable to the kind of matter with which he is dealing. In the absence of such specific familiarity, there are many traps for the unwary.

In the extreme case, an agency's rules may bar *ex parte* contacts in a matter that is not and may never be adversary, in the sense of involving mutually exclusive applications or petitions to deny or oppositions to a proposed course of action. The *ex parte* rules of the

FCC[24] may be a fair example of this very strict category. Under those rules, "restricted proceedings," in which *ex parte* contacts with decision-making personnel are prohibited, include these broad categories:

1. Adjudications (from the time designated for hearing); proceedings involving construction or operation of broadcast facilities; transfers of control of station licenses; revocations of licenses; issue or suspension of licenses of station operators; proceedings involving interlocks between boards of directors of communications utilities (called "common carriers"); complaints against common carriers; authorization of construction or operation of a common carrier line; consolidations, acquisitions, and mergers among telephone companies and among telegraph companies; any proceeding involving the technical characteristics, construction, additions, or operation of the international communications satellite system[25] and associated ground stations.
2. Applications for and modifications and renewals of broadcast licenses where there is a petition to deny or a conflicting application.
3. A broad category of restricted rule-making, including proceedings involving common carrier routes, charges, and connections; complaints against and investigations of carrier services or charges; rate increases; suspensions of rates; valuation of rate base property; consolidation or merger of telegraph companies; carrier access to the international satellite system and charges therefor, including rate-making; *any* informal rule making involving "competing claims to a valuable privilege."

Oral and written *ex parte* representations are barred in restricted proceedings. The FCC personnel who are placed "off limits," i.e., barred from receiving *ex parte* representations, include really everyone who would be likely to decide or to advise the decision makers or to evaluate legal issues, appeals, technical merits, etc.[26]

It is worth giving considerable space to these FCC *ex parte* rules, since they afford a vivid example of the extreme, even exaggerated, restraints that an agency can impose upon *ex parte* contacts made by private sector advocates with agency personnel. In matters in which *ex parte* rules are applicable (covering nearly everything in the FCC), the advocate must carefully conform his conduct to the rules or risk destroying his effectiveness with, and even access to, the agency.

Desirable as it is to keep agency actions clean by closing side door access to agency personnel, severe *ex parte* rules can work very unevenly and unfairly from the viewpoint of the private sector advocate. Senior officials of other agencies, congressional committee members and staff, and White House staff all have various means of conveying their views to members and staff of the regulatory agency. These means run little risk of disclosure, much less public censure or discipline. Some of these means are quite open and have been touched on earlier. They include interrogation at congressional hearings, press conferences, speeches, and public statements for attribution. Parties to the proceeding or parties in interest (such as contractors of applicants) have too much to lose to warrant serious breaches of the *ex parte* rules. For this reason, *ex parte* rules of agencies are sometimes regarded—not without some justice—as rules made to disadvantage parties without champions on Capitol Hill or in the executive branch.

From what has been said about the *ex parte* rules thus far, it should be clear that the advocate may be able to seize a tactical advantage before an agency if he can identify an adversary party who has committed a breach of those rules. For this purpose, common recourse is had to the Freedom of Information Act through requests served upon the agencies under the authority of that Act to disclose the records relating to all contacts and communications from outside sources with agency personnel in connection with a specified proceeding or action of the agency.[27] Occasionally these efforts are successful (though in a small minority of cases) in turning up evidence of improper contacts that can embarrass an adversary or taint or delay a decision of the agency. Since the maker of the record, if a record there is, normally would be the agency employee who received the improper contact, one would correctly surmise that the employee usually follows the most convenient course and is content to admonish the contacting person, make no record, and dismiss the matter from his mind. In any event, that there is a slender volume of material disclosed under

FOIA showing culpable breaches of the *ex parte* rules seems indisputable and will occasion no great surprise to students of human nature.

In most informal agency actions, contacts with agency personnel are freely made without fear of violation of *ex parte* rules. The processing of applications for export licenses, for example, takes place with entire propriety within an *ex parte* procedure. The applicant, OEA personnel, and the consulted agencies play their respective roles in a pattern of bilateral exchanges of information, views, and restricted meetings. Similarly, requests for rulings and for interpretive guidance addressed, for example, to the federal agencies regulating financial depositary institutions[28] are not normally placed on public notice or thrown into an adversary or restricted mode of proceeding. It seems highly desirable that such consultations retain a candid give-and-take character and should be free of the delay and record building that characterize on-the-record procedures.

Except in clearly adversary situations, rigid and far-reaching *ex parte* rules, such as the FCC's, appear to interfere unduly with the mutual education process that enables business and government to understand one another's problems. Such rules contribute to the paper burden, the delay, and the expense that characterize our excessively ritualized regulation processes. Looking at it in the large, it seems to this writer that in such rules we have distorted our processes in order to seal off the possibility of relatively minor abuses of *ex parte* contacts, and that the cure is worse than the disease. There is no compelling reason why informal rule-making by agencies exercising delegated legislative power should follow such rigidly judicialized *ex parte* rules, while in the legislature itself the members and the staff are open to all channels of education within the limits of honesty and common sense. As the saying goes: "If you have a large hole in the door for the large cat, you don't need a small hole for the small cat."

THE SYMPATHETIC ISSUE

If agencies do not have souls, at least they or their principal members and staff have points of view on major regulatory issues.

Often those points of view can be brought to bear, in a helpful way, on the matter that engages the advocate. Each point of view has a history. Each such history begins with the enabling act of Congress that brought the agency into the world and gave it its original mandate. Each history continues through the subsequent delegations of legislative power that add up to the agency's current mandate. To these legislative delegations are inevitably linked congressional attitudes that were built into the legislation and continuing attitudes that characterize congressional committee oversight. These attitudes become part of the intellectual ambience of the agency. Often these attitudes rise to the level of explicit agency policy and become accepted by the agency principals and staff as part of their mission.

Examples and variations can be seen in our familiar illustrations, the FCC and the OEA. During the 1960's and early 1970's, the FCC staff and a majority of the commissioners, reflecting the militancy of the antitrust and communications subcommittees of the Congress, evolved a strong commitment to weakening the "monopoly" position of the Bell System in domestic telecommunications. This attitude was reinforced by a degree of activism in the Antitrust Division of the Department of Justice. It did not take long for these attitudes to find their reflection in the advocacy addressed to the FCC on issues touching the Bell System's position in the telecommunications industry structure. Applications submitted to the Commission during that period for new domestic common carrier (satellite or microwave) services that would be competitive with the Bell System regularly emphasized that a grant of the application would strengthen competition with the Bell System and dilute the Bell System's market position. These applicants had hold of a "sympathetic issue" of considerable force and straightforward simplicity. Thus, an exploding technology conjoined with an anti-monopoly attitude in government brought about a new regulatory policy—competition in common carrier services. MCI's Chicago-St. Louis microwave line was authorized and the "specialized common carrier" phenomenon took hold and grew.

Like radioactive substances, however, attitudes in agency regulation have finite half-lives that terminate, or at least yield to other, sometimes contrary, attitudes or to drift. So with the antimonopoly emphasis of the FCC. Today, the prevailing attitude seems to be ambivalence, a deregulation spirit coupled with nervousness about deregulation's consequences. The FCC appears to have clustered rather loosely around a policy of letting risk-takers go forward with new services in a market characterized by innovation and diversity, putting their capital behind their market faith. Such a philosophy is seen in the "open skies" policy in domestic satellite telecommunications, in the granting of numerous specialized microwave carrier proposals, and in progressive deregulation of cable television. It has more recently found further expression in FCC actions on direct broadcasting by satellite.[29] But also present at the FCC and in Congress is the fear that deregulation of any consistency and breadth will run the risk of freeing the Bell System from its constraints and allowing Bell to trample the smaller animals in a stampeding market of telecommunications married to data processing capability. Thus, the sympathetic issue to which the underdogs could confidently appeal ten years ago seems to have been supplanted by a qualified pro-competition sentiment "sicklied o'er with the pale cast of thought," in Hamlet's phrase, the fear that all-out competition will leave Bell on top. The agency attitude is, predictably, a reflection of congressional ambivalence.[30]

The OEA example affords a different, but instructive, sidelight on the matter. The OEA is charged by statute with the duty of serving two masters. (This is meant in a wholly nonpejorative sense.) These are the national interest in a free flow of exports, on the one hand, and on the other hand the nation's interest in barring from the export trade commodities and technology that may strengthen potential enemies. Both interests are explicit objectives of the 1979 Export Administration Act and reflect the inevitable ambivalence of the Congress in seeking to promote aims that are necessarily conflicting.

The "sympathetic issue" vehicle for advocacy, therefore, is not present in export license applications in a clear or simple sense, since at no time is there likely to be a dominant mind-set in OEA or in its congressional constituency that provides a lifting tide for the license applicant's boat. Generally speaking, the intellectual ambience in which applications are considered is set by the President's policy on trade with the Soviet bloc and the degree of visible tightening up that the President wishes to apply to high technology exports to the Soviet bloc. While this ambience has undergone changes in degree in the recent past—in both directions—it has not changed in kind for some years and does not seem likely to change in kind for some years to come. This leaves the personnel of OEA and the consulted agencies in the position of judging the career risks of licensing actions on a one-way scale. Denials of licenses can aggrieve only the private applicant. Grants of licenses that one day might be seen to have resulted in the release of useful military technology to potential enemies might produce that worst case of all career horrors, a search by Congress and the press for a scapegoat, a search leading to the grantor. On this scale it is easy to give much weight to the reasons to err on the overly strict side.

Thus, there are situations in which the sympathetic issue can take hold and become an advocate's vehicle; in other situations, the nature of the mission of the agency—an ambivalent mission in the case of the OEA—militates against such a prevailing force and leads to official caution that cannot help the private party seeking relief.

In any event, the advocate must explore whether a useful sympathetic issue exists and where, considered as a vehicle, it might be moving. Insight can begin from talking with personnel of the agency and with staff of the congressional oversight committee in circumstances that will permit a discursive, exploratory conversation. Is the matter at hand part of a topic that is presently a serious preoccupation of the committee or the agency? Is the preoccupation of recent vintage, or has it been around a while? Is a policy settled, is it in the process of settling, or is intramural opinion scattered? To what extent do emerging policy views depend upon a dominant individual protagonist? To what extent do views represent a broad consensus? Are any dominant protagonists likely to remain on the scene for a time, or are terms of office or electoral tenure of key personnel—committee, staff, or agency—likely to lead to the departure of a key player? These matters can be explored in unhurried conversation in a fashion that may yield a sense of present policy attitudes and the direction and pace of shifts, eddies, and undertows.

If policy commitments or trends of the agency or committee can be discerned from reconnaissance of this kind as currents that might move the advocate's interest in the desired direction, care must be taken to distinguish between policy trends that represent agency orientation and merely individual predilections or "kicks" of particular—even important—figures in the agency. It can be a serious mistake to stake one's case on policy initiatives of the latter type. Expirations of terms, changes of the party in power, congressional criticism, and many other currents can sweep such sands away. Before the advocate makes a tactical commitment to a "sympathetic issue," he should be satisfied that it is one that has durable support in one or more overseeing congressional committees and thus some promise of durable commitment in the agency.

CONTACTS AS SOURCES

Many lawyers and Washington corporate representatives think of their agency contacts as sources of information to be tapped, rather than as the other parties in a bilateral dialogue. The latter concept bodes far better for the productivity of the relationship. It is one thing to know who has the information one wants and quite another thing to get it. Apart from a generalized wish to be of service to taxpayers, what motivation does the agency or committee staff official have to impart helpful and considered information, particularly after the second or third visit?

The answer usually is that the staff official will be motivated by getting in return something that enhances *his* effectiveness in doing *his* job. That something is the same kind of information that the advocate wants from him. If the advocate is diligent in his reconnaissance among several agencies, offices within a single agency, and congressional staff, it does not take long for him to acquire information, impressions, educated guesses, and reflections that will be interesting and useful to nearly any public official working in that topical area. If the advocate is far-sighted, his visits thus become mutual education sessions, with each party to the visit coming away better oriented than before, more sophisticated, and better able to do his job. Each is thus serving his profession; each is in fact performing a public service.

A common stereotype pictures the businessman or his advocate on one hand, and the public official on the other, as natural enemies who should maintain arm's length relations or run the risk of seeming to consort and traffic with the enemy. This is wholly wrong.

The duties of official and advocate to their respective principals require each to educate himself in about the same way. If they exchange observations, everyone gains and duty is served just as, in a general sense, the public weal cannot help but gain from free dialogue and improved understanding between the public sector and business.

Naturally, both advocate and official will hold something back—confidences, tactical reflections, information which is as yet uncertain. It would be improper, in the sense of a breach of duty, for either to divulge confidential or privileged information. An experienced advocate does not pry for "hot" or "inside" or confidential information. Except in rare cases of well-established personal relationships, the advocate would make a mistake to try to engage his contact in gossip about the personal politics among individuals in the agency or about specific actions still under consideration. Not only are these efforts unprofessional, but they are good ways to alarm the public official, to make him feel that the advocate is slippery or untrustworthy, to make him fear the risks of continuing the dialogue. Future exchanges of information will, in such a case, become dry and unforthcoming, or the door will be shut altogether.

It is natural to think of writers and reporters for the trade press as promising sources of information. In the great majority of cases, however, barring close and long personal friendships, they will prove disappointing. These writers often know a great deal about what is brewing within an agency or a congressional committee, but they work under special constraints that predictably make them unforthcoming. They or their publications are in the business of selling information to subscribers, not giving it away. They live by information given them by government officials, many of whom insist upon remaining unidentified as the sources. Any valuable information imparted by a writer prior to publication date will augment two risks: the identification and consequent stoppage of his source for that information; and the possible leakage and denial of the information by the agency, which may spoil a potential story for publication. The reporter, therefore, has absolutely no motivation to give information to the advocate and very little motivation to exchange information, since the reporter's will nearly always surpass by a wide margin the volume and quality of the advocate's information.

THE CHANNEL SELECTION JUDGMENT —HIGH RANK OR LOW?

In the normal course, responsibility within an agency for its jurisdictional regulatory matters is spread over a long vertical chain of command; that is to say, a given jurisdictional activity reaches well down to junior officials and all the way up to the senior staff and to the head, or heads, of the agency. Press stories about changes of command in federal agencies often convey the impression that new agency heads originate the ideas, programs, and policies and set the drumbeat to which the agency marches. It is true that new agency heads often engage in such rhetoric for publication. It is also true that, on matters of philosophy or perspective, agency heads of unusual force and persuasiveness can often set a direction or an intellectual ambience that will mark the work of the staff. It remains to the staff, however, to initiate by far the greater number of specific actions in rule-making, enforcement, and licensing, even if they do so under general policy objectives established by the agency head or heads. While it is in the name of the latter that final action is taken (except in matters formally delegated to the staff), the ideas often, though not always, start with the staff. They are developed, written up, reviewed for comment, and "massaged" by a considerable span of junior and senior personnel, much as one would expect. Thus, whether the agency or the private advocate makes the first move in a given matter, the advocate must decide at what level or to which person in the agency he should address himself in order to commence his dialogue with the agency. (This refers to discussions of a substantive nature, not mere reconnaissance.) It is a decision that can have beneficial or troublesome consequences and should be approached with care. Where to start?

In each case the analysis that yields the answer to this question will involve considerations unique to the particular case; nevertheless, there are durable principles that will be important, often controlling. These tend to weigh on the side of starting the dialogue at the career working level, rather than at the level of a Presidential appointee in the agency, such as the Secretary, Administrator, Chairman, Deputy, or Assistant.

First, the career official will probably have had more familiarity with the subject in detail and will likely have more time, on a continuing basis, to devote to understanding and following it. If an important part of what the advocate seeks is attention to his matter, he is far more likely to get it from a career official.

Second, it is likely that the matter will loom larger on the career official's horizon than on that of the political appointee; it will be vested with more importance and will represent to him more interesting work than to the senior official already burdened with plenty of weighty matters. The political level official is usually running behind. More often than not, desire is not for a larger workload, regardless of the importance quotient. The career official is more likely to see in a given matter a path to greater responsibility and commensurate status in the agency and thus feel the necessary motivation to give the matter serious study.

Third, there is a considerable risk that, even if a political level official is the selected contact, he will, after a perfunctory audience, pass the matter back to a staff official. This official, being human, may feel demeaned that he was by-passed in the first instance, or he may feel challenged to show that end-runs do not pay. Such a frame of mind is not soil from which sympathetic treatment of the matter is likely to grow.

Fourth, in the end, the agency head will surely consider staff recommendations before taking final action. Better that such recommendations come from a staff assistant whom the advocate has consulted early in the game rather than from one who has been left outside the consultative process or who has been brought in only by his own chief.

Fifth, on other occasions the advocate will have other battles to fight at the agency. In those encounters, a staff official is more likely to be well-disposed and helpful if he was brought into the process by the advocate on the first matter than if he was by-passed. Moreover, he is more likely to survive as a player, well-disposed or not, than a political appointee with limited tenure.

These considerations have, over the years, produced much support for a rule of thumb: "Start at the lowest competent and responsible level in the relevant chain of command."

Against the advantages of beginning the dialogue with the agency at the career or "working" level, certain risks must be weighed. If the career official has too narrow a responsibility, or is too close to the trees to see the forest, or if he has formed intellectual commitments that are opposed to the advocate's cause, the risk is that the career official will start the ball of agency action rolling in the wrong direction. If the advocate then takes his case to a higher level, he will already have activated an opponent on the staff and must undo that opponent's work. If the only otherwise suitable choice on the staff is believed in advance to fit this description, this consideration may provide a compelling reason to go first to the agency head or at least to the political level. Such cases will not be many.

Second, the career staff official may be powerless to help because he is under specific policy guidance from above which can only be changed by persuading his seniors. In this case, however, first resort to the staff official is not likely to impair the chance of ultimate success, since it will only have disclosed that he is neutralized.

Third, the political level official, perhaps the agency head, might have come to office with well-known views in favor of precisely the action that the advocate now seeks, and it may be that these views run counter to well-known views of the staff. In these circumstances, why waste energy with the staff, when the advocate's chief asset is the top level official's ability and inclination to move in the right direction? These cases will be extremely rare, and even some of those may evaporate as the staff goes to work on their boss. If the top level access maneuver is to work at all, therefore, time may be of the essence.

One temptation that sometimes prompts advocates into starting at the top in an agency matter is the belief that the client will be favorably impressed with the advocate's access and clout. Without exception, this temptation should be resisted resolutely. The risk of backfire is too great to warrant assuming it for such meretricious reasons. The top level official will know the matter is not an appropriate one for his initial involvement, but he may hear the advocate out for reasons of civility. He is likely then to refer the matter back to the staff for advice, facts, recommendations, etc. The advocate then faces the "end-run" syndrome, mentioned earlier. A staff that will often be helpful if consulted initially can be expected to wish to establish the principle that there is no profit in trying the boss's side door. The top level official will usually follow their advice, and an embarrassing fiasco will result for the advocate. Next time, when he may genuinely be needed, the top level official will not be so accessible and the staff will not be motivated to be helpful. If the advocate's self-confidence is so undernourished that he feels that he needs a demonstration of clout, he is well-advised to choose name-dropping, dinner parties, or football tickets as his tools and keep exhibitionism away from his serious business.

In the majority of cases, the advocate will find that he is following the rule of thumb mentioned above and starting his dialogue with the agency at the staff working level. He should not follow the rule of thumb woodenly, however, but should approach the question from the vantage point of the analysis suggested in this section. If his case clearly fits circumstances that argue for the high-level access decision or for the working-level access decision, then he should be governed by the analysis and act accordingly. Rules of thumb are useful when the governing circumstances are not known or not recognized or when counterbalancing considerations make the case too close to call.

THE FREEDOM OF INFORMATION ACT[31]

Advocates who handle discretionary matters before the federal agencies, as well as advocates who handle formal rule-making and litigation with the government or with private parties, will have frequent recourse to the Freedom of Information Act (herein "the Act" or "FOIA").[32] The Act is a tool of many uses, and the substantial amount and utility of the information that an advocate can reach through its procedures can be very valuable in a broad variety of professional matters. The Act, passed in 1966, is the outgrowth of a movement that combined the curiosity of journalists about the unseen acts of government with the view of certain legislators holding that openness in government is a value to be promoted. The movement has been said to have sprung from the publication in 1953 of a book[33] commissioned by the American Society of Newspaper Editors. Congressman John Moss of California picked up the theme in the mid-1950's and thereafter legislative hearings, proposals, and activity snowballed until the passage of the Act.

Ironically, considering its early history, the Act has been of little use to journalists. The response time of agencies to requests for information is typically much longer than the time allowed by the deadline that the journalist must meet. The sophisticated journalist has frequent access to public officials who wish to "leak," or put out anonymously, their own versions of their agencies' doings that are favorable to themselves. This phenomenon continues to operate in a fashion independent of the Act. It is also questionable how much the Act has worked toward the accountability of government to the public. The tools of congressional investigation and hearing, of committee subpoenas, and of informal demands and requests for information by the Congress to the executive and to the independent agencies are resources that still operate quite independently.

If the press and the civic-minded monitors of "openness in government" have not made conspicuous use of the Act, a number of others have, chiefly consumer and environmental groups, many single-issue pressure groups, researchers of various kinds, corporate representatives, and lawyers. The discussion of the Act that follows will be oriented to the purposes of lawyers and other professional advocates, but will also have relevance to anyone else considering the uses of the Act.

Any treatment of the Act should draw perspective from some aspects of its early history. This was characterized by a generally grudging receptivity on the part of the agencies. A pattern of evasion and delay in compliance, purported ignorance of the agency records, supervisor pressure, and judicial caution in review proceedings were noted by a report of The Association of the Bar of the City of New York in 1974.[34] The reaction swung rapidly on both the legislative and the judicial fronts. As the judicial trend ran increasingly to greater disclosure, the legislative attitude ran to stiffer pro-disclosure legislative requirements, culminating in the 1974 amendments of which the final episodes were a Presidential veto and a legislative override.

The 1974 amendments narrowed the exemptions from disclosure and introduced some remedies for non-disclosure that seem quite energetic: a 10-day response time for the agencies, *in camera* review by the courts, the segregation of non-exempt portions from exempt material, and indexing requirements.[35]

The Act requires each agency to publish currently in the Federal Register descriptions of its organization, and directions enabling the public to make requests for information; statements of its functions;

and its procedural and substantive rules.[36] Each agency is required to make available for public inspection and copying final opinions and orders, statements of policy and interpretations, and manuals and staff instructions that affect the public.[37]

Subsection (a)(2)(C) requires each agency to "maintain and make available for public inspection and copying current indexes providing identifying information for the public as to any matter issued, adopted, or promulgated after July 4, 1967. . . ."

The heart of the Act is contained in §552 (a)(3), which reads as follows:

> (3) Except with respect to the records made available under paragraphs (1) and (2) of this subsection, each agency, upon any request for records which (A) reasonably describes such records and (B) is made in accordance with published rules stating the time, place, fees (if any), and procedures to be followed, shall make the records promptly available to any person.

It is apparent that the request for records is a document to be crafted with great care, since it will establish the conditions for treatment of the request by the agency and will provide or deny to the agency, depending upon the care with which the request is framed, the means of resisting a request, or narrowing it, or stalling for time.

Under clause (A) of subsection (3) the request must "reasonably describe" the records sought. This clause has not been interpreted to lay down the impossible condition of requiring the requester to know the records that he is requesting, though he has never seen them before. Rather, all that is necessary to comply with clause (A) is a request that describes the subject matter in a way that will enable the custodian of the records to look the material up. If the requester is uncertain how to describe the records in a way that will enable the custodian to identify the file, he should serve a request upon the agency for the index or indices of all records that touch upon the designated subject. The agency has an obligation to provide an index, and the requester can work from there.[38]

Clause (B) of subsection (3) requires that the requester comply with the published rules of the agency that state the procedures and the conditions for lodging a request, including the fees for making the materials available. It hardly needs saying that an agency disposed to delay or resist requests will be encouraged to do so all the more if the request does not comply with the agency's rules. The requester would do well to put a ceiling on the fee liability that the request will incur, i.e., to state in the request that he wishes that the agency not incur fees of more than a stated sum, without further consultation. In this way, the requester can avoid an open-ended liability that could otherwise result from a request for materials of unknown volume.

As is apparent from subsection (3), if the requester complies with the conditions stated therein it is mandatory that the agency "make the records promptly available" to the requester. What "promptly" means depends, of course, upon the dimension of the request, the specificity with which the request is made, the volume of the source files, the duration of the search, etc. Nevertheless, "promptly" is further affected by subsection (6). That section requires each agency to determine within ten days of the receipt of the request whether it intends to comply with the request and to notify the requester "immediately." The requester is given twenty days within which to appeal an adverse determination to the head of the agency. In practice, agencies often negotiate extensions of time with the requester, particularly in cases where it is clear that all, or most, of the request will be complied with and a reasonable response time, as opposed to a controversy, would work in favor of both sides. In such a case, particularly where the scope of the search is quite broad, the requester usually has little alternative but to agree to allow the time that is necessitated by the backlog of prior requests, and by the search and assembly of the material. This can often run into months.

In cases where the agency is disposed to resist the request, the agency's initial response to the request will very often follow one of several well-versed bureaucratic forms. These include responses designed to dead-end or delay any further concern with the request, such as:

- the request is not sufficiently specific;
- the records requested are not in the agency files;
- the search indicates no such records;
- more time is necessary for processing and search;

- query as to reasons for the request;
- acknowledgment and postponement;
- acknowledgment and postponement to notify the file subject;
- grant of request, with postponement for assembly;
- grant of request, with deletions;
- grant of request, with postponement of delivery until large search fee is paid.

O'Reilly's treatise[39] suggests tactics for dealing with these forms of agency response. Specificity may or may not be adequate, and perhaps can be narrowed across the board or that part of the request that is adequately specific can be identified. If the records are missing, they can be traced and pursued where relocated or, if not traceable, suit can be filed and the agency called to account. Excessive requests for more time can be met by taking an administrative appeal. A demand for the reasons for the request can be met the same way and is an improper demand, to be met only if the agency is in a legally strong withholding position.

The administrative appeal from an adverse agency determination can be a crucial document. The appeal is taken by letter to the appellate official designated in the agency regulations or to the head of the agency. It should be as specific as possible in rejecting the exemption, or excuse for delay, or deletion, or other nonresponsiveness appealed from. It should marshal all available legal authority so as to maximize the chance of forming or changing the legal perspective of the appellate official and so as to make the most compelling administrative record in the event of a suit to enforce the request. In the appeal, the requester should aim to strengthen his case by stating reasons why the request should be met, why the description is reasonable, why some claimed exemption does not apply, and why the agency is not in compliance with the Act, so as to put the request in its most compelling and reasonable light. Since the appeal will be determined by someone other than the person who received and passed upon the request initially, it is far from inevitable that the appeal will encounter the resistance that the officials at the initial level may feel. On the contrary, the official determining the appeal must examine it on the assumption that the requester will resort to judicial review if the request is not met. Such a perspective may bring to bear quite different considerations than those in the mind of the official who received the request in the first instance. In this regard, the appeal official will presumably be guided by the Justice Department's standards governing the treatment by federal agencies of requests under the Act. The edition of these standards mentioned by O'Reilly was set forth by the Office of Information Law and Policy in the Department of Justice (January 29, 1979).[40] Those standards were drawn to minimize the chances of the government losing FOIA litigation and of suffering court decisions further limiting the discretion of the agencies. If the agency does not comply with the standards, the Department of Justice will not undertake to defend the litigation. The requester has reason to hope, therefore, that the administrative appeal will be determined by rules that seek to be objective and that are designed to avoid needless controversy.

The agencies are not required to disclose exempted material. The exemptions are specified in subsection (b) of the Act.

For the purposes of this Chapter only exemptions (b)(4) and (5) will be discussed, since they comprise a high percentage of the requests and of the controversies that arise under the statutory exemptions.[41]

Exemption (b)(4) provides that the disclosure requirements are not applicable to "trade secrets and commercial or financial information obtained from a person and privileged or confidential; . . ."[42]

In examining the (b)(4) exemption, the advocate's point of view will depend upon whether he is seeking disclosure of the information and thus trying to narrow the exemption, or whether he is seeking to protect from disclosure information submitted by his client to the agency, information now sought by a competitor or a pressure group. It is in connection with exemption (b)(4) that private parties are most likely to fight out the information request with each other. The advocate can just as easily find himself fighting disclosure as seeking it, since the interests involved are chiefly private interests. In most of the other exemptions, except those raising privacy issues, the adverse interests are normally those of the agency itself and the requester.

Information that has been found to be in the (b)(4) "commercial" category includes business and investment plans and strategies, sales figures, technical and product information, research data, details of employee structure and pay scale, prices, suppliers, customers and union authorization cards. In the financial category are loan and accounting information, profit and loss data, information regarding interest rates, operating costs, imports, income payments, income sources and credit.[43]

The case law has given a strong and expansive definition to "trade secrets,"[44] though a federal court would presumably look to the applicable state law to determine whether the facts at hand involve a "trade secret." To fit within the categories of (b)(4), the information must have been closely guarded by the submitter and there must be a demonstrable adverse competitive impact upon the submitter if the information is disclosed. *National Parks and Conservation Association v. Morton,* 498 F.2d 765 (D.C. Cir. 1974). If the party seeking disclosure can establish that the information has not been guarded or that disclosure would not have an appreciable injurious effect upon the submitter, then the information is likely to be disclosed.

In the case of most of the exemptions, again putting aside those subject to Privacy Act[45] issues, the effect of the exemption, once established, is not to bar disclosure but only to make disclosure not mandatory, leaving it to the discretion of the agency. This is not the case with (b)(4). If the information is found to be confidential or in the nature of trade secrets, disclosure is barred by 18 U.S.C. §1905, the so-called "Trade Secrets Act."[46] Moreover, the considerations weighing toward protection are heavily reinforced by the inescapable proposition that disclosure would amount to a taking of property without compensation, though that proposition has not yet been decided squarely by a federal appeals court.

So far what has been said deals with substantive standards. Problems are likely to arise, however, on the procedural side, since the agencies vary widely in the degree of protection that they afford to the (b)(4) categories of information and in the notice and opportunity given to the submitter to move to protect the same against disclosure. For example, the attitude and procedures of the Food and Drug Administration, the Federal Trade Commission, the Environmental Protection Agency, Consumer Products Safety Commission, Federal Communications Commission, and Department of Transportation are far from uniform and may be seen to pose for the submitter the practical problem of uncertainty as to whether he can expect notice of a request to disclose, or possibly of the agency's intention to disclose, or whether disclosure might take place without warning.[47] Generally speaking, however, the submitter is likely to have notice of a request for disclosure, particularly if the material has been submitted in the first instance with confidential marking and subject to a written request that it be accorded confidential treatment. Some agencies permit a "pre-submission review," an informal procedure in which the agency may be asked for its concurrence that information about to be submitted or reported to it is in fact confidential and exempt from disclosure under (b)(4). It behooves the submitter, therefore, to prepare material carefully for submission, to seek pre-submission review where possible, to mark the material "confidential," to request confidential handling by letter, and to ask in writing for notice of any requests for disclosure from third parties.

On balance, although there is no ironclad protection for confidential material submitted to government agencies, neither is FOIA a profitable avenue for competitors, researchers, and others seeking to pry into trade secrets and financial confidences. The sensitivity of the courts to protecting trade secrets and confidential information appears to be increasing; at this writing, Congress has before it various legislative proposals, not without opposition, to give added protection to confidential information and trade secrets.

As mentioned earlier, the exemptions in the Freedom of Information Act (with the exception of the "trade secrets" exemption) do not *require* an agency to withhold disclosure but merely remove the exempt records from mandatory disclosure, leaving the agency with the discretion to disclose or not. The initiative for blocking disclosure rests primarily with the party that submitted the information.

Assuming that the submitter is notified of a disclosure request, he normally initiates such action through a request to the agency that the information not be disclosed. If the agency does not concur in the nondisclosure view, the submitter of the information must then protect its confidences by judicial action. The Act does not, of its own terms, give such a party a right of action to prevent disclosure. A right of action has been implied, however, by the case law and rests upon two bases. One is the Administrative Procedure Act and the right to judicial review thereunder; the other is the prohibition upon agencies against disclosing proprietary information protected by the Trade Secrets Act,[48] although the latter act is a criminal, rather than a civil, statute.

To be effective, a right of action must depend upon the moving party having timely notice of the request for disclosure and of the agency's intention to disclose the information. In *Chrysler Corporation* v. *Brown*,[49] the Supreme Court has implied such an obligation of the agencies. Such an action is known as a "reverse-disclosure suit," now a familiar phenomenon in information practice before the federal courts.

Subsection (b)(5) of the Act exempts from disclosure "inter-agency or intra-agency memorandums or letters which would not be available to a party other than an agency in litigation with the agency; . . ." This is, in O'Reilly's view, the most controversial exemption in the Act and one of the most frequently invoked. In exempting material which is not available in discovery to a party in litigation, (b)(5) adopts the standard of Rule 26 of the Federal Rules of Civil Procedure. This rule exempts from disclosure advisory communications from one government officer or employee to another. The case law under (b)(5) applies this standard on the basis of pre-deliberative communications (advisory) as opposed to post-deliberative communications (not advisory). *EPA* v. *Mink*, 410 U.S. 73 (1973). Thus, material containing intra-agency or inter-agency arguments about a proposed ruling or course of action, or posing alternatives, or containing recommendations, would be exempt from disclosure under subsection (b)(5). A simple example would be a memorandum from the Chief of the Common Carrier Bureau of the FCC to the Commission recommending and outlining a proposed decision in a disputed common carrier application like the MCI Chicago - St. Louis service case, mentioned earlier in this chapter. These pre-deliberative materials, i.e., subjective advisory materials submitted to agency principals prior to final decision, are protected in order to protect the confidentiality and integrity of agency decision-making and to enable agency staff to give their most candid advice to their principals without having to account for it in public.

Postdeliberative materials, such as opinions, interpretations of rulings, and commentary upon decisions, are not exempt. Purely factual reports and materials, even if predeliberative, are not exempt under (b)(5). In this group fall materials such as applications for government research grants; unclassified portions of reports on underground nuclear tests; records supporting an SEC staff study on "off-board" trading (a finding critical to disclosure was that the material did not contain any substantive "exchange of ideas," such as proposals or arguments, thought to be the hallmark of predeliberative advice); and work notes, written data, and computations pertinent to a Bureau of Customs laboratory report on imported fibers and fabrics. Where materials include some factual material and some advisory or subjective material, the factual material is not exempt if it is capable of segregation from the remainder.

If advisory predeliberative materials are explicitly adopted by the agency as, or in, its decision, the materials are not within the (b)(5) exemption, on the theory that they then become postdeliberative.[50] This category covers, for example, memoranda (and related documents) by National Labor Relations Board staff counsel proposing and drafting Advice and Appeals Memoranda dismissing complaints, when the staff memorandum is incorporated by reference in the operative dismissal Memorandum. *NLRB* v. *Sears Roebuck & Co*. 421 U.S. 132, 95 S. Ct. 1504, 44 L.E. 2d 29 (1975). Memoranda that conclude that the agency will take no action upon a certain matter or will not commence enforcement proceedings—so-called "no action letters"—are not exempt under (b)(5), again on the post-deliberative theory. Documents examining agency compliance with established policies, sometimes called "compliance monitoring," are not protected by the exemption. For example, Civil Service Commission studies and reports evaluating the way that different agency managements were performing their personnel management responsibilities were held non-exempt on the ground that those materials were not part of any specific deliberative process. *Vaughn* v. *Rosen*, 523 F.2d 1136 (D.C. Cir. 1975).

Exemption (b)(5) is of particular interest to the advocate because of the high degree of natural curiosity that he and his clients might have about the activities of the regulatory agencies in the sectors affecting them. This would include curiosity about who may have filed complaints, whether there are differences of view among the agencies, what public comments on, or protests of, actual or intended agency action may exist, what directives within the agency may govern agency practice, who may have directed *ex parte* communications to the staff or agency members, and a host of other matters in the nature of tactical intelligence. Even if curiosity is absent, the advocate may well wish to establish his own diligence in exhausting available resources.

In passing over the remaining seven exemptions in the Act, we do not wish to imply that they are unimportant or that they must not be studied in detail when they are encountered. The two exemptions (b)(4) and (b)(5) have been selected for discussion solely because of their prominence in work before the agencies in a business-oriented practice.

It should be emphasized, as previously indicated, that the materials protected under the Privacy Act of 1974[51] are in most cases barred from disclosure, whereas most of the exemptions in FOIA leave the agency with discretion to disclose or not. The advocate who is seeking to protect information in the categories covered by the Privacy Act should concentrate, therefore, upon the provisions of that Act rather than on FOIA as the basis of his legal right to bar disclosure.

It should be pointed out also that the fact that exemption (b)(5) of FOIA exempts predeliberative interagency or intra-agency communications does not mean that the predeliberative proceedings of agencies will invariably be protected from disclosure. The reason for this is the Government in the Sunshine Act.[52] This Act applies to agencies headed by collegial bodies of two or more individual members, such as the FCC, and requires open meetings of such agencies with notice to the public, except in unusual situations. It may be, therefore, that the substance of some material that would be exempt from disclosure under exemption (b)(5) of the Freedom of Information Act might be disclosed, at least partially, to the alert observer in a "sunshine" meeting of a collegial body agency under the Sunshine Act. This resource should not be overlooked, though it is not likely to provide a detailed insight into staff advice of a predeliberative nature.

THE RELATION OF ADVOCATES TO THE SYSTEM

Americans have long been, and still are, ambivalent about their citizen relationships with regulatory bureaucracy. While it is commonly thought that we have too much regulation, it is also commonly thought that it is somehow suspect for businessmen, or their advocates, to seek to exert persuasion upon regulatory agencies or their parent legislature, the Congress. This ambivalence long antedates the antiphonal exchanges between the Ralph Naders and the Irving Kristols, or, if you will, between Common Cause and the American Enterprise Institute. The roots lie in the conflicting philosophies of laissez faire and anti-corporate populism that remain as unresolved, authentic presences in the American psyche, a Yin and a Yang coexisting in our national life.

In the process of advocacy before the agencies, these conflicting streams find a form of reconciliation. The advocate seeks to interpose his skills between the bureaucracy and the object of regulation in order to test the validity of proposed action, to try the power of the state, to keep government from overreaching, and to put forward alternatives and compromises—and to do it with regard for the rules, for propriety, and for professionalism. In this role, the advocate must be seen as an indispensable part of the governmental process, a part which would have to be invented if it did not exist. He becomes, in microcosm, the mediator between the Jeffersonian and the Hamiltonian models of government. His work becomes a part of what government does. The advocate should always work with an awareness of the responsibility that must accompany this role. It is in this role, not in the perspective of parochial advantage, that the advocate is to be understood by society.

FOOTNOTES

[1]Such as the power to ". . . take Care that the Laws be faithfully executed. . . ." Art. II, Section 3.

[2]For example, the power in Article I, Section 8, C. 3, "to regulate Commerce with foreign Nations, and among the several states . . . ."

[3]McGowan, *Congress, Court and Control of Delegated Power*, 77 Col.L.R. 1119, 1126 (1977).

[4]Beyond the scope of a book on Washington representation is the controversy over the problems of judicial review caused by "standardless delegation" of rule-making authority to executive and independent agencies by Congress, and over the "legislative veto" and proposed structural substitutes for legislative veto. For an astute and thorough treatment of this bundle of related subjects, including legislative and judicial remedies, see Judge McGowan's article, *supra*.

[5]McGowan, *supra*, 1167.

[6]In this chapter, both male and female advocates are encompassed by the pronouns "he," "his," and "him," following anthropological usage and sense of the word "man," as in *The Ascent of Man*.

[7]Professor Antonin Scalia has made the interesting suggestion that the pressures upon rule-making, chiefly the legislative veto and judicial review hostile to standardless delegation, will make it increasingly attractive to agencies to proceed instead by

adjudication in particular matters. Scalia, *Back to Basics: Making Law Without Making Rules,* Regulation; American Enterprise Institute Journal on Government and Society (July/August, 1981), p. 25. This writer has his doubts. Adjudication would seem insufficiently appealing to the zeal of the regulator to play his role on a large scale, an urge that has its origin in human nature, perhaps even in our simian ancestry. The urge would not seem likely to yield to tactical calculation. To paraphrase Clarence Day, if we were descended from the great cats, perhaps a trend to less flamboyant regulation by adjudication might be in the cards.

[8]Pub. L. No. 96-72, 93 Stat. 505 (codified at 50 U.S.C. app. §§2403 *et seq.* (1980)).

[9]50 U.S.C. App. §2404-5 (1980).

[10]15 C.F.R., pts. 370, 371 (1981).

[11]15 C.F.R., pt. 399 (1981).

[12]15 C.F.R., pt. 379 (1981).

[13]47 U.S.C.A. §214 (1981).

[14]47 U.S.C.A. §309 (1981).

[15]47 U.S.C.A. §721(c)(9) (1981).

[16]*In Re Application of Microwave Communications, Inc.*, 18 F.C.C. 2d 953 (1969).

[17]Agency actions of such sweeping dimension, decided under virtually standardless authority, naturally attract an exacting scrutiny on judicial review, as judges look for ways to place limits upon seemingly open-ended delegated legislation. The intellectual process of such review has been described by Judge McGowan, *supra*, pp. 1125-26:

> . . . This record tends to resemble nothing so much as the record made in a legislative committee hearing on a proposed bill. By the same token, it can be said with some plausibility that the vote of a judge scrutinizing that record resembles nothing so much as the vote for or against a bill by a conscientious legislator who has done his homework. In such circumstances, the conclusional labels to be affixed by the court—"arbitrary," "capricious," "an abuse of discretion," or "discriminatory"—can slide very easily into the same value judgments as are made by legislators in casting their votes, or by administrators in formulating their statements of reasons for doing what they are doing.

[18]15 U.S.C.A. §80a-17(d).

[19]15 U.S.C.A. §77e-5 sets forth the Act's registration requirements and contains broad prohibitions against the use of any means of interstate commerce to sell unregistered securities. The term "interstate commerce" as set forth in 15 U.S.C.A. §77b-2(7) ". . . means trade or commerce in securities or any transportation or communications relating thereto among the several states or between the District of Columbia or any territory, or between any foreign country and any State, Territory, or the District of Columbia, or within the District of Columbia."

[20]29 Fed. Reg. 9828 (1964) [SEC Securities Act Release Nos. 33-4708 and 34-7366; 1 Fed. Sec. L. Rep. (CCH) ¶1361].

[21]The quoted phrase is from The Export Administration Act of 1979, §3(2)(A), 50 U.S.C. App. §2402(2)(A).

[22]In the first nine months of 1981, 48,096 printed pages.

[23]E.g., *The United States Attorneys Manual*, a publication for the United States

Attorneys (who are responsible to the Attorney General) setting out prosecution criteria, modes of working with the divisions of the Department of Justice, recommended methods of organizing litigation, etc.

[24]47 C.F.R. §§1201 *et seq.* (1980).

[25]The Communications Satellite Act of 1962, Pub. L. No. 87-624, 76 Stat. 419 (codified at 47 U.S.C. §§707 *et seq.*), is regarded as applying only to the international system maintained by INTELSAT (International Telecommunications Satellite Organization), while domestic satellite systems and maritime systems (in respect to United States-based operations) are viewed as falling under the coverage of the Federal Communications Act as radio or common carrier facilities.

[26]The categories of "decisional" personnel are listed at 47 C.F.R. §1.1205, 1.1209 (1980).

[27]Resourceful use can be made of FOIA discovery procedures for a variety of purposes beyond the scope of this immediate context. See the discussion in this chapter, "The Relation of Advocates to the System."

[28]The agencies referred to are Comptroller of the Currency, Board of Governors of the Federal Reserve System, Federal Deposit Insurance Corporation, and Federal Home Loan Bank Board.

[29]Docket No. 80-603, *Report and Order*, 90 F.C.C. 2d 676 (1982).

[30]See, for example, the Packwood Bill, S.898, 97th Cong., 1st Sess. Sec. 2:

> . . . (2) competition is a more efficient regulator than Government of the provision of diverse telecommunications services and, as competition continues to develop, deregulation of telecommunications carriers and services should occur;
>
> . . . (4) the transition to competition and deregulation must be accompanied by appropriate safeguards to assure that basic telecommunications services are universally available at reasonable charges throughout the United States.

[31]Throughout this section, the author is heavily indebted to James T. O'Reilly's definitive treatise, *Federal Information Disclosure* (Shepard's, Inc. 1977) (hereinafter "O'Reilly").

[32]5 U.S.C. §552.

[33]Cross, *The People's Right to Know* (AMS Press 1953).

[34]O'Reilly, pp. 3-11.

[35]Id., p. 3-30.

[36]5 U.S.C. §552(a)(1).

[37]5 U.S.C. §552(a)(2).

[38]5 U.S.C. §552(a)(2). In addition, in litigation under FOIA to compel disclosure, the Court may order the agency to index the documents being withheld, and to supply cross-references to the exemption claimed by the agency for each document, or portion thereof. *Vaughn* v. *Rosen*, 484 F.2d 820 (D.C. Cir. 1973) *cert. denied*, 415 U.S. 977 (1974).

[39]O'Reilly, pp. 7-24 through 7-29.

[40]Now the Office of Information and Privacy, reporting to the Assistant Attorney General for Legal Policy.

[41]O'Reilly's treatise discusses all the exemptions in detail with agency position, court decisions and Department of Justice guidelines.

[42]5 U.S.C. §552(b)(4).

[43]O'Reilly, pp. 14-27 through 14-29.

[44]*Kewanee Oil Co.* v. *Bicron Corp.*, 416 U.S. 470, 94 S. Ct. 1879, 40 L.Ed. 2d 315 (1974).

[45]5 U.S.C. §552a.

[46]*Chrysler Corp.* v. *Brown*, 441 U.S. 281, 99 S. Ct. 1705, 60 L.Ed.2d 208 (1979).

[47]O'Reilly, pp. 14-51 through 14-75.

[48]18 U.S.C. §1905.

[49]*Supra,* n. 46. Successive remands have sent the matter back to the Department of Labor for findings as to whether disclosure would violate 18 U.S.C. §1905. *Chrysler Corp.* v. *Schlesinger*, 611 F.2d 439 (3rd Cir. 1979). There it rests at this writing. See Braverman, "*Chrysler Corporation* v. *Brown*: Protecting Business Secrets in the '80s," 4 Corp.L.Rev. 23 (1981).

[50]O'Reilly, pp. 15-35.

[51]5 U.S.C. §552a.

[52]5 U.S.C. §552b.

Chapter 2

EFFECTIVE REPRESENTATION IN AGENCY PROCEEDINGS

EDWARD J. GRENIER, JR.*

Over the last 10 years, the importance of agency proceedings has grown considerably. This is reflected in part by the proliferation of administrative agencies. The American Bar Association's Commission on Law and the Economy has reported that by 1977 there were approximately 85 federal agencies with authority to regulate some aspect of our daily lives.[1] Over one-fourth of these agencies were created between 1969 and 1975. Accompanying this growth in the sheer number of agencies has been a quantum increase in the scope of federal involvement in the activities of both individuals and corporations.

Despite efforts by Presidents Nixon, Ford, Carter, and Reagan to reduce the burden of federal regulation, much of the business in Washington is still being transacted in the context of agency proceedings. Some of these proceedings affect broad classes of persons, such as a Food and Drug Administration proceeding to determine whether a new prescription drug should be approved for public consumption. Other proceedings affect only the rights of one

---

*Edward J. Grenier, Jr. is a partner in the firm of Sutherland, Asbill & Brennan, Washington, D.C. He has had extensive experience in the administrative and legislative phases of energy law relating to gas, electricity, coal and petroleum and has frequently appeared before the Federal Energy Regulatory Commission and its predecessor.

person, such as an Equal Employment Opportunity Commission proceeding to determine whether an individual has been the victim of unlawful job discrimination. The stakes in these proceedings are often high in both monetary and human terms.

In this chapter, we shall explore some of the more important considerations that can spell the difference between effective and ineffective representation in an agency proceeding. By "agency proceeding" I mean a more-or-less formal administrative process—such as an adjudication, a rule making, or some type of "hybrid" containing elements of both adjudication and rule making—which is usually open to public participation and which is used by federal officials to determine how best to implement Congressionally mandated public policies. Excluded from consideration in this chapter are those types of discretionary agency actions discussed in Chapter 1.

Some readers will undoubtedly approach this chapter believing that agency proceedings are mysterious, unfathomable arenas in which outsiders have virtually no chance of suvival when pitted against experienced practitioners. Others will assume that agency proceedings can be easily mastered by virtually anyone who has access to the agency's rules of practice and procedure. The truth, of course, lies between these two extremes. As in most human endeavors, experience can be an invaluable "tool of the trade." However, experience alone will not ensure success. It must invariably be accompanied by thoroughness, attention to detail, and, in short, just plain hard work. Indeed, in some cases, a lack of experience can, to some extent, be compensated for by such diligence and aggressiveness.

Not all of the considerations identified and discussed below will be present in each and every case. One key to success lies in determining *which* factors are important in a particular proceeding, *when* those factors become important, and *how* they can be used to advantage. This often requires creativity and resourcefulness in even relatively straightforward and uncomplicated proceedings.

Before proceeding further, three general observations should be made. First, as will be pointed out periodically throughout this chapter, one of the most important considerations confronted by the Washington lawyer will often be whether his client should participate at all in a particular agency proceeding. The "do nothing" option is frequently available. When it is, it should be carefully considered. Not all problems can be solved in the context of an agency proceeding. Indeed, as Stanley Marcuss correctly points out in Chapter 5, a decision to participate in an agency proceeding can, in some situations, be as big a mistake as a decision not to participate at all.

Second, the stereotype of the Washington lawyer as "fixer"—the well-connected influence peddler who solves problems with timely campaign contributions and a few quick phone calls to the "right people"—is a part of our national folklore that is greatly overdrawn. A more accurate description of the Washington lawyer is the professional called upon daily to use a variety of skills in an effort to persuade decision makers of the virtue inherent in a client's position while silmultaneously establishing that this position is consistent with the public interest.

Third, it is important to recognize that a variety of factors have recently converged to make this a period during which important changes are taking place in the nature of agency proceedings. There is, of course, nothing unique about the fact that the administrative process is undergoing change. For decades, politicians, judges, lawyers, scholars, and others have discussed and debated the need for, or wisdom in, change. What is unique today is the direction and nature of the proposed changes and the fact that some of these changes are already being put into practice. Public support for these changes appears to be on the upswing. Much of the support is the result of attention recently focused on the issue of regulatory reform by Presidents Carter and Reagan.

The potential for further and even more profound changes in the administrative process is also evident from the increasing attention given to regulatory reform by Congress. The Administrative Procedure Act, which provides the foundation for most federal administrative law, was enacted in 1946.[2] The first major amendments to the Act did not occur until 1967, when Congress made effective the Freedom of Information Act.[3] Since then, Congress has enacted several major pieces of legislation designed to control the nature and course of agency proceedings, including The Sunshine Act,[4] The Small Business Flexibility Act,[5] The Privacy Act,[6] The Ethics in Government Act,[7] and The Paperwork Reduction Act.[8] In addition, Congress has, of course, enacted the National Environmental Policy Act,[9] which requires agencies to consider the environmental effects of their actions, and the Congressional Budget and Impoundment

Control Act of 1974,[10] which has important implications for the conduct of agency business. More recently, Congress has enacted legislation which deregulates important sectors of our economy. This legislation includes the Airline Deregulation Act[11] and the Trucking Deregulation Act.[12] These Congressional initiatives grow out of an increased concern over the impact of regulation, a concern which underlies continuing Congressional study of the administrative process.

For its part, the organized bar has also recognized the need for reform. Thus, the American Bar Association established a special commission—the Commission on Law and the Economy—and charged it with responsibility for studying the process and recommending possible changes.[13]

The principal goals of this reform movement are to decrease the burden of regulation by deregulating activities formerly subject to agency oversight and control, to improve public input into the decision-making process, to improve agency procedures by making them more efficient, to increase agency accountability, to coordinate the actions of different agencies, and to make the regulations intelligible to a greater portion of the public.[14] As a result, proposals for reform of the administrative process cannot be viewed as "legal theory" but rather as a force that must be dealt with in the context of agency proceedings on a daily basis.

THE ROLE OF AGENCY PROCEEDINGS

Generally speaking, agencies are expected to play not one but several roles—the roles of adjudicator, rule maker, and enforcer. Hence, the statement that agencies are "quasijudicial," "quasilegislative," and "quasiexecutive" institutions.

When functioning as an adjudicative body, an agency is most like a court, in the sense that it decides the merits of claims brought before it. Sometimes the claimants are private parties with opposing interests, such as commercial airlines seeking to maximize their respective shares of take-off and landing slots in proceedings before the Federal Aviation Administration. In other cases, there is only one claimant, such as a defense contractor seeking reimbursement for additional costs in proceedings before the Armed Services Board of Contract Appeals. Regardless of the number of participants, adjudicatory cases typically present material issues of fact which require the presentation of sworn testimony and the opportunity for cross-examination by opposing counsel.[15] In order to resolve proceedings of this nature, the agency must generally make findings of fact based upon record evidence and must provide an adequate explanation of how it reached its decision.

By contrast, when the agency proceeds as rule maker, it functions as a kind of minilegislature, adopting rules and regulations which have the same binding force as a statute.[16] The rules and regulations adopted usually reflect the exercise of a considerable degree of discretion as the agency searches for the most effective way of achieving broadly formulated Congressional policies and goals.[17] Unless the agency is expressly required by statute to follow procedures more commonly used in adjudicatory-type proceedings, it usually resorts to less formal procedures in adopting rules and regulations. These procedures can vary from the simple notice and written comment procedure used in informal rule making to more elaborate procedures which involve legislative-type hearings and presentations by panels of experts.

When serving in the role of enforcer, the agency acts most like officials in the executive branch of government.[18] The agency's primary mission is to see that the laws are faithfully observed. When potential violations are discovered, an agency will, depending upon its statutory authority, institute its own investigation and initiate proceedings to determine whether a violation has occurred, or it will institute an investigation and submit its findings to the Department of Justice for a determination as to whether enforcement proceedings should be commenced in the courts.

The characterization of an agency as adjudicator, rule maker, or enforcer is helpful because it focuses attention on the fact that the agency is a multipurpose institution. The characterization may also be a clue to the type of procedures that will be observed. On the other hand, such a characterization can be misleading. For example, the practitioner who assumes that the agency as adjudicator will function in the same manner as a trial court may be surprised and disappointed to learn that the agency has no formal rules of evidence or discovery and observes the Federal Rules of Evidence and Civil Procedure only in a very loose fashion.[19]

This same practitioner may also be blinded to the potential importance of public policy to the outcome of the adjudication. By definition, agencies that administer national programs will expressly or implicitly decide cases with reference to the policy implications of their actions. This is not to say that all adjudicatory proceedings are a battle of policy arguments. In some cases, the law will be clear and the relevant policies will be firmly established. In such cases, the attorney's principal concern will be with developing a factual record to demonstrate that his client comes within, or falls outside of, the parameters of the law and the policies that the law embodies. In other cases, however, the client's situation may not fit so neatly within a particular legal pigeonhole or under a particular policy. Or, the law and/or relevant policies may be unclear. In these instances, greater attention will have to be paid to identifying relevant legal and policy reference points and extrapolating from those reference points in order to achieve a favorable result. For example, the issue in a proceeding to determine whether an individual qualifies for Supplemental Security Income may be as simple as determining whether the applicant's "resources" are valued at more than $1,500.[20] On the other hand, a company whose operations are subject to the Occupational Safety and Health Act may face considerable legal and regulatory uncertainty because of ambiguities inherent in either the applicable statutory standard or the implementing regulations under which the adequacy of safety measures is determined.[21]

Similarly, to say that an agency is performing the role of rulemaker may suggest that the agency has more power than is actually the case. Generally speaking, agencies are not free to adopt any rule that they think is in the public interest. In addition to observing constitutional limitations which bind even Congress, an agency must stay within the confines of its statutory authority. It is also denied the luxury of being arbitrary and capricious and, in most cases, must have some kind of record upon which to defend its decisions before a reviewing court. Moreover, attention must be paid to the possible applicability of *ex parte* restrictions.[22]

Finally, the enforcement role of an agency often differs considerably from the enforcement role of the executive official by virtue of the fact that the agency is frequently empowered to decide whether a violation has occurred. Thus, while it may be true that there are limitations upon the agency's ability to serve as both prosecutor and judge,[23] it would be a mistake to assume that the agency can demonstrate the same degree of impartiality as a court before which the prosecutor is required to overcome a presumption of innocence. In addition, the agency is once again required to consider not only the propriety of the accused's conduct but the impact of punishment of the accused on the public interest.

For example, a public utility may operate its facilities in a negligent manner. This negligence might warrant a determination that the utility's customers should not be required to pay certain portions of the company's cost of service. By denying recovery of some of these costs, the agency could enforce the obligation of the utility's management to operate all facilities in a prudent manner. At the same time, however, this type of enforcement action could jeopardize the utility's ability to provide future service. This is not to suggest that utilities that operate their facilities in an irresponsible manner should be insulated from financial loss. What is being suggested is that a critical factor in the agency's decision-making process—i.e., the public interest in assuring adequate and reliable future service—is of potentially greater importance to the agency than to a trial court.

In short, an agency is a unique forum for the consideration of disputes and the problems of a complex interrelated society. In a very real sense, agencies therefore continue to function in our society as the "fourth branch of government." As such, agencies do more than merely apply law; they make law.[24] This should not be surprising. Given the broad statutory mandates under which most agencies operate; given the expectation that the agency will demonstrate flexibility in dealing with rapidly changing political, social, economic, and technological developments; and given the fact that the public interest is always lurking in the background, it is inevitable that agencies formulate new law. From the perspective of the practitioner, this fact—that agencies make law—requires sensitivity as well as creativity and imagination in representing clients before an agency.

THE CONTEXT OF AGENCY PROCEEDINGS

The institutional context in which an agency operates can be of decisive importance to the outcome of a particular proceeding. In representing a client before an agency, it is therefore essential to understand that context, to be able to identify the individuals with the potential power to influence the ultimate decision, and to understand the extent and limits of their power. Included in the "institutional context" in which a particular agency operates are Congress, the courts, the executive branch, and other agencies.

As the source of all laws administered by federal agencies, Congress has an obvious potential interest in agency proceedings. The agencies recognize this interest and, generally speaking, will not go out of their way to antagonize members of Congress. The agency's sensitivity to the opinions and desires of key members of Congress reflects the power that these members, individually and collectively, can exercise. This power can take any one of several forms.

It is quite common for members of Congress to attempt to use the confirmation process as a means of influencing an agency official's subsequent conduct. Thus, a key member of Congress may question a nominee extensively with respect to a particular area of interest. Such questioning can be used to make a nominee go on record in favor of a particular philosophy or viewpoint. It can be used to explore a nominee's familiarity with issues of importance to the law maker and to make known to the nominee the law maker's views and depth of concern over a particular issue. Such questioning can even, on occasion, be used to obtain an express commitment by the nominee to take a particular course of action or to refrain from taking particular actions.

In addition to confirmation hearings, members of Congress also have the option of conducting oversight hearings to explore an agency's actions and policies. Such hearings can be an effective forum for bringing public pressure to bear upon the agency and its officials. To assist in preparing a case against the agency, interested congressmen have not only committee staffs and their personal staffs but also the resources of the General Accounting office, the Congressional Budget Office, and the Congressional Research Service readily available. In addition, private parties often have the opportunity to appear before Congressional committees during oversight hearings to explain their grievances.

Perhaps the simplest way for members of Congress to put pressure on an agency is through a letter to the top agency officials. Such letters can alert the appropriate officials to a congressman's concerns and will often demand information or explanations regarding agency actions or proposals. Agencies routinely receive such communications and have established procedures for placing such correspondence in publicly available files. It is often difficult to assess the impact that such a communication has on the decision maker. In some uncontested cases, an inquiry from a member of Congress may be all that is needed to get the agency to take action—any action—on a pending matter and may contribute to a favorable result. In other cases, particularly contested cases involving complex competing claims, each of which represents valid strands of the public interest, it becomes more difficult to ascertain whether competing expressions of interest by members of Congress have any demonstrable effect upon the ultimate decision. At the very least, however, Congressional inquiries may motivate an agency to give serious consideration to a proposal that might otherwise be lost in the shuffle as the more vocal participants in the case aggressively argue their positions.

Assuming that such Congressional efforts fail to get the agency's attention or to influence the agency's deliberations, more drastic means remain available to Congress to change the course of agency action. One of the more obvious devices for influencing agency action is to control the agency's budget. If, for example, a particular program or activity is viewed with disfavor, Congress always has the option of reducing or eliminating funding. If, on the other hand, Congress desires to see more of the particular type of activity, it can authorize and appropriate increased funds and require the agency to spend those funds on the desired activities.[25]

A more direct way of influencing an agency's actions is to amend the statute which the agency administers. However, this can be a cumbersome and highly uncertain process. One or more interest groups may oppose the revisions sought, and the whole effort may fail for reasons having nothing to do with the merits of the issues.

In addition to these more traditional methods of controlling agency activity, Congress has over the last few years resorted with increasing frequency to two other devices. First is the one-House legislative veto under which an agency regulation is subject to review by either House of Congress for a specified period after promulgation. During this period, if either House, by simple majority, adopts a resolution disapproving the regulation, it is prohibited from going into effect. There has been a considerable amount of litigation recently over the constitutionality of the one-House legislative veto.[26] If ultimately upheld, it will provide private parties with a further opportunity to prevent undesirable regulations from going into effect. If, on the other hand, the one-House veto is ultimately held to be unconstitutional, it is possible that a substitute mechanism—a "constitutional legislative veto"—may yet be adopted.[27]

A further device, which has been used at the state level and may sooner or later be adopted by Congress, is the so-called "sunset review"[28] provision typically provided for in a statute establishing an agency. A "sunset review" provision limits the existence of the agency to a specified period of years. Prior to termination, a report is prepared and submitted to the legislature for review in order to determine whether the existence of the agency should be extended or whether other amendments should be made to existing legislation that would affect the programs which it administers. Building upon the concept of a "sunset review" for an entire agency have been several recent proposals for legislation which provides for similar reviews of specific regulations or regulatory programs.[29]

Having identified some of the more notable means by which members of Congress, individually or collectively, can seek to influence agency actions and policies, it should be quickly pointed out that the use of the "Congressional connection" to achieve favorable results in an agency proceeding is subject to important legal as well as practical limitations, not the least of which is finding the influential member or members of Congress willing to pursue a particular cause. This latter limitation is beyond the scope of this chapter and is discussed instead in Chapters 5 and 6. We shall return to consider some of the legal and practical limitations later in this chapter. At this point, suffice it to say that there exist considerable opportunities for members of Congress to influence agency proceedings in a lawful and appropriate manner and that effective representation in an agency proceeding requires the attorney to be sensitive to those opportunities.

In addition to Congress, the courts have historically played a significant role in directing the course and outcome of agency proceedings. As the only branch of the federal government constitutionally empowered to declare agency action unlawful, the courts are indeed the final arbiters of the extent of agency authority. At a minimum, the courts have the obligation to determine (a) whether the agency has acted in a manner consistent with the Constitution, including the question of whether the delegation of authority to the agency is constitutional, and (b) whether the agency has acted within the scope of its statutory authority. Beyond this, the courts are often empowered to review other aspects of the agency's decision or decision-making process in order to determine whether the agency has acted properly. The standards of review are quite often set forth in the substantive legislation under which the agency purports to act. In the absence of such specific statutory review procedures and standards, the courts will, generally speaking, observe the standards set forth in the Administrative Procedure Act.[30] The standard of review is often a function of the type of proceeding conducted by the agency. For example, agency action that results from an informal rule-making proceeding will often be subject to judicial review under the "arbitrary and capricious standard," under which the agency can sustain its action if it makes a minimal showing that its action was not unreasonable.

While the courts are not free to substitute their conception of the public interest for that of the agency, they have exercised a considerable amount of control over agency action. One danger that flows from this is that the attorney practicing before an administrative agency may rely too heavily upon the process of judicial review to clean up errors committed by the agency during the course of the administrative proceeding. The assumption that judicial review can be routinely relied upon as a safety net tends to obscure the need for careful work *during* the course of the agency proceeding. Careful attention to the details of the administrative proceeding will not only maximize the chances for success at the agency level but is a prerequisite to the development of the kind of record needed to succeed on appeal. We shall return to this subject in more detail later.

Presidents, like congressmen and judges, have for a long time attempted to influence agency actions and policies. Presidential control of agency actions has, however, traditionally been limited to those agencies that are part of the executive branch.[31] This authority to control executive branch agency action grows out of Article II, section 3 of the Constitution, which states that the President has the power to "take Care that the Laws be Faithfully Executed." The courts have long recognized that this provision authorizes the President to "supervise and guide" executive officers in "their construction of the statutes under which they act in order to secure that unitary and uniform execution of the laws which Article II of the Constitution evidently contemplated in vesting general executive power in the President alone."[32] By contrast, independent regulatory agencies are not subject to this kind of direct control by the President. Indeed, the purpose of establishing independent regulatory agencies was to insulate these agencies from control by the President.[33]

While the President's direct control is limited to executive branch agencies, the degree of control over such agencies is, in a very real sense, even greater than the degree of control which Congress and the courts are capable of exercising. Thus, the heads of executive branch agencies can be removed by the President with, or without, cause.[34] In short, if the President is unhappy with the manner in which an executive branch agency head is exercising his authority, the President can simply replace him with someone whose views are more in tune with the President's desires. There are, of course, obvious legal limitations on the President's authority within the executive branch. For example, the President could not direct an agency head to violate the provisions of the statute under which the agency was acting.[35] As a practical matter, however, the statutes administered by executive branch agencies permit the exercise by the agency heads of a significant amount of discretion. Given a choice between two lawful courses of action, the agency head in the executive branch can be expected to carry out the wishes of the President.

Recently, there has been growing support for exercise by the President of more systematic control over the actions of executive branch agencies. The support for Presidential control has coincided with an effort by both Presidents Carter and Reagan to begin exercising such control. In his Executive Order No. 12,044, issued March 23, 1978, President Carter directed all executive branch agencies and departments to adopt certain procedures intended to improve existing and future regulations and to make these changes in a manner that would minimize paper work.[36] Specifically, agencies were directed to publish a semiannual agenda of significant regulations under development or review; to exercise greater policy oversight in the development of regulations; to improve the opportunity for public participation; to establish criteria for identifying significant regulations; to prepare a regulatory analysis of significant regulations that includes a careful examination of alternative approaches to the proposed regulations; to establish a systematic review program for existing regulations in order to ensure that they are necessary and effective; and to promulgate regulations in clearly written and understandable language.

On November 30, 1979, President Carter issued a further Executive Order, No. 12,174, entitled "Paper Work."[37] The purpose of this order was to account for and control in a more coordinated fashion the information burdens that federal programs place on the public. The responsibility for overseeing this regulatory reform effort was vested in the Office of Management and Budget (OMB). Assisting OMB were such newly created agencies as the Office of Regulatory and Information Policy, the Regulatory Analysis Review Group, the Council on Wage and Price Stability, and the United States Regulatory Council.[38]

A little over one year later, on February 17, 1981, President Reagan issued his Executive Order No. 12,291.[39] The purpose of that order was, among other things, "to reduce the burdens of existing and future regulations, . . . provide for presidential oversight of the regulatory process, . . ., and insure well-reasoned regulations . . . ." To accomplish these goals, President Reagan terminated the policies and procedures previously ordered by President Carter by revoking Executive Order No. 12,044; in their place, he established his own policy and procedural mechanisms. Specifically, the President required executive branch agencies and departments to base their consideration of new or existing regulations upon "adequate information" regarding the need for and consequences of the proposed regulatory action. To the extent permitted by law, the agencies are required to engage in a cost-benefit analysis. Potential benefits to society must outweigh potential costs, with maximization of the net benefits to society the ultimate goal. Where alternative approaches to regulation exist, the alternative representing the least net cost to society is to be chosen. The only rules and regulations covered by these policies are those which are considered in the context of an informal rule-making proceeding.

While the focus was upon *agency* administration of these requirements, Order No. 12,291 substantially expanded the role of OMB in the review process (subject to direction from a newly established Presidential Task Force on Regulatory Relief chaired by the Vice President). OMB can, for example, designate a rule as a "major" rule, thereby requiring the agency to promulgate a Regulatory Impact Analysis (RIA) to assess the costs and benefits of the rules. OMB can also evaluate the adequacy of the RIA, require the agency to consider additional data, and prevent publication of the proposed or final rule until the agency has responded to OMB's concerns. OMB cannot substitute its decision for that of the agency. However, as a practical matter, OMB displeasure with a proposed agency action is not likely to be ignored.

Since issuance of President Reagan's Executive Order, the momentum in favor of Presidential control of executive branch departments and agencies has been given an added boost by a decision by the United States Court of Appeals for the District of Columbia Circuit in *Sierra Club* v. *Costle*, 657 F.2d 298 (D.C. Cir. 1981). In that decision, the court had occasion to review the propriety of various contacts between the White House and the Environmental Protection Agency prior to adoption of regulations governing emissions from coal-fired or oil-fired electric utility boilers. In upholding the President's right to engage in such consultations, the court made the following observations:

> The court recognizes the basic need of the President and his White House staff to monitor the consistency of executive agency regulations with Administration policy. He and his White House advisors surely must be briefed fully and frequently about rules in the making, and their contributions to policymaking considered. The executive power under our Constitution, after all, is not shared—it rests exclusively with the President.
>
> The idea of a "plural executive," or a President with a council of state, was considered and rejected by the Constitutional Convention. Instead, the Founders chose to risk the potential for tyranny inherent in placing power in one person, in order to gain the advantages of

> accountability fixed on a single source. . . . The authority of the President to control and supervise executive policymaking is derived from the Constitution; the desirability of such control is demonstrable from the practical realities of administrative rulemaking. Regulations such as those involved here demand a careful weighing of cost, environmental, and energy considerations. They also have broad implications for national economic policy. Our form of government simply could not function effectively or rationally if key executive policymakers were isolated from each other and from the Chief Executive. Single mission agencies do not always have the answers to complex regulatory problems. An overworked administrator exposed on a 24-hour basis to a dedicated but zealous staff needs to know the arguments and ideas of policymakers in other agencies as well as in the White House. (*Id.* at 405-406.)

The lesson to be learned by anyone who practices before an executive branch department or agency is that the White House, and particularly the Office of Management and Budget, must be considered as a possible means of gaining access to the hearts and minds of executive branch administrators. This is not to say that legal restrictions do not exist. On the contrary, anyone who seeks to influence an executive department or agency through the White House or OMB must be extremely careful to observe those applicable legal restrictions. However, the practitioner who chooses to ignore such opportunities may soon find that his client's adversaries are actively cultivating such contacts in a perfectly lawful manner, to his client's serious disadvantage. Failure to use the same avenues could at least constitute poor practice. Indeed, under some circumstances, the failure to use these avenues to influence the ultimate agency decision could run afoul of the ethical requirement that an attorney represent his client aggressively to the best of his ability.[40]

In addition to considering the potential impact of the courts, Congress, and the President on agency proceedings, the experienced practitioner must be alert to the possibility that other agencies and departments may, directly or indirectly, play a role in the ultimate outcome of a particular administrative proceeding. This possibility arises from several sources.

First, the prolification of "single-mission" agencies has increased the number of situations in which a particular activity or proposal will fall under the jurisdiction of more than one regulatory body.

Such cases typically present numerous potential pitfalls, as well as opportunities to use the position taken by one agency to influence a decision by another.

A further source of multiple agency involvement in a particular activity or proposal can be found in statutory provisions which require one agency to consult, or to act in concert with, a sister agency or department. For example, the Export Administration Act of 1979[41] gives the Secretary of Commerce primary responsibility for the administration of export controls imposed for reasons of national security, foreign policy, or domestic shortages. However, the Act requires extensive consultation with the Secretaries of State, Defense, and Energy.[42]

The desirability of input from another agency, either formally or informally, will, of course, vary from case to case. Depending upon the circumstances presented, it might be useful to encourage input by another agency. For example, input from an agency dedicated to aiding certain constituencies or activities might be of benefit to a private party from that constituency in a proceeding before another agency. A case in point was the input given to the Federal Energy Regulatory Commission (FERC) by the Secretary of Agriculture regarding the uses of gas that should be considered "essential agricultural uses" and therefore eligible for a preferential natural gas allocation during periods when interstate pipeline suppliers are experiencing shortages.

On the other hand, suggestions by another agency could prove to be a serious disadvantage—for example, a suggestion by the Council on Environmental Quality that an agency action your client is urging is a "major federal action" affecting the human environment, thereby requiring preparation of an environmental impact statement and considerable potential delay. In either event, the possibility of input from another agency or department cannot be ignored.

Nor can the likelihood of input from a state or local agency be overlooked. In some cases, the governing statutes require such input. For example, major environmental legislation enacted during the 1970's promotes, and in some cases requires, input from state and local authorities.[43] In other cases, such input, while not required, is actively solicited. For example, President Carter's Executive Order No. 12,044 was intended, in part, to increase participation by state and local governments.[44] With the Reagan Administration's emphasis upon "returning government to the people," we can only expect that input from nonfederal governmental authority will continue to be encouraged.

THE NATURE OF AGENCY PROCEEDINGS

The nature of agency proceedings is determined by the interaction of the Administrative Procedure Act, the agency's enabling statute, relevant court decisions, and agency practice. These "converging elements" have been correctly referred to by the United States Court of Appeals for the District of Columbia Circuit as a "baroque structure" within which "there is admittedly some room for confusion."[45]

The basic underlying procedural charter of most administrative proceedings is the Administrative Procedure Act (APA), which has been in effect since 1946.[46] The Act has four basic purposes: (a) to require agencies to keep the public currently informed of their organization, procedures, and rules; (b) to provide for public participation in the rule-making process; (c) to prescribe uniform standards for the conduct of formal rule-making and adjudicatory proceedings; and (d) to restate the law of judicial review.[47] The Act applies, with certain exceptions, to every agency and authority of the United States government. In general, the procedures required by the Act apply unless overridden by other statutory requirements.

Under the APA, there are basically three types of agency proceedings: (a) informal rule-making proceedings (governed by section 553);[48] (b) formal rule-making proceedings (governed by sections 556 and 557);[49] and (c) adjudicatory proceedings (governed by sections 554, 556, and 557).[50] The distinction between informal rule making, on the one hand, and formal rule-making and adjudicatory proceedings, on the other, is of particular importance because of the marked difference in the procedures applicable to each.

Informal rule making under section 553 requires nothing more than notice of the proposed rules that the agency plans to adopt and an opportunity for interested persons to comment on the proposals. With certain exceptions, no substantive rule may be made effective until at least 30 days after its publication in the *Federal Register*.

There is no requirement that oral hearings be held or that trial-type proceedings be conducted.

By contrast, those rule makings and adjudications that are required by statute to be determined "on the record after opportunity for an agency hearing" are subject to the more formal procedures provided for in sections 556 and 557.[51] Those latter sections provide, among other things, for the taking of evidence before certain agency personnel, the conduct of agency hearings, the allocation of the burden of proof in the proceeding, the issuance of a decision on the basis of the record developed during the proceeding, the right of a party to present evidence and to conduct cross-examination, the issuance of initial decisions, and the review of those decisions by the agency. Generally speaking, the provisions in sections 556 and 557 contemplate, even if they do not always require, trial-type proceedings.

While classification of a particular agency proceeding as an informal rule-making, formal rule-making, or adjudicatory proceeding has played an important role in determining the propriety of the procedures employed, the courts have often rejected such classification as the sole basis for determining the lawfulness of the procedures used. For example, in *Mobil Oil Corp.* v. *FPC*, 483 F.2d 1238 (D.C. Cir. 1973), the United States Court of Appeals for the District of Columbia Circuit expressly rejected an argument by the agency that notice and comment procedures, without more, were necessarily adequate in all informal rule-making proceedings. Instead, the court viewed the APA as "providing the outer boundaries of administrative procedures."[52] Thus, section 553 specified "the minimum protections upon which administrative action may be based. . . [and] . . . [a]t the opposite end of the spectrum lie the requirements of sections 556 and 557. . . [which] may be viewed as representing the highest degree of administrative protection that Congress believed would be necessary to protect interested parties."[53] The court refused "to conclude that Congress in establishing these limits intended to preclude all the possible formulations that might lie in between the two extremes."[54] Instead, the court concluded that the adequacy of the procedures employed by the agency must be judged against the complexity of the issues presented and the adequacy of the record developed by use of those procedures. In short, the courts were becoming increasingly less reticent about telling the agencies how to conduct their proceedings.

At the same time that the courts were beginning to require agencies to observe more formal procedures than the absolute minimum required by statute for informal rule makings, the agencies began searching for ways to avoid formal procedures in proceedings covered by sections 556 and 557 in order to expedite proceedings and cut through the growing regulatory backlog.[55] There emerged from these conflicting trends a growing tendency to employ "hybrid procedures." For example, in an informal rule-making proceeding, the agency might require, in addition to the submission of written comments, an evidentiary hearing on certain specific material issues of fact. Indeed, in certain types of informal rule makings, it has become the practice for the agency to hold a conference of parties or a legislative-type hearing, in addition to providing for the filing of written comments. For example, the Federal Energy Regulatory Commission recently successfully employed a series of technical conferences and legislative-type hearings featuring panels of witnesses (with fruitful crosscomments among the panelists and Commission personnel) in adopting rules to implement a series of regulations governing the pricing of natural gas to industrial users.[56] Or, in an adjudication, an agency might attempt to narrow the scope of the trial-type hearing by providing that certain issues would be the subject of written submissions or legal briefs.

It was against this background that the Supreme Court issued its 1978 decision in *Vermont Yankee Nuclear Power Corp.* v. *Natural Resources Defense Council, Inc.*, 435 U.S. 519 (1978), a decision with important implications for future agency proceedings. In *Vermont Yankee*, the Court overturned an appeals court ruling that the Nuclear Regulatory Commission, in an informal rule-making proceeding, had unlawfully failed to employ procedures beyond the minimum notice and comment procedures required by the APA. In reversing the lower court, the Supreme Court declared emphatically that, save in extremely rare cases, the notice and comment procedures were "the maximum procedural requirements which Congress was willing to have the courts impose upon agencies in conducting rule-making procedures."[57] The Court also relied upon a line of cases which for four decades had emphasized "that the formulation of procedures was basically to be left within the discretion of the agencies to which Congress had confided the responsibility for substantive judgments."[58]

The *Vermont Yankee* decision stands as a serious obstacle to future efforts by appellate courts to compel agencies to go beyond the minimum procedural requirements specified in the APA for informal rule making. This will undoubtedly encourage agencies to resort more frequently to informal rule making in order to expedite agency proceedings.

Should such a trend develop, the courts will likely be called upon to articulate standards for identifying the "extremely rare" cases which the Supreme Court in *Vermont Yankee* conceded might arise in which the courts would be justified in requiring observance of more formal procedures in the informal rule-making context. It is also conceivable that the courts may find alternative bases for reversing agency action under more traditional standards. For example, courts could reverse agency action for failing to address critical issues without telling the agency what procedures must be employed in order adequately to address those issues. The practical effect of such rulings could be to require agencies to employ more formal procedures.

In contemplating what is likely to occur in the wake of *Vermont Yankee*, we should not be so cynical as to assume that agencies will never accord procedural protections in informal rule-making proceedings that exceed the minimum requirements of section 553 of the APA. Such an assumption is predicated upon the belief that the *only* thing that administrators want to do is shuffle paper, and that they are completely indifferent to the consequences of their actions as long as their docket is current. While a premium is currently being placed upon administrative efficiency, we should not overlook the fact that most administrators take their oath of office seriously and do endeavor to further the public interest in carrying out their statutory duties. Consequently, we should not be surprised to find agencies continuing to experiment with procedural devices in an effort to give all participants in agency proceedings a fair opportunity to persuade the administrators that their positions should be adopted, while at the same time trying to avoid "undue" delay in the resolution of the proceedings.

Such experimentation with "additional" procedures (procedures beyond the statutory minimum) in informal rule-making proceedings may be mirrored by experimentation with "fewer" procedures in formal rule-making and adjudicatory proceedings. In short, we may see a trend toward procedures falling somewhere between the minimum and maximum required by the APA.

Experimentation with agency procedures may receive added impetus from participants in the agency proceedings. Experience has shown that a participant's interest in the procedures employed in a particular proceeding is closely related to his position on the merits. In some cases, participants will favor more informal procedures, such as cases in which the participant believes that the agency is inclined to decide in his favor. In other cases, these same participants may be wary of the agency's approach and may desire to see more formal procedures employed in order to develop a record that will convince the agency of the wisdom of their positions (or, alternatively, of the folly inherent in the positions of their adversaries) or that will increase their chances of convincing a reviewing court that the record will not support the agency's action in the event of a nonfavorable decision. It is also noteworthy that Congress, in a number of recent statutes, has required procedures beyond mere notice and comment in certain informal rule makings.[59]

UNDERSTANDING: A PREREQUISITE TO EFFECTIVE REPRESENTATION

According to an ancient proverb, "Wisdom is the principal thing: therefore get wisdom and with all thy getting get understanding."[60] This admonition, while it dates back many centuries, has special relevance for the Washington lawyer. In an age and in a city in which technical knowledge abounds, it is all too easy to mistake such "wisdom" for genuine understanding. The Washington lawyer is as vulnerable as anyone to this shortcoming, particularly when he handles matters which require a working familiarity with technical information. To represent his client effectively, the Washington lawyer must go beyond the mere mastery of such technical information and develop a fuller understanding of the client, his interests, and his problems; the legal framework; the agency (as well as other potential governmental players); and the practicalities of the situation.

Understanding the Client's Interests and Problems

Every lawyer should understand his client's interests and problems. While this admonition may appear to be painfully self-evident, almost trite, it is precisely because it is so obvious that a conscious effort should be made to avoid an "understanding" which is, in reality, little more than a superficial familiarity based upon erroneous assumptions and outdated facts.

A common human failing, which can be disastrous in the context of an agency proceeding, is to assume that we know more about something than is actually the case. Thus, for example, we assume that we understand the client's interest merely because we have heard the description of a problem confronted by one division, or one affiliate, of the client. Or, we assume that we understand the relative importance of a problem to the client simply because we are told that the problem is "significant." As lawyers, we are trained to identify assumptions and test their validity. As human beings, however, we routinely fall victim to the same traps that we criticize laymen for failing to avoid.

The danger of making erroneous assumptions is perhaps smallest when we are initially confronted with a potential problem. During this early stage of a lawyer's involvement in a potential case, he is inclined to ask questions and to identify and evaluate assumptions. There is, nevertheless, a danger that the lawyer will fail to ask important questions for fear that he may, in his client's eyes, appear to lack sufficient familiarity with the particular type of problem being discussed. What is called for at this point is a tactful and skillful method of probing all potentially relevant areas of inquiry without appearing to be ignorant of the subject matter. This can be particularly difficult when the employee or representative of the client with whom you are speaking has a vested interest in avoiding certain areas where he may be vulnerable to accusations that he has "dropped the ball."

A second, and perhaps even greater, danger is that the lawyer will at some point gain an adequate understanding of his client's interests and problems and will erroneously assume that his understanding is somehow absolute and unaffected by subsequent developments. As a result, his interpretation of the client's position becomes etched in granite and may eventually produce a result which no longer fits the problem. In order to minimize the possibility of such a result, it is essential to recognize that "understanding" is something that must be constantly updated and re-evaluated and that can best be achieved through the exercise of a good healthy skepticism.

In addition to these general admonitions, special mention should be made of the problems inherent in representing a corporate client. A corporation's perception of a regulatory problem (and the appropriate solution to that problem) will depend to a greater or lesser extent upon the identity of the department or individuals within the corporation with whom the lawyer deals. For example, a problem which in the eyes of Corporate Purchasing is the biggest single threat to the corporation may in the eyes of the Marketing Department be considerably less important. Accordingly, the attorney representing a corporation in a regulatory proceeding must be particularly sensitive to the possibility that the corporate representatives with whom he deals are overstating or understating the problem as well as the even more unsettling possibility that they are mischaracterizing essential elements of the problem. There is, unfortunately, no single fail-safe way of avoiding this potential problem entirely. Its danger can be minimized only by critical analysis and the exercise of independent judgment.

One of the potential pitfalls that must be guarded against is the temptation to define the client's problem too narrowly. The problem with which you are dealing will often influence, and be influenced by, developments in other areas. Identifying these other areas may provide alternative means of dealing with the problem. For example, by recognizing the relationship between environmental and energy policies, an electric utility facing air pollution control problems under the Clean Air Act (because of a proposed conversion to coal) may secure substantial relief from the Department of Energy. Such relief would be in the form of a prohibition order from DOE mandating the conversion to coal. Facilities subject to such prohibition orders are not treated as "new sources" under the Clean Air Act and are therefore subject to less stringent emission standards.[61]

A corollary to this suggestion is that an attempt should be made to understand the relevant history of the problem, the manner in which the client attempted to cope with the problem in the past, and the reasons why the client can no longer continue coping with the problem in this manner. It is also useful in this connection to determine whether other persons or corporations share your client's problem or whether they have opposing interests. These determinations will play an important role in formulating the strategy for dealing with the problem.

In attempting to develop his understanding of the client's interests and problems, the Washington lawyer frequently has the opportunity to increase the client's understanding of the manner in which the government operates and the reasons for agency action. What sometimes may appear to the client to be mindless bureaucratic action, or inaction, can frequently be explained as a very reasonable process from the perspective of the government official. Positioned as he is between private parties and government agencies, the Washington lawyer is, in a very real sense, an intermediary in an ongoing dialogue between citizens and their government. Through the process of representing his client, the Washington lawyer can help the two sides understand each other. In order to increase understanding on both sides, the Washington lawyer must himself begin the process by gaining, and maintaining, an understanding of his client.[62]

Understanding the Legal Framework

The need to understand the legal framework should be obvious. However, many "outsiders" view Washington lawyers as influence peddlers and, as a consequence, fail to appreciate the importance of understanding the legal framework. They assume, incorrectly, that because the agency administers broadly drafted enabling statutes, effective representation in an agency proceeding consists essentially of finding a sympathetic official who can be prevailed upon to take the desired action. While none would dispute the desirability of locating and gaining access to a "sympathetic official," there are nevertheless legal limitations upon agency authority, procedures, and discretion. These legal limitations play an important role in determining the actions that agencies can and do, in fact, take.

One reason that agency officials, generally speaking, do take the law seriously is that there is usually someone involved in the proceeding who has an interest in invoking legal precepts that place boundaries on their actions. That "interested person" could include an agency staffer who opposes a proposed action; a journalist; a member of Congress or a Congressional committee staff member; the President; other agencies; a private citizen or "public interest group"; and, last but certainly not least, an individual or corporation with a financial interest in the outcome of the proceeding.

From the agency official's perspective, the sanctions for failing to observe the law range from various degrees of bad publicity (a potentially devastating sanction in a media-conscious city like Washington), to Congressional investigations, to judicial sanctions that grow out of lawsuits.

In short, our national preoccupation with the rule of law perceived over 100 years ago by de Tocqueville[63] will, at some point, influence even the most cynical of twentieth-century agency administrators by forcing action in a manner that is at least arguably "lawful." As a result, the skillful use of "the law" in an agency proceeding is an invaluable weapon in obtaining a desired result.

The most obvious source of law in an agency proceeding is statutory law. The principal sources are the specific statute or statutes under which the agency is authorized to act and, to the extent applicable, the Administrative Procedure Act. Together, these statutes provide the basic foundation upon which the agency acts. They determine the agency's authority to act, the goals that Congress is trying to achieve, and the procedures that can be used in reaching a decision.

In addition to these principal statutes are what shall be referred to as "secondary statutes." Secondary statutes are those statutes that do not expressly authorize or require the agency to take specific actions but which nevertheless articulate federal policies that are properly considered by the agency in carrying out its functions. The importance of these secondary statutes arises because of the broad delegations of authority in numerous enabling statutes which require that agency actions to be "required by the public convenience and necessity," be "just and reasonable," and be either "in the public interest" or "not inconsistent with the public interest."

In carrying out their responsibilities, agencies are routinely called upon to give content to these standards; in doing so, they must look to other statutes for guidance. For example, in determining whether a regulated utility's rates are "just and reasonable," the FERC may (and, some would argue, must) determine whether those rates are inflated because of past discrimination against minorities—discrimination that is "contrary to the public interest" as embodied in the nation's civil rights laws.[64]

Answers to questions such as when and to what extent such secondary statutues permit or require particular agency actions are obviously complex and must be made on a case-by-case basis. The important thing for the practitioner is to recognize that effective representation in a particular agency proceeding may require familiarity with more than just primary statutes.[65]

Closely related in importance to primary and secondary statutes is the legislative history of statutes. Considerable care, however, should be exercised in the use of legislative history, which is often ambiguous at best. While a superficial analysis of legislative history might convince some administrators of the merits of your client's position, there is a danger that, sooner or later, you will run into an administrator or judge who is not only left unpersuaded by your legislative history argument but who may actually feel that the legislative history is so weak as to undermine the strength of your other arguments.[66]

Familiarity with relevant statutes and legislative history is, of course, only the starting point. Not until you have become acquainted with the important judicial and prior administrative interpretations of those statutes will you be prepared for your agency proceeding. Generally speaking, this admonition should not be necessary to lawyers schooled in the common law system, under which the importance of case law has been emphasized since the first day of law school. However, there is one aspect to keeping up with the case law which may be less apparent. Given the interrelated nature of many agency cases, the prudent practitioner will stay on top of judicial case law developments in cases other than the one in which his client is participating.

In view of the steady stream of court decisions involving review of agency action, this can be a formidable task, even when all of the related cases are before the same agency. Moreover, the private or corporate practitioner may find himself at a decided practical disadvantage vis-à-vis the agency counsel in staying abreast of these developments since the agency, as a party to much of the litigation, has immediate access to the relevant decisions. Perhaps the best advice is to subscribe to a good reporting service and to receive all slip opinions from a court which hears large numbers of agency cases, such as the United States Court of Appeals for the District of Columbia Circuit.

Equal in importance to knowing the statutes and their history is knowing the rules, regulations, and precedents of the agency. Unless overruled by a reviewing court, these agency pronouncements constitute "the law." While a decision by a federal appeals court may be surrounded by considerably more majesty, the key to your case may lie in a relatively obscure but legally binding regulation.

The relatively easy task is to research rules and regulations published in the *Federal Register* and *Code of Federal Regulations*. More difficult is the task of uncovering relevant agency decisions, particularly because of considerable backlogs in the printing of formal agency reports and because of less than ideal indices to more recent agency decisions. The problem of legal research varies from agency to agency, and it is impossible to offer general guidelines or shortcuts to assist the unfamiliar practitioner except to suggest that the neophyte seek to discover the parameters of available research tools from an experienced practitioner. You should be able to find at least one staff attorney who can give you an overview of possible research tools. Beyond that, your progress is largely a matter of trial and error. Some comfort can be found in the fact that even seasoned practitioners often find that researching agency decisions depends upon the more-or-less fortuitous knowledge that an acquaintance was involved in a case in which the same or analogous issues were presented.

Understanding the Agency

Having considered the context in which agencies operate, let us turn our attention to the agency itself.

Familiarity with the agency's organization and the manner in which the agency operates is extremely valuable. Often an organizational chart can be used as a good starting point for learning about an agency's structure. It is, however, a terrible ending point. What you really need to know is how the agency offices and bureaus work together in practice with respect to particular problems. Without long familiarity with the agency and its workings, there is no simple magic formula for acquiring this vital information. The best approach to this challenge is to find a knowledgeable and sympathetic staff member who is willing to give you an overview of how problems similar to yours are handled by the agency. If a single such staff member is not available, a series of conversations with various staffers should aid in illuminating the course your matter is likely to take through the agency.

It is also essential to know who the key personnel are. Even though an agency's ultimate decision will be issued by the top official or officials, certain key staff members may be the real shapers of the decision. By knowing the key players and their relation to each other, it is sometimes possible to tailor your presentation in a manner that will maximize the weight accorded to your client's position. For example, there may be situations in which an unsympathetic agency administrator can be persuaded by the agency staff to recognize an exception in a particular case. In such a case, it would be a mistake to attack the administrator's general views. Instead, you would be better advised to prepare a presentation that persuades the staff that an exception is warranted and that gives the staff adequate information with which to justify an exception in the eyes of the administrator.

The question that occasionally arises is how, and at what level, the initial approach to the agency should be made. In many cases, the answer to this question is determined by the agency's regulations, including specifically its Rules of Practice and Procedure, and the type of proceeding involved. Thus, for example, an agency's regulations may contain detailed procedures for submitting certain types of proposals to the agency. Or a particular proposal may be handled in the context of an adjudicatory proceeding governed by particular rules of practice and procedure.

Sometimes, however, you will have a choice of where and how to approach the agency—for example, in uncontested cases or in informal rule-making proceedings involving questions of policy. The choice is usually presented in terms of "starting at the bottom" or "starting at the top." Generally speaking, it is best to avoid going over the heads of front-line staff, at least initially. If your client has a good proposal, the staff will usually be reasonable. Moreover, if you convince the staff of the wisdom of your proposal, this will usually increase the proposal's chance of success as it goes through successively higher levels of review. There may, however, be occasions when it is better to start at a higher level. Even so, it is usually better to start at the lowest level possible. This will avoid unnecessarily using up "chips" at the higher levels. It will also avoid guerrilla warfare by disgruntled staffers whose only real gripe may be their displeasure with your allegedly heavy-handed tactics. In short, it is usually best to avoid making enemies unnecessarily. Moreover, to the extent that you pick up lower-level support for your proposal, these allies can be useful in later stages of the agency review process.

It should also be recognized that high-level initial review of the proposal may be hard to obtain. In large, controversial matters, the high-level people may be reluctant to touch your proposal without prior review and acquiescence by lower-level staff because of the danger of adverse publicity, a likely danger in a truly significant matter. On the other hand, if your proposal is a small matter, the higher-level personnel may not want to be bothered with it and prefer seeing lower-level staff process it.

In any event, if you decide to go to a higher-level official initially, you are well advised to have a good reason—a reason that sounds convincing and which warrants engaging high-level personnel in the basic review of a proposal. Otherwise, you will only antagonize the higher-level officials, secure a remand to the staffer you passed over, and get the opportunity to see bureaucracy at its worst.

In shepherding a proposal through an agency, it may also be necessary to make a special effort to coordinate with agency attorneys, since they may not be in the same office as the technical personnel who process your proposal. Do not underestimate the importance of the staff attorney. In the first place, attorneys usually speak the same language, something which may facilitate making your case before the agency. Second, if you antagonize the staff attorney unnecessarily, he may have the opportunity to repay you by recommending formal proceedings that bog your client down for an extended period.

Like your understanding of the case law, your understanding of the agency should be constantly updated. This applies to seasoned practitioners as well as to newcomers to agency proceedings. It applies particularly during these days of regulatory reform. One of the most obvious potential changes is a change in top agency personnel. A new chairman or top administrator will likely have an agenda and set of priorities different from those of his predecessor. New commissioners or administrators appointed by a new President are likely to reflect the new President's philosophy. Reorganizations of the agency could well signal a possible shift in agency policies or attitudes—to the benefit or detriment of your client. The careful practitioner will watch carefully for all such signs of possible future shifts in the agency's direction. A great deal of information can be gleaned from whatever specialized trade press covers the agency. You can pick up a good deal of information by chatting with reporters from those publications. (Remember, of course, that reporters are in the business of gathering information, not giving it. A reporter will be of help to you only if you can be of at least occasional help to him.) In addition to opinions and orders issued by the agency, another good source of information is, again, the friendly or sympathetic staffer. I do not mean to imply that you can, or should, seek out secrets through "leaks." However, a great deal can be learned from these sources without anyone leaking any confidential information or committing any impropriety.

A discussion of agency organization and operations would be incomplete if mention were not made of the opportunity to use the agency itself as a source of information. Agencies maintain extensive case files and routinely require the filing of potentially useful reports containing many different types of data. Some idea of the types of reports and data available through the agency can be gained by simply reviewing the description of an agency's reporting forms set forth in the Code of Federal Regulations. Some of the information collected by the agency is used by the staff to produce reports and studies on a variety of subjects. Much of this information can be obtained with little difficulty through an agency's Office of Public Information. In those cases in which the agency is reluctant to make information available, the Freedom of Information Act can be used to obtain access to the desired material. Time invested in learning how to use the agency's informational resources can pay a high return in the long run. Indeed, effective representation of a client in an agency proceeding will often hinge upon the attorney's ability to track down information, staff reports, and case files in the agency's possession.

EFFECTIVE USE OF AGENCY PROCEEDINGS

As should be apparent by now, effectiveness in an agency proceeding is no accident. It is the result of careful planning and preparation, attention to detail (without losing sight of the big picture), and sensitivity to the factors that influence decision makers. We have previously discussed the context of agency decision making, as well as some of the more notable developments and trends in the agency decision-making process. In the discussion that follows, we shall identify some of the considerations and techniques that can contribute to effective participation in an agency proceeding.

These factors are obviously not the only ones that can contribute to effective representation. Of particular importance to the practitioner will be those considerations and techniques that are peculiar to a specific agency or type of agency proceeding—considerations and techniques that are beyond the scope of this chapter. Nevertheless, the factors identified below have wide, if not universal, application and are therefore worth exploring.

Having become familiar with the client's situation, the effective Washington lawyer should have a fairly clear idea of the client's goals. Once the goals have been identified, he must assess the potential of an existing (or possible) agency proceeding for furthering the client's interests. He must then propose a strategy that will maximize the likelihood of achieving a favorable result. This is obviously a complex process involving numerous considerations.

In assessing the potential impact of an agency proceeding for achieving desired goals, it is useful to distinguish between agency proceedings that have already been instituted (including those that have been ongoing for some time) and potential agency proceedings that the client has the opportunity to request.

Existing or Ongoing Proceedings

The principal difference between an existing proceeding and a proceeding that has not yet been instituted is the relative lack of control that the client has over the scope, thrust, and nature of the proceeding. Thus, for example, if the agency has already decided to consider a particular issue in the context of a rule-making proceeding, the client will in general be less able to convince the agency or a reviewing court to consider a broader or narrower issue or to review the issue in a different type of proceeding, such as an adjudicatory proceeding. In short, the proceeding will be a given to which the client is required to respond.

This situation has important implications for the types of factors that must be considered in assessing the potential impact of the proceeding. The first thing that must be considered is the background and history, if any, of the proceeding. What gave rise to the proceeding—a statutory command, a problem perceived by the agency, a complaint or petition by a private party, pressure from another branch of government? What type of proceeding did the agency institute—a rule making, an adjudication, a hybrid proceeding—and what is its scope? How did the agency frame the issues? What type of factual or policy information did it expressly request? How does the agency propose to solve the problems presented? Finally, who has been participating (or who intends to participate) and what positions have the parties and the agency's staff been advocating? Answers to these and other questions regarding the direction and course of the proceeding will provide valuable insights into its possible outcome.

For example, consider a situation in which your client desires to bring about a change in the FERC's policy regarding the circumstances under which costs incurred during the construction of an electric utility generating plant will be included in the utility's rate base (thereby determining whether the utility will earn a return on its investment in the plant during construction). In such a case, the decision on whether to participate, as well as on the nature of participation, could easily depend upon whether the issue is raised in a general rule making or an individual utility rate case. If the commission has an ongoing general rule making, then you and your client will have to judge whether the scope of the proceeding, the questions raised by the commission in its notice of proposed rule making, the schedule for the filing of comments, and other parameters established by the agency will permit your client to achieve its goal in that particular proceeding. The answer to these and related questions will also help the client determine whether it should commission a study by experts in the field or limit its efforts to the filing of comments directed to the broad policy issues. On the other hand, if the issue is raised (or could be raised) in a particular utility rate case, you and your client should first determine whether a decision on this issue in this particular case is likely to have precedential value. If not, and if your client's interest in the particular utility system is only marginal, you might advise your client not to get into the proceeding.

Care should also be taken to identify other proceedings before the agency which could have an impact upon the proceeding in which you are interested. Similarly, you should consider proceedings before other agencies and the courts, as well as Congressional or Presidential actions, that could bear upon the outcome of the agency proceeding of interest.

Armed with this information, the lawyer can attempt to predict the range and likelihood of potential outcomes. Such predictions will be based upon an analysis of such items as the agency's authority, its policies (both present and foreseeable), and the form of the proceeding.

In assessing the potential outcomes, special attention should be paid to the opportunities that exist for the client to influence these outcomes through his participation in the proceeding. The assessment of a client's potential impact on a proceeding will play an important role in determining whether and to what extent a client will participate in a proceeding, as well as in determining the client's overall strategy.

Two aspects of an agency proceeding that must also be constantly borne in mind are the time required to complete a proceeding and the likelihood that the client will be able to enjoy interim relief (or continued freedom from agency sanctions) prior to conclusion of the proceedings. Despite the best of intentions, agency proceedings rarely adhere to an optimum schedule from a client's perspective. The agency practitioner and the client must therefore be prepared to deal with delays or unexpected (and sometimes undesired) expedition. In cases in which delay is harmful, you may be able to obtain some kind of interim relief. For example, in a case in which your client is seeking a license or other type of authorization, you may be able to persuade the agency to use its statutory authority to grant a temporary authorization. Thus, an applicant for a television license under the Communications Act of 1934 may be able to obtain a temporary license from the FCC pending the outcome of permanent licensing proceedings.[67]

If, on the other hand, unexpected expedition is the problem, there may be ways to preserve your right to participate in a proceeding or to delay the effectiveness of an adverse decision. For example, if your client is called upon to file testimony more quickly than expected, you might seek to persuade the agency or presiding officer to provide for reply testimony later on (if you cannot obtain an extension of time to file the initial testimony). Some of the material you had hoped to file initially might still be usable in the context of reply testimony. Or, if an adverse decision is issued, it may be possible to obtain a stay from either the agency or a court pending judicial review.

Finally, account must be taken of the possibility that the various potential outcomes could be modified by subsequent actions, such as a legislative veto, a court remand or reversal, or even new legislation. While assessment of the likelihood of any one of these developments is largely conjecture, the possibility of their occurrence cannot be ignored, and their potential impact must be kept in mind.

New Proceedings

By "new proceedings" I mean proceedings that have not yet been instituted but which the client can request (or, in some cases, demand) the agency to institute. Because the request (or demand) originates with the client, this affords a valuable opportunity to seek to define the issues as well as the scope and nature of the agency proceeding. For example, a client can seek to raise an issue in the context of a particular trial-type adjudicatory proceeding, or he can petition the agency for institution of a rule-making proceeding.

In theory, there are four basic options available to a client interested in seeking to institute an agency proceeding: (a) request institution of an informal rule-making proceeding, (b) request institution of a formal rule-making proceeding, (c) request institution of a formal, trial-type adjudicatory proceeding, and/or (d) request some kind of hybrid proceeding.

Under the Administrative Procedure Act, a request for institution of a rule-making proceeding, whether formal or informal, can be made on an *ex parte* basis unless the person making the request has knowledge that the matter has been, or will be, noticed for hearing.[68] The same is true of a request for formal adjudicatory proceedings.

While it might be assumed that an *ex parte* request for an agency proceeding would give the person making the request a significant advantage, such an advantage can be substantially mitigated by statutory limits on *ex parte* communications (not to mention restrictions contained in a particular agency's regulations) and by the practice commonly followed by many agencies of giving potential opponents an opportunity to respond to the request.

This fact, when coupled with the broad discretion traditionally accorded by reviewing courts to agencies to institute (or refuse to institute) proceedings, to frame the issues presented, and to structure the proceedings, means that the ability to obtain the desired proceeding will in the final analysis depend largely upon the discretion of the agency.[69] Accordingly, a client's request for initiation of a proceeding must be carefully prepared and structured in a manner that will maximize its persuasiveness. The persuasiveness of the request can be increased, for example, by keying the request into important policy questions, by relating the request to known concerns of agency officials and staff, and by persuading other persons (both potential allies and adversaries) to support institution of the requested proceeding.

The type of agency proceeding that you request will be heavily influenced by your client's goals and the type of proceeding best suited to attainment of those goals. For example, if your client desires the adoption of a particular policy standard, an informal rule-making proceeding might be preferred. In general, such proceedings are well suited for cases in which there are no issues of material fact and the primary focus is upon the weight and interpretation of data and statistics of the type generally agreed to be adequate to support such policy decisions.

Other factors could, of course, encourage the client to seek to have the issues decided in a more formal proceeding. For example, the client might conclude that critical flaws in an opponent's case could best be brought to light if cross-examination of witnesses in trial-type proceedings is permitted. In that case, the client might try to raise the issue in a complaint or by opposition to an opponent's application.

The client might also fear adoption of an unfavorable policy statement but nevertheless conclude that it can make out a case for individualized relief that would be difficult for the agency to deny. In such a case, the client may prefer inducing the agency to make its decision on the basis of a more detailed record developed in an adjudicatory proceeding.

The form of agency proceeding will also have important implications for the nature of your client's participation, including the opportunity to deal with agency decision makers on an *ex parte* basis, as well as for the standard of review before an appellate court.

In its pristine form, informal rule making under the APA requires only notice to the public and receipt by the agency of written comments.[70] Generally speaking, the APA does not prohibit *ex parte* communications between interested persons and agency decision makers in proceedings of this type.[71] Restrictions under the APA on *ex parte* communications have, however, been recognized by the courts in the narrow class of cases in which the informal rule-making proceedings are concerned with competing claims by opposing persons to a valuable economic privilege. These cases have been characterized by the courts as "quasiadjudicative."[72] In addition to possible APA restriction on *ex parte* contacts, restrictions may also be found in an agency's enabling statutes or regulations.[73]

Agencies also frequently hold legislative-type hearings in informal rule-making proceedings before the decision makers themselves or before panels of agency staff members. In most cases, the standard for judicial review is whether the agency's action is arbitrary or capricious—a standard that makes it difficult to challenge such agency actions successfully.

Given these general parameters, effective representation is a function of the advocate's ability to draft clear, concise, and persuasive comments; to make effective oral presentations when hearings are held; and to use *ex parte* opportunities effectively. Moreover, the relatively difficult judicial review standard substantially reduces the opportunity to overturn agency action, thus placing more of a premium upon convincing the agency initially to decide in your client's favor.

By contrast, the APA requires agencies to observe much more formal procedures in formal rule makings and adjudicatory proceedings. These procedures are specified in APA Sections 556 and 557. Generally speaking, these sections provide for evidentiary hearings at which oral or documentary evidence is received; cross-examination to the extent necessary for a full and true disclosure of facts is permitted; recommended decisions, whether initial or tentative, are issued by the presiding officers or law judges; exceptions to recommended decisions are entertained; and strict limitations on *ex parte* communications with decisional employees are imposed. Moreover, judicial review is under the "substantial evidence standard," a standard generally more favorable to the challenging party than the "arbitrary and capricious" standard.

The skills needed to participate effectively in formal rule makings and adjudications are much closer to the trial skills of the courtroom practitioner. Legal briefs, motions, and other pleadings require drafting techniques of the adversarial type employed in a judicial setting. And, although not strictly applied, the rules of discovery and rules of evidence are often observed in a loose but important manner. Similarly, the advocate must be proficient with the courtroom skills of examining and cross-examining witnesses.

In deciding which type of proceeding—informal rule making, formal rule making, adjudication, or some kind of hybrid proceeding—would best suit the client's interests, it is essential that the attorney consider the foreseeable outcome of each type of proceeding, the likelihood of each potential outcome, differences in the amount of time required to complete each type of proceeding, differences in the cost (both direct and indirect) of each type of proceeding, and the ability to defend or successfully attack the agency's ultimate decision.

Closely related are questions of strategy. The threshold question in each case is whether to participate in a proceeding or attempt to institute a proceeding. This is, in a very real sense, the ultimate strategic question. It can often be the most difficult. On the one hand is the possibility that participation will make a perceptible and positive contribution to the advancement of the client's interests. On the other hand is the danger that participation will be futile and that the client will have wasted valuable and limited resources or, worse yet, that participation will produce an even more unfavorable result than would otherwise have been the case.

In advising a client regarding the wisdom of participating in an agency proceeding, the attorney must often overcome a bias in favor of participation, a bias rooted in the natural and sometimes excessive optimism that we attorneys have in our ability to persuade decision makers to follow the course of action that we recommend. What must be cultivated is the ability to assess both the pluses and the minuses inherent in participation in an agency proceeding in a dispassionate, objective, and realistic manner. Such a healthy skepticism is important at every stage of an agency proceeding, but no more so than at the threshold when the decision to participate, or not to participate, is made.

Related to the question of whether to participate in a particular proceeding is the question of whether to participate in other related proceedings. Individuals as well as corporations often make the mistake of limiting their participation to one case. The reason for this narrow approach is usually laudable: to focus the client's effort, while at the same time keeping down costs. This approach unfortunately overlooks important relationships between cases and results in the loss of valuable opportunities to use one proceeding to influence the outcome in others.

An example of the use of related proceedings to influence ultimate agency policy occurred during the 1970's in the extended litigation before the Federal Power Commission (later, the FERC) over natural gas curtailments. In early 1973, the Commission adopted a policy statement calling for curtailments to be based in part upon the end use of the gas, that is, how the gas was used at the burnertip (for example, as boiler fuel, as a process fuel, or in home furnaces). However, the policy statement for identical end uses gave a curtailment preference to gas purchased under a "firm" contract instead of under an "interruptible" contract. In the latter instance, the gas supplier had the contractual right to interrupt service whenever necessary, usually in the supplier's sole discretion. Some industrial gas users believed that curtailments should be based exclusively on the end use of the gas, regardless of whether the gas was purchased under firm or interruptible contracts. Through persistent participation in virtually all of the major individual pipeline curtailment cases (which involved lengthy hearings and several court appeals), these industrial users largely achieved their goal. Notwithstanding the policy statement (which is still on the books today), the end result was that most of the curtailment plans on the major interstate pipeline systems have abolished the distinction between firm and interruptible service.

In many instances, lost opportunities to participate in related cases are doubly distressing because selective participation in more than one case does not necessarily require a significant increase in the client's financial commitment. The client can, for example, choose one case in which to make his principal effort and simultaneously monitor other cases with the intent of participating when and if advantageous, and then only to the minimal extent necessary.[74]

The extent and form of participation in the case involve important considerations of strategy. In some cases, other parties or agency staff can be relied upon to "pull the laboring oar" with respect to issues of interest to the client. In such cases, the client need merely supplement the presentations of these other participants. In other cases, effective participation will require the client to take a more active role, either to overcome the presentation of adversaries or to ensure that a unique position will be brought to the agency's attention.

Five rules of thumb should be kept in mind in planning and executing the strategy for participating in an agency proceeding.

First, attempt to influence the agency at the earliest possible time. Critical decisions are made by the agency both before and at the time it institutes a proceeding. These decisions have important implications for the ultimate outcome. They involve such important factors as the scope and nature of the proceeding, the manner in which the issues will be formulated, and the direction of an agency's proposed course of action. To the extent possible, efforts should be made to influence the agency to decide these matters in a manner that favors your client's interest.

A device being resorted to more and more frequently by agencies is the "Notice of Inquiry" procedure under which the agency either convenes informal public conferences or invites written submissions (or both) prior to the institution of a rule-making proceeding in order to gather information that will assist the agency in determining the need for, and thrust of, proposed rules. These conferences can provide a valuable means of getting the agency moving in the right direction.[75]

Informal contacts with agency personnel can also be an effective way of advocating a particular course of action. As noted earlier, such informal contacts are generally permitted under the APA prior to the institution of a proceeding, although it is essential to check limitations on *ex parte* contacts in the agency's enabling statute and regulations. After proceedings have been instituted, the APA prohibits most *ex parte* contacts in formal rule makings and adjudications.[76] By contrast, informal rule makings are subject to APA *ex parte* restrictions in only narrow situations.[77] Once again, however, the agency's enabling statute and regulations should be consulted for limitations beyond those contained in the APA.

In considering the possibility of making a formal *ex parte* contact with the agency decision makers, there is a tendency among lawyers to avoid such overtures altogether. Such scrupulous avoidance of these types of contacts may not only be unnecessary but in some instances may constitute a departure from the attorney's duty to represent his client aggressively.[78] In short, the agency practitioner has an obligation to ascertain the limits on *ex parte* contacts and to attempt to use such contacts if lawful and helpful to the presentation of his client's case.

A second rule of thumb is to make every reasonable effort to maintain flexibility in the position taken by your client. Never discount the importance of the element of time. Despite strong agency efforts to the contrary, it can often take years for an agency to issue a final decision. A great deal can happen during those intervening years—new policies can be adopted, old policies can be discarded, important judicial and legislative developments can occur. To the extent that you can formulate a basic position that permits your client to change with the times, you minimize the danger that such changes in related policy areas will devastate your case.

Perhaps the best way to protect against such unnecessary disasters is to try to identify foreseeable changes in policy areas that have implications for the arguments that you plan to make on your client's behalf, and then to see if you can structure your case to permit small but important changes in direction that may be able to accommodate such developments. The second thing you could do is avoid taking positions on issues gratuitously. Sometimes, in attempting to dot every *i* and cross every *t*, you end up addressing points that are only peripherally related to the basic issues in your case. When those tangential points are undercut by subsequent developments, this could needlessly harm your basic position.

A third rule of thumb is to concentrate on presenting the basic elements of your case in a clear and intelligible manner while avoiding the kind of showmanship common in jury trials. Success in an agency proceeding usually depends upon presentation of the client's position on a complex issue in a simple and straightforward manner. Anyone who has attempted to make such a presentation will confirm that it is an art.

While your client might derive a sense of satisfaction from seeing you castigate opposing parties or the agency, it is rarely, if ever, effective in an agency proceeding. In the first place, the ultimate decision maker will never see your Academy Award-winning performance in the hearing room. In the second place, your empassioned jury argument, while itself an impressive piece of rhetoric, will probably fade into insignificance when the decision maker sits down to consider all of the policy implications of his decision on the basis of the record before him.

A corollary to this rule is to cultivate credibility with the agency whenever possible. Indeed, credibility of both the attorney and the client is one of the most important weapons in a lawyer's arsenal. Even small clients arguing relatively small causes can be surprisingly effective if their positions are credible. Such credibility is fostered by such things as consistency, candor, and avoidance of overstatement. If your position is credible, it will be considered.

Fourth, you should endeavor to use the flexibility inherent in agency proceedings to be creative. Such creativity can be invaluable within the context of a particular proceeding—for example, by using the Freedom of Information Act as a discovery tool or by using the "nonunanimous settlement" as a vehicle for resolving otherwise protracted cases.[79] By "nonunanimous settlement" I mean the well-established procedural vehicle under which those parties who desire a particular result join forces by entering into a settlement among themselves which is presented to the agency as suggested resolution of the case. The agency can then base its decision on the terms of the settlement without going through extensive briefing before an administrative law judge and without awaiting an initial or recommended decision by the judge. A decision by the agency upholding such a nonunanimous settlement must still be supported by substantial evidence of record in order to withstand a court challenge by a dissenting party. But if care is taken to assure that there is such evidence in the record, that type of settlement can be a very useful device to advance your client's cause.

Creativity can also be used to orchestrate the interplay between related cases, for example, by establishing policies in one case that further your goals in another case or by accumulating a series of small victories in successive cases and thereby erecting a much larger policy edifice. The gas curtailment litigation described above is one concrete example. Demonstration of such creativity is the hallmark of an effective Washington lawyer.

Fifth, never underestimate the importance of developing a good record. The record is the foundation upon which everything is built—findings of fact, ultimate findings, and the rationale of the ultimate decision.

The record is important not only at the agency level but at the appellate court level as well. If you do not have a critical fact in the record by the time you get before the court, it will, barring extraordinary circumstances, be too late.

Nor will a careful advocate be content with merely getting all of his facts and arguments into the record. Rather, he must attempt to put all of his facts and arguments into the record in an intelligible manner. By so doing, he will maximize the impact of his client's position at the time the presentation is being made, at the time the record is reviewed by higher-level agency personnel, and months or years later when the record is reviewed by an appellate court.

POST-AGENCY PROCEEDINGS: THE ART OF SNATCHING VICTORY FROM THE JAWS OF DEFEAT

As a practical matter, many agency proceedings (cynics would say "most," but that is plainly not so) do not end with the issuance of a final rule or order. Instead, they continue on, albeit in a different form, as disappointed parties seek to overcome the adverse agency decision.

In most cases, the disappointed participant has several options from which to choose. He can continue to pursue his original goal or an alternative goal in other proceedings before the same or a different agency. He can seek a legislative solution in the form of a legislative veto (if available) or through corrective legislation of some type. He can seek to influence the President to overrule the agency (in those cases in which the agency decision is subject to Presidential review and modification). Or he can seek redress of his grievances in the courts. In this section, we shall consider the last alternative: an appeal of agency action to the courts.

Over the years, much has been written about judicial review of agency action. In the brief space available in this chapter, we obviously cannot hope to provide an adequate summary of this literature or an in-depth look at the more notable facets of this complex and interesting subject. Instead, we shall attempt to give the reader a feel for the role and nature of judicial review as seen from the perspective of the Washington lawyer and to highlight some important general considerations that should be borne in mind during an appellate proceeding.

In considering judicial review of agency action, it is useful to think of the review proceeding as a further stage or phase of the agency proceeding. The supremacy of law and the primary role of the courts in interpreting and applying the law are, of course, notions that are deeply rooted in our national heritage. In the area of administrative law, they are given expression through the legal doctrine that agency actions are subject to judicial review of some type, even in the absence of a statute expressly providing for such review.[80] Even more concrete expressions of these notions in the agency-court context are the numerous substantive agency statutes that expressly provide for judicial review and applicable provisions in the Administrative Procedure Act.[81]

Several important implications flow from this view of the courts as an integral part of the administrative process, not the least of which is that the agency lawyer must be familiar with the nature and role of judicial review. Even the lawyer who specializes in agency proceedings and leaves appellate proceedings to his litigation partner must have sufficient familiarity with the judicial process so that he can lay the appropriate groundwork for pursuing an appeal (or for defending against someone else's appeal).

A second and extremely important implication of this agency-court relationship is that, to a greater or lesser degree, courts are legally bound by some of the agency's actions. For example, substantive enabling statutes typically provide that an agency's findings of fact are to be deemed conclusive if supported by substantial evidence.[82] These same statutes also routinely limit the courts to a review of agency action solely on the basis of the record compiled before the agency. Moreover, as the Supreme Court decision in *Vermont Yankee* makes clear, the agency's choice of procedures is something that a reviewing court will be unable to second-guess, except in extremely rare cases. Finally, there is the presumption of validity that is traditionally imputed to agency action.[83]

In other words, while reviewing courts possess the awesome power to declare agency action unlawful (and are therefore, in a sense, superior to the agency), they generally cannot overturn agency action merely because they would prefer another result. While they provide a check and balance to agency action, they are *not* the absolute masters of the agencies.

Because of the deference that reviewing courts are required to show to agencies, the attorney appearing before the agency must take the proceeding seriously and pay scrupulous attention to developing the best record possible for his client. The assumption that you can "clean it up on appeal" is both unfounded and dangerous. The federal court reporter system contains many examples of agency decisions that passed judicial muster because of failure by an attorney to lay an adequate foundation for a court challenge while the proceeding was still before the agency.[84]

A further consequence of this judicial deference to agency action is that an attack on the agency decision must be sharply focused if it is to be effective. Generalized denunciations of the agency will not be enough to secure a judicial reversal or remand. This is especially true before such courts as the United States Court of Appeals for the District of Columbia Circuit which routinely entertain challenges to administrative agency actions. These courts are extremely sensitive to the difference between appeals that quarrel with the agency's choice of one of several potentially acceptable results and appeals in which the agency is guilty of the kind of conduct that requires reversal or remand.

In order to make a persuasive attack on the agency decision, it is absolutely essential to understand the standard of review. There is a potentially big practical difference between the "arbitrary and capricious standard" applied in review of most informal rule makings and the more demanding "substantial evidence standard" applied in review of formal rule makings and adjudications. Whereas the former standard recognizes the existence of considerable agency discretion and thus can present a significant bar to reversal, the latter standard affords significantly greater opportunities to obtain a reversal or remand. However, some recent court decisions, particularly by the D.C. Circuit, have somewhat blurred this distinction and have required agencies to take a hard look both at what they are doing and at available alternatives, even when the court is reviewing the matter under the "arbitrary and capricious" standard.[85]

In either case, however, one cannot lose sight of the ultimate goal of an appeal: to convince the court that the agency committed an error which, under the applicable standard, requires the court to set the agency action aside.

The task of convincing the court that the agency acted unlawfully is complicated considerably by the fact that agency decisions frequently deal with extremely technical economic, scientific, or financial matters that are difficult for nonexperts to understand. Even if, by chance, one or more of the judges hearing an appeal happen to have formal training in one of these specialized disciplines, their review of the agency's decision will be frustrated by a massive record developed over a period of several years. Becoming sufficiently familiar with such a record could be a substantial accomplishment even for an expert. In short, there are significant hurdles that must be overcome in order to attack an agency's action successfully.

A determination of whether to appeal involves consideration of numerous factors. Two factors bear special mention at the outset—time and expense. With respect to time, it must be recognized that several months or even years can elapse before the reviewing court issues a decision. This is particularly likely in an appeal of a complex agency determination. Moreover, even if you successfully challenge the agency's decision, the court may simply remand to the agency for further proceedings. The delays inherent in the appeal process can sometimes be the determining factor in deciding whether to appeal. This is particularly true in cases in which the relief would be prospective only. The second factor worthy of special mention is expense. An appellate proceeding can be quite costly. In some cases, the time and money that would be spent on the appeal would be better spent on compliance with the agency's decision and on planning some alternative strategy before the agency.

Other considerations routinely encountered in deciding whether to appeal an agency ruling include the importance of the issue in both a practical and precedential sense; the likelihood of success, or the danger of an even worse result; the question of which court is most likely to issue a favorable ruling; the form of relief that can be expected—i.e., reversal or remand; the value, if any, of keeping the issue alive despite the likelihood of an unfavorable ruling; the possibility of bad publicity; and the likelihood that the agency will decide more favorably if the court were to remand the case for further proceedings. Balanced against these considerations are the advantages and disadvantages of available alternative courses of action.

Assuming the decision is made to pursue an appeal, there are a number of things that could be borne in mind in order to maximize the chances of success. First, the experienced practitioner will recognize from the outset that the nature of the judicial review proceeding is considerably different from that of the agency proceeding. Addressing the agency, the practitioner was immersed in the details of complex technical evidence and agency precedents. Moreover, he was arguing to an expert decision maker (or, at least, to a decision maker who was advised by an expert agency staff). At the appellate level, however, he is arguing to nonexperts, generally regarding court precedents and how the agency failed to observe the requirements embodied by those precedents.

In short, you are no longer arguing *to* the agency. Instead, you are arguing *about* the agency and *about* a proceeding that went so badly as to require invalidation of the agency's results. This is a critical difference with important implications for both the content and method of presentation on appeal.

Generally speaking, presentation on appeal will be made through legal briefs and oral argument before one or more judges who decide the case. Quite often, the biggest single challenge confronted at the appellate level is to present the case in an understandable and preferably nontechnical manner that clearly and persuasively exposes the deficiencies in the agency's action. In order to do this, several unwritten rules should be observed.

First, in planning an appellate presentation, the experienced practitioner will carefully balance his desire to raise all genuine issues against the critical need to present a focused and forceful attack. Inexperienced counsel often focus on the former without paying adequate attention to the latter. The result is a presentation that strikes the court as a confusing conglomeration of arguments, subarguments, and sub-sub-arguments that lack clear direction and force. While appellate cases may be won despite this approach, there is no excuse for pursuing an appeal with such self-imposed handicaps.

Instead, a concerted effort should be made in every case to identify the major defects in the agency's action and to organize your arguments around the principal issues raised by those defects. Emphasis should be placed on the major arguments. Minor arguments should either be left for textual footnotes in your brief or dropped completely. While these suggestions are elementary, they are critical. It is surprising how many appellate briefs, for example, seem to ramble on endlessly, mixing major and minor arguments in what appears to be an unpersuasive stream of consciousness.

A further, and often devastating, error reflected in far too many appellate briefs is the error of assuming that the court understands fundamental and critical aspects of a case, such as the nature of the problem with which the agency was dealing; the reasons why the issues being raised on appeal are important; and the differences, if any, between the goal that the agency tried to achieve, the goal the agency was legally obligated to achieve, and the result that was actually achieved.

Related to these defects is the error of using technical terms without providing the court with an adequate explanation of both their meaning and importance. The mere definition of a critical technical term tucked away somewhere in a footnote can be totally inadequate. Without an explanation of how the concept embodied by that term fits into the case and the reason for its importance, you create an unnecessary and dangerous risk that the significance of the term (and the underlying concept) will be seriously misapprehended by the court.

This situation points up once again how absolutely essential it is for the attorney to recognize that his success or failure at the appellate level may depend upon his ability to translate agency action and "technocrat-ese" into terms that are readily comprehended by non-expert judges.

Implicit in translating what happened before the agency into a comprehensible and compelling tale on appeal is the process of simplification. Extensive involvement in an agency proceeding gives the attorney a detailed familiarity with the arcane aspects and nuances of the case. It simultaneously creates the danger that those arcane aspects and nuances will find their way into the appellate presentation, even if they are only tangentially relevant. Couple this with the desire to appear erudite before the appellate tribunal by citing as many precedents as possible, and the predictable result is a presentation that is needlessly complex and that distracts attention from the principal thrust of your case. Make every effort to simplify and to be concise. Then test your result. For example, have another attorney in your office who is totally unfamiliar with the case read your appellate brief. If he cannot follow your argument, chances are the judges will not be able to either. If he is unpersuaded, chances are the judges will also be left unpersuaded.

Having extolled the virtues of selectivity, simplicity, and conciseness, it is now appropriate to pay homage to the god of thoroughness. While unnecessary arguments and details should be omitted from your presentation, necessary arguments and details must be included, particularly in your briefs, unless there is an overriding tactical or strategic reason for omitting them. Inadvertent or careless omissions are often rationalized on the ground that "we'll pick it up on oral argument."

This excuse is inadequate. First, appellate courts are eliminating or severely limiting oral argument in increasing numbers of cases. Second, developments that must be brought to the court's attention during oral argument frequently occur between the date when you filed your brief (or briefs) and the date of oral argument. By the time the case is argued, you may have your hands full bringing the court up to date. Third, time flies at oral argument, particularly if the court asks a great many questions. This is not the time to correct omissions in your brief. Fourth, the court may be interested in discussing matters other than the principal ones presented at oral argument, and you may never find time to get back to the omissions. Fifth, it is to your advantage to have important arguments and details available for the judges (and their clerks) at the time they prepare for oral argument. This could result in the formulation of some difficult questions for your adversaries.

My final observations will be directed at oral argument. It is not uncommon to hear even experienced attorneys question the value of oral argument. Simply put, they believe oral argument is a waste of time. In my view, however, oral argument can afford an extremely valuable opportunity to the advocate handling an agency appeal, provided that he recognizes the unique contribution that oral argument can make to his case.

The most common mistake made by a surprising number of lawyers is their use of time during oral argument to restate, sometimes even quote, arguments from their brief. This approach not only fails to advance the client's cause but actually detracts, by preventing a dialogue with the court. In view of the number of oral arguments that are presented in this manner, it is not surprising that many attorneys, including some of the principal offenders, criticize oral argument as useless.

Instead, oral argument should be viewed as an opportunity to anticipate and to answer questions that the judges might have after reading the briefs; to clear up misconceptions that may have been created by opposing counsel (i.e., tell the judges what the case does *not* involve); to correct erroneous impressions apparent from questions asked by the judges; to drive home your major (not minor) points; and to bring the court up to date with respect to any recent developments of importance.

Viewed from this perspective, oral argument is not a formal oration requiring the skills of Pericles but a surprisingly informal encounter with the decision makers—a chance to explain, to persuade, to bring life into a controversy which, until oral argument, was held captive by inanimate printed words.

In order to maximize the impact of your presentation at oral argument, five suggestions are offered. First, know the record and come to the argument prepared to point the judges to specific record pages that deal with critical aspects of the case. Second, reacquaint yourself with the principal authorities (both statutory and case law) shortly before the argument. Third, plan a simple, straightforward presentation that includes only major points. Fourth, try to relate your argument to the real world and anticipate questions regarding the practical implications of your position. Good judges are sensitive to the impact that their decisions will have in the real world. Fifth, anticipate difficult questions that may point out weaknesses in your case and be prepared to answer those questions candidly and in a manner that will adequately explain why your position should be accepted.

In this chapter, we have explored the concept of effective representation in the context of agency proceedings. In doing so, we have identified a number of techniques and considerations which foster an effective representation. The broad goal has been to deepen the reader's understanding of how Washington lawyers approach agency proceedings. Practice before a federal agency is among the most challenging types of legal practice in the country today. This chapter will have served its purpose if it promotes a better understanding of the nature of the agency process and the role of the Washington lawyer in that process.

FOOTNOTES

[1]Commission on Law and the Economy, American Bar Association, *Final Report 1979 With Recommendations, Federal Regulation: Roads to Reform* at p. 16 (1979) [hereinafter cited as the Commission on Law and the Economy].

[2]Administrative Procedure Act, codified as amended at 5 U.S.C. §§551, *et seq.* (1976).

[3]Freedom of Information Act, codified as amended at 5 U.S.C. §552 (1976).

[4]Government in the Sunshine Act, codified as amended at 5 U.S.C. §§551, 552, 552b, 556, 557a (1976).

[5]Small Business Act, codified as amended at 15 U.S.C. §§631 *et seq.* (1976).

[6]Privacy Act of 1974, codified as amended at 5 U.S.C. §552a (1976).

[7]Ethics in Government Act of 1978, codified as amended at 2 U.S.C. §§701, *et seq.* (Supp. IV 1980).

[8]Paperwork Reduction Act of 1980, 44 U.S.C. §3501, *et seq.* (Supp. IV 1980).

[9]National Environmental Policy Act of 1969, codified as amended at 42 U.S.C. §§4321, 4331-4335, 4341-4347 (1976).

[10]Congressional Budget and Impoundment Control Act of 1974, codified as amended in various portions of U.S. Code, including 31 U.S.C. §§1301 *et seq.* (Supp. III 1979) [hereinafter cited as Congressional Budget Act].

[11]Airline Deregulation Act of 1978, codified as amended at 49 U.S.C. §§1301, *et seq.* (Supp. III 1979).

[12]Motor Carrier Act of 1980, 49 U.S.C. §§10101, *et seq.* (Supp. IV 1980).

[13]The Commission on Law and the Economy was established in 1975 by the American Bar Association's House of Delegates to explore the relationship between the nation's regulatory processes and the performance of the economy, with particular emphasis on the growth and operation of federal regulatory agencies. It consisted both of experienced lawyers and economists.

[14]*See, e.g.,* Executive Office of the President, Office of Management and Budget, *Improving Government Regulations–Current Status and Future Directions* (November, 1980).

[15]E. Barrett Prettyman, *Trial by Agency* at 19 (1959) (reprint by Virginia Law Review Association of three lectures delivered at the University of Virginia Law School).

[16]*Id.* at 9.

[17]For example, contrast the rules and regulations promulgated by the Federal Energy Regulatory Commission under Section 4(a) the Natural Gas Act, 15 U.S.C. §717c(a)(1976) with the rules and regulations promulgated by the Federal Energy Regulatory Commission under title IV of the Natural Gas Policy Act of 1978, 15 U.S.C. §§3391, *et seq.* (Supp. IV 1980).

[18]*See, e.g.,* 1 K.C. Davis, *Administrative Law Treatise* §9 (2d. ed. 1978).

[19]*See, e.g.,* Federal Trade Commission, Rules of Practice for Adjudicative Proceedings, 16 CFR §§3, *et seq.* (1981); National Labor Relations Board, Rules and Regulations, 29 CFR §§102.34, *et seq.* (1981); Securities and Exchange Commission Rules of Practice, 17 CFR §§201, *et seq.* (1981).

[20]*See, e.g.,* Supplemental Security Income for the Aged, Blind and Disabled, 20 C.F.R. at §416.1205.

[21]*See, e.g.,* American Textile Manufacturers Institute v. Donovan, 452 U.S. 490 (1981).

[22]1 K.C. Davis, *Administrative Law Treatise* §6.18 (2d. ed. 1978).

[23]*Id.* at §2.7.

[24]Prettyman, *supra*, at 6.

[25]Congress has passed legislation in order to ensure that money appropriated for activities is actually spent by the agencies responsible for those programs. *See* Congressional Budget Act, §1002, codified at 31 U.S.C. §665(c)(2) (Supp. III 1979), which provides that "reserves may be established solely to provide for contingencies, or to effect savings whenever savings are made possible by or through changes in requirements or greater efficiency of operations." Sections 1011-1017 of the Congressional Budget Act establish procedures for Congressional approval of rescissions and deferrals of budget authority proposed by the President.

[26]*Consumer Energy Council of America* v. *FERC*, 673 F.2d 425 (D.C. Cir. 1982) *appeal docketed*, No. 81-2008, *et al.* (U.S. April 29, 1982); *Chadha* v. *Immigration and Naturalization Service*, 634 F.2d 408 (9th Cir. 1980), *appeal docketed*,

No. 80-1832 (U.S. Oct. 5, 1981). Some statutes require passage of resolutions of disapproval by *both* Houses in order for the regulation to be rejected. *See, e.g.*, Section 122 of the Natural Gas Policy Act of 1978, 15 U.S.C. §3332(c)(1) (Supp. III 1979).

[27]The Commission on Law and the Economy proposed a type of legislative veto which it believes to be constitutional. Specifically, it proposed that powers be delegated to the President for ". . . a specific term of years and that, during a brief period before any presidential action under a delegated power takes effect, the President may withdraw or modify his action in the light of any resolution that Congress or either House thereof may have voted during that period. Any such resolution would not invalidate the presidential action, but the Congress could, of course, decline to renew the President's delegated authority if he failed to respect congressional reactions." Commission on Law and the Economy, *supra*, at 88. Also, some recent Congressional proposals for administrative regulatory reform include legislative veto provisions that take the form of joint resolutions to be passed by both Houses of Congress and signed by the President. *See, e.g.*, H.R. 746, 97th Cong., 2d Sess. §201(a) (1982).

[28]*See, e.g.*, Colo. Rev. Stat. §§24-34-104, *et seq.*; Fla. Stat. Ann. §§11.61, *et seq.*

[29]Commission on Law and the Economy, *supra*, at 110-111; Davis, *Review Procedures and Public Accountability in Sunset Legislation: An Analysis and Proposal for Reform*, 33 *Ad. L. Rev.* 393, 401-407 (Fall 1981); *see, e.g.*, S. 2, 96th Cong., 2d Sess., §§303, 501 (1980); H.R. 5858, 96th Cong., 2d Sess. (1980). Another version of "sunset" procedures is Congressionally required periodic reports regarding agency programs. These reports must be made by the agency and submitted to a relevant Congressional committee in order to facilitate Congressional review of programs administered by the agency. *See, e.g.*, Department of Energy Organization Act, 42 U.S.C. §7351 (Supp. III, 1979).

[30]Administrative Procedure Act, 5 U.S.C. §706 (1976).

[31]*Sierra Club* v. *Costle*, 657 F.2d 298, 405-406 (D.C. Cir. 1981).

[32]*Myers* v. *United States*, 272 U.S. 52, 135 (1926).

[33]Verkuil, *Jawboning Administrative Agencies: Ex Parte Contacts by the White House*, 80 *Colum. L. Rev.* 943, 964 (1980).

[34]*Sierra Club* v. *Costle, supra,* at 405.

[35]Verkuil, *supra*, at 956-958.

[36]Exec. Order No. 12,044, 43 *Fed. Reg.* 12661 (1978).

[37]Exec. Order No. 12,174, 44 *Fed. Reg.* 69609 (1979).

[38]Executive Office of the President, Office of Management and Budget, *Improving Government Regulations–Current Status and Future Directions*, Chapter 1 (November, 1980).

[39]Exec. Order No. 12,291, 46 *Fed. Reg.* 13193 (1981).

[40]American Bar Association, Code of Professional Responsibility, Canon 7 (1981).

[41]50 U.S.C.A. App. §§2401-2420.

[42]*See* specifically §5(c) and (d), 50 U.S.C.A. App. §§2405(c) and (d) [Secretary of Defense]; §6(a), 50 U.S.C.A. App. §2406(a) [Secretary of State]; and §7(b)(3),

50 U.S.C.A. §2407(b)(3) [Secretary of Energy]. *See also* Murphy and Downey, *National Security, Foreign Policy and Individual Rights: The Quandary of United States Export Controls, The International and Comparative Law Quarterly* (October, 1981).

[43]*See, e.g.,* Clean Water Act, 33 U.S.C. §1314(b) (Supp. III 1979); Clean Air Act, 42 U.S.C. §7410(a)(1) (Supp. III 1979).

[44]Exec. Order No. 12,044, 43 *Fed. Reg.* at 12661 (1978).

[45]*Mobil Oil Corp.* v. *FPC*, 483 F.2d 1238, 1250 (D.C. Cir. 1973).

[46]Administrative Procedure Act, 5 U.S.C. §§551, *et seq.* (1976).

[47]United States Department of Justice, Attorney General's Manual on the Administrative Procedure Act, at 9 (1947).

[48]5 U.S.C. §553 (1976). To reduce confusion when referring to the sections of the APA, the section number used by the United States Code is used herein rather than the original APA section number. For example, Section 4 of the APA will be referred to as Section 553; APA Section 5 as Section 554, etc.

[49]5 U.S.C. §§556, 557 (1976). Excluded from discussion in this chapter are those agency actions, such as the issuance of interpretative rulings, which are more advisory in nature and which are not binding in a precedential sense upon other persons or upon the agency. Moreover, such rulings are usually the product of more informal interactions between the agency and an individual or corporation. This is not to denigrate the importance of agency interpretations or private rulings. Indeed, there may often be situations in which the risks or delays inherent in an agency proceeding are unacceptably high and in which an interpretative ruling is far preferable.

[50]5 U.S.C. §§554, 556, 557 (1976).

[51]Administrative Procedure Act, 5 U.S.C. §554(a) (1976).

[52]*Mobil Oil Corp.* v. *FPC*, at 1253.

[53]*Id.*

[54]*Id.*

[55]Brandt-Rauf, *Ex Parte Contacts Under the Constitution and Administrative Procedure Act*, 80 *Colum. L. Rev.* 379, 383 (1980).

[56]*See, e.g.,* Regulations Implementing Incremental Pricing Provisions of the Natural Gas Policy Act, Docket No. RM79-14.

[57]*Vermont Yankee Nuclear Power Corp.* v. *NRDC* at 524.

[58]*Id.*

[59]*See, e.g.,* Department of Energy Organization Act, 42 U.S.C. §7191(b)(1) (Supp. III 1979).

[60]Proverbs 4:7.

[61]42 U.S.C. §8341, as amended.

[62]*See generally,* Charles A. Horsky, *The Washington Lawyer* (Little, Brown & Co., Boston 1952), especially at pp. 119, *et seq.*

[63]A. de Tocqueville, *Democracy in America* (London 1835-40).

[64]*NAACP* v. *FPC*, 425 U.S. 662 (1976).

[65]For example, in successfully defending an association of soft drink bottlers before the Federal Trade Commission against charges that they had violated the Sherman Antitrust Act, my partners successfully argued, among other defenses,

that the bottlers' actions were environmentally sounder under the policies of the National Environmental Policy Act.

[66]Friedman, *A Look at Abner J. Mikva, District Lawyer*, May-June 1980, at pp. 37, *et seq.*

[67]*See, e.g.*, 47 CFR §73.3542.

[68]Administrative Procedure Act, 5 U.S.C. §557(d)(1)(E) (1976).

[69]*Vermont Yankee, supra,* at 524-525; *FCC* v. *Schreiber*, 381 U.S. 279, 290 (1965); *FCC* v. *Pottsville Broadcasting Co.*, 309 U.S. 134, 138 (1940).

[70]Administrative Procedure Act, 5 U.S.C. §553 (1976).

[71]*Id.*

[72]*Home Box Office, Inc.* v. *FCC*, 567 F.2d. 9, 51-59 (D.C. Cir. 1977), *cert. denied*, 434 U.S. 829 (1977), *rehearing denied*, 434 U.S. 988 (1977); *U.S. Lines* v. *Federal Maritime Commission*, 584 F.2d 519, 537-542 (D.C. Cir. 1978); *National Small Shipments Traffic Conference, Inc.* v. *ICC*, 590 F.2d 345, 350-351 (D.C. Cir. 1978).

[73]*See, e.g.*, Federal Trade Commission Organization, Procedures and Rules of Practice, 16 CFR §4.7 (1981); Federal Communications Commission, *Ex Parte* Presentations, 47 CFR §§1.1201-1.1251 (1981).

[74]It should be noted that in formal rule makings and adjudications, such monitoring and subsequent participation is possible only if the client is a "party" to the proceeding. Since agencies place deadlines on seeking party status, this means that the client sometimes becomes a party before it is clear whether or not issues of interest will in fact be presented. In most cases, however, the cost of simply becoming a party is nominal and does not commit the client to active and expensive participation. The key is to identify cases of potential interest in advance so that the deadline for becoming a party is not missed.

[75]*See, e.g.*, Notice of Inquiry, issued by Federal Energy Regulatory Commission, Docket No. RM82-13, January 29, 1982, regarding the use of data filed by electric utilities under Section 133 of PURPA, 47 *Fed. Reg.* 5437; Notice of Inquiry, issued by Federal Energy Regulatory Commission, Docket No. RM 82-26-000, April 28, 1982, regarding the production, distribution, and pricing of natural gas, 47 *Fed. Reg.* 19157-19171.

[76]Administrative Procedure Act, 5 U.S.C. §557(d)(1) (1976).

[77]*Sangamon Valley Television Corp.* v. *U.S.*, 269 F.2d 221 (D.C. Cir. 1959).

[78]American Bar Association, Code of Professional Responsibility, Canon 7 (1981).

[79]FERC Rules of Practice and Procedure, 18 CFR §1.18(e)(4)(i) (1981).

[80]*Association of Data Processing Service Organizations* v. *Camp*; 397 U.S. 150 (1970); *Abbott Laboratories* v. *Gardner*, 387 U.S. 136 (1967).

[81]*See,* Administrative Procedure Act, 5 U.S.C. §706 (1976); *see, e.g.*, Securities Act of 1933, 15 U.S.C. §77(i) (1976); Clayton Act, 15 U.S.C. §21(a) (1976).

[82]Administrative Procedure Act, 5 U.S.C. §706(2)(E) (1976); *e.g.*, Natural Gas Act, 15 U.S.C. §717r(b) (1976).

[83]*Environmental Defense Fund* v. *Costle*, 657 F.2d 275 (D.C. Cir. 1981); *Natural Resources Defense Council, Inc.* v. *SEC*, 606 F.2d 1031 (D.C. Cir. 1979). It should be remembered that there have been proposals to eliminate this presumption of

validity which has been accorded to agency action by the courts. The best known of these proposals is the "Bumper's Amendment," a version of which was recently passed by the Senate. *See,* S. 67, 97th Cong., 1st Sess. (1981).

[84]*See, e.g., Cisternas-Estay* v. *Immigration & Naturalization Service*, 531 F.2d 155 (3d Cir. 1976), *cert. denied*, 429 U.S. 853 (1976); *Patsis* v. *Immigration & Naturalization Service*, 337 F.2d 733 (8th Cir. 1964), *cert. denied*, 380 U.S. 952 (1965), *reh'g denied*, 381 U.S. 921 (1965).

[85]*See, e.g., Loyola Univ.* v. *FCC*, 670 F.2d 1222 (D.C. Cir. 1982).

Chapter 3

COMMUNICATIONS WITH THE AGENCY—SEEKING GUIDANCE AND ADVISORY OPINIONS

JOHN H. SHENEFIELD*

Much of Washington law practice consists of communications with the agencies and departments that make up our federal government. While to the cartoonist and columnist, a Washington lawyer's communications with agencies smack of influence-peddling and lobbying, by and large this is serious lawycr's work, requiring high degrees of skill and sensitivity.

Communications take many forms, ranging from courtesy calls and sensitizing sessions to pre-suit settlement negotiations. Every four years new presidential appointees populate the enormous offices that signify power and status in our federal establishment. And every four years Washington lawyers find an excuse to meet these new officials in preparation for the time—which will inevitably come—when name recognition and personal familiarity will make the difference between getting in the door or not.

Quite different but equally common is the sensitizing session—the

---

*John H. Shenefield is a partner in the Washington, D.C. office of Milbank, Tweed, Hadley and McCloy. During the period 1977 to 1981, he held various positions in the Justice Department, first as Deputy Assistant Attorney General and then as Assistant Attorney General in charge of the Antitrust Division, later becoming Associate Attorney General. He specializes in antitrust litigation, a field in which he was an active practitioner prior to entering government service.

effort to prepare a government official well in advance of the time when he will need to make any decision on a topic of which the decision-maker is ignorant or whose political implications he may need to be taught. Other communications and meetings include the last minute plea to avoid the issuance of harmful regulations, negotiations prior to decisions on whether to seek indictments or file suit, the tough bargaining sessions over the language to be proposed in an administration bill, and even attendance at department social functions or farewell receptions. All have their purpose and all may be useful to an enterprising lawyer.

But just because they are common does not mean they are necessarily easy to undertake or successfully manage. There are rhythms and conventions that govern each of these communications, and the Washington lawyer enjoys nothing better than trading stories of how some practitioner, whose skills were less finely attuned to the meeting of the moment, was undone by an unfortunate gaffe at a crucial meeting. Not that Washington lawyers are necessarily any better or more adept than other lawyers—it is just that at least some of them have had more experience with government agencies and are more successful at communicating with them. Many have also served in the agencies. While this almost never results in favored treatment, it does supply an awareness, indeed familiarity, between lawyer and agency that can serve a client very well indeed.

One of the most important communications with the agency and perhaps the most difficult—consultation in search of legal guidance—is unique in strategy and approach. The rewards for a successful communication can be very great for the client. By the same token, the penalties for error can be severe. So here, as elsewhere, it will be the lawyer's skill and sensitivity to the dynamics and demands of the process that will stand between the client's access to maximum benefit, and disaster.

CONSULTATION IN SEARCH OF ADVICE: THE NATURE OF THE PROCESS

Seeking advice and guidance from a government agency is one of the most important techniques of the successful Washington practitioner. What can be more reassuring to a lawyer and his client working in a murky area of law than to have the responsible law enforcement official give a clear indication of where the borderline between the lawful and unlawful is deemed to be—at least for the moment? Beyond that, while no government official will ever tell a lawyer that the law will not be enforced, an indication of enforcement priorities frequently will give a lawyer a strong sense of the lower risk to a client venturing into an area that the agency views as largely irrelevant to its primary mission.

Despite the welcome reassurance that is possible from this kind of advice, the technique for obtaining the advice is poorly understood outside Washington and imperfectly practiced even by experienced Washington lawyers. Detailed knowledge of the consultation process is important, and each department and agency is likely to have conventions and usages, familiarity with which will enhance the usefulness of the results. Treating law enforcement officials at the Department of Justice the same as industry advisers at the Department of Energy is likely to risk suspicion, at the very least, and perhaps even formal investigation. For example, law enforcement officials are charged with responsibility for enforcing the law, not providing formal advice and assistance. When presented with a fact situation, they are likely to probe deeply to determine whether a possible violation of the law has occurred or may occur in the future. These are very different government officials, and attention to those important differences is highly advisable.

Access is never guaranteed, and access to the wrong officials may be useless, or even harmful. The quality of the results from this process varies enormously. The primary variables include the lawyer's skill, his knowledge of the agency and his credibility with the department officials who must be involved in the process.

Why Seek Guidance from an Agency?

An important fact that is sometimes overlooked is that seeking guidance of an agency can be useful to the agency itself. Indeed whether the agency decision-maker sees it as helpful or informative to talk with some important company or constituency outside of the government may be the essential predicate for the meeting. Whereas the client may learn something about its proposed course of conduct, the agency may learn more about the real-world impact of its policies. And the lawyer in any event will have learned more about the process, acquainted himself with the relevant government officials and quite possibly produced a result for the client that will seem unusually efficient because it is achieved in an office—as the client is used to achieving results—and without the seemingly wasteful trappings of courtroom process or expensive discovery.

It may be necessary to get guidance from government agencies because of the nature of their authority. For many very important regulatory decisions, although the words of the statutes and the tenor of the regulations seem clear, broad agency discretion may be key.

Or the regulations may not yet have been written. Consider the enactment of a wholly new regulatory statute calling on the agency to give life and content to broad and general policy statements. At this early point in the life of the regulatory scheme, the lawyer for affected companies has presumably done careful analysis and study in the course of congressional consideration. He will therefore be well placed to approach the implementing agency at an early date with proposals for the new regulations.

Even if the regulations have been on the books for years, there may still be wide discretion lodged with an agency decision-maker and few precedents to guide him. Every lawyer has been faced at one time or another with a client who simply does not believe his advice that enforcement will swiftly follow a proposed course of action. Why not offer to consult the government agency—with the client in tow if appropriate—to confirm this advice? Nothing makes a more vivid impression on a client than to have the law enforcement official not only come to the same legal conclusions on the spot, but do so with reference to the severe penalties likely to ensue from a violation.

A lawyer may find himself confronted with a wholly novel problem, or a problem that has novel aspects. Although a company's chances, based on an analysis of precedent, might seem poor, the lawyer may recognize that there is an unprecedented aspect to the situation, one that argues for a wholly different approach. If he can persuade the agency to that effect, he has engineered a legal coup.

Take an investigation that may develop into a serious dispute between our government and the government of a powerful ally as an example. The criminal investigator, unaware of the foreign relations and national security aspects of the investigation, may move so far down the investigatory path that his agency is committed to a conventional conclusion oblivious of the gathering foreign relations stormclouds. It might well be unfair to impose a standard penalty if, for instance, the activity the United States government is investigating has been mandated by a friendly foreign government. There is room for creative lawyering at the outset—long before an investigation is pursued very far—to reassure a client that blind following of conventional precedent will not produce a result that is, in the larger context, nonsensical: a company being prosecuted for doing what another government has required. But only the most sensitive evaluation of the case, the players and the agency will enable the lawyer to recognize the novel aspect that will make the essential difference, to frame the case in terms first plausible, then persuasive to the public official, to deliver the message credibly and persuasively all in order to produce the correct result.

A request for guidance can also be put in a policy context. Frequently the public policy component of a problem will be crucial, and it is likely in those situations that personal contact with the decision-maker will be the only effective way to communicate the nature of the policy issue and to suggest the appropriate result—one that will incidentally be of benefit to the lawyer's client. A lawyer relying on policy implications to gain agency approval for a proposed course of conduct requires an intimate knowledge of the agency's policy priorities as well as of his client's situation. Policy positions of departments and agencies change frequently, and very markedly, with changes in administration or appointments to key positions. Anyone at all conversant with a particular field will understand the larger policy shifts, but these will frequently be far too crude a basis on which to approach an agency with any hope of getting a precisely calibrated result. A far more finely tuned sense of the policy predisposition of particular officials and the bureaucracies beneath them will be required before the seeking of advice is anything more than a crap-shoot. A smart lawyer in Washington never likes to seek guidance from an agency without a substantial degree of certainty as to how the issue will eventually be resolved.

Perhaps a new office is developing its enforcement policy for the first time. A lawyer representing a firm, or a trade association, will be asked by the department to address a certain policy issue. The far-sighted lawyer may have induced such a request, having looked through his client's experience to find an appropriate reason for approaching the agency to inquire about its policy. Frequently, the responsible officials will have given the issue only the barest thought, and the lawyer may find that he is working virgin territory altogether. Here the emphasis in presenting the problem must be on that aspect that most interests the agency—what is a sensible enforcement policy in this area. The public official will, no doubt, expect to hear some discussion of the effects of various policies on particular businesses or individuals, but he must consider the issue primarily in the larger context of benefit to the public at large—and thus the lawyer's normal instincts to argue in detailed and specific terms must be resisted. It is always possible to contend for a particular interpretation because any other will put a single client in economic difficulty. But it is far more effective to make the same argument generalizing from the experience of a single business firm to derive conclusions about whole industry sectors, with policy recommendations thus based on a broad factual foundation rather than a weak reed of an individual experience.

As an aid to considering different views, the public official may create an adversary process. The lawyer may find himself in a comparative hearing, replete with presentation of opposing viewpoints and oral argument, and punctuated by skeptical cross-examination from the agency staff. More commonly, the lawyer will be told that others with different viewpoints—and with paying clients—have preceded him in a particular public official's office, and indeed the first lawyer on the scene may have made some headway. The job is then to assess what kinds of arguments were made, why they struck responsive chords with particular officials, and how to reverse and undo any damage that may have been done.

Sometimes a lawyer can take advantage of a problem that is surprisingly common in Washington. Shocking as it may seem, it is frequently the case that prior decisions have not been recorded. That means that each time a particular problem arises there may be the opportunity for renewing arguments that have been less than successful in the past. Even more curiously—or perhaps it should be expected—newly appointed personnel in an incoming administration may actively disagree, or think they disagree, with the decisions of their predecessors. This situation is fertile ground for a lawyer who wishes to change the direction of decision-making and can argue that policy components were incorrectly decided by an earlier administration, or that a recent election produced some sort of mandate for an entirely new approach.

Finally, there may be a rare but important reason to approach an agency for guidance in some especially important life-or-death situations for your client. Ninety percent of all efforts to seek the guidance of an agency will yield results that can be predicted with good confidence. But in some situations, even where the result of an agency decision is fairly predictable, the investment or effort that will be required for a project is so massive that the price of a miscalculation is simply too high to proceed solely on the basis of a lawyer's opinion. In these cases, an extra margin of reassurance is essential—both to the well-being of the project and to the mental health of the lawyer and his perspiring clients.

The project may not be large enough to require the absolute certainty that can be produced only by congressional action to amend the relevant law, but it can still be too large to risk any chance of agency disapproval. In these situations, rare though they may be, the presentation to the agency must emphasize the conventional nature of the effort, rather than its unique size. For instance, the more comfortable an official decision-maker feels with the shape and form of a proposed transaction, the more likely the conventional approvals will be orderly and routine. The agency's perception that the proposed activity is extraordinary is likely to trigger an unusual reaction. From the lawyer's point of view, that is the least desirable possibility in this circumstance.

And so it seems clear beyond doubt that there will be times when seeking the advice of an agency, far from catapulting a firm into danger, as many lawyers assume is inevitable whenever the sleeping bureaucratic beast is aroused, instead is a productive, even necessary aspect of effective Washington representation. The techniques for executing this aspect of the lawyer's mission are not altogether obvious. But before we examine them closely, it is wise to have at least a glimpse of the perils of this course of action—perils that, while they can be minimized, can never entirely be eliminated and therefore must be weighed in the decision to seek the advice of a government agency.

Reasons Not to Seek Guidance from a Government Agency

The process is not risk-free. Lawyers sometimes blithely assume that there is no danger from asking a question, that only benefits can result. These lawyers run the risk of subjecting their clients to unforeseen calamity, no matter how skillfully they use the process. The risk must always be carefully evaluated and in certain situations seeking guidance should be avoided altogether.

If the consultation is the sort involving government approval of a proposed course of action, there is the obvious danger that the agency may say no. When the plan would likely not have attracted the agency's attention in the first place, the consultation has the effect of producing a disapproval, instead of the client's simply taking his chances.

The factor that must be weighed, of course, is the importance of having government approval nailed down in advance. It does little good to proceed with a massive investment in a huge construction project, only to find that the government is going to disapprove the entire proposal. The investment is lost, management loses its credibility and the government is inclined prospectively to regard the company and its lawyers as unreliable and unsophisticated.

It is the essence of judgment in this area to discern which proposals really do need some kind of government approval in advance, and which proposals can risk government rejection after the fact. This judgment is most reliable when based on close contact with the decision-makers and their record of approval and disapproval in similar situations. This is one of the reasons that Washington lawyers are constantly studying the steps that government agencies did not take—the bureaucratic dogs that did not bark. When an agency decides not to proceed adversely, you can count on the fact that lawyers most closely connected with that agency are making notes and filing away that precedent for future use.

A very different kind of risk is possible where the agency consulted is a law enforcement agency. Imagine the thoughts that would race through your mind as a lawyer when, in an initial meeting with a government lawyer, you are carefully laying out a proposal for exchange of information to promote a self-regulatory goal, only to hear your client volunteer that no harm can come from the exchange of information because prices long ago were agreed on by industry members. The meeting that would have begun so hopefully, as a step to a new and more efficient way of doing business, perhaps, would have ended with your client being read his *Miranda* rights. You would be kicking yourself for failing to brief your client adequately and for failing carefully to research the facts, and your client, between thoughts of jail and trial, would be wondering whether he had a defense in ineffective representation.

The key, then, to deciding whether to consult a law enforcement agency is to know the facts—all the facts, including the unattractive ones. Any potential violation of law even remotely related to the subject to be discussed with the agency ought to be revealed and evaluated before the meeting. Some are so inconsequential or of such age as to offer no basis for concern. Others can only be deadly if they are revealed, and steps can perhaps be taken to avoid having the government agency stumble onto them. But if there is sufficient likelihood that a potentially incriminating situation will be opened up by consulting a government agency, it is time to reevaluate the plan to consult. Seeking guidance is not supposed to result in an indictment!

There is another kind of risk to the consultation process. The process may simply be so long and drawn out, or so expensive and detailed, that the result, even if favorable, will not come soon enough or be worth the trouble. One can easily imagine the frustration of a company, wanting reassurance of the legality of a proposal, instead finding itself so bogged down in the consultation process—supplying documents, answering questions, responding to inquiries in marginally related areas, producing studies, perhaps even computing new data or working up new plans—all involving expense, executive time, and lawyer time out of proportion to the risk of proceeding without approval. This is one reason why, with very small projects or very insignificant operations, the consultation process is rarely very useful. This is also one reason why government agencies ought constantly to be pressured to simplify the process and to go to the heart of the matter. There is nothing in the Washington legal scene more discouraging than observing a government agency that could be helpful instead becoming part of the problem by erecting complications and piling intricacy on irrelevancy so that frustration on all sides is the only result.

These are not arguments against using the resources of government when they are important. Rather they are caution signals indicating that prudent reflection in advance of the consultation can forestall futile regret afterwards. The skilled Washington lawyer will have his own calculus of benefit and cost for each agency, for each kind of consultation and for each category of communication. These are largely developed through experience, but careful advance analysis will avoid having that category of consultations that blow up in the lawyer's face become too large a part of his experience.

Varieties of Consultation Processes

There are as many different kinds of consultation as there are government agencies or government officials. They range from the most formal to the completely unstructured, happenstance conversation at a social function. There is no necessary relationship between formality and usefulness of the result. Sometimes the most formal occasions are the least useful, whereas the chance encounter at a garden party in Georgetown—perhaps it is the unguarded moment or the relaxed setting—may prove to be the most revealing.

The more formal occasion may involve large retinues of civil servants, so that posturing, rather than candid communication, is the order of the day. Or the results from a formal consultation process may by tradition be too narrow to be useful—framed in some historic formula that is no longer in touch with reality, or hedged by numerous protective caveats and qualifications, which may seem to the government official to be necessary but which deprive the guidance of any life and utility. In addition, the more formal processes tend to require more lawyering—more applications in writing, legal memoranda in support, perhaps the taking of evidence or at least the supplying of documents and data, culminating perhaps in some kind of final argument. More lawyering necessarily means more lawyer's fees. A client can be pardoned for welcoming the less structured, less formal but more affordable results that come from the casual conversation or chance encounter.

On the other hand, informal results may bind no one. Or they may be so off-hand as to give very little assurance. How much will a client be willing to risk on the basis of a comment at a cocktail party delivered after a drink or two? The government official is perhaps justified in claiming later that information he got was sketchy or uninformative or even misleading. And it is doubtful that a government agency should consider itself estopped, either legally or morally, if a lawyer attempted to transmute an off-the-cuff remark into official agency approval.

Nevertheless, off-the-cuff remarks are not to be ignored. Sometimes they are more revealing than is ever the case with a more formal consultation process. This may be intentional, or not, but the result is the same. A government official may choose to deliver his opinion on an informal basis, knowing it will not be quoted and cannot be cited. He may suggest either that the formal process ought to be foregone, or that it is unnecessary. The popularity of Washington parties self-evidently does not depend on their ample drink, comfortable surroundings or good food, as anyone knows who has ever attended one. Rather, business is being done at all levels in what is quite literally a bazaar of information and high-level persuasion.

In choosing the kind of consultation process most beneficial to the client, probably the most important judgment to be made at the outset is whether the opinion will be favorable or not. The situations in which it is necessary to go into an agency blindly are far less frequent than is generally presumed. Almost always some indication of outcome is available, through testimony before congressional committees, speeches, interviews and the like. An informed lawyer can often predict with a fair degree of accuracy the kind of meeting likely to result.

Once the general tenor of the result is known, it becomes important to find out in what form the advice will be made available. Frequently this is the subject of the most intense negotiation, even before the process begins to grapple with the merits. It may well be that the only possible result is a formal, highly stylized departmental opinion in writing, or even less useful, a statement that the authorities are aware of certain facts, without any conclusion on the agency's position. Perhaps least useful of all is the letter from the lawyer to the government agency confirming that an official was told certain plans and expressed no objection. Indeed, that kind of a letter, although it may have some limited use in infrequent situations, is likely to bring down the curtain on any future meetings with that particular official. Government officials who have decided that they are unable to render more formal advice do not like their inaction or muteness transmuted into agency policy. Before any such device is adopted, the long-run disadvantages—as well as the more immediate advantages—ought thoroughly to be considered.

Another general rule based on anticipation of results is that the more significant the possibility of disapproval, the narrower the request or proposal for review. One reason why many prefer to precede the submission of a proposal with a face-to-face meeting with the bureaucrat involved is to take his pulse—to get a sense of whether he is reacting affirmatively or is likely to be the bearer of bad news. If the signs are good, thought should be given, perhaps even during the meeting, to withholding the narrow request that had been prepared for submission at the meeting, and instead, volunteering to have a properly drafted proposal, "taking into account all of the information you have learned at the meeting," brought round to his office by messenger that afternoon. This enables you to get back to your law office, consider in what ways the proposal could usefully be broadened, without losing a step in the consultation process.

If the meeting is more ambiguous, or even shows signs of a sour response, the proposal is best described in the narrowest possible way so that options for restatement to avoid the agency difficulty are easily available. It is not at all unusual for a lawyer to come to a meeting of this kind armed with two different versions of the same proposal, one more expansive and the other less, with an on-the-spot decision made at the last moment as to which written proposal will be left on the desk of the decision-maker at the conclusion.

The same set of calculations is brought to bear in choosing the level for a meeting—and this is one of the most sensitive calculations to be made. One dimension of it is quite simple: a lower-level disapproval is not as damaging as a high-level disapproval, but a lower-level approval is not as useful either. So some part of the choice of the level for a meeting depends on the anticipated result.

Never forget the ego of a bureaucrat. Like any other person, the decision-maker needs to be made to feel important and needs to be catered to, particularly if you intend to revisit his office. Thus, in choosing the level, be aware that mischief can be caused by a lower-level bureaucrat who feels that he has been ignored, or that he has been vaulted in the hierarchy by a lawyer in search of a more favorable audience. Many Washington lawyers, who fully intend to pursue a matter to at least the sub-cabinet level if necessary, religiously start off at the staff level. They know this builds good will, improves connections, may make the later stages unnecessary and in any event avoids putting someone's nose out of joint.

Two kinds of officials are especially sensitive. The first is the seasoned bureaucrat who has worked throughout his professional career to get to a senior level in the civil service and is highly jealous of his turf and prerogatives. He is knowledgeable, a tough in-fighter, with good connections on the Hill, and with the press and the interests groups. Irritating him on a major matter can carry a very high price.

The second kind of official to be wary of is the highly ideological young lawyer who sees a conspiracy and a Watergate scandal whenever someone from the private sector visits a political appointee's office. These people will gradually mature as they learn how the world really works, but during this period of fevered suspicion, they too can be major headaches if their suspicions are fanned by being by-passed.

The other determinant in choosing the level for a meeting is the question of access. Getting access to a very senior official's office for a meeting may be very difficult. And this is where some Washington lawyers really earn their fee. Many of them are former office-holders themselves and have done their best to stay on good terms with their successors. Usually they have been successful. There are lawyers in Washington who simply will not be turned down when making a request for a meeting.

Curiously, for certain people, the more junior staff officials are more difficult to meet with than a department secretary. A staff member may studiously avoid responding to a lawyer's request for a meeting, sensing that he is about to lose control in his agency over the pace or direction of agency action with respect to a certain project. He may not have in mind the broader implications of turning down certain petitions for a fair hearing. A department secretary or sub-cabinet official may be acutely aware of the broader import of such a rejection—political trouble at a later date—and, as a result, may be willing to set aside twenty minutes or half an hour on a special request.

Timing is crucial. The first question will be whether guidance should be sought before the plan is implemented. The easy answer is "Of course!"—but not so fast. In certain kinds of cases, the fact that investment has been undertaken, or that one's competitors have already begun, will sway judgments. In a close case, the waste of calling off a major project or the unfairness of preventing one firm in an industry from proceeding may be a decisive consideration. On the other hand, many agencies simply refuse to consider a request for guidance if the project is already underway. As we shall later see, the Department of Justice's Business Review Procedure requires that the plan be prospective and will refuse even to process a request for a business review of past or present conduct. The gamble is that, if there is any significant chance of disapproval, it is far better to go about it before extensive investment has been sunk in a plan that must ultimately be shelved.

Framing the Question

Many of your clients will have the notion that all that is involved in consulting a government official is walking into his office and popping the question. It is never that simple. Framing the issue may be the most important decision of all. As much attention should be paid to that as is devoted to wording argument headings in a brief for the United States Supreme Court.

We have talked about the narrow versus broad distinction. But the reality is even more subtle. Consider the question of emphasis. It is possible to highlight a policy component of the issue, or to downplay it, or even to modulate it in order to engage the interest of a particular official or to generate the support from a segment of the bureaucracy. Should budget impact be alluded to? What kinds of code words or buzz words should be avoided, or included?

Again, it is essential to know in detail the policy views and the preferences of the officials with whom you will speak. Every government office puts out press releases by the bushel, and those of the relevant office should be examined in detail. Most Washington lawyers keep up with the latest twists and turns of particular government offices or officials as a matter of course. Indeed, public officials are often astonished to find out how closely their every action and word is watched and analyzed by the Washington lawyer. And yet it is simply a means of preparing for the most persuasive presentation at that next meeting. The analysis of speeches, testimony and articles by the relevant officials should be a prerequisite to framing the issue.

Problems can arise when it will be necessary to check with different government offices. Because the offices may have differing responsibilities and contrasting policy concerns, the temptation will be overwhelming to vary the question, depending on which office is being consulted at the moment. There is nothing wrong with this as long as one important risk is confronted and understood. While you need not frame the question identically for all reviewing officials, you must avoid the impression that there has been a lack of candor or that one or the other official has been misled. Thus, though the formulations of the issue may vary somewhat, the presentations should be recognizably related, and not so different in tone or content that your client will be regarded as having tried to pull a fast one on a government official.

You should always be prepared to bargain over the framing of the question. You may be able, in advance, to ascertain whether a particular formulation will meet with the approval of the relevant official. It may well be that some advance consultation with a special assistant or with others who have had similar problems before the same government agency will give clues to the best way of presenting the issue for review.

And just as the nature of the question is subject to negotiation, so also is the nature of the response. It is ideal if you can be shown a draft, but that is rare. Instead, it may be possible to advise that it would be helpful if the answer contained this boiler plate or that standard provision, or not. The suggestion that trade secrets be omitted will be perfectly appropriate, and there may even be provision in the relevant regulations for keeping part or all of the response off the public record—which may be important in a competitive context. In any event, the lawyer should never be afraid to try to assist the government official in organizing a useful response.

Other Considerations

Although the client is certainly going to derive some value from the process, he will also be concerned about the expense and intrusiveness of the consultative process. Inevitably, whenever the government is consulted, there is some chance that the citizen is going to become enmeshed in the bureaucratic toils and lose all control over the process.

The fear is not an idle one. While some agencies will act quickly on the basis of what a lawyer presents to them, others are far more deliberate, even lead-footed. Volumes of information may be requested in the absence of some previous understanding with the government official as to how much information will be necessary. Company officials may be interviewed. Much of this can be worked out and planned before the process is initiated. But if not, the client ought to enter the process with his eyes open.

Nor should the businessman expect his dealings with the government to remain secret. Some agencies act as if they are conducting their business in the anterooms of the Washington Post and the other influential dailies that write about government activities. Some government officials display their roster of visitors publicly in the department press rooms, perhaps with a note as to the nature of the business to be discussed. And then there is always the Freedom of Information Act, pursuant to which your client's competitors can make requests for information concerning your client from every department and, in due course, expect to receive some indication that you and your client have business pending and some clue to what the pending business is all about.

Clients may also worry that they will be unable to extricate themselves from the consultation process if it takes an unfavorable turn. The best answer to this concern is that there are no guarantees, although sometimes the request can be withdrawn with little or no damage to client interests. The result is that the process is stopped in its tracks, the file closed and nothing more thought of it. In other situations, however, although the formal request can be withdrawn, the agency may continue the inquiry on its own motion or establish in its agency suspense file a schedule for some later check to see whether there has been a violation of law. The very act of withdrawing the request may accelerate this process.

Once the issue is broached to a government official, the client in a sense has taken an irreversible step. The formalities of the process may permit reconsideration, but no-one can guarantee that that will be the end of the matter.

Summing Up

The consultation process is inevitably complicated. Skillfully used, it can do wonders for a client's peace of mind, produce government approval of private initiatives or avert enforcement actions based on inadequate information and insufficient consideration. Misused, it can be disastrous. Attention may be called to problems that might escape the notice of government altogether. Sensitivities may be raised but not adequately handled. The client may be damaged, the lawyer, discredited.

As a means of seeing how the general lessons we have derived can play out in actual practice, it makes sense to look at a specific kind of consultation process—the Business Review Procedure at the Antitrust Division. A close examination of the Business Review Procedure makes it clear that it can be very useful indeed, that it is underutilized mostly as the result of misunderstanding and that a skillful lawyer can play the process as though it were a cello. The key to successful use is intimate knowledge of the process and the rules of the game, familiarity with those who are likely to be making the decisions within the Division and awareness of the dangers and pitfalls of proceeding in the wrong way. All this information can yield enormously impressive results in the hands of an able practitioner.

THE BUSINESS REVIEW PROCEDURE OF THE ANTITRUST DIVISION: ONE MODEL OF FORMAL GUIDANCE

Of all the formal processes for gaining guidance from our federal government, one of the best known and most highly developed is the Antitrust Division's Business Review Procedure. Through a process detailed in 28 C.F.R. § 50.6, business entities can inquire of the Division as to its enforcement intentions with respect to any arrangement, merger, joint venture or other piece of commercial conduct. At the end of the process, the client has frequently gained a clear verdict, one way or the other, and the process reveals to the lawyer the considerations that will govern the Antitrust Division's analysis of the conduct proposed as well as similar conduct in the future.

The Business Review Procedure had its origin in 1939 in the practice of issuing "railroad release" letters. Under that procedure, the Division would review business conduct and then state whether it would forego criminal prosecution against the persons engaging in the conduct. Over the years a merger clearance procedure was added, and in 1968 these practices were formalized with accompanying regulations. Today, the Antitrust Division receives a variety of business review requests every year, responds to them diligently and seriously and, thus, can be quite helpful to a businessman who is contemplating a particular project or manner of doing business. The procedure provides an opportunity to discover the intentions of a law enforcement agency without the pain of prosecution. As such, it is a relatively unusual and highly useful procedure.

The Business Review Process

In the ordinary case, the process is initiated by a letter to the Assistant Attorney General, requesting a business review of proposed conduct. While it is not required that the letter be addressed to the Assistant Attorney General, this is the most effective way to begin, since it is then a matter that has had his personal attention, however briefly, and the attitude of the staff lawyers will be correspondingly different. Diligence in timely processing, for one thing, is far more likely.

The request itself should set out in some detail the conduct proposed, its industry context, the fact that it is unlikely to have major anticompetitive effects and why, therefore, it should be approved. Any contracts or documents directly relevant to the conduct, including studies of competitive effect or industry analyses, should be attached to the original request.

The Division is not required to respond to the request. If, for instance, the conduct is ongoing, rather than proposed, the Division typically will not assess its enforcement intentions, because then it would be in the business of giving advisory opinions on conduct that could become the subject of litigation at a later time, raising the possibility that the business review process was being manipulated rather than consulted. Or, if regulatory approvals are required from other federal agencies, the Division is reluctant to take an enforcement position before these approvals have been obtained. But these factors can be dealt with. If there is some danger that the request will be turned down for these or other reasons, it is important for the lawyer to anticipate that and to move quickly with a direct communication to the Division addressing the question of why this specific business review request is appropriate and should be handled by the Division on its merits.

It is sometimes assumed that a meeting with Division personnel is mandatory early in the process. That is certainly true if the proposal has major national security implications or involves something truly extraordinary such as a project of unprecedented size, scope and expense, or if there is an emergency aspect to the proposal. Then, a meeting requested on an emergency basis with the Assistant Attorney General himself may be quite appropriate. At any such meeting, the nature of the special problem, emergency or national interest involved can be explained to an official who can greatly accelerate the process. In the unique circumstances of a major national industry proposing conduct with national security implications, the Antitrust Division has been known to process a business review request within 24 hours.

Ordinarily, any such early meeting is more profitably held with the staff to whom the business review request has been assigned. Such a meeting should be directed toward explaining the proposed conduct, offering to be helpful in furnishing the initial round of information, and setting up a contact point and a procedure for staying in touch.

Following the initial request to the Assistant Attorney General, the lawyer should in fact make every effort to stay close to the process. This is the secret of working this process to the maximum advantage—at all times be up to date. Be helpful and responsive to the government lawyers who must process the request. How the lawyer monitors the process can make all the difference in whether he is viewed as meddling or helping, and obviously the better one knows the institution and the people involved, the more skillful and therefore effective one can be. But it is possible for the lawyer to assist and accelerate the process greatly by supplying the right information or analysis at the right time.

Unless the lawyer is keeping in very close touch with the Division from the moment the request is filed, the first notice that he will have that the request has been considered appropriate for business review treatment is when the Office of Operations in Washington refers the request to a section or field office having commodity or geographic responsibility for the product or service involved in the request. The Office of Operations is the clearinghouse for the Division and traffic cop for all its litigation. As a result, the director and his co-equal—at least in responsibility—the deputy director, know virtually everything that is going on in the Antitrust Division, from inquiries and informal investigations to cases in trial and mergers being considered for challenge. Thus, they are best equipped to assign responsibility for considering a business review. Once they have done so, the staff will be identified and can begin to focus on the merits of the request. That formal step will be signaled when the assigned section submits to the Office of Operations a formal memorandum requesting investigative authority—as they would for a preliminary inquiry at the beginning of an investigation—together with a request to seek clearance from the Federal Trade Commission.

Because the FTC in many areas has dual responsibility for antitrust enforcement, neither agency undertakes an examination or investigation without getting clearance from the other. Because the Commission has its own advisory procedure, there is always a chance that a business review request directed at the Antitrust Division will wind up being considered by the Federal Trade Commission. If this is a result the client would very much wish to avoid, as is sometimes the case—the FTC may historically be more inclined to investigate conduct in some industries than the Justice Department—an effort should be made to communicate both with the section involved and the Operations Office, setting forth arguments why the request is best not referred to the Commission. A particularly crucial contact at this stage is the deputy director in the Operations Office who has responsibility for managing the clearance process with the FTC.

At the time clearance is sought from the FTC, a file is formally opened and the whole matter is entered into the ACES system, the Division's internal computerized status report system. This sets the stage for the next key point for intervention by the lawyer—the assignment of a deadline. When authority is granted to one of the sections, an "action date" is established. This is a scheduled target date for completion of the investigation and business review letter. That target date varies depending on the size and complexity of the review to be undertaken, and substantial discretion is lodged in the Operations Office to choose a date. Typically the date will be 60 to 90 days off, although if the review concerns export-related requests, the Division has a policy that it will respond within 30 business days from the date that it receives all relevant data.

A client may have a special need for getting the response within a much shorter time. This can be arranged in exceptional cases, although it will be difficult and it can never be guaranteed. A lawyer in this situation should make clear to the Operations Office and to the staff at the outset that a quick response is essential and the reasons why. The experience of most lawyers faced with this kind of problem is that if the Division can move quickly, it will certainly try.

Once the action date is assigned and the section staff is selected, the process of investigation begins. The requesting parties have the obligation to supply the Division with all the information and documents in their possession that are needed for review of the matter. In all likelihood, the Division will request additional information and may seek to interview several officials or experts from the client's company. Other sources will be consulted, including industry experts, other firms in the industry and perhaps other parts of government.

The job of the lawyer at this stage is to become virtually an arm of the staff. The staff's needs must be anticipated, its confidence gained, its education furthered and its conclusions shaped. For instance, a great deal of time can be saved at this stage if the lawyer for the requesting party assembles a neat and well-organized package of all relevant materials in several copies and submits them simultaneously to the Operations Office and to the two or three lawyers who may be working on the request. The mechanics of document reproduction in the government are notoriously inefficient and, surprisingly, a great deal of time can sometimes be saved by this kind of shortcut.

Each time documents are delivered, it is helpful to use the opportunity for conversation to get some sense of which way the wind is blowing. These informal meetings may be more revealing than the more formal consultation sessions. Lower-level staff people may feel freer to talk, and their questions and comments will have an air of practical significance that is sometimes absent from the larger, more formal meetings. When possible, you should respond fully and frankly to concerns expressed on such occasions. It may be necessary to offer to supplement an oral response with a more reasoned memorandum within a day or two or to deliver some additional documents. In any case, their questions must never be ignored.

As the investigation process continues, and the outlines of any staff concerns become clearer, you will increasingly have to assist the staff by preparing analytical memoranda that array the facts and apply the law. Almost always you will have done the more thorough thinking over a longer period of time than a staff that has recently come to the problem. And thus, not only can time be saved but analysis sometimes shaped and conclusions assisted by augmenting the review process with the results of your own research and reflection.

It will sometimes be the case that the staff seems to be headed off in an irrelevant direction. What better way to convince them of that than to write a memorandum showing why the line of inquiry on which they are embarked will make no difference to the ultimate decision. Or suppose the staff is focusing on the right question but seems to misapprehend some of the relevant facts. You should be closely enough in touch with the process to see this developing and to step in to correct the misimpression. Offer supporting evidence to strengthen your arguments. In fact, you may at this point wish to volunteer your client's employees for interviews or offer to retain an independent expert who will address the staff's concerns.

The point is that, whichever way the issue seems to be headed, you will want to know about it immediately and be in a position to take suitable steps if a mistake is about to be made, or otherwise to influence the development of the correct conclusion. How closely the lawyer can be involved in the process rests on many different factors, including the general reputation of the lawyer at the Bar and his special reputation for candor and credibility within the Division itself. There are lawyers whose reputations in the Division are less savory because of reports of events in the past, handed down by word of mouth from one generation of young lawyers to the next. The word of others, regarded as thoroughly reliable, is very much respected by the lawyers in the Division. In the end this is a tribute to those lawyers and also of enormous benefit to their clients. Perhaps no single factor is more important than credibility and a reputation for candor in practicing before a government agency. These assets should not be squandered in the service of any client.

Even the lawyer whose reputation is good and whose face is welcome in the attorney's offices must make it a habit to stay in touch with the agency staff. Antitrust lawyers frequently make appearances at Division parties or at staff retirement parties, not only because they enjoy the chance to see old friends—and certainly not to find out what is going on in their particular case—but also to maintain the closeness that at some later time may be of great assistance when it is appropriate to pick up a telephone and inquire of a long-time friend what progress has been made with a certain business review. No Division lawyer is going to say anything improper on such occasions simply because he knows you. But many Division lawyers are competent and confident enough to know that there can be no harm in informing a lawyer about progress made on a business review request or predicting the probable schedule. Many will feel quite free to describe the current problems of analysis, hoping to receive informed assistance.

Obviously the lawyer/agency relationship is a very delicate one, with the potential for all sorts of risks. It is equally true, that when it is well-managed it can be exceedingly useful. And perhaps most obviously, when it is sufficiently current and informative so that problems can be disposed of as soon as they arise, this kind of close contact with the agency can be the difference between success and failure in seeking guidance for your client.

As the investigation moves toward conclusion, the pace will quicken and intensify. The staff is preparing a memorandum with its recommendations, together with a draft business review letter, which will be forwarded to the section chief. The lawyer who has been close to the process will surely anticipate that the staff effort is coming to a climax and that responsibility is about to move toward a higher level.

Anything that can be done at this stage to change a negative recommendation to an approval is worth the time and effort that it takes. Once a negative staff recommendation is in place, salvaging the situation becomes much harder. Staffs are not infrequently reversed, but the fact that you must persuade a supervisor that his staff's conclusion is in error is one more—and substantial—obstacle to a favorable result.

Persuasiveness is now at a premium. Contrary to what some lawyers seem to think, bluster or contempt is not effective. A patient, factual, well-prepared presentation, which takes into account the Antitrust Division's lawyer's real interest in promoting competition, will be by far the most effective tool.

If a lawyer senses that a negative recommendation is being prepared, a meeting with the staff should be sought at once. If the memorandum has already been submitted to the section chief, a meeting with him may be advisable. Whether such a meeting should be sought is a judgment that can only be made by those who know how he is likely to react. Some always sustain their staffs' recommendations; others approach them in a more neutral spirit. It does no one any good to meet with a section chief whose mind has been made up for him by his own staff, but most of the Division's section chiefs are experienced and independent thinkers and a meeting with them can be very worthwhile. Quite frequently, the rationale for a negative recommendation will be somewhat altered by such meetings, and even if the negative recommendation goes forward, an altered rationale may be easier to deal with at the higher levels of the Division.

If the section chief, after his review, agrees with the position recommended, he will add his own memorandum and pass it on to the Office of Operations. After Operations has reviewed the matter, further review will take place by the appropriate Deputy Assistant Attorney General and, ultimately, the Assistant Attorney General. At each of these new levels, there is an opportunity for intervention and persuasion. As a general rule, one should take each new opportunity to make one's views known as long as there is the possibility for persuasion. The character of the argument may change subtly, with greater emphasis on the policy component, or the importance of the project proposed, or the strong views of other parts of the government, or the importance of precedent. But in the Antitrust Division at all levels, there will be a rigorous interest in the applicable law and its economic implications, and an unwillingness to sacrifice significant competition benefits for other competing values, unless the imbalance in favor of the non-competition benefits becomes too great. Once again, the skill of the lawyer, his sensitivity to the special dynamics at each level, his awareness of the personalities and their concerns and interests and his energy in staying as close to the process as possible will be vital to the outcome in a close case.

The bottom line phrasing of the Division's conclusion is generally not subject to negotiation. The three business review formulae are (1) that the Division does not presently intend to bring an enforcement action against the proposed conduct; (2) that the Division declines to state its enforcement intention; or (3) that the Division will sue if the proposed conduct is implemented. Generally one of those conclusions is contained in a letter that also sets forth the procedural history of the request, a short summary of the representations made by the party requesting the business review and a description of the procedures for making public the information in the business file. The letter is signed by the Assistant Attorney General or, in his absence, by the Acting Assistant Attorney General.

Ordinarily no one outside the Division is involved in the Business Review Procedure, but that is not an immutable rule. One can conceive of situations of such importance or so great an urgency that unfavorable results at the Division level would suggest the desirability of moving the level of decision beyond the Division. Clearly only the exceptional case would be considered for such treatment. But at least one business review request that I know of was initiated in a meeting with the Attorney General, and there is no reason why in such a situation the Attorney General should not be responsible for making the final decision. In appropriate cases, therefore, you may wish to consider requesting a meeting with the Attorney General, but these circumstances will be very rare indeed.

At the time of final decision, not only does the Division notify the requesting party of its action on the business review but a press release is issued describing the matter in full and attaching a copy of the Division's letter of response. At this point also the initial request and the responsive letter are placed in a public file, and, within thirty days thereafter, all the information supplied in support of the request is placed in a public file in the Division's Legal Procedure Unit.

At this point another major struggle can arise. The regulations provide that information submitted by a requesting party may be protected from disclosure if it can be shown that disclosure would have a detrimental effect on the operations or relations with customers, employees, suppliers, stockholders or competitors of the requestor. 28 C.F.R. § 50.6 (10)(c). This generally covers confidential commercial or financial information, which is not subject to compulsory disclosure under the Freedom of Information Act. Nevertheless, here too there is room for some negotiation and creative lawyering.

Presumably the less information about the client that is revealed publicly, the better. This concern has to be balanced during the investigation process against the desire to furnish as much information as possible to persuade the Division to take favorable action. But it does not help much if, following favorable action, a great deal of confidential information is spilled out onto the public record. The effort here, then, is to negotiate both with the legal staff and with the Division's freedom of information staff to see to it that as much of the information as is possible is classified as protectible commercial or financial information not subject to release.

One might be pardoned for thinking that, after all the investigation and analysis involved in a business review, the result would be permanent, and, if favorable, would endow the conduct with immunity. Unfortunately, that is not the case. The letter states only the present enforcement intention of the Division as of the date of the letter. And the Division unashamedly claims the right to withdraw a letter and to bring whatever action or proceeding it subsequently comes to feel may be in the public interest. The courts have confirmed that even a favorable business review does not shield the requestor from subsequent antitrust action. *United States* v. *Grinnell, Corp.*, 30 F.R.D. 358 (D.R.I. 1962).

You may be virtually sure, however, that after the Division has stated a present intention not to sue, it is extremely unlikely to bring criminal action, that is, assuming there was full disclosure of the facts when the business review request was presented to the Division. In the absence of full disclosure, of course, all bets are off.

On one occasion judicial review was sought of the Division's conclusions in the business review letter. In *Holly Farms Poultry Industries, Inc.* v. *Kleindienst*, 1973-1 Trade Cas. ¶ 74,535 (M.D. N.C. 1973), where the Division had declined to state a present enforcement intention, Holly Farms sought judicial review claiming jurisdiction under the Administrative Procedure Act. The court dismissed the suit, holding that the issue of whether to bring an action for violation of the antitrust laws was so clearly within the discretion of the Attorney General as to make it judicially unreviewable. The court's opinion placed major reliance upon the fact that the conduct was proposed for the future, not engaged in as a past practice. The court suggested in dicta that a different result might be called for where there was both reliance on an earlier ruling and conduct under way that subjected the inquirer to prosecution.

CONCLUSION ON SEEKING GUIDANCE FROM THE AGENCY

The usefulness of guidance from a government agency is clear enough. When a statement of clear intention can be obtained, a client's confusion and uncertainty are minimized and energy can be devoted to moving ahead with the plan of action, rather than worrying about its legality. If at the end of the day the reaction from the government is unfavorable, that too is useful because investment and commitment to the project are avoided and alternative means of accomplishing the necessary ends can be considered.

The Business Review Procedure of the Antitrust Division is an example of the consultation process in one of its purest forms—one focusing on the merits of a proposal to the exclusion of political implications, one that is neutral—contrary to the general view held outside the Division—and one in which proposed conduct, even though it embodies some danger to competition, may well be approved.

But it is important to realize that the opinions of a government agency do not emerge automatically, as Chiclets out of a gum machine. Rather they are developed and shaped by interaction among client, lawyer and government officials. They are evolved in a dynamic process that can be influenced by sound argument and persuasive formulation. And therein lies the secret of successful lawyering in this area—glimpsing the opportunities for persuasion and having the wit and the skill to use them. Casualness or insensitivity will not only waste the opportunity for a favorable result but may make each new approach by the same client or the same lawyer to the Antitrust Division more difficult.

It is the art of effective representation that uses a lawyer's skill and effectiveness to translate a client's proposal into its most persuasive form, to anticipate and deal with the concerns and skepticism raised by the reviewing authorities, and to emerge at the other end of the process with an approval that permits the client to proceed on a proposed course of conduct that might just as easily have been disapproved. But such skill and effectiveness require detailed and close knowledge of the agencies and their processes. When that constellation of knowledge and ability is present, the opportunity exists for a lawyer, in achieving successful results, not merely to surprise the client but to amaze him.

Chapter 4

THE IMPORTANCE OF THE OFFICE OF MANAGEMENT AND BUDGET

JAMES T. McINTYRE, JR.*

Lobbying OMB, until very recently, was an unknown art. OMB was an introverted, self-insulated agency, priding itself on the intellectual purity and neutral competence of its staff work. Such independence has not always been the reality at the top political level of the agency, but it is the source of OMB's greatest institutional pride.

OMB's influence has ebbed and flowed, depending on the needs of the President and the style of the OMB director, as well as on the trust and confidence that the President has in an OMB director. Throughout its history, OMB has generally been viewed as politically naive. That view has resulted in successive attempts to make OMB more politically responsive.

The Office of Management and Budget was originally established by the Budget and Accounting Act of 1921 as a small staff agency, called the Bureau of the Budget, in the Treasury Department. Under the Act, executive branch agencies were required, for the first time, to submit their budget requests to the Bureau of the Budget, which

---

*James T. McIntyre, Jr. is a partner in the Washington, D.C. office of the law firm, Hansell & Post. He served for three years as Director of the Office of Management & Budget, Executive Office of the President and as a member of the Cabinet of President Carter. Prior to serving as Director, Mr. McIntyre served as Deputy Director of OMB.

then assembled the requests and submitted them to the Congress.

In 1939, the Executive Office of the President was created and the Bureau of the Budget was transferred there from the Treasury. The Executive Office of the President was established to help the President carry out his responsibility to manage the executive branch. OMB is the oldest institution in the Executive Office of the President. It has the largest professional staff of the EOP agencies, with substantial stability at the top career staff levels. OMB has historically attracted the cream of federal employees who look at issues from an objective government-wide basis and thereby give OMB its institutional edge over other departments and agencies.

It was during the 1940's that the Bureau became an indispensable staff arm of the President and that the director became established as a key Presidential advisor, thereby exercising significant influence in the executive branch decision-making process. That influence grew when the Bureau of the Budget became the Office of Management and Budget in 1970 and took on the additional responsibility of coordinating a wide variety of agency actions to insure that they were consistent with the President's overall policies.

Historically, the director's access to the President and his personal relationship with the chief executive have directly affected OMB's influence and power. The influence of OMB has risen and fallen in both Democratic and Republican administrations. For example, after FDR and Director Lewis W. Douglas split over policy issues, Douglas ceased to be an intimate advisor. However, Harold Smith, who was appointed to succeed Douglas in 1939, was an intimate advisor to FDR and therefore wielded significant influence over a wide range of domestic, economic, and budgetary issues. Similar fluctuations in OMB's influence occurred in the Eisenhower Administration. Director Brundage was unable to get beyond the President's personal staff, but Director Stans had significant clout because he did have personal access to the President.[1]

OMB's lack of access to and influence with the President can work both for and against it in terms of the agency's influence outside the White House. During the Watergate years, for example, it was OMB's ability to survive at arm's length from the White House that kept the government running smoothly. Yet it was this very neutrality that led the incoming Carter Administration to add more "political" layers to the agency in an attempt to make it more responsive to political direction from the top.

In addition to the importance of the director's relationship with the President, it is equally important that OMB be a part of the "paper loop" and play a key role in the analysis and recommendations of various issues to be presented to the President. In this role, OMB has a unique position among the other agencies in the Executive Office of the President because of its mandate to give impartial advice to the President. Although OMB is firmly ensconced in this paper loop, the director must remain vigilant to prevent against another agency's effort to short circuit OMB, because of concern for the weight its recommendations may carry with the President.

While it has always been an important agency, the Office of Management and Budget was not in the public eye until recent years. Subsequently, with the emphasis on improved governmental management, balancing the federal budget, this office has attracted significant public attention. Regardless of OMB's place in the White House political hierarchy, it will always be an essential contact point for someone trying to affect federal policy. If others in the White House carry their own weight, OMB may not be the only place to lobby inside the Executive Office of the President, but it will always be one necessary stop.

WHY GO TO THE OMB?

OMB's decisions and recommendations obviously carry a great deal of weight in the final outcome of questions of federal policy. Because of the director's personal access to the President, OMB's role in the paper loop, its governmentwide overview of Presidential policy, and its role in allocating money and staff to various executive branch departments and agencies, OMB is involved in practically every major federal decision. One would therefore look to OMB, among other executive office agencies, to communicate facts and information about an existing policy, a proposed policy, or a budget question. For instance, the number of subsidized housing units to be supported annually is usually subject to intense debate. If an organization were interested in seeing a certain number of units proposed by the President, it would be advisable for the organization to meet with OMB officials and present its arguments before OMB made its recommendations to the President.

One might also approach the Office of Management and Budget to induce it to review an existing policy or agency decision, with a view to changing the decision or policy. For instance, the Davis-Bacon Act requires payment of prevailing wages for workers on federally supported construction projects. The policies of the Department of Labor for determining prevailing wages have been subject to much criticism over the years. Inquiry by OMB into these policies could be instrumental in getting the Secretary of Labor to review and perhaps modify the policies. In such an instance, OMB serves as a catalyst for action, since Presidential interest is implied. This role as catalyst is a very important part of the budget development process in which challenges by OMB of existing policies and programs can result in changes in current policies.

OMB is also the place to discuss circulars that establish general policy, especially in regard to the federal government's dealings with state and local governments and nonprofit organizations. OMB circulars deal with ongoing requirements and are known by number, such as Circular A-76, which deals with contracting out services to the private sector. OMB also issues directives for one-time needs, usually an agency procedure or the collection of certain information. One might also wish to present to OMB facts on legislation that has been passed by the Congress and which OMB is reviewing before recommending Presidential action. Because of OMB's responsibility for reviewing paperwork requirements and agency regulations, one could also approach OMB with information helpful in deciding whether to approve a form or a proposed regulation.

The director of OMB may also use his power of inquiry to affect federal agency rule making. By merely inquiring into an agency's rationale for a particular ruling and questioning its projected impact in terms of technological feasibility and economic practicality, the director informally but effectively conveys OMB's position on the affected issue. The agency may react to the director's inquiry in any number of ways, depending on how controlling its administration perceives OMB's authority and influence to be. If the agency is unsure whether it is acting with procedural correctness and within the proper bounds of its authority, it may respond by changing its policy directives in line with what it understands the director's implied position to be.

Such accommodation might be subtle. It might take the form of extended administrative hearings in which witnesses favorable to OMB's position would be called in. More drastic accommodation might lead to the agency's calling a halt to the entire rule-making process until further investigation were completed. As a case in point, this latter situation arose when a former director sent a letter of inquiry to the Environmental Protection Agency (EPA) regarding a noise pollution standard it had set for garbage truck manufacturers. OMB's position was generally favorable to the industry on this issue because of the significant financial impact the standard would have caused. OMB also reasoned that setting this type of standard was not the business of the federal government. In a letter, the director questioned whether the EPA should have issued such a standard since it encompassed an information collection plan, which statutorily came under the review powers of the OMB. Upon receipt of the letter, the agency had good reason to fear that it had failed to follow certain procedural steps required for the issuance of the standard. In fact, the letter had been prompted by a petition from the industry to the OMB citing statutory authority that indicated that the EPA had failed to follow procedural guidelines. As a response to this inquiry from the OMB, the agency promptly withdrew the proposed standards.

To see exactly what OMB does, let us examine OMB's roles and look at various points of access.

ROLES OF THE OFFICE OF MANAGEMENT AND BUDGET

The role of the Office of Management and Budget is much more complex and extensive than the archetypal image of "green eyeshade accountants" suggests. It is the only place in the federal government, besides the Oval Office, where budgeting, management information and control systems, and foreign and domestic policy issues come together. The Office of Management and Budget makes important decisions every day of the year on virtually every program of the federal government. While OMB does not establish national policy, it does interpret, coordinate, and implement policy that has been set by the President or the Congress. In other words, OMB translates the President's general policy into specific government actions.

OMB is responsible for setting budgetary objectives. In the course of making decisions on allocating resources to the various departments and agencies for carrying out their programs, OMB emphasizes Presidential priorities among competing objectives. For example, the President's policy emphasizes law and order. In setting the budget for the Department of Justice, OMB could therefore deemphasize the federal government's role in antitrust regulation by reducing the dollars and personnel recommended for the Antitrust Division and increasing the resources available to the Federal Bureau of Investigation. In such a case, it would be the President rather than OMB who established the policy to focus more on general law enforcement and less on antitrust enforcement. Nevertheless, it would be OMB that would transform the Presidential priorities into a dollars-and-cents reality. In some cases, OMB makes the final decision about what actions implement Presidential policy; in others, OMB is the synthesizer of conflicting views from the agencies, serving as focal point for analysis and recommendations before the President himself decides an issue.

The President gives OMB his general policy guidance during the spring budget review process. OMB's initial direction is derived from campaign statements, personal instructions from the President, and meetings with the President and his advisors. OMB makes its detailed decisions and recommendations within the framework of these policies. OMB usually has significant discretion in choosing among alternatives for achieving a policy objective as long as the alternative is substantively and politically acceptable to the President.

As a result of this broad charter, OMB has long been staffed by highly qualified professionals of diverse backgrounds, varying from economics to public administration to international affairs. OMB generally provides staff support to the President and management assistance to other parts of the executive branch. In addition, OMB staff works in the following broadly defined areas:

1. budget development and execution
2. legislative coordination and clearance
3. information and regulatory management
4. clearance of executive orders
5. establishment of federal procurement policies.

In some way, all of these roles directly affect people, especially those who have to deal with the government. Every decision affects someone's potential or current benefits, one's rights under laws or regulations, or the way in which one does business with the federal government. It is important to understand the organizational structure of the Office of Management and Budget in order to know where decisions are made. (A copy of OMB's current organization chart can be found in Appendix 1 at page 142. Very general information about OMB and the budget process can be obtained from its Office of Public Affairs.)

The Office of Management and Budget evaluates issues with a knowledge of the President's policies. While all departments and agencies are at least theoretically knowledgeable of the President's policies, their proposals are usually couched in ways that serve the agency's goals and objectives, which may not be the same as the President's. OMB is supposed to be the objective analyzer whose primary goal is serving the President and protecting his interests. OMB is also not as swayed as departments and agencies are by program beneficiaries or client groups. But OMB also brings to bear its own institutional views, which may on occasion be somewhat in conflict with those of the President. OMB's institutional memory can be an invaluable resource when dealing with the White House and other agencies in the Executive Office of the President. For example, when examining budget issues, OMB gives great weight to cost-benefit analyses developed over years of program evaluation experience. In management areas, OMB has been consistently concerned about the fairness and consistency of the regulatory process, cutting out unnecessary regulations, reducing government paperwork burdens, and improving federal productivity. In its various roles, OMB attempts to see that the President's policies are reflected in the actions of the federal government.

Appendix 1
EXECUTIVE OFFICE OF THE PRESIDENT
OFFICE OF MANAGEMENT AND BUDGET

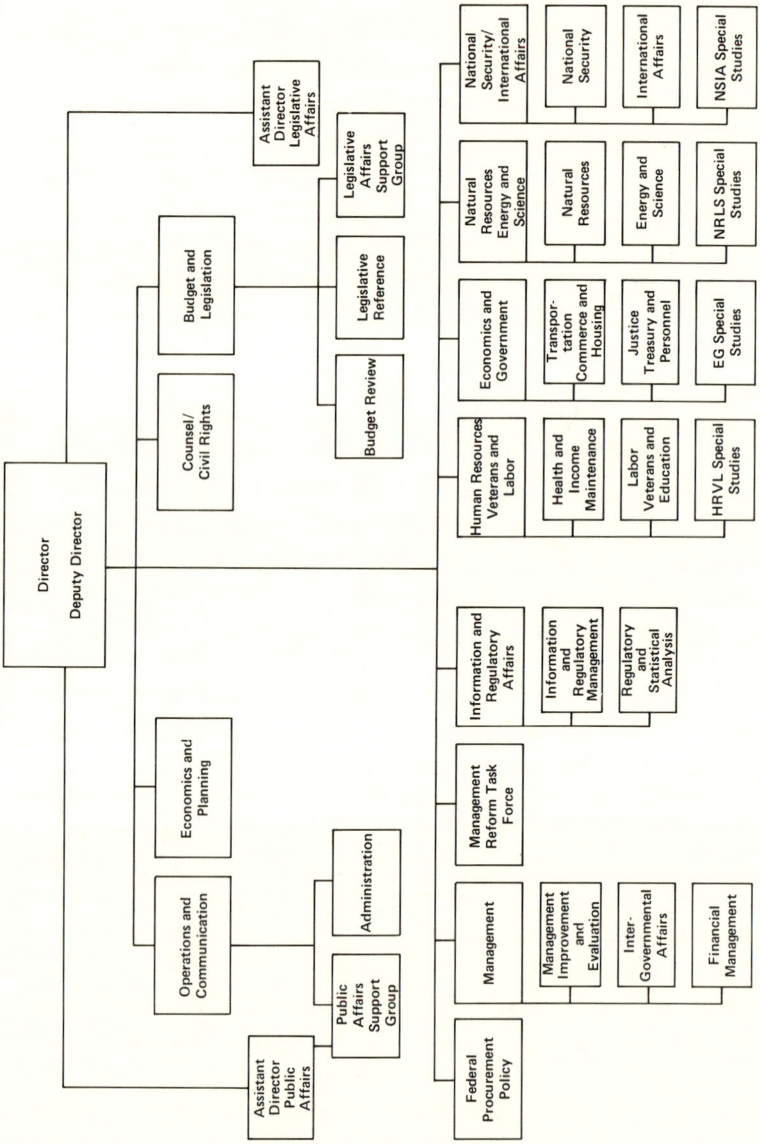

BUDGET DEVELOPMENT AND EXECUTION

OMB is best known for its roles in budget development and execution. By law, OMB has the responsibility for coordinating and supervising for the President the budgeting activities of all federal departments and agencies; resolving issues and conflicts between them; advising the President on major programatic issues and choices concerning spending levels; and preparing the federal budget and ultimately defending it before the Congress.

The budget development process is not a public process and therefore appears to some people to be cloaked in mystery, but there are several important points in each annual budget cycle that the outsider should be aware of. In the spring of each year, OMB conducts planning reviews with the President. The purpose of these reviews is to highlight the major issues that the agencies will address during the summer as they begin preparations for submitting to OMB their budget requests for the following fiscal year. A second set of reviews with the President is conducted each fall, at which time final decisions are made on budget recommendations for the January submission of the budget to Congress. In between these two sets of reviews is a "window" of three to four months during which the OMB staff prepares the spending recommendations it will make to the President. The second review reflects changes in economic conditions, program decisions, and Presidential priorities that have occurred since the spring review. It is important that an agency raise issues with OMB in time for them to be taken into account during one of these two reviews.

To appreciate fully the budget development and execution roles within the OMB, it is necessary to understand that the executive budget process can be divided into two major steps. The first step is executive preparation and submission by the President of his budget proposals to the Congress; the second step is implementation and control of the budget by the executive branch after enactment by the Congress. Step one is in turn composed of two principle parts: preparation of the budget request by the agencies and submission to OMB and submission of the review, analysis, and recommendations by the Office of Management and Budget to the President. Let us briefly look at the actions comprising each of these two parts.

The federal fiscal year begins on October 1 and ends on September 30. In March, 18 months before the beginning of a fiscal year, an agency begins to review its current operations, various program objectives, and issues of concern. Taking these considerations into account, the agency begins planning for its upcoming annual budget request, which it will submit to the Office of Management and Budget. In the latter part of the spring, the agency incorporates into its plans any suggested alterations that it has received from the Office of Management and Budget as a result of OMB's spring planning reviews with the President. The agency then identifies major issues and various alternatives for resolving them, along with the appropriate cost-benefit analyses. In the early part of the summer, the department head issues internal instructions regarding the preparation of the annual budget request, emphasizing program initiatives and objectives the head wants to accomplish during that year. In September, the agencies submit formal requests for their annual budget to the Office of Management and Budget. From September until early December, the agencies and OMB engage in constant communication and negotiation over the budget requests in an attempt to achieve an acceptable compromise incorporating agency needs in the recommendations by the OMB to the President. It is out of this process of negotiation that the final budget estimates come.

To ensure adequate consideration of a specific budget request, it is essential that the agency incorporate the request into the budget proposal submitted to the OMB. Most often, the Office of Management and Budget limits itself to analyzing and reviewing an agency's request and only rarely encourages including funds in an agency's budget that the agency itself has not requested. There are some exceptions to this general rule, however. If an item is a high Presidential priority and the agency has, for some reason, failed to include it in the budget, then the OMB will suggest its inclusion in the agency's budget. Secondly, if an agency head is playing the proverbial "Washington Monument game" and has purposely left something critical out of the budget, the Office of Management and Budget will see that it is reinstated. And thirdly, because Presidential initiatives are sometimes concluded too late for the agency to incorporate a budgetary proposal in its request, the Office of Management and Budget will recommend that such amounts be included. In such cases, however, the recommendation is usually jointly made by both the agency head and the OMB.

The Office of Management and Budget begins its budget year in the spring with what is known as the "spring review process." During the course of spring review, the Office of Management and Budget develops economic assumptions, issues, and policy objectives that it or the President feels needs specific review by the Congress. During the course of the spring planning review, issues are presented to the President for his consideration and direction. These issues are matters of Presidential policy, matters involving large sums of money, or questions of general government direction, such as personnel ceilings. After the President has given his guidance on the spring planning issues, the OMB issues policy guidelines for the agencies to incorporate into their budget submissions in the fall, as outlined above.

During the summer months, the Office of Management and Budget discusses with the agency program officers the various program issues and objectives raised during the spring review process. In addition, OMB personnel travel around the country, inspecting projects that will be the subject of budgetary discussion in the fall.

OMB also must issue what is known as the "July Update." This update is a re-estimate of the President's budget proposals that were submitted the previous January. The Office of Management and Budget staff compiles outlay estimates, new economic assumptions, and budget authority estimates and issues a new set of estimates for the President's budget.

The Office of Management and Budget begins receiving agency budget requests in September. It analyzes budget submissions and begins meetings with the agency representatives on their budget requests. Beginning in October, the director begins a series of reviews of agency budgets in preparation for his recommendations to the President. These reviews are known as "the Director's Review," in which the economic assumptions underlying the budget and its basic fiscal policies are examined. The development of program recommendations is made within a framework of trying to accomplish Presidential objectives, comply with Congressional mandates, and incorporate the administration's fiscal policy. In the reviews, the director makes basic decisions about what he will recommend to the President.

These decisions are communicated to the agencies through the "OMB passback." An agency head who disagrees with the director's decision may appeal the decision to the director himself. In such cases, the director holds a meeting with the agency head to discuss the reasons for his recommendations. The director then makes a decision on the agency appeal. If the agency head still disagrees with the director, he may appeal the director's decisions to the President. In such instances, the appeal may be presented either in writing or in person. Personal meetings with the President are usually limited to heads of agencies that are involved with significant public policy issues or large sums of money.

Once the President has made his decisions on the agency appeals, the Office of Management and Budget begins the final details of assembling the President's budget. OMB prepares drafts of the President's budget message and all of the attendant budget documents, including the budget of the United States, the budget appendix, special analyses, and the budget in brief. The budget is then transmitted to the Congress, within 15 days after Congress convenes.

Under the Congressional Budget Act, the Congress has a specific timetable for consideration of the President's budget. Appropriating funds is accomplished by a three-part process in the Congress: (a) program authorization, which is done by the authorizing committees, (b) the development of the Congressional budget resolution, and (c) appropriation of funds by the Congress.

After receiving the President's budget, the budget committees, the appropriation committees, the Joint Economic Committee, the Senate Finance Committee, and the House Ways and Means Committee may request the director of OMB to appear to testify and defend the President's budget proposals. These hearings are usually held in late January and February. By March 15, the budget committees must receive the proposals and estimates of all the committees and begin drafting the first concurrent resolution on the budget. The Congress must adopt the first concurrent budget resolution by May 15.[2] The first resolution is designed to establish budgetary targets and objectives. After the first resolution has been adopted, the appropriations committees act on all regular appropriations bills. After passage, they are sent to the President for his approval or veto. If the Congress cannot complete appropriation action by September 30, then the effected programs are covered in a continuing resolution until an appropriation bill is approved by the Congress and the President. In the fall, the budget committees prepare and submit a second concurrent resolution on the budget reflecting the action of the Congress on authorization and appropriation bills to date. The second concurrent resolution is supposed to be adopted by September 15.

Under the Budget Act, if the actions taken by Congress exceed the authority provided for in the second budget resolution, a reconciliation resolution must be passed. The reconciliation resolution directs various Congressional committees to take action either to reduce programs or to increase revenues to make them consistent with the totals in the second budget resolution. The totals and functional spending levels in the second resolution are binding. This means that they establish a Congressional spending ceiling and a revenue floor. The effect is that once the binding totals have been adopted by the Congress, no legislation can be passed that would be inconsistent with these totals, unless Congress passes a subsequent budget resolution. Assuming that all has gone well in the budget process, and that Congress has complied with the deadlines established in the Congressional Budget Act, the appropriations process has been completed as the new fiscal year begins on October 1.

As a practical matter in recent years, many appropriation bills have not been passed before the beginning of the fiscal year. In fact, for the last three years, the second budget resolution has not been adopted before the beginning of the new fiscal year. Thus, much of the government has run on a continuing resolution.

To make sure that a particular program is incorporated into the budget, it is necessary to know and understand all of the various steps of the budgetary process, both in the executive and the Congressional branch. It is important to know how, when, and where to act in the budgetary process. In addition, once a program has been authorized, it is important to follow the program through its execution stage. Many things can happen to interfere with the successful implementation of a program, such as OMB's recommending a rescission or a deferral of funding for a program, or a "reprogramming of funds," which causes the funds appropriated for a particular program to be used for some other purpose within the same program category. To implement a program initiative successfully, an agency must request funds for the particular initiative in its annual budget. Then the program must survive the OMB budget review process, including efforts to cut the program request or change the purposes or objectives of the proposal. After the President has included the budget request in his recommendations, the agency must work with the Congress to ensure that the funds are authorized and appropriated. In following a proposal through the Congress, it is important to work with the authorization committee, the budget committees, and the appropriation committees. The most important people in these committees are the subcommittee chairmen, who actually handle the authorization and funding for a particular program.

There are many pitfalls along the way, and an agency head must be in communication with the individuals in the executive branch and the Congress who are able to affect a particular matter. It is important to be in constant communication with these individuals and to keep abreast of the matter as it moves through the Congressional process. One way to do this is to get to know the individual staff members in the Congress and let them know of the agency's interest and concern about a particular program. Developing good relationships with the program people in the executive branch who are responsible for administering the programs enables an agency to stay abreast of the program's current status.

Legislative Coordination and Clearance

OMB's legislative clearance function is an inseparable part of its budget and management functions. But this function operates year round, independently of the budget cycle. The basic procedures and guidelines for carrying out this function are established in OMB circular A-19. These procedures have remained basically unchanged for over 40 years. The clearance function originated in the early 1920's as an outgrowth of the 1921 Budget and Accounting Act. Initially, it was confined largely to bills involving expenditures, but President Roosevelt extended its coverage to all bills. Now the clearance function covers agency legislative proposals, agency reports and testimony on pending legislation, and enrolled bills.

Essentially, the function is a staff service for the President to assist him in fulfilling his legislative responsibilities. The legislative clearance function also assists the Congress and executive departments and agencies in these ways:

1. Providing an institutional procedure for bringing together and

staffing agency legislative proposals to be included in the President's legislative program;
2. Assisting agencies in developing legislative proposals that are consistent with the President's policy objectives;
3. Informing the Congress of which bills are consistent with the President's program;
4. Providing a procedure for the Congress to get coordinated information about agency views on pending legislation;
5. Assuming that bills submitted to the Congress by one agency take into account the concerns and interests of other affected agencies to ensure support by all executive agencies; and
6. Providing a way to reconcile divergent agency views on proposed legislation and in agency reports and testimony.

The President's legislative program is usually contained in his three regular annual messages to the Congress—the State of the Union and budget and economics reports—plus any other special messages (for example, a special message on crime or social security) or communications to the Congress requiring legislation. The President's recommendations may originate from many sources, including studies, commissions, panels, and task forces established by law or administrative order to examine and make recommendations on particular matters. One major source of recommendations is the executive departments and agencies. Each year, along with their budget submissions, the departments and agencies submit to OMB proposed agency legislative programs for the coming session of Congress. Working with the agencies, OMB utilizes its clearance function to assist the White House staff in developing the President's program.

Through a coherent, consistent set of goals, the existence of the President's program provides the framework for the clearance process to function in a meaningful manner. Through this process, guidance can be provided for the executive branch in shaping or commenting on proposals before the Congress.

Legislative Proposals

Any bill that an executive branch agency wants to submit to Congress must be cleared by OMB. Agencies that may be affected by or have an interest in the proposed legislation are given an opportunity to review and comment on the proposal. They may favor the proposed legislation, have no objection, or, as is usually the case, propose substantive or technical amendments. In some instances, the agencies may propose a complete substitute. Divergent views are reconciled by the OMB legislative clearance staff, usually by letter or by telephone. In some cases, a meeting of the interested agencies may be required.

OMB advises agencies whether a legislative proposal is consistent with the President's program. There are five types of advice given by OMB: (a) that there is "no objection" in the Administration's viewpoint to submission of the proposed legislation; (b) that a proposed bill is "consistent with the Administration's objectives"; (c) that a proposed bill is "in accord with the President's program"; (d) that the bill would be consistent with the Administration's objectives if certain revisions were made; or (e) that the bill is either not in accord with the President's program or it conflicts with an important Administration objective. In the first four instances, the OMB advice is conveyed to the Congress in its transmittal letter by the submitting agency. In the fifth instance, an agency may not transmit the bill to the Congress. The first category normally consists of the agency's legislative program, as contrasted to the President's program, which includes proposed bills in the second and third categories. OMB may give advice that falls between these ranges, including suggestions for amending proposed legislation to eliminate other agency objections.

Reports on Pending Legislation

Agencies are often requested by Congressional committees to testify or report on pending legislation. Sometimes agencies even ask to testify on such legislation. In such instances, agencies must transmit their testimony to OMB for clearance. Similar clearance procedures are followed for agencies and any advice on what should be included in their testimony or reports. In the case of the reports, an agency is not required to change its view in the event that OMB gives opposing advice. However, an agency is expected to review its position.

Enrolled Bills

After a bill has passed the Congress, it is enrolled and sent to the President for his approval or disapproval. According to the Constitution, the President must take action within 10 days after receipt of the bill, excluding Sundays. To assist the President in deciding what action to take on the bill, OMB may request each interested agency to submit within 48 hours its analysis and recommendation in writing. OMB then prepares an "enrolled bill memo," transmitting these views and recommendations to the President.

Presidential Policy

The method of determining the President's policy varies from administration to administration. The normal processes established over the years result in the President's State of the Union message, the budget message, and the economic report. Each President uses different machinery for developing policy or positions on various questions. For example, in the Reagan Administration, the cabinet councils are emerging as important policy decisions-making bodies. There are currently seven cabinet councils: Food and Agriculture, Human Resources, Economic Affairs, Commerce and Trade, Natural Resources and Environment, Legal Policy, and Management and Administration. Each is headed by a cabinet officer and has a staff director who is in the White House. In addition, there is OMB with its budget process, the National Security Council with its process, and the White House Office of Policy Development.

In addition to using these entities to develop policy or decide a disputed issue, less formal decision-making processes exist. There are the senior White House staff meetings every morning at which many decisions are made. There are regular legislative strategy meetings with the Director of OMB and White House legislative staff. Policy is also derived from campaign promises and platforms.

From these various sources, a body of information develops called the President's Program or Policy. If there is a conflict on a budget issue, "an options memorandum" outlining the issue arguments is prepared for the appropriate OMB program associate director. If the question is significant, it could go to the deputy director, the director, or the White House staff. A decision is made based upon an understanding of administration policy. If an agency disagrees, it can appeal the decision where it was made or to the next higher level, ultimately appealing to the President.

To influence the decision-making process in the case of legislation, communications with the White House, particularly the congressional liaison staff, can be effective. Talking with White House staff involved in the decision-making process can also be effective. Sending telegrams, mailgrams, or letters is important, as are meetings with the staff who will make the decision.

Information and Regulatory Management

OMB's responsibilities for and power over the federal regulatory process have grown significantly over the last several years, in large part as a result of Presidential efforts to reduce and manage regulatory development. A major expansion of OMB's regulatory role came under President Carter's Executive Order No. 12044, "Improving Government Regulations" (43 F.R. 12661, March 23, 1978).

This executive order had three objectives: (a) regulations should be as simple and clearly written as possible, (b) they should achieve legislative goals effectively, and (c) they should not impose unnecessary burdens on the economy, individuals, public or private organizations, or state and local governments. Agency heads were told to oversee the development of significant new regulations carefully to ensure that such regulations were needed and that the direct and indirect effects of those regulations had been adequately considered. They were also required to assure that alternative approaches had been considered and that the least burdensome alternative had been adopted. OMB was directed to assure the effective implementation of the executive order and to oversee agency procedures for revising their existing regulatory processes as necessary.

An Office of Regulatory and Information Policy was created within OMB to implement E.O. 12044 as well as to fulfill OMB's other information management responsibilities. The office was given a statutory basis by the Paperwork Reduction Act of 1980, which created in OMB a single control point for the management of federal information resources. The Paperwork Reduction Act assigned the following information management functions to the director of OMB and to the statutorily designated Office of Information and Regulatory Affairs: general information policy, clearance and paperwork control, statistical activities, records management, privacy, and federal automatic data processing and those telecommunications related to the collection of information.

The Paperwork Reduction Act also gave OMB potent leverage over federal regulations containing forms by requiring that after January 1, 1982, all government forms be reviewed and approved by OMB. If an agency fails to obtain OMB approval, evidence of which must be displayed on the form, the form can be disregarded without fear of penalty. In reviewing proposed forms, the Office of Management and Budget must determine whether the questions being asked are necessary or required by law and, if so, whether that information is available from another government source. The general objective of this provision is to try to reduce the number of forms (and the burdens they impose) that an individual or company is required to fill out by requiring the submission of only information that is necessary to comply with the law and for the government to act. These strengthened authorities are an important new power vested in OMB that can be used effectively by those who feel that agencies are asking for information that already exists or that agencies are going beyond the scopes of their authority in asking for information.

The Reagan Administration has continued the trend of consolidating OMB's authority over the regulatory process and information management. Like E.O. 12044, which it replaced, Executive Order 12991 (46 F.R. 13193, February 17, 1981) is intended to ensure that all regulatory agencies set priorities with the aim of maximizing the aggregate net benefits to society and choose the alternative approach involving the least net cost to society. Under E.O. 12991, agencies must submit all proposed and final regulations to OMB for review before publication. Generally, agencies cannot publish the proposed or final rule until OMB has completed its review. A regulatory impact analysis must be prepared for each "major rule"—one that will have a significant economic effect—and the analysis must be submitted to OMB for review both before publication for comment and again before it becomes final. The regulatory impact analysis must describe the potential costs and benefits of proposed rules, describe alternative approaches that would achieve substantially the same regulatory goals at lower cost, and briefly explain the legal reasons why the less costly alternatives had not been adopted, if such was the case. The director of OMB, subject to the direction of a Presidential Task Force on Regulatory Relief headed by the Vice President, is empowered to review the following: any preliminary or final regulatory impact analysis, notice of proposed rule-making, or final rule based on the requirements of the Executive Order. The director can prevent agencies from publishing such rule makings until OMB has completed its review.

Subject to the direction of the Task Force, the director of OMB can and has promulgated standards for the identification of major rules and the development of regulatory impact analyses by agencies. OMB can also designate any proposed or existing rule as a major rule (thus triggering the requirement for a regulatory impact statement), even if the issuing agency does not agree. The OMB director may also require that any set of related rules be considered as a major rule. In connection with a regulation, an agency can be required by the OMB director to obtain and evaluate any additional relevant data from any appropriate source.

The Executive Order also gives the director authority to identify duplicative and conflicting rules that are inconsistent with either statutory policies or the purposes of the executive order. The director can require interagency consultation to minimize or eliminate burdens and can establish procedures for estimating the annual benefits and costs of agency regulations for purposes of compiling a paperwork budget used to establish a base from which government-wide paperwork burden reductions may be made. In a provision similar to features of "sunset" reviews, E.O. 12291 empowers OMB to designate regulations for review in accordance with the purposes and criteria in the order and to establish schedules for such reviews and regulatory analyses so that inconsistent rules may be reviewed at the same time. Lastly, the director is authorized to monitor agency compliance with E.O. 12291 and to advise the President with respect to such compliance.

A recent memorandum issued by the Justice Department to the OMB in response to a request for an opinion concerning the application of the Paperwork Reduction Act of 1980 (the Act) to regulations that impose paperwork burdens substantially curtailed OMB's power to review agency regulations in existence at the date of enactment that authorize data collection and record-keeping requirements.

OMB requested the opinion after a dispute arose with the Treasury Department over what constituted an "information collection request" (ICR). The Treasury Department argued that written forms constituted ICRs, but not the regulations that authorized the information to be obtained by the use of such forms or that required any other type of disclosure not obtainable by a written form. The OMB maintained that the regulations as well as the forms were reviewable under the Act since both eventually led to the imposition of a paperwork burden on the public.[3]

The Justice Department concluded that forms and regulations were to be viewed separately under the Act, and thus existing regulations prior to the Act were off limits to the OMB. The opinion, however, does stipulate that new regulations must be developed in accordance with the OMB coordination process created by §3504(h) of the Act and that OMB retains broad powers to initiate and review changes in existing regulations as well as full authority to review all written forms. After some negotiations, a compromise was arrived at whereby it was agreed that OMB can perform its paperwork review for all regulations so long as the public comment provisions of the Administrative Procedure Act are complied with. Thus OMB will not be able to require the rescission or substantial modification of ICRs in existing regulations promulgated in compliance with the Administrative Procedure Act until the promulgating agency has conducted an informal rule-making on such rescission or modification. OMB is completing rule-making to implement this agreement.

Combined with OMB's authority under the Paperwork Reduction Act, the authority granted by E.O. 12291 has made OMB the principal central control point for the entire regulatory process. OMB's current emphasis in exercising these powers is to deregulate, to rely heavily on cost analyses in evaluating proposed rules, and generally to reduce the regulatory and information burden imposed by the federal government. Anyone seeking to influence OMB's actions on a proposed or existing rule would do best to present information and cast arguments in ways compatible with that mandate.

At the time requests are sent to OMB for clearance to conform with the regulations or the information collection request, the agencies must give notice in the Federal Register of the submission and include a brief description of the subject matter. In the Federal Register, one can see a notice of the fact that an agency has submitted to OMB an information collection request on specific subjects for clearance. Therefore, one way to keep abreast of what OMB is involved in clearing is to check the Federal Register.

When OMB gets a proposal or a request from an agency, it opens up a public docket on the request. All of the public comments that it receives in response to the notice of the agency go in there, as well as all of the agency's submissions. Any factual material prepared by OMB is also included in this docket. The docket is public; there is a staffed reading room with this information located in the New Executive Office Building. Anyone who is interested in what comprises a docket can either write OMB for information or visit the docket reading room and examine the contents of the record. To influence the process, one should review the collection request, then write OMB commenting on why the request is unnecessary, or why it is too burdensome or too costly, or how it can be improved. Such comments are very useful to OMB staff in analyzing and commenting on the request.

As a practical matter, OMB staff does not have the time to make phone calls to everyone who might suggest improvements. Instead, the staff must rely on the agency and the public's comments in making decisions.

Ex Parte Communications In Informal Rule Making

The OMB issued a memorandum on June 11, 1981 instructing federal agencies in the proper procedures to follow regarding *ex parte* communications pursuant to Executive Order 12291. It outlines how ". . . the Presidential Task Force on Regulatory Relief and the [OMB] will communicate with the public and the agencies . . . [and] . . . describes certain obligations of the public and the agencies in this regard."

In keeping with this memorandum, it must be remembered that although the Task Force and the OMB may review factual materials related to regulatory proposals, both the public and the agencies should understand that the proper forum for reviewing such factual material is the agency proposing the rule making, not the OMB or the Task Force. Thus, any factual information sent to the OMB or to the Task Force should also be sent to the agency proposing the rule making for its evaluation and subsequent inclusion into the rule making record.

In the event that the Task Force or the OMB compiles its own factual materials which it considers relevant to the agency's decision-making process, then it should submit such materials to that agency. Factual materials thus submitted, however, should be properly sanitized so as to ensure the confidentiality of the donor agency's deliberative process in compiling such information.

The above guidance applies only to informal rule-making procedure. The *ex parte* rules applicable to agency adjudication and formal rule making are not affected since such proceedings are expressly intended by Congress to be carried out in a formal judicial setting.

Clearance of Executive Orders

The executive orders and substantive proclamations by which the President exercises the authority provided by the Constitution or the laws of the United States are processed by the OMB for the President's consideration. Executive orders typically delegate Presidential authority to Cabinet level officials and to agency heads, establish interagency task forces and advisory bodies, and structure and organize the executive branch.

Similar to the manner in which views are developed on pending or proposed legislation, draft executive orders are sent to concerned agencies for examination of their contents. Their views are considered by OMB, and issues are resolved and disputes settled in the process of preparing a final draft and alternatives for the President. The final orders are reviewed by the Attorney General for proper form and legality.

Establishment of Federal Procurement Policies

In 1974, Congress created the Office of Federal Procurement Policy within OMB to improve the federal procurement system by providing overall direction of procurement policies, regulations, procedures, and forms. OFPP's authority applies to procurement by executive agencies and recipients of federal assistance or property (other than real property in being); services, including research and development; and construction, alteration, repair, or maintenance of real property. In 1979, Congress directed the administrator of OFPP to develop a proposal for a uniform procurement system that would promote economy, efficiency, and effectiveness in procurement by both civilian and military agencies, and to submit legislative recommendations to effectuate such a system.

The administrator of OFPP implements procurement policies through policy letters, with which the director of OMB must concur. Agencies must make sure that their regulations are consistent with these OFPP policy directives. The director of OMB is authorized to reject agency regulations if they fail to conform to the OFPP policy guidelines. For example, OFPP issues guidance to federal agencies on when they should acquire goods and services from the private sector instead of developing the capability to provide or produce them within the government (Circular A-76). Major recent efforts by OFPP have been to eliminate, as much as is possible, conflicting or inconsistent regulations, procedures, and forms used by the various procuring agencies; and to have those agencies buy what the private sector makes for its commercial customers rather than to contract to have the private sector make something different for the government. The statutory charter of OFPP requires that OFPP operate in carrying out its important functions in a manner designed to permit public participation.

EXTERNAL RELATIONSHIPS

OMB has cautiously begun to reconcile its seemingly conflicting roles of "neutral competence" on one hand and promotion of the President's budgetary, legislative, and regulatory initiatives on the other.

WITH THE CONGRESS

OMB's enhanced role in the regulatory process and the Congressional Budget and Impoundment Control Act of 1974 setting up the new budgetary process in the Congress has significantly altered OMB's role in its relationships with the Congress. Before the enactment of the Budget and Impoundment Control Act, OMB rarely had to appear publicly before congressional committees. Now OMB representatives must appear regularly to explain and defend Presidential budgetary decisions.

The role of the House and Senate Budget Committees—and thus OMB's relationship to these committees—in setting overall budgetary totals and initiating reconciliation bills that affect substantive legislation has taken on new importance with the advent of the reconciliation process in 1980 and its use in 1981 to cut back substantially on entitlement programs. OMB appears before the Appropriations Committees in connection with consideration by those committees of the amounts to be appropriated to each agency by budget function. Before the substantive authorization committees, OMB appears to promote cost-saving measures or to help pass legislation such as the Paperwork Reduction Act of 1980. Understanding the congressional budget process is essential to knowing when and how to approach OMB, because OMB's role before each type of committee varies with the function of that committee. Even more important, one should know how to approach OMB on issues while there is still time for OMB to affect their outcome in Congress.

The President's budget must be submitted to the Congress not later than 15 days after Congress convenes each year. Congressional action is then driven by two concurrent budget resolutions; the first must be adopted by May 15 and the second by September 15. The total amount of revenues, new budget authority, outlays, the deficit (or surplus), and public debt of the government are contained in each resolution. The amount of spending is allocated among 19 "functions," budget terminology for spending categories such as defense and transportation.

After receiving the President's budget, the House and Senate Budget Committees hold hearings on its spending priorities and its underlying assumptions as a preliminary to drafting the first resolution. This is an appropriate occasion for interested organizations to testify on the impacts of the budget. The authorization committees, the appropriations committees, and the revenue raising committees must report to the House and Senate Budget Committees on their estimates of new budget authority (appropriations levels) or revenue changes needed for the coming fiscal year. These reports are due to the budget committees by March 15. The first budget resolution should be completed by the Congress by May 15, setting nonbinding spending targets and revenue projections for the next fiscal year. The first resolution has not been adopted on time in the last several years; instead, the Congress has adopted the resolution by the middle of June. It is important, however, to have the program contained in the first resolution. Even though it is not binding, the first resolution is built upon assumptions about programs in or out of the budget. If a program is excluded from the first resolution, it is more difficult to get it considered by the authorization and appropriations committees.

While by statute the President proposes to the Congress the budget for the executive branch of the federal government, the Constitution gives Congress the responsibility for budget decisions. Not one penny can be spent by an agency of the federal government unless the expenditure has been approved by the Congress. The "Budget of the United States Government," published each January, contains the President's proposals for the federal government's expenditures and budget authority for the ensuing fiscal year. The Congress can take whatever action it desires on the President's proposal. It can change funding levels, amend or eliminate programs, or add new appropriations not requested by the President, as well as act on revenue-raising measures. The results are the authority for the expenditure of federal funds. The Congress, however, does not vote on outlays directly, even though outlays are a determining factor of the federal deficit, but rather acts on requests for budget authority. The appropriations bills adopted by the Congress grant budget authority to the agencies, pursuant to which agencies are permitted to incur obligations and therefore to spend federal funds.

Before any agency may spend funds or Congress can appropriate funds for a purpose, Congress must first enact legislation authorizing an agency to conduct a particular activity. The so-called authorizing legislation sets limits on amounts to be appropriated, or it can provide for "such sums as necessary," but it cannot appropriate money itself. Some activities are authorized for a period of years whereas others, such as defense procurements, are approved on an annual basis. In some cases, such as appropriations for social security, the appropriations committees are in effect bypassed because the law provides for continuing appropriations. There are anomalies such as highway expenditures, which are authorized in terms of "contractual authority" as opposed to "appropriations." If Congress cannot agree upon an appropriation by the beginning of the new fiscal year, it passes what is called a continuing resolution, which usually authorizes agencies to continue their activities at the then-current level.

The Budget Act added two important new procedures for dealing with appropriations once Congress has acted. In response to President Nixon's impoundment efforts, Congress required that the President notify the Congress if he decides for any reason not to spend money appropriated. In the case of a decision not to spend an appropriation, the President must send a rescission proposal to Congress. Congress must pass a rescission bill within 45 days of continuous sessions after receiving the proposal, or the President must make the money available to the agency for expenditure. If a rescission is agreed to by the Congress, it cancels an existing appropriation. If the President is simply postponing expenditure until some future date, the President must send a deferral proposal to Congress. A deferral proposal is effective until the end of the fiscal year, unless either house of Congress disapproves the President's request. If either house disapproves the President's request for deferral of budget authority, the President must immediately make funds available to the agency for an extended period.

Responsibility for overseeing compliance with impoundment control is vested in the Comptroller General. He reviews executive branch actions and reports to the Congress any errors in Presidential transmissions or any failures of the President to report an impoundment. The Comptroller General has issued a ruling that the Act "does not purport to invalidate the exercise of reasonable administrative discretion in the adoption of program provisions and regulations.[4] In addition, he has ruled that failure to spend the entire amount of an appropriation does not by itself constitute an impoundment. He said that "[t]here must be sufficient evidence of behavior on the part of responsible Executive Agency officials that demonstrates an intention to refrain from obligating available budget authority."[5] The Comptroller General is empowered to bring suit in the counts to enforce the Act.

Another significant change authorized by the Budget Act is the provision for reconciliation. A reconciliation bill requires the authorization committees to make changes in legislation that has already been enacted or enrolled. As originally contemplated, reconciliation was to be used in the second budget resolution to direct appropriate committees to raise or lower taxes for expenditures to achieve desired economic policy. The reconciliation process was first used effectively in 1980 as a part of the historic attempt of the President and Congress to balance the FY 1981 budget. In that case, the reconciliation measures were contained in the first budget resolution and were geared to achieving the tax increases and spending cuts required to balance the budget. The reconciliation process was used effectively in 1981 to reduce spending by some $35 billion over three fiscal years, in both entitlement programs and traditional discretionary programs.

With Private Individuals and Organizations

Historically, OMB preferred to leave meetings with outside groups to the White House staff. Recently, however, OMB has been more receptive to meeting with outside organizations because of the complexity of many of the programs and its need to know more about the actual impact of its decisions. Information from trade associations, businesses, and state and local governmental organizations can be very helpful to the OMB staff in making decisions, and thoughtful letters and memoranda to the OMB staff are well received. By contrast, uninvited, orchestrated campaigns by interested parties usually become readily apparent and thus have less impact. Each director organizes OMB to suit his own style of management and operational needs, and each director has a different style and emphasis in dealing with outside groups. Outside organizations should very carefully consider the style of a particular OMB director when deciding whether and how to approach him.

In approaching OMB, it is important first to determine one's objectives. The director and his senior staff are extremely busy, so it is important for outsiders to use their meeting time effectively. There are many purposes for which a meeting with OMB staff may be desirable—for example, to get acquainted or to provide information for an upcoming decision.

Assuming that most meetings are for the purpose of getting some idea of staff thinking or providing information on an upcoming decision, one should provide relevant facts and arguments in as short and concise a manner as possible. Credibility is the most important asset for effectiveness in Washington. Arguments should be substantive, factually correct, and accurate in all respects. One should never deliberately mislead; if a factual error is discovered, it should be corrected immediately. Positions should be backed with facts, figures, and other information.

It is important to anticipate opposing arguments and to be prepared to deal with them. OMB does have institutional experiences in addition to current administration positions. Those biases and positions should always be considered. One should try to find out if there have been prior decisions by OMB on related matters. It is also useful to read speeches, budget documents, new releases, circulars, and bulletins to get background on any OMB policy before meeting with OMB staff. One should also be familiar with budget jargon. A useful tool is a booklet on budget terminology published by GAO.

In requesting meetings with OMB, one must decide which level of staff to begin with. Most of the OMB staff are career employees, with only the top people being political appointees. Out of 610 employees, only 40 are noncareer. The OMB staff takes pride in its objectivity, neutrality, and impartiality in dealing with issues. It is left to the political appointees to put "the political spin" on decisions.

As a general rule, it is advisable to start with the working level staff. In the case of budget decisions, these people are the budget examiners. The budget examiners have day-to-day supervision over and contact with the agencies and are therefore most familiar with the issues. If the budget examiner supports a decision, it is much easier to get the decision through the hierarchy. Furthermore, if one goes to a senior-level official, that official may buck the issue back to the examiner. In accordance with basic human and bureaucratic nature, the budget examiner may resent an outsider's going over his head. Such an approach could adversely affect any desirable long-term relationships with career staffers.

At times, however, it is necessary to go to senior OMB officials, possibly political appointees. At OMB, the senior officials and political appointees are the Associate Directors, the Administrator for Federal Procurement Policy, Information and Regulatory Affairs, the

Executive Associate Director, the Deputy Director, and the Director. One can contact people at the higher levels in OMB to discuss political considerations (which should rarely be set out in writing), to discuss issues with significant national impact, or to argue for reversal of a decision that has been made at a lower level. However, there is obviously a risk in going to a political appointee first, if the decision in question can be easily reversed after the political appointee leaves office.

Who should attend a meeting at OMB depends upon the level of the meeting. It is not necessary for the chief executive officer of a company to meet with a budget examiner; however, the presence of the chief executive officer is almost mandatory for a meeting with the OMB director.

Technical experts, of course, should also attend when necessary to explain details. However, the total number of outside attendees should be limited to those officials and technical people absolutely necessary to present the case adequately. It is never a good idea to try to overwhelm the staff with a show of force. Often such an effort backfires and is seen as a lack of supporting evidence for the position asserted. It also causes the staff to be overly cautious and reticent, so that they may not give the useful insight and direction one may be seeking.

It is helpful for OMB staff to know the nature of the subject matter of a meeting in advance. Presentations at meetings should be supported by written position papers. It is a good idea to leave a memorandum outlining the position so that the staff can consider the points made with the written material at hand as a constant reminder of the facts and recommendations. One should always follow up on these meetings by making oneself available to help the staff. For example, assisting the budget examiner by supplying information that can be helpful in carrying out his responsibilities or in dealing with superiors often makes the staff member more receptive to listening to the position asserted.

Do not take any action that would result in an OMB employee's appearing to use his office for personal gain or to give preferential treatment to anyone. Naturally, OMB staff cannot accept any gifts, gratuities, or favors from one doing business with OMB or from one who has an interest that may be substantially affected by the employee in the performance of his official responsibilities. An employee can "accept food or refreshments of nominal value on infrequent occasions in the ordinary course of a luncheon or dinner or other meeting . . ." (Section 1300.735-14(b)(2), OMB Manual). The OMB has set forth general standards of conduct for its employees with which one dealing with OMB should be familiar. (Part 1300 *et seq*. OMB Manual.)

In dealing with OMB and for that matter with other agencies as well, it is essential to avoid taking any action that would even suggest impropriety. To guard against this danger, one must be knowledgeable of, and sensitive to, the ethics laws. The OMB staff is extremely sensitive about its professionalism, objectivity and neutrality, and would be offended by any perceptions to the contrary.

I have not yet dealt with what is perhaps the most important consideration in dealing with OMB, and that is the point at which one should approach OMB rather than the appropriate Cabinet agency. To an ever-increasing degree, OMB not only exercises tremendous influence over all policy, program and legislative decisions in the Executive Branch, no matter where they originated, but also represents the President as court of next-to-last resort. Indeed, OMB is often the final authority on an Administration decision, because it is only the rare case that actually reaches the President. In the legislative review process, for example, it is actually OMB's responsibility to hammer out the Administration's position. On the other hand, where a program recommendation one is interested in influencing has originated in a Cabinet agency, it makes sense to deal with decision-makers at that agency, because OMB may not even be involved at that stage of the process. Unless a matter falls in an area for which OMB has primary responsibility, it may not make sense to approach OMB before an agency has formulated a recommendation or made a decision about a program.

In short, there is no single set of rules to follow. The strategy and tactics for each intervention should be carefully tailored to the situation. They should reflect the timing of the decision, the relative influence of the players, the decision "loop" into which the issue falls and the level of political interest in it. But it is almost inevitable that part of effective Washington representation will be communication with OMB.

FOOTNOTES

[1]*See generally,* Larry Berman, *The Office of Management and Budget and the Presidency, 1921-1979* (Princeton, N.J.: Princeton University Press, 1979).

[2]However, in recent years, the Congress has failed to meet this deadline, though without any penalty. For example, in 1982, the Congress said in the first resolution that if no second resolution were adopted, the numbers in the first resolution would substitute for a second resolution.

[3]In its response to the Justice Department's memorandum, OMB stressed that the legislative intent of the Act was to prevent the imposition of any kind of reporting in record-keeping requirements that placed unnecessary paperwork burdens on the public regardless of whether the reporting was required to be done orally or in writing or even if the regulation was silent as to the required medium of reporting.

[4]*Decisions of the Comptroller General of the United States.* June 11, 1975, *Reprinted in the General Accounting Office, Review of the Impound Control Act of 1974 After 2 Years,* June 3, 1977, p. 173.

[5]Letter from the Comptroller General to Rep. James J. Florio, September 28, 1976, Reprinted *ibid.,* p. 217.

Chapter 5

WORKING WITH THE WHITE HOUSE

STANLEY J. MARCUSS*

Working with the White House is one of the most intriguing and delicate aspects of effective Washington representation. It is also perhaps the riskiest. For failure at the White House can permanently extinguish all hope for success—no matter how meritorious the issue. Hence, caution is called for when 1600 Pennsylvania Avenue comes into view.

This might seem a strange admonition. After all, we are accustomed to thinking of the White House as the center of power, the place where all issues are ultimately decided.

While that view is often held by those who do not realize that there are many other power centers in Washington, it contains within it a germ of truth—and that is, to its *occupants*, the White House is believed to be the center of all big issues and, hence, the place where there is time for only the most important issues. However important your issue may be to you, unless it is important to the White House as well, you are unlikely to be heard at all. Worse still, if your hearing provokes no White House interest, the chances of achieving favorable action or reversing adverse action by another

---

*Stanley J. Marcuss is a partner in the Washington, D.C. office of Milbank, Tweed, Hadley & McCloy. He was Senior Deputy Assistant Secretary of Commerce under President Carter and from 1973 to 1977 was Counsel to the Senate International Finance Subcommittee. He currently specializes in international trade law.

executive branch agency are likely to be slim. Indeed, a demonstrated absence of White House interest is a clear signal to the bureaucracy that it has a relatively free hand in dealing with your problem. It is reminiscent of the little boy who boasted to his friends that he would get an electric train for Christmas because he had prayed for one all year long. When Christmas arrived and no train appeared, his stock as a communicator to the Almighty declined. Sometimes it is better not to ask and leave the door ajar than to ask and have the door slammed shut with a resounding thud heard round the block.

WHAT THE WHITE HOUSE IS

To understand what is important to the White House, it is essential to understand what the White House is. To start with, it is a large institution. While the number of employees varies from one administration to the next, the White House often has over two thousand people on its payroll. And that number reflects only those who are formally on the payroll. Many more, formally on the payrolls of other government agencies, are "detailed" by their agency to work directly for the White House. So to a considerable degree, the White House staff is much larger than it may seem.

The White House is not a single institution. It is made up of dozens of constituent parts, each with its own interests, assignments and responsibilities, each with its own point of view on matters, and each engaged in a more or less continuous struggle to gain the ear of the President.

Some of its parts are generally well-known, such as the National Security Council and the Council of Economic Advisers. But others, such as the Office of Counsel to the President, the Office of Science and Technology, the Council on Environmental Quality and the Office of the U.S. Trade Representative, are not. And often overlooked is the fact that OMB, the Office of Management and Budget, that powerful arbiter of literally thousands upon thousands of decisions about how the Federal Government will raise and spend its money, is also part of the White House and can have a significant influence on what is decided and what is not.

Often overlooked as well is the Office of the Vice President. It is an integral part of the White House and can have a significant effect on its decisions. The Vice President who does not have his eye on the office down the hall has probably yet to be born, so he can be expected to act. And however careful he may be to conceal his ambition, he inevitably is surrounded by staff who have eyes on offices down the hall for themselves.

In dealing with the White House, it is essential that one be aware that it is constantly changing. Applying your understanding of yesterday's White House to today's problem is like using last week's Dow Jones average to decide whether to sell your portfolio today.

Each administration's White House is different, reflecting the different interests and operating styles of its principal occupants. And unlike other agencies where only the top echelon generally turns over with a new administration, there is a nearly complete turnover of White House personnel when a new President is elected. Moreover, the structure of every White House as an administration enters the second half of its term is seldom the same as the day it took office. Issues change; priorities change; experience is gained; mistakes are made; successes are noted; and structure and personnel are rearranged accordingly. All this adds up to a constantly moving target. The ball that was carefully aimed at the receiver when the play began may be wide of the mark by the time it gets downfield.

A large part of understanding the White House is an appreciation of the fact that it is filled with very ambitious men and women, not the least of whom is the President himself. This aspect of the institution has several dimensions.

One is that most of the people who work at the White House have struggled long and hard to get there. Many, but not all, got there by laboring in the campaign vineyards, where each day was a struggle to be noticed by the candidate and where the competition from others was often fierce. The mental attitudes and ambition that ultimately made them successful tend to remain with them once they are in office.

To a large extent, the same is true of those who got to the White House by other routes. Years of hard labor on the conference circuit hoping to gain recognition as noted authorities in their fields have left habits of mind and ambition that tend to persist once these people arrive at the center of power.

Another factor is the relative youth of many who work on the White House staff. Presidential political campaigns tend to require vast quantities of unpaid labor, labor that can typically be provided only by those whose years have not yet brought on the financial and other responsibilities that accumulate over time. This is much less true of those who hold their White House jobs because of recognized expertise in a particular area, but even they tend to be surrounded by youthful campaign aides for whom a job at the White House is their reward. The consequence is that the White House tends to be peopled with hard working, ambitious and bright young men and women who, of necessity, have often had limited experience with the vast range of issues with which they are expected to deal in doing their jobs.

Moreover, they are intensely loyal to the President. To be sure, each member of the staff probably defines that loyalty differently—some seeing it as their duty to insure that the President is fully aware of all the facts and options that bear on a particular decision, and others seeing loyalty as requiring them to shield the President from aspects of decisionmaking that might subject him to criticism. But each member of the staff knows that he serves at the pleasure of the President—no civil service protection here!—and that an act of disloyalty is likely to find him out on the street looking for work before sundown. As a consequence, White House staff strive mightily to pick up and reflect every nuance of Presidential or senior White House staff thinking on a matter. And they are often careful—at least those who survive are careful—to submerge their personal views on matters of any consequence.

Finally, there is the political dimension: The White House is first, foremost and lastly a political institution. The people who work there, from the President on down, are there to advance the political interests of the President. No matter will knowingly be resolved in a manner that affects the President's political interests adversely. Put another way, every effort will be made to deal with an issue in ways that are believed to advance the President's political fortunes.

This may sound somewhat cynical, but it is not. The President is elected to advance and protect the nation's interests. He will be forgiven if he tends to see his interests and those of the nation somewhat synonymously, but it is, after all, virtually impossible for him to do otherwise. He holds his office because a majority or plurality of those who voted think he will advance their interests. Thus anything that detracts from that perception undermines the very basis for his being there. And anything that adds to that perception confirms the wisdom of the people in the choice they made. As a consequence, the basic marching orders in the White House are clear, at least conceptually, and matters brought to the attention of the White House will be viewed and dealt with in light of those basic marching orders.

WHY ARE YOU GOING TO THE WHITE HOUSE?

Where does all this lead in trying to deal with the White House? Above all, it should lead to an awareness of the complex assessments that are needed in trying to decide on how or whether to engage the White House in a problem. The caution light that flashes in front of the White House is more like the signal at the railroad crossing that warns the traveller to stop, look and listen. Unlike other executive branch agencies whose mandate and jurisdiction are more precisely defined, the mandate and the jurisdiction of the White House are virtually unlimited, except for matters that fall within the purview of the independent regulatory agencies or are subject to legally-prescribed rules for decisionmaking. Predicting how the White House will react to a problem—and therefore deciding whether it is wise to approach the White House at all—is impossible without assessing all the factors that will affect the individuals in the White House to whose attention a problem is first and ultimately directed.

The first step is to ask yourself why you are bringing your problem to the White House. Most matters in Washington are the responsibility of a particular agency. Congress and the White House establish the overall policy of the government in broad-brush terms. Execution is carried out by the departments and agencies. If you are thinking about approaching the White House on a matter, be sure you know why you are going there instead of dealing with Congress or with the department or agency that has immediate responsibility for that matter. Knowing why you are going there is the first step in analyzing the prospects of success and the potential pitfalls. It is also essential in fashioning the approach you will want to take.

For example, the way you deal with the White House may be very different if an agency has already dealt with your problem but in a way that you regard as unsatisfactory. Then you will be seeking to overturn an agency decision. On the other hand, an agency might not yet be aware of your problem or may just be starting its analysis of the issues. In that case, you might be going to the White House to see if you can get the White House to prod the agency to look upon your problem favorably.

Alternatively, you might find yourself caught in a situation where two or more agencies are involved in your problem but cannot agree on how to resolve it. In that case, you might be asking the White House to mediate or arbitrate a dispute, or to decide the matter itself.

Another possibility is that you are seeking to have the administration adopt a new policy on a matter so that agencies acting within that policy framework will have a basis for taking actions that are favorable to your interests. In that circumstance, you might be seeking to overturn pre-existing administration policy—or the policy of a previous administration—or you might be seeking a new policy on a matter that has had no direction in the past.

Finally, you might find yourself in a situation where Congress—through legislation or otherwise—has taken action that affects you adversely or, alternatively, has failed to solve your problem. In that case, you would be seeking White House help in your dealings with Congress.

Some situations consist of combinations of some or all of the above. Knowing how you fit in—and going through the mental discipline of identifying precisely where you fit in—is essential to planning your strategy. It is not enough to say "I have a big problem and because it's a big problem I need to go to the White House." Going to the White House, and failing, can be very costly indeed because there is likely to be no place else to go for a second hearing. So knowing the risks you run and balancing them against the chances of success are absolutely essential.

QUESTIONS TO ASK

In that connection, it is useful to ask a series of questions:

1. *Has another agency dealt with your problem, and has it reached a definite conclusion on the matter?*

If the matter is one that falls within the jurisdiction of another agency that has not yet been apprised of the matter, one possibility is that the White House will send you packing to the appropriate agency and ask you to come back only after it has made its decision. In other words, your visit to the White House may be premature, and the White House will understandably wish to avoid getting involved if the matter can be dealt with elsewhere. The same will be true if the matter is one that is already being considered by another agency, but no final decision has yet been rendered.

On the other hand, after assessing the probable final decision of the agency that is handling or would handle the matter, you may conclude that the chances of success with the agency are practically nil. In that event, you might conclude that your only real opportunity for a favorable outcome requires contacting the White House before the agency deals with the matter at all, or, if the agency already has the matter under consideration, before it reaches a final decision.

Here is where shrewd analysis of agency attitudes becomes crucial. If you conclude before you have brought your matter to an agency's attention that its reaction is likely to be unfavorable, it may be better to go to the White House first. Otherwise you run a serious risk that, once the machinery of the bureaucracy has been engaged, it will be difficult to turn off. For even when the White House speaks, the bureaucracy may not care to listen, and it has ways through the press and Congressional contacts to embarrass anyone who attempts to interfere with its prerogatives.

For example, were the White House to attempt to reverse an agency decision to deny a loan or grant application that the agency had carefully analyzed and decided was not meritorious, there is a considerable risk that someone in that agency will contact the press or the Congressional committees with jurisdiction over the program to complain of White House interference. Not only could that be embarrassing, but it could also make both the White House and the agency wary of further dealings with you on this or other matters.

Going to the White House before the agency has become involved in the matter also risks charges of White House interference, but to a considerably lesser degree, since the nature of the request to the White House at that stage will be different. Since the White House in most instances cannot actually make the decision for an agency, all you would be seeking at that stage is an expression of White House interest in, and sympathy for, your cause. It is difficult to fault that kind of effort, and the bureaucracy is much less likely to resent that effort than it would if the White House were to attempt to interfere with a matter in midstream or after a final decision had been made. Indeed, it can often be the case that an early expression of White House interest will help condition an agency to look more favorably on your matter, or at least give you a better hearing than it otherwise would, since there is still some magic, even for the most independent hard-nosed bureaucrat, in having his secretary announce "the White House is calling."

If you are bringing your problem to the White House because another agency has already dealt with it in a way you regard as unsatisfactory, it is important to ask yourself why.

If it did so for reasons that are similar to those that are likely to be given by the White House, you may be wasting your time. For example, an agency may have turned you down because it was acting with clear Presidential instructions or guidelines that reflect a fundamental political decision. Worse than wasting your time, you may confirm to the White House the wisdom of its decision and thereby reduce the latitude of the agency in attempting to accommodate interests of a similar nature in other matters that you may have on your agenda.

For example, assume that you are a regular exporter of machine tools to the Soviet Union and that the Commerce Department has turned you down on an application to export a particular machine for use in a Soviet steel mill. Assume its reason is that the machine is too sophisticated for the job and might be diverted to the fabrication of metals for military uses. Assume further that the administration is firmly on record as opposing all exports to the Soviet Union that might enhance its industrial base and thereby, in even marginal ways, contribute to its military capability. But despite this general policy, the Commerce Department has the latitude to make case-by-case decisions on items like machine tools so that more often than not you are able to secure approval for the bulk of your exports. Under these circumstances, one of the risks you will run in attempting to overturn the Commerce Department's rejection of your export license application is that by bringing the matter to the attention of the White House, you may cause it to be concerned about the latitude it has given the Commerce Department in other similar matters. If the consequence is that the Commerce Department's export licensing latitude is narrowed or revoked, not only will you have failed to achieve your objective on this particular matter, but you will also have made it difficult if not impossible for the Department to help you in the future.

On the other hand, you may feel that the Commerce Department has applied the Presidential mandate too narrowly or incorrectly and that only the White House can rectify the situation, or that the basic policy is misguided. Under these circumstances, an approach to the White House, while still running the risk that the Commerce Department's freedom of action will be further circumscribed, may be wise if the transaction is so important to you that the adverse Commerce action is unacceptable. For example, the rejection of your license application may be of crucial importance because of the value of the transaction to your business or because of the precedent it sets for future decisions. On the other hand, if it appears to be an isolated decision based on circumstances that are unlikely to arise again, it might not be worth the risk of circumscribing Commerce's future freedom of action to go to the White House to seek a reversal.

2. *Is more than one agency dealing with your problem, and is there a conflict in their positions?*

One of the more important roles of the White House is to iron out differences among agencies. A member of the White House staff is far more likely to want to get involved in a matter where such a conflict exists than he would be otherwise. To engage his attention, however, it is often necessary to put the issue into a political or policy framework so that it is seen as something other than a squabble among bureaucrats. That is not to say that the White House will not step in to settle even petty squabbles—it can and often does—but it is far more likely to get involved if it sees the matter as an important political or policy issue.

Hence, the next question.

3. *Is there an important policy or political dimension to your problem?*

Because the White House necessarily sees itself as the center of major policy and political issues, it is much more likely to look at a matter that is brought to its attention from that perspective. This has two consequences: one is that an issue that is not seen as presenting such major issues may tend to be ignored; the other is that any issue that is seen as raising such major issues will tend to be resolved in accordance with current administration policy and political interests.

This presents opportunities as well as pitfalls. Opportunities arise if you are able to place your issue in such a posture that the White House believes that it must be resolved in accordance with your desires in order to carry out broad administration policies or in order to protect or advance basic administration political interests. For example, a company might be confronted with the possibility of an Environmental Protection Agency ruling that would require the installation of devices to achieve a particular level of emission control the company believes could be achieved through less costly devices. EPA might be well within its rights to insist on the kind of controls it desires, but if administration policy is to maximize opportunities for individual companies to meet performance standards in accordance with their own best judgment about methods, objection to the EPA proposal might strike a responsive chord at the White House.

Pitfalls arise if, upon examination of a matter, the White House decides that your interests are inconsistent with administration political and policy objectives. For example, you may be seeking Export-Import Bank assistance for a major investment in a country like Libya, a country with which the United States has been at foreign policy odds for years and against which various administrations over the years have imposed sanctions of one kind or another. Sometimes such action has come about because of strong Congressional pressure; at other times it has been initiated by the State Department; and at other times it has been the product of independent White House initiative. Any effort to seek White House help in getting assistance from the Export-Import Bank for the project may trigger instant and fatal White House opposition on the ground that help from that quarter risks outcries of opposition from the Congress, the State Department or elsewhere.

Such a situation can present extremely difficult dilemmas. For example, you may conclude, rightly, that a proposed export to another country, say Iraq, involving millions of dollars of investment in plant and equipment in the United States, can be made without U.S. Government approval. But knowing that U.S. export control regulations can be changed at any time and without notice, and knowing that U.S. relations with Iraq have been volatile, you might wish to seek high-level assurances that export controls toward Iraq will not be changed midway into your project and thereby destroy the value of your investment. However, by seeking assurances, you may be alerting the administration to a project that might otherwise escape its attention and forcing it to consider the political and policy ramifications of any support it might appear to give. Having done so, it could easily conclude that a project that would otherwise have gone unnoticed must be stopped lest it appear to have administration blessing.

Unfortunately, there is no easy way out of such dilemmas. The most that can be said as a general proposition is that no matter should be brought to the attention of the White House without first analyzing how the White House would assess it. Nor should a matter be brought to the White House unless you are prepared to show how what you seek is consistent with administration policy and interests. Of course, should you fail to alert the White House to potential political or policy problems associated with a matter and problems of that sort should later materialize, you run the risk of a favorable decision being reversed. You also run the risk of your access to the White House on other matters in the future being totally foreclosed.

A frontal attack on policy is generally no easy task. It is rare that a major policy is reversed because of a single instance of adverse consequences for an individual company. An example is the widespread loss of jobs that was suffered by Caterpillar Tractor Company because of its inability to export pipelaying materials to the Soviet Union in the wake of the Reagan Administration's decision to bar U.S. exports for Soviet petroleum development. The administration was not moved by Caterpillar's plight to change its basic policy; the policy remained intact despite the hardship it caused.

If a frontal attack on policy is to be made, it is crucial that allies be formed and the issues be framed as ones in which the administration's policy is harmful to its political interests. Such efforts are notoriously unsuccessful where the matter involves significant foreign policy issues on which the White House has taken a highly publicized stance and the interests to be served by a change in policy can be characterized by the press and others, however incorrectly, as serving narrow parochial interests. The Reagan administration's determination during most of 1982 to maintain its ban on exports for the Soviet natural gas pipeline to Europe, despite the hardship it caused for a number of major U.S. companies, is an example. The ban was lifted only after the outcry from Europe convinced the administration that its continuation was harming America's relations with its allies. Among other things, that suggests that any dealings with individuals at the White House be limited to those individuals who are able and willing to deal with your matter on a technical basis, as an issue of correctly *applying,* rather than modifying, existing Presidential policy. For example, during the Soviet pipeline ban, at least one U.S. company was permitted to export pipeline-related equipment after apparently demonstrating that it did not precisely fall within the technical specifications of the regulations issued to implement the ban.

Upon examination, you may find that there is no one at the White House who can deal with your issue on that basis and you would be better going elsewhere. In the export control area, for example, where many agencies other than Commerce are involved in making decisions, you might more readily find a technical expert at the Defense Department or the State Department who can be helpful.

4. Are there other matters on which you may need White House assistance in the future?

Winning the battle but losing the war is, alas, all too common a phenomenon in Washington. It is often difficult to see beyond the immediate issue and assess how its resolution will affect other matters down the road. The matter at hand always seems to be more important than the matter yet to be decided. And it is tempting to dismiss those who counsel putting the present matter into a larger context as dreamers, incompetents, cowards or worse.

Yet the fact of the matter is that there are limits to the number of occasions on which the White House can be engaged on your behalf. This is true in part because those whom you ask to take up your cause have to be concerned about appearing to be your front-man in the White House. And the White House as a whole must concern itself with appearing to be the guardian of special interests. This means that White House assistance must be sought with a full realization that the reservoir of willingness to help starts to dry up as soon as the tap is turned on. For some, of course, such as those who are personal friends of the President, substantial campaign contributors or particularly respected for their expertise and wise counsel, the reservoir may be deeper, and more trips to the well may be possible. But eventually the well will run dry.

No matter should be looked at in isolation from other matters for which you may need help in the future. Decide now what issues will be most important to you over the next year or so, and ask yourself whether approaches to the White House on other matters now will jeopardize your ability to go to the White House on more important matters in the future. If so, you might pass up the first train out of the station and save your ticket for the one that can carry the heavy baggage.

5. Is there an individual in the White House with a special interest or expertise in your problem?

Most generalizations about dealing with the White House, or with any other agency for that matter, founder upon rocks—more often pebbles—in shallow water. Any contact with the White House obviously starts with an individual. If an individual willing to listen to and try to understand your problem cannot be found, then the exercise is doomed from the outset. That much is obvious.

Less obvious is the danger that you will encounter an individual who either cannot understand or sympathize with your problem or who is diametrically opposed to your view of the matter.

For example, assume you represent an organization that is seeking increased resources for the Export-Import Bank as a means of improving U.S. export performance. Assume also that it is administration policy to encourage U.S. exports and to that end, White House staff have been instructed to find ways to be helpful to exporting interests. Your first approach to the White House happens to be to someone on the Council of Economic Advisers who is spearheading the administration effort but who has already firmly concluded that Export-Import Bank assistance is too costly and inefficient a way to deal with the problem. Instead he believes that an overvalued dollar is the real cause of poor U.S. export performance and thus turns aside all plans for changes in policy in other areas. It may not be pointless to approach such an individual, for powers of persuasion vary. Who knows, you may be able to turn this individual around. But the failure to know in advance that you were up against a firmly held personal point of view can be costly.

You will have tipped your hand and set forth your best arguments for the opposition to deal with. More important, you will have alerted him to your effort and will have given him an incentive to redouble his efforts elsewhere in the Executive Branch to thwart acceptance of your point of view. That need not be fatal, but it is both undesirable and avoidable.

The lesson here is that it is important to know in advance the viewpoint of the individual in the White House with whom you will be dealing. Look at his writings, speeches or other decisions. Consult with others who have dealt with him. Sometimes there is no alternative but to deal with someone whose views are hostile to your own, but there is no excuse for not knowing in advance what those views are. It can make a big difference in how you proceed.

For example, you might consider avoiding the White House altogether until you have had a chance to consult with or marshall forces elsewhere in the Executive Branch. Often you will find allies outside the White House who can give you valuable insights into dealing with hostile forces within the White House. Members of your trade association, members of Congress or their staff or another agency that has an interest in your problem may be helpful. You may also find that individuals outside the White House know of other points of access in the White House that should be tried despite the nominal responsibility for the matter that a particular individual may have. For example, other companies that have had similar problems may be able to identify who has been helpful to them and who should be avoided. Congressional staff members or employees of other agencies that deal with the White House on issues such as yours may be able to provide similar advice.

Knowing in advance of a hostile White House reception may make it possible to frame the issues in ways that avoid a head-to-head confrontation and seek an avenue that acknowledges differences of point of view while admitting the possibility of different approaches to a solution. In any event, thinking about the specific and practical aspects of bringing your problems to a particular individual—not just "the White House," but John Jones who works at the White House—will help you in understanding why you have decided to go there in the first place. It should also force you to think about what you hope to gain and what you have to lose. The latter is always the most difficult, for hope is eternal, and failure is difficult to contemplate.

HOW TO APPROACH THE WHITE HOUSE

Whom to See

After you have clearly identified why you are bringing your problem to the White House and what the possible pitfalls may be, the next step is to decide how you will approach the White House.

As with approaches to other parts of the Executive Branch, it is tempting to think that only those at the highest levels can effectively deal with your problem. While it may sometimes be true that only the President or his closest aides can resolve the matter, the Oval Office and its immediate environs is seldom the place to start.

Throughout the White House, there are offices and individuals charged with responsibility for dealing with particular kinds of matters. And while the White House is constantly undergoing change, institutions such as the Council of Economic Advisers, the National Security Council and Office of Management and Budget, among others, are permanent fixtures, and other groupings, such as domestic policy staff, tend to survive in one form or another from one administration to the next. Each of these has its own area of responsibility, and it is to each of these that senior White House aides tend to look for the resolution of problems falling within their jurisdiction. Thus, it is seldom necessary to seek out White House aides whose names appear in the newspapers as the President's closest advisers, since others of lesser renown and status embody the power and authority of the White House and can often be as effective as the more exalted in dealing with your problem.

In contrast to other Executive Branch agencies, the White House is considerably less hierarchical. This means that you can be less worried about offending someone by appearing to go over his head than you should typically be in dealing with another Executive Branch agency. If you have a particularly good contact at senior White House levels, it might prove valuable even if the matter falls within someone else's direct area of responsibility.

In addition, issues that are appropriate for White House consideration often affect more than one individual's area of responsibility. For example, if you go to the White House to seek reversal of an agency refusal to provide adjustment assistance to relieve the burdens in your community of unemployment due to foreign imports, White House staff dealing with labor, budget matters, trade, foreign relations and federal-local relations are likely to become involved. As a consequence, it may be necessary to deal with more than one person simultaneously in order to avoid duplication of effort. Indeed, such duplication should be avoided, for if you have to make a series of visits to each of the individuals involved, there is a real danger that some of them may reach conflicting conclusions. In that circumstance, it might be difficult to re-enlist those who sided with you at the outset against those who are against you later on.

Getting Advice

Figuring out whom you should see in the White House is a formidable task. The wisest approach is probably to seek out someone with experience who can help you. Such a person can be an individual in a company's Washington office, a lobbyist, a consultant or a lawyer. Far more important than the category into which he fits is his familiarity with the current workings of the White House.

It can sometimes also be helpful if he has personal familiarity with the individuals who will be involved in your issue. Familiarity should not be looked on as a means of influence but more as a means of access, although this can be overemphasized for familiarity can be a double-edged sword. Sometimes, in order to avoid the appearance of favoritism, government officials will be more cautious about acting favorably on a request from someone they know than from someone they do not. Nonetheless, familiarity with individuals in the White House can be the key to opening a door and has to be considered in evaluating who can provide you with effective assistance. At the very least, an individual who is familiar with relevant White House officials can provide useful insight into developing a strategy for dealing with the White House if he has a good sense of their basic interests and inclinations.

Evaluating someone's knowledge of the White House in order to judge the quality of his advice is also a formidable task. To a large extent, you have to rely on the person's reputation. But to a significant extent, you can form judgments based on what he has to say about how he would go about dealing with your problem at the White House.

So far as reputation is concerned, the key thing is an individual's reputation among his colleagues. What you should look for is an individual who is respected as a thoughtful student of issues and politics and has a record of respected accomplishment in Washington. To be avoided is the person who has the reputation of being a "wheeler-dealer," for rare are the occasions when "wheeler-dealers" are successful without engaging in influence-peddling of a type that can cause embarrassment to his client's reputation. Moreover, the days when influence-peddling stood a significant chance of success are to a large extent past. What is called for these days is a person who has a reputation for honesty and integrity so that those with whom he deals in the White House need not fear being tarnished by acting favorably toward his interests.

It is not essential that you seek out a person who belongs to the party in power in the White House. While the White House is an intensely political institution, its political concerns revolve around the political interests of the President—or to the extent they are different—the Vice President. What is crucial is that the Washington representative, be he a Democrat, Republican or unaffiliated with any party, understand how to put the favorable resolution of an issue into the broader context of the President's political interests.

For example, a company that is seeking modification of the law that prohibits compliance with the Arab boycott against Israel must show that such a change will not harm the President's standing with those who strongly support that law (assuming the President values his standing with the law's supporters). To do so, it must convince the White House that the change it seeks is not a matter of concern to the law's supporters or that it will be seen by the law's supporters as either strengthening the law itself or strengthening overall support for the law. Alternatively, it must convince the White House that whatever opposition such a change would engender from the law's proponents would be outweighed by increased support for the President by the law's opponents. If he cannot make such a showing, the party credentials of the company's representative will be of little avail.

The credentials that count most are those that reflect the Washington representative's knowledge of the substantive, as well as the political, issues involved. For White House staff will rely—in some instances to a considerable degree—on what he *says* will be the effect of a proposed change in the law and what reactions can be expected from the various interests that are affected. If he is wrong on these matters—or has a reputation for being wrong on such matters in the past—he will do little to advance his or his client's interests. Indeed, he will probably be a serious impediment to their achievement.

Who Makes the Contact?

Once you have decided whose advice to follow, the next step is to decide who will actually make the contact with the White House. Two steps are involved here. The first is the initial contact—probably by telephone—to set up an appointment for a visit. The second is the visit itself.

As to the first, the Washington representative who knows the White House is the clear choice to make the telephone call. As to the second, it is almost a cardinal rule that the principal—not just his representative—should attend the meeting.

This goes for similar meetings with any government agency. Government officials seldom like to act on issues for faceless interests. The lobbyist, the lawyer, the consultant and the Washington office representative are all seen as guns for hire—necessary, to be sure, but not sufficient. Officials like to see constituents in the flesh. It is thus essential that a representative of the organization be present. He should be as high up the corporate or organizational ladder as possible—demonstrating the intensity of the company's interest—and he should be fully conversant with the issue.

He should also be fully prepared for an environment that is different from the corporate environment. It is seldom the case that White House officials will see the issue in exactly the same terms as the corporate executive. At the White House there will be a number of political, bureaucratic and other factors to be considered that may be extraneous to the business world. A first encounter with a government official can be frustrating when these other factors are cited as obstacles to a solution. The temptation to walk out in anger can sometimes be almost overwhelming. But it is to be avoided at all costs. The corporate executive, with help from his Washington representative, must make every effort to understand the issue from the White House perspective and, if necessary, to fashion and accept a compromise solution that meets the needs of the White House as well as those of his company.

For example, assume an agency is seeking to impose sanctions on a company for what it sees as a violation of a regulation but that the White House has the discretion legally to intervene in the agency decision. And assume further that the administration is under fire for failing to enforce that regulation vigorously. The White House may agree with you that at best it is a close question as to whether a violation occurred. It may also agree with you that the agency is probably being overzealous in this particular matter, perhaps because of criticism for being less than vigorous in the past. Under those circumstances, it will be difficult in the extreme for the White House to overturn the agency's decision, and some face-saving solution must be found. Among the possibilities would be a consent agreement whereby you do not admit a violation of the law but promise that you will not violate the law in the future.

Sending a Memorandum in Advance

In advance of any meeting at the White House, it is usually important to send in a short written description of the problem, the proposed solution and why the proposed solution makes sense from the standpoint of the administration. An often fatal error is to bring such a statement along with you to the meeting to be handed over for the first time. At that juncture, it is a simple matter for the presiding official to accept the paper graciously, indicate that, of course, he and his staff would like to study the paper carefully and announce that he will get back to you when he has done so. If that happens to you, you won't have to worry about sitting next to the phone to avoid missing his return phone call. You've given him a perfect excuse to avoid the issue, and you've squandered a useful opportunity.

The purpose of submitting the paper in advance is to try to smoke out any objections to your proposed course of action. The paper gives the bureaucracy an opportunity—and indeed will impose on it something of a moral obligation—to identify its concerns at the meeting or forever hold its peace. Thus it is important that it set out not only the arguments in favor of your position but also the arguments that can be marshalled against it. Having identified those arguments, you can then deal with them and thereby show that you are not oblivious to the concerns of the opposition.

Dealing with the political dimensions of the issue requires some delicacy. Needless to say, you should avoid such crass statements as "support for my position will generate votes in the upcoming Congressional elections." That may very well be the case, but saying it on paper is not very wise, not only because it tends to cast doubt on the intrinsic merits of your position, but also because, whatever their hidden motivations may be, government officials like to think that their actions are motivated by a higher purpose. Moreover, it will immediately convey to the reader a degree of insensitivity on your part to the embarrassment that would result if the paper were to become public. He will worry about what you may be saying to others, and he will worry about being able to defend to the public and a critical press a decision that is favorable to you were one to be made. There will be appropriate opportunities to convey the political aspects of a decision during the meeting, and so any such observations along those lines should be reserved until then.

In this connection, any paper that is submitted should be analyzed before it is submitted from the standpoint of how you and the White House would feel if it were to become available to the public. A rule of thumb is that any paper you submit will in due course become public. That may not happen, but you must be prepared for that eventuality. There is virtually no such thing in government as a document that does not see the light of day if someone wants it to. So after you have put your best arguments down on paper, step back and ask yourself how you would feel if that paper were photocopied and sent to *The New York Times* or *The Washington Post*.

Who Will Attend the Meeting?

Once the meeting has been set up, it is important to know precisely who will attend. Seldom is it the case that a government official will come to the meeting alone. Usually he will be accompanied by an aide or two when he meets with someone from the public seeking government assistance. While it can happen that he will come alone, you should not count on it. Failure to know in advance just who will be at the meeting can result in surprise and confusion.

You may suddenly be confronted with a person who has been studying issues such as yours with great intensity and has formulated a strongly held position. For example, he may have been hired by the White House to devise a way to bring the Export-Import Bank's activities back under the federal budget. Perhaps he even did a doctoral thesis on the issue. You can be sure that he will come to the meeting with strongly held views on the subject and with a degree of vigor that is strongly reinforced by both his past work on the subject as well as his current mandate. Needless to say, a meeting with such a person in attendance will require far more by way of preparation and will require a different cast of mind than one in which those in attendance are generally competent in their field but do not come to the table with points of view carved in stone or preconceived positions to uphold.

Unfortunately, it is not always possible to know exactly who will be present. And things change so rapidly in government that even if you do know who is scheduled to attend, the list of attendees may change at the last minute. So even if you expect a useful supporter to be present, it may be that he will be called away at the last minute.

Alas, that is one of the variables with which one must contend in dealing with the White House or with any other governmental agency. Nonetheless, this element of uncertainty can to a degree be reduced by the simple expedient of asking the person with whom you are to meet who else will attend the meeting and then asking his secretary, usually on the day of the meeting, who is actually scheduled to attend.

Are Other Agencies Involved?

A related question is that of whether other concerned agencies know you are going to seek White House assistance. The issue principally arises in circumstances where another agency is already dealing with your problem. And it is akin to the problem of appearing to go over someone's head in another agency. But as a general matter, one can minimize possible adverse consequences by letting him know in advance what you propose to do. He may still resent it, but usually he will understand your right as a citizen to seek redress wherever you legitimately can. The worst situation is one in which you appear to be forum-shopping without the knowledge of the person who is immediately responsible for dealing with your problem. He will resent such action as a frontal attack on his authority.

Conduct at the Meeting

At the meeting it is important to be succinct. Many government officials are beseiged by persons with special problems caused, quite often, by government regulation. Over the years government officials develop a knack for avoiding problems and passing them off to others if they can. Being succinct can help convince them that you understand their situation and that you are, in a sense, a kindred spirit. It is important to combine succinctness with earnestness so that you are seen as a force to be reckoned with, not one that will go away at the first negative response. Coupling brevity with the impression of an earnest determination to pursue the issue to a final resolution—whatever that may take—is essential if one is to make headway with individuals who must fend off myriad special interests.

In that connection, it is essential that the meeting be carefully planned. Strategy and tactics should be discussed and agreed upon well in advance, not just in the car on the way over. The person who is to make the presentation should be briefed on everything he needs to know about the problem. He should have a clear concept of the goal of the meeting and should be carefully instructed to limit his remarks to matters that bear directly on the problem. He should resist the temptation to discuss extraneous matters, particularly other matters that he may have pending before the government. Either he or the person accompanying him should open the meeting with a statement as to exactly what the White House is being asked to do. That way, all participants will have a clear idea of the issues and objectives. Only then should the substantive presentation begin.

Succinctness also has another value. Whenever one is talking to the federal government one has to be wary of saying something that could generate a legal inquiry. For example, in describing the way you do things by way of arguing for governmental assistance or relief, you may inadvertently say something that indicates that you have been violating the law, however inadvertently, in the way you conduct your affairs. Government officials who hear of such activity are generally duty-bound to bring the matter to the attention of the proper authorities. Thus by talking too much you may not only fail to achieve your objective, but you may find yourself on the defensive as well. At a minimum, you may alert the official to activities that are currently legal but are of a kind the government might prohibit if it thought about them.

The lesson here is that one should be absolutely sure that any of his current activities that he wishes to talk about with the government are clearly and unequivocally legal. He should steer away from discussing matters where there is any doubt whatsoever.

Another lesson is that he should avoid bringing to anyone's attention aspects of current governmental practice that work to his advantage but that could be changed if someone decides that that practice should not continue. For example, if an agency generally manages to deal with your problems in ways that, while bothersome, eventually work out to your satisfaction, it may be a mistake to attempt to get the White House to change the system so as to eliminate those bothersome aspects of the process altogether; someone may decide, having been apprised of what is going on, that the agency has been too lenient in the past and that what is called for is more tightening up, not greater flexibility. Having ventured into the territory, you may find yourself sitting in stunned silence as the baby goes out with the bath.

The basic lesson is to plan what you wish to talk about and how you wish to talk about it in advance. Examine the possible pitfalls. Once you are satisfied you are on the right track, do not deviate from it once you are in the meeting. A cordial atmosphere may tempt you into being effusive. But effusiveness can land you in jail—or at the least close off the escape routes.

After the White House Meeting

A meeting at the White House is often only the first step in trying to resolve your problem. There is a temptation to think it is the last; that because you have had a "successful" meeting, things will work out all right. But nothing could be further from the truth.

Actually, you may be only at the start of a process that will ultimately involve other governmental agencies. It is essential, therefore, that you find out who will ultimately make the decision and that you find out what factors will govern the decision. Also, you must know who will advise the person who makes the decision and exactly how the issues will be presented.

Will there be an "options paper" for the President? If so, who will prepare it? Will it be highly detailed or will it be cast in more general terms? Will the agencies that are directly responsible for the issue prepare the options paper or will it be prepared in the White House? Will dissenting points of view be expressed directly to the President or will a consensus paper be developed? Will the matter actually be decided by the President or by someone acting in his name under delegated authority? These are crucial issues.

For example, if another agency is preparing the paper for the President, it may be possible to work with that agency to put the issues in a light that is most favorable to you. This assumes that the agency is favorably disposed to your point of view. If an agency that is opposed to your position is charged with preparing the paper, you might want to encourage a more sympathetic agency to intervene in the process, either with a paper of its own or by way of insisting that it review the paper being prepared by the other agency. In any event, you should not leave the crucial process of presenting the issues to the decisionmaker entirely to others if you can possibly avoid it. Axes that are ground by others can have edges that cut the wrong way—or that are exceedingly dull.

The Media

A larger part of the process that ultimately leads to a White House decision involves the media generally and the press in particular. As a political institution, the White House generally pays careful attention to how it plays back home—as interpreted by *The New York Times*, *The Washington Post* and other influential newspapers. A well-timed favorable editorial or column can be enormously helpful to your cause; an adverse one can be devastating.

Unfortunately, there are few who can generate the appearance of a favorable editorial or column. And many who try fail miserably and end up generating adverse media commentary. The press, and the media in general, think of themselves as being fiercely independent, so no attempt to influence them should be made without expert advice. And even with such advice, no attempt should be made to influence them except on a thoroughly intellectually sound basis.

The media know an issue when they see one. And they generally know when someone is attempting to influence them. But they generally like to deal with sound points of view on a matter, even if those points of view are ones with which they disagree. And they like to ventilate issues of importance that are controversial. Therefore, if there is possible media interest in your problem, it is worth considering bringing it to their attention, but only if you are reasonably confident that you can make a persuasive case that it should be seen and written about in a way that is sympathetic to your position. The best way to gauge your media prospects is by contacting a columnist, editorial writer or reporter you know and trust and who has confidence in you. You can describe to him the general outlines of a story on an off-the-record basis and, if he evinces an interest that makes it clear he might write a story favorable to you, release him from the off-the-record stricture. The risks inherent in contacting someone you do not know are simply too great to be worth the chance. So without a good media contact, you should probably stay away from this minefield, tempting as it might be.

Congress

Akin to media assistance is the assistance that can be provided by Congress. Few people in the bureaucracy, including few people in the White House, like to go out on a limb. They like to be supported—or at least not opposed—in the decisions they make. There is nothing like that well-timed call from an important member of Congress to vault the hesitant White House official over the hurdle.

Before going to the White House, it is essential to know what Congressional attitudes are toward your matter. If they are adverse, the White House is likely to react by saying that it would like to help you, but "Congress won't stand for it." In that event, your trip to the White House will be premature; Congress is your first hurdle. If Congressional attitudes are favorable, a member of Congress or his staff can ease your way considerably.

To have a real impact, it is important that the Congressman have influence on matters of the kind you have brought to the attention of the White House. Often that will be the chairman of a Congressional committee or subcommittee that has jurisdiction over such matters and who has a degree of leverage that he can exercise. However, other members of Congress can also have influence depending on their position within Congress and their relationship to the President.

For example, a senior member of the minority party in the House of Representatives can wield considerable influence with an administration if his party is in control of the Executive Branch. Similarly, members of Congress who have acquired a solid reputation for expertise in an area can exercise considerable influence within an administration regardless of party affiliation. The key thing is to lay the groundwork with the member of Congress at an early stage so that when it comes time to make contact with the White House, he will be fully conversant with the issue.

One should bear in mind that members of Congress are understandably often reluctant to get involved with individual matters unless on behalf of a constituent or unless the matter is one of great principle involving a legislative area for which the Congressman has responsibility in his capacity as an important member of a committee or subcommittee. As a consequence, the range of possible Congressional champions is quite limited, and it may very well be that there are no realistic possibilities.

Before you reach that conclusion, however, it is useful to consider Congressional staff rather than a member of Congress as a possibility. Many members of the Congressional staff, especially the staff of committees and subcommittees, are well-respected professionals in their fields and exercise considerable influence in their own right. A matter that is not sufficiently significant to move a Congressman to take action on your behalf may nonetheless be of great interest to a staff member. His assistance can sometimes be as useful—sometimes more useful—than that of a Congressman. So that possibility should never be overlooked.

Follow-up

Once your meeting at the White House is over, it is essential to follow up with whatever was agreed upon at the meeting. You may have agreed to produce a paper that can be used in the decisionmaking process. Be sure that paper is done on time. Also be sure that it conforms to the needs of the White House staff member who asked for it. Consult with him in advance as to form and content. And once you send it over, follow up with a phone call to confirm that it is satisfactory. If not, be prepared to redo it expeditiously.

You should also secure guidance from the staff member as to any additional efforts on your own behalf he would recommend. If he is supportive of your position, he should have a good feel for what it will take to succeed. He may know, for example, where the opposition lies and what the nature of the opposition is. He should have useful ideas as to what, if anything, you can do to try to overcome that opposition. So explore with him an overall strategy for dealing with the problem and be sure to follow through with your assignments.

One should never assume that the staff people with whom you have met are fully supportive of your position or are willing to do what is necessary for success even if they appear to be supportive. For one thing, with the thousands of matters that come to their attention, they necessarily have to pick and choose among those to which they are willing to commit substantial time and resources. Hence while they may support your point of view, they may simply be unwilling to make the kind of effort that is called for.

In addition, because it is generally easier to say "yes" rather than "no" to a request for help, you may obtain an indication of support that is so lukewarm in reality that it will be of little avail. Follow-up phone calls or other contacts with the White House can be useful in giving you a feel for how vigorously your matter is being supported. They may also suggest different avenues of approach if interest appears to be flagging. They can also serve as a prod or reminder to the staff member who promised to help. And they show that you really care and will not quietly go away. In any event, follow-up phone calls or contacts to see how things are going are an important part of dealing with the White House and with any other governmental agency. Alas, it is one that is often overlooked.

As with so many things, the failure to do the seemingly little things risks the entire enterprise. One of the things that can be fatal is the failure to follow up to see to it that a document reaches its intended destination in time. You may have prepared a paper to be delivered to a White House staff member in advance of your meeting only to discover when you arrive at the meeting that for some mysterious reason it never arrived. Or you may have committed yourself to preparing a memorandum for someone in the White House who is charged with responsibility for putting together an options paper for the President. You dutifully deposit it in the post office or with a courier or transmit it on a telecopier machine assuming all is well only to discover to your horror that it never arrived and that the decision was made without benefit of your views.

There is really no excuse for such failure. A simple phone call to the office of the intended recipient will determine whether the document has arrived and has been placed in the recipient's hands. It is not enough to confirm that it has arrived in the building or that it was delivered to the recipient's secretary. You must confirm that it has actually been brought to his attention. Many are the cases where the sender is cheerily told that the document has arrived only to discover later that the mail room misdirected its delivery or that the recipient failed to fish it out from the bottom of his in-box.

IN SUMMARY

Dealing with the White House is unquestionably complex, especially because it involves so many variables. What may be appropriate in one setting may not be appropriate in another. But the basic principles are relatively clear, and you can apply them with careful planning and analysis.

Before approaching the White House, you should draw up a checklist of steps you plan to take, the assumptions behind each step, the risks associated with each step, the rationale for proceeding in one fashion as compared to another, the alternatives available if obstacles are encountered and the follow-up actions that will be required. The plan can be altered as you proceed, but, by going through the exercise and developing a checklist, you will have a set of guidepoints against which progress can be measured and pitfalls avoided.

Chapter 6

WORKINGS OF CONGRESS

DR. ROBERT W. RUSSELL*

Trying to understand and work with the United States Congress drives nearly every Washington representative to despair at one time or another. Getting to know individual Congressmen is hard enough (office appointments are worth as much as $100 per minute in the private calculus of one Washington professional); getting to know how Congress really works sometimes seems beyond the capacity of mere mortals.

The Congress consists of 535 or so individuals of diverse backgrounds and talents elected to two large, unwieldy bodies, subdivided into 260 subcommittees and regulated by an elaborate system of rules and precedents completely understood by no one. These individuals are collectively charged by the First Article of the Constitution with all the legislative powers granted thereunder: They may tax. They may spend. They may regulate. They may license. They may declare war. They may accept or reject treaties and appointments. In short, they are free to wreak government upon the people.

The responsibilities are awesome; the members of Congress are

*Dr. Robert W. Russell has served on the staff of two Senate committees. He was Minority Staff Director of the Committee on Banking, Housing and Urban Affairs from July 1982 to January 1983, having previously served as Counsel to the International Finance Subcommittee of the Banking Committee from June 1977 to January 1981. He was Staff Director of the Subcommittee on International Economic Policy of the Senate Foreign Relations Committee from January 1981 to July 1982.

human and political. Their personal goals range from the crass to the lofty. Members collectively charged with responsibility for the welfare of the nation have too often been individually charged (and convicted) for offenses ranging from drunken driving to fraud and influence peddling.[1] A popular representative institution should not, after all, be expected to differ greatly from the general populace in its proportions of saints and sinners. Mark Twain no doubt exaggerated when he claimed the United States had but one native criminal class—the Congress.

Members of Congress do differ from the "normal" people who elect them, however, in at least one important respect: most seek the votes and political support of their fellow citizens more or less incessantly. Just as small children can tell you by spring how many more days it is until Christmas, politicians have internal clocks ticking off the days until the next election. The countdown begins the morning after the euphoric victory night and builds in a slow but mighty crescendo toward the next evening of celebration or gloom or, occasionally, until an irrevocable decision is made not to run again.

Electoral politics is only the beginning, not the end. The internal politics of the Congress offers a rich outlet for the political drive of ambitious politicians. For some, getting elected is the price of admission to play the game of influence in the Congress or to wrestle with great national and international issues. For others, serving in Congress is just an unwelcome cost that must be paid in order to enjoy the status and perquisities of office that come with being elected.

Making sense of the jumble of rules, roles, and reputations of the Congress requires an acceptance of complexity, a willingness to master dry details, and an alertness to new, unexpected factors which can reshape the political terrain. The first step is to acquire a coherent view of Congress as a functioning body.

CONGRESS AS A POTENT AND POTENTIALLY DANGEROUS FORCE

Citizens as well as Congressmen feel ambivalent about the broad powers of the Congress. Perhaps the most common viewpoint is reflected in the old adage that "no man is safe while Parliament sits." Will Rogers is said to have commented: "This country has come to feel the same when Congress is in session as when the baby gets hold of a hammer." Congress, like other assemblies throughout history, can be dangerous to the life, liberty, and property of citizens.

The long-term growth of the Presidency and the more recent "activism" of the Supreme Court have tended to obscure the basic potency of the Congress. The Constitution itself places the legislative branch first and, in addition to the lengthy list of broad powers enumerated in Article I, section 8, confers upon Congress the additional, highly elastic power: "To make Laws which shall be necessary and proper for carrying into Execution the foregoing Powers, and all other Powers vested by this Constitution in the Government of the United States, or in any Department or officer thereof."

The Supreme Court, in a lengthy series of decisions only practicing attorneys and law students need remember, has repeatedly demonstrated its tolerance for all manner of statutory extensions of federal authority on the basis that such enactments either fall within the broad enumerated powers of Article I, section 8 or were "necessary and proper" to carry out such powers. Nearly everything produced or consumed in the United States today is subject to a host of federal regulations stemming from acts of Congress.

Suppose, for example, you are having a cigarette while you skim the pages of this book. The label on the cigarette package which warned you against the harmful effects of smoking is only the visible tip of the iceberg. The tobacco you are smoking was grown on acreage "allotted" by federal regulations the privilege of growing commercial tobacco. The factory which processed the tobacco was subject to federal regulations concerning air and water pollution, occupational health and safety, and labor standards and practices. The truck which carried the tobacco to the factory and the cigarettes to your local store was probably a carrier regulated by the federal government, making its trip on highways built to federal government specifications and financed by the federal government, in part from taxes paid by the trucker and in part by you through gasoline taxes.

The company producing and selling the cigarettes is subject to federal antitrust and fair trade statutes, which are presumed to help indirectly hold down the price you paid for the cigarettes. The federal government in turn imposes a stiff tax on the final sale of the cigarettes to help pay for everything else the government is doing while you are enjoying a cigarette.

Should you develop lung cancer, you may enjoy the benefits of federally funded cancer research and receive treatment in a hospital built in whole or in part with federal funds, staffed with personnel whose training was supported in whole or in part by the federal government. You may pay your bill through Medicare or a federal employee insurance plan; if you must pay it directly yourself, you may deduct the amount in excess of 3 percent of adjusted gross income from federally taxable income. Should you fail to recover, however, you may take some comfort from the fact that the funeral industry is one of the least federally regulated industries in America. Efforts are under way to change that, of course.

You are not just smoking a cigarette, you are consuming a product whose origins, production, transportation, price, and ultimate consequences are intimately linked to 100 or more statutes enacted by Congress. Incidentally, I hope you are not seated in the nonsmoking section of a federally regulated air carrier.

Congress has done much more than enact measures to regulate the private pursuit of pleasure and profit. No one needs to be reminded of the scope and impact of federal legislation intended to secure civil rights and liberties for all Americans. Some of the most difficult and dramatic legislative struggles in the history of the Congress were waged over civil rights legislation.[2]

New contests are looming over another agenda of "rights" legislation: right-to-life, right to pray in school, right to privacy, and others. What Congress can do, it can also undo. The power to make laws will not rest quietly; it seems to insist upon regular exercise, and the "Mr. Smiths" who come to Washington are ever ready to oblige. The effect on our lives is monumental; unless closely watched, it can become monstrous.

The power to make laws of all sorts is nurtured by the power to tax and, increasingly, by the power to borrow. Nearly every American with an elementary school education recalls John Marshall's dictum that "the power to tax is the power to destroy." Few remember that Marshall applied the dictum in denying the right to a state to tax the federal government.[3] No similar limitation exists on the power of the federal government to tax an individual or his company to the point of bankruptcy. Congress has generally found it simpler to regulate or prohibit undesirable conduct directly, but the power to tax in order to control behavior is there.

Congress has even—on rare occasions, fortunately—permitted its processes to be used to destroy the personal lives of citizens without benefit of the judicial process. Witch-hunting and character assassination when waged by the Congress observe none of the rules laid down by the Marquis of Queensberry. Senator Joe McCarthy of Wisconsin earned so infamous a reputation for bullying witnesses before his subcommittee that "McCarthyism" is sometimes mistakenly thought to have been his work alone. In the past, Congress has shown a distressingly large tolerance for hearings, statements, and other actions by members who "in the performance of their official duties" have succeeded in damaging the reputations and ruining the lives of unlucky citizens who incurred Congressional wrath.[4] Having a Congress with such awesome powers is like keeping a large, vicious dog: it is great protection as long as it is pointed in the right direction.

The Founding Fathers were well aware of the potential for legislative assemblies to run amok. They had had their share of misfortunes with the legislatures created by the new state constitutions after the Revolutionary War. The wiser among them also knew that the Revolution itself was precipitated by actions of the British parliament, not the monarch. Accordingly, they designed the Constitution of 1787 to ensure that the new Congress would not exercise its vast powers precipitously. They separated the powers of government into legislative, executive, and judicial branches, assigning the bulk of each power to the appropriate branch, but also giving each branch a share of the others' responsibilities in a system of checks and balances. Congress was divided into two chambers, equal in power, with members to be elected on a different basis.[5]

CONGRESS AS A STALEMATE MACHINE

The division of Congress into two houses with members chosen by different electorates was one of several compromises struck at the Constitutional Convention of 1787 to safeguard the interests of small states and reinforce the separation of powers; it was seen as a protection against tyrannical government. The Congress, once elected, proceeded to organize itself into committees for consideration of particular subjects. Rules of procedure and precedents were developed to provide thorough deliberation before laws were passed. The dangers of swift action by narrow majorities were thought to be far greater than the risks of inaction.[6]

By the 1950's there were complaints that Congress was so bound by its procedures and precedents that even propositions strongly favored by majorities in both Houses could not be enacted. A system of "multiple vetoes" was said to have developed. Chairmen of committees could block measures from reaching the Senate or House floor. Barbara Hinckley charged that "by multiplying centers of power down to the level of committee chairmen, [the seniority system] contributes to the fragmentation of power which frequently makes any attempt to form a governing majority impossible."[7] In the House, the Rules Committee with its venerable and sometimes autocratic chairman, Judge Smith of Virginia, was an additional high hurdle. On the Senate floor, the basic rule of unlimited debate could only be overcome by a vote by two-thirds of the total membership to impose cloture. Successful filibusters against civil rights bills gave rise to a reaction against the structure and rules of the Congress itself.[8]

Senator Joseph S. Clark, writing in March 1965, saw the critical question as

> How can we organize our legislative process so that it responds to the wishes and needs of the American people? How can we be certain that when a majority of the members of the House and Senate wish to act they will be able to, unencumbered by a skillful minority employing outmoded rules and procedures?[9]

The reform movement pressed for easing the requirements for cloture in the Senate, curbing the power of the House Rules Committee to keep measures from reaching the House floor, election of committee and subcommittee chairmen instead of selection by seniority, and strengthening of the elected party leadership of each body. The reformers succeeded to a considerable degree in achieving the changes they advocated. Both the House and the Senate are considerably more democratic than they were formerly.[10] Together with redistricting and changes in election laws, the Congressional reforms have made the Congress more representative of the electorate.

The stalemates on issues persist in many cases, however, despite the reforms. The side effects of dispersing power more widely and easing the movement of legislation to and through the floor of each House have been to increase the independence of each of the more than 200 separate legislative subcommittees in the two chambers, to increase the proportion of legislation which has little chance of enactment in the form in which it is reported from committee, and to reduce the stability of Congressional decisions.

The reformed Congress passes more legislation than the old Congress, but it also passes more legislation which is poorly drafted and poorly conceived.[11] The more open floor procedures, together with the frenetic pace of legislative activity, lead to adoption of more floor amendments without sufficient deliberation on their merits. Conference committees have wide latitude which, given the weakened committee and floor leadership, can be used to alter radically the products of either or both Houses. Because the majorities which enact legislation are often ephemeral, frequent revisions become probable. Interested parties look forward to each newly elected Congress to reverse the losses they suffered at the hands of the previous Congress. Consequently, the pulling and hauling which went on within committees in the old Congress goes on in the new Congress as well, but it is fought out within the statute books from year to year. More frequent change has meant that any single change is less likely to endure.

CONGRESS AS ONE SIDE OF AN "IRON TRIANGLE"

When conversation about the Congress turns from jokes to substance, one is most likely to hear a version of the "Iron Triangle" theory. The simple formulation is that organized interest groups, Congress, and the executive branch form three sides of a conspiracy against the public interest. In particular, it is argued that each subcommittee of the Congress forms a symbiotic relationship with the vested interests affected by matters within the subcommittee's jurisdiction and the bureau in the executive branch responsible for the same subject matter.[12] The cynical view is that the subcommittee passes the legislation drafted by the vested interest group and the executive bureau interprets and administers the law for the benefit of the vested interest group. In this view the vested interest group helps the members of the subcommittee get re-elected, helps the executive bureau defend their ever larger budget, and invites everybody involved to the annual Christmas party. The three sides join to form an iron triangle of mutual support and vigorous defense against attacks by rival claimants to the federal purse.

Iron triangles exist at times, but they are much less formidable than the image implies. Many factors can bend and even break the links that hold such triangular associations together. In the first place, the vested interests affected by the statutes within a particular subcommittee's jurisdiction seldom agree. Within a single industry, labor and management groups are often at loggerheads. The emergence of consumer groups and other "public interest" groups as active lobbyists adds additional divergence to the views presented to Congressional subcommittees.

Subcommittees themselves are seldom so cohesive and pliable as the iron triangle theory implies. The weakening of seniority rules and the powers of committee chairman have affected subcommittee chairmen as well. National political party organizations have also become steadily less influential. Individual members of subcommittees often feel free to defy the wishes of the chairman or ranking member from their own political party. The atomization of political power in the Congress makes the behavior of subcommittees less consistent and predictable than formerly was the case, while enhancing the relative importance of subcommittees compared with full committees and floor leaders.

When formed, iron triangles can be crushed by an aroused public or a determined President. The news media search ceaselessly for too-cozy relationships between industry and government. Exposure of unseemly transactions can lead to an outcry which cannot be ignored. Similarly, a President who takes a strong personal interest in a given subject can usually make a strong impression on policy, iron triangles notwithstanding.

Finally, there are inevitable conflicts between iron triangles over limited budget resources or the distribution of regulatory burdens.

Not all costs can be passed on to an unorganized public, although they probably will be, if possible. As stronger iron triangles prevail over weaker ones, coalitions of interests tend to be redistributed, forming new triangles to wage new contests or renew old ones. Thus, the relationships among Congress, the interest groups, and the executive branch are much more fluid and multifaceted than the term "iron triangle" would imply. A better image would be a nine-sided Nerf ball, the foam ball which can be squeezed into various shapes without losing its basic form.

Subsidization and regulation of the United States merchant marine offers a good example of both an iron triangle and a nine-sided Nerf ball. The merchant marine subcommittees in the House and the Senate, the merchant marine industry, and the Maritime Administration in the Department of Transportation often appear to form an iron triangle defending and promoting shipping and shipbuilding interests against other modes of transportation, perhaps even against the public interest. But the iron triangle becomes less firm when the choices are between the advancement of shipping and shipbuilding or between benefits to workers in the merchant marine industry and profitable operations for shipping companies. Merchant marine subcommittees in the Congress become splintered when policies are debated which could favor West Coast ports over East Coast ports or East Coast ports over Gulf ports. Crosscutting interests lead to continuous realignment of coalitions, although on many basic, recurring issues certain coalitions persist long enough to give the appearance of iron triangles. Through careful study, Washington representatives can discern not only the existence of such triangles but their strengths and weaknesses as well.

None of the three images commonly associated with Congress provides an adequate guide to the essential features of Congress. The first image—Congress as a potent and potentially dangerous force—merely warns of the wide sweep Congressional action can take. The second image—Congress as a stalemate machine—is partially outdated by reforms of the Congressional process but remains helpful in reminding us that consistent Congressional action depends upon the continuing presence of a stable majority. The third image—Congress as one side of a series of iron triangles—gives a first but very rough approximation of what to expect from the legislative process.

CONGRESS AS AN INSTITUTION

Getting to know Congress as an institution apart from its three images requires an understanding of all of its functions. The primary function of Congress is clearly law making, but there are many other functions which also shape the institution. These functions form part of the context in which laws are passed.

Congressional Oversight of the Executive Branch

The President is required by Article II, section 3 of the Constitution to "take care that all Laws be faithfully executed," but it is the Congress which has developed an extensive practice of overseeing the execution of laws by the executive branch. Oversight includes frequent Congressional hearings to review policies being carried out by executive agencies; it also includes reports prepared by the Congress or its supporting agencies: the General Accounting Office, the Congressional Research Service of the Library of Congress, the Congressional Budget Office, and the Office of Technology Assessment. Hardly a day goes by without release by one of these agencies of a critical study of executive branch execution of one or more statutory responsibilities delegated to it by the Congress.

In addition to hearings and reports, oversight is exercised through correspondence between members of Congress and officials of the executive branch; through reports to the Congress required by statute; and through frequent consultations, some required by statute, others a matter of prudential responsiveness by executive branch agencies to Congressional interest. The result is a mammoth flow of paper and endless hearings and meetings.

The significance of the oversight function lies in the constant communication of Congressional intent and the corresponding adjustment of executive branch practices. The broad delegations of authority which are typical of modern legislation are offset in part by the increased oversight activity of the Congress. By the same token, final outputs from the federal government are less predictable on the basis of the passage of legislation alone. The further adjustments which occur through executive branch implementation—and which are influenced by Congressional oversight, together with the threat of new legislation—not only increase the flexibility of law and its administration but also the uncertainty and impermanence of results.

The executive branch takes Congressional oversight more seriously because Congress has added to its oversight kit a major tool which was not contemplated by the drafters of the Constitution: the legislative veto. There are many variations, ranging from veto of proposed executive action by concurrent resolution of the two Houses to the veto of an executive branch decision by a single Congressional committee. As of 1980, the Congressional Research Service had identified 272 legislative veto provisions contained in statutes.[13]

Congress has even considered adopting a statute which would apply the legislative veto to every major regulation or interpretation made in the executive branch. The proposal for a generalized veto over regulations has not gotten far, but it hangs like the sword of Damocles over recalcitrant executive branch agencies. So too do threats to deny appropriations, hold up nominations, or pass new legislation. Members of Congress have numerous opportunities to press their views upon the executive branch, and there are few actions an executive agency can take that are not shaped to some degree by the anticipated reactions of Congress.

The federal judicial process is also subject to Congressional oversight. Congress has the power to establish federal courts other than the Supreme Court (Article II, section 1 of the Constitution) and to fix the number of justices who shall constitute the Supreme Court, as President Franklin D. Roosevelt reminded the nation in 1937 when he proposed that the number of Supreme Court justices be increased from 9 to 15.

Nominations

The nomination process is so important a part of Congressional responsibility that it deserves discussion apart from Congressional oversight, although the review of nominees is an important aspect of oversight. The House of Representatives has no role in nominations, except to the extent that members may use their influence on their colleagues in the Senate. Appointments of the higher officers of the federal government (generally those at or above the level of Assistant Secretary), all ambassadors and other Foreign Service appointees, all military officers, and all federal judges are subject to the advice and consent of the Senate.

The practice of Senate committees in reviewing nominations varies but usually consists of the following steps: first, the President submits to the Congress the official nominating papers together with background information concerning the nominee. The papers are referred to the Senate committee with jurisdiction over the agency or office to which the person has been nominated. The committee may, and usually does, conduct its own investigation of the nominee's qualifications. If the position warrants, a hearing will be held; if the nomination becomes controversial, hearings on the nomination can stretch out indefinitely, with many witnesses called to testify. The committee will next consider the nomination at a committee business meeting and recommend to the Senate that it give or withhold its advice and consent to the appointment. The nomination is placed upon the Executive Calendar of the Senate, where it remains until the Senate is prepared to consider it. When called up, the nomination may be debated, but no amendments are in order. If the nomination is controversial, or if the position is of sufficient importance, a roll call vote will be held; otherwise, the nomination will be consented to by voice vote. If a majority of those senators present and voting agree, the nomination papers are returned to the White House with "the advice and consent of the Senate." Should the nomination be disapproved, the papers are also returned to the White House, but with the notation that the Senate does not give its advice and consent.

That is the procedure, but the by-play is infinitely more interesting. Every position to be filled has its own history and creates impressions about the sort of person who should occupy it. Some positions are created at the insistence of Congress—the Assistant Secretary of State for Human Rights and Humanitarian Affairs, for example. Others are established by executive reorganization and acquiesced to by the Congress—the Under Secretary of Commerce for International Trade, for example. In most instances, there is a historical record of what purposes the position would serve, which in turn gives clues as to the kind of person various interested parties would like to see occupy the position, or would like to prevent from holding the position.

The selection of a nominee does not occur in a vacuum. Members of the Congress with an interest in the position to be filled or in the subject matter likely to be affected by the person occupying the position take an active part in identifying and recommending candidates to the White House. For example, a recommendation from the Chairman of the Senate Banking Committee of an individual to serve on the Board of Governors of the Federal Reserve System will be taken seriously by the President, although the person will not necessarily receive the nomination. Such recommendations from Congress are avidly sought by those who seek appointment to top posts in the federal government.

Senators must consider a number of factors when deciding whether and how strongly to recommend an individual for a position. Do they owe the person a favor? If so, is the recommendation a cheap and safe way to discharge the obligation? Will the person prove to be a crook, a fool, or an incompetent, thus harming the reputation of the senator who supported him? How will other important constituencies respond when they learn of the senator's recommendation? (The basic rule is not to expect anything to remain secret very long.) What will be the response of others who are seeking the position and of other senators who are supporting other candidates? How will the President and his advisers respond? If appointed, will the candidate take positions on policy issues consistent with the senator's views? Last but not least, is the candidate the best person available to fill the post?

The White House, in turn, must consider a number of points when weighing the recommendations of senators. The starting point is "senatorial courtesy," a concept often misconstrued. The basis for senatorial courtesy is the belief that a senator ought not to be forced to accept as an appointee to a federal position *in his state* a person who is personally offensive to the senator. The rule is informal, depending upon the mutual accommodation of senators for its enforcement, but, in fact, Presidents seldom wish to test it. Senators have often construed senatorial courtesy more broadly to mean the ability to name federal appointees in their states, and some have taken it to mean the right to veto the appointment of anyone *from* their state to a federal office. Presidents have often challenged the broader notions of senatorial courtesy, and have often prevailed. Still, the senators from the state in which the nominee resides or in which the nominee will serve are always important participants in the nomination process.

Even more important are the senators who chair or who are ranking minority members of the committees or subcommittees with jurisdiction over the agency in which the nominee will serve. They are presumed to have the strongest feelings about, and the greatest influence over, the policies in which the nominee will have a say. The White House will sometimes pre-clear a nominee with the relevant senators on a private basis. Usually the purpose is to avoid a difficult battle over the nomination which can end only in embarrassment for the President or embitterment of key senators toward the President.

Once the nomination has been announced by the White House, it is customary for the nominee to make a series of "courtesy calls" to senators sitting on the committee which will review the nomination as well as to other key senators known to have an interest in the agency involved. The prudent nominee would call, for example, on the chairman of the relevant subcommittee of the Senate Appropriations Committee. During the same period, the nominee would usually call upon key members of the House of Representatives as well, including the representative from the district in which the nominee resides.

Courtesy calls can be very time-consuming at the beginning of a new administration and can therefore be a considerable nuisance to senators and representatives, as well as to nominees. They are usually more useful to nominees for lesser posts or posts at less well-known agencies. The nominee may find the courtesy call offers the best chance to get acquainted with a key senator, as well as a chance to do some early lobbying for a particular policy or agency funding. It is a chance to make friends, to pacify potential adversaries, and to educate senators to the merits of the nominee and the agency in which he will serve. It is a common mistake to overestimate how much senators or representatives know or care about an agency or program over which they have formal legislative responsibility.

Senators can find courtesy calls useful as well. They can be used on occasion to extort promises from nominees as to their future behavior. Senators can impress upon nominees their views on the appropriate policies to pursue and do so in a climate in which the nominee has little choice except to mumble agreeably. Finally, courtesy calls can enable senators to resolve their concerns about nominees privately. That is the primary purpose of the visits, of course.

Senators who are interested in following through will do so at the nomination hearing, either by appearing in person to direct questions to the witness or by submitting written questions to be answered for the record. It should come as no surprise that the questions asked of nominees are frequently submitted by interested private groups. A truckers' association, for example, might suggest questions for a senator on the Commerce Committee to ask a nominee to the Interstate Commerce Commission. The nomination hearing can become a contest to pin down the nominee's views on controversial questions.

Nominees are frequently ill-prepared for the questioning they receive during courtesy calls or at hearings. This is surprising, considering the importance of first impressions as well as the risk of getting locked into a poor policy stance. It is the responsibility of the Congressional relations staff at the agencies in which the nominees will serve to provide "coaching." Other interested parties, such as industry representatives and Congressional staff, can help, but the nominee must ultimately face the questioners alone.

One further aspect of the nomination process deserves mention. The "new ethics" of public office requires the nominee to make extensive disclosures of his financial holdings and past affiliations. The nominee will be required to place most of his or her holdings in a blind trust if the position involves financial matters. The nominee may also be asked to "recuse" himself or herself from taking part in policy decisions on matters in which the nominee has had close association in the private sector or in which the nominee holds a significant financial interest. Nominees usually need help from legal counsel in order to draft (and sometimes to negotiate) an appropriate arrangement on these subjects.

Senators have been embarrassed in the past by acceding to nominations when the nominee's background ought to have been investigated more thoroughly. Most Senate committees have, therefore, charged their investigative staff with probing the backgrounds of nominees. In addition, most committees have developed supplementary questionnaires for nominees covering finances, affiliations, and political activities. Nominees have sometimes expressed surprise over the extent of the information they are required to reveal. Washington representatives should do a better job of briefing their clients or officers on what to anticipate in the nomination review process in the Senate if they seek appointive federal office.

Most nominations are handled without a written report, but in controversial cases or for major appointments, a report may be required. Any senator on the committee reviewing the nomination may insist that the committee prepare a written report. There is no rule to that effect; it is a right established by custom. Committees will sometimes consider the report in draft form when they vote on the nomination; at other times the committee will vote on the nomination and direct the staff to prepare the report later. The nominee will probably not see the report before it has been filed by the committee. If he or she is concerned about the content of the report, the best chance to gain access to it is via a sympathetic senator or staffer on the committee. Of course, any senator on the committee may insist on an opportunity to review the report before it is filed.

Senators may decide to delay a nomination in order to make a policy point, even if the point is unrelated to the nominee and his qualifications. Any senator can slow the progress of a nomination for a time, but the delay can be considerable if the senator is a member of the majority party and the committee reviewing the nomination. If the chairman of the committee is seriously opposed to the nomination, the nominee and the President should be prepared for a long fight with slim prospect of victory. Ordinarily, the President will take care not to submit a nomination to which the committee chairman objects strongly.

Nominees sometimes bring witnesses before the committee to testify on their behalf. When the political rapport with the nominee dictates, the senators from the nominee's home state appear in person at the hearing to "introduce" the nominee to the committee. Members of the House often appear as well. Nominees and their supporters often expend great effort to obtain such endorsements, and there is no doubt that they can be helpful in some cases. But nominees need to remember that such testimonials are an inconvenience to all the senators and representatives involved, and nominees sometimes stir resentment by aggressively seeking a personal appearance by a senator when there is no controversy over a nomination. Perhaps the easiest way for a nominee to avoid mistakes is to remember that the nomination process is the beginning of continuous interaction with the Congress, not a set of hurdles to be quickly run over and promptly forgotten.

Investigations and Educational Hearings

Another function of Congress is to speak to and for the public interest. Hearings and reports are used to attack corruption, waste of taxpayers' money, and the "special interests." Both the Government Operations Committee of the House and the Governmental Affairs Committee of the Senate have large staffs specializing in reviewing the operation of federal government programs. Other committees frequently launch investigations into subjects more or less within their jurisdiction; there are few limits on who may investigate what.

Congressmen have learned that exposing a scandal is the surest way to gain television coverage and the applause of constituents. The public seems to have an insatiable appetite for revelations of misdeeds. The suspicion that something is rotten in Washington, and in the federal government in particular, runs deep. Congressmen spend considerable effort devising ways to tap that sentiment.

Investigative and educational hearings and reports are actually distinct parts of the oversight process. Legislation is usually not the immediate objective, although the possibility of follow-up legislation must be kept constantly in mind. For example, the Senate Foreign Relations Committee conducted extensive "educational" oversight hearings in the mid-1960's on national commitments. The hearings and reports led to the National Commitments Resolution of 1969 and War Powers Act of 1973 (P.L. 93-148), highly controversial legislation which may have a major impact on the way the United States goes to war in the future.[14] Likewise, exposure in investigative hearings of bribes paid by corporations to foreign government officials to secure sales led directly to the Foreign Corrupt Practices Act of 1977.

Treaties

Another function which devolves only upon the Senate is the consideration of treaties. Article II, section 2 of the Constitution provides that the President may "make treaties, provided two-thirds of the Senators present concur." George Washington experimented (unsuccessfully) with personally presenting draft-negotiating instructions to the Senate for its review.[15] Presidents ever since have wrestled with the problem of how to consult with the Senate sufficiently in advance to ensure a favorable reception for treaties, yet still preserve the ability to negotiate treaties which are in the national interest even if they are not universally popular.

Current practice varies considerably from one case to the next. The United Nations Convention on the Law of the Sea involved extensive consultations by the United States delegation with the Senate Foreign Relations Committee. By contrast, until procedures were recently revised, the Committee was unaware of most bilateral tax treaty negotiations until signed treaties were presented to the Senate.

The development of international agreements other than treaties to handle most international questions has diminished the importance of the Senate's power to review treaties but has added new problems at the same time. International agreements (executive agreements) must be executed by the United States to be effective, which frequently means that implementing legislation is needed. Congress can be as recalcitrant in the implementation stage as the Senate alone can be in considering treaties. Equally troublesome is the risk that Congress will take the initiative to pass legislation which prevents implementation of, or which violates, international agreements previously entered into by the executive branch. While there are no guarantees that Congressional involvement in the negotiation and approval of international agreements will yield smooth implementation, the chances are better when there is consultation.

A striking example of successful Presidential-Congressional cooperation in concluding and implementing international agreements is the Multilateral Trade Negotiation concluded in 1979 and the Trade Act of 1979 which implemented the agreements. Congress authorized United States participation in the negotiations by passing legislation in 1974. The legislation spelled out the procedures for consultation between the Senate Finance and House Ways and Means Committees and the executive branch, the participation of private sector advisory groups, and finally, special rules for expediting consideration of the implementing legislation in both the House and Senate. The procedures worked well, and there have been suggestions that similar procedures should be tried in other areas.[16]

Constituent Service

Congressmen are also ombudsmen. Their constituents encounter the most amazing array of difficulties in dealing with the federal government. Members of Congress spend considerable time and effort trying to help their constituents with Social Security or Medicaid problems or retrieving lost records or getting applications reconsidered. Much is done by Congressional staff, but members must shoulder a major share themselves.

Congressmen also obtain and distribute funds and favors to their friends and constituents. Patronage is largely a thing of the past, but the President still makes many appointments, and so do his appointees. Therefore Congressmen send forward many recommendations and see many federal job seekers.

Funding for programs which benefit the member's state or district is a constant preoccupation. Some members spend more than half their time working on ways to provide direct economic benefits to their constituents. When a member is presented with a problem of national interest, in most cases he will inquire first about his constituents' interest.

Miscellaneous Functions

Finally, Congress has a variety of rarely exercised functions that can be important and time-consuming when they must be exercised. Since Congress has the power of impeachment, in 1972 the Watergate episode became the major business of Congress for months. A member of the committee investigating Watergate would not have had time to go to a Commerce Committee hearing on flood insurance, for example.

Congress has ceremonial functions as well. Visiting foreign heads of state must be entertained, funerals must be attended, ships must be launched and ribbons cut. These may not be matters of eternal significance, but they are a significant part of what the Congress does and what Congressmen think they should do. Passing bills can sometimes seem dull by comparison.

GETTING TO KNOW THE PLAYERS

Knowing the nature of the institution needs to be joined with a knowledge of the players and the rules by which they play. In addition to getting to know individual members of the Congress, it helps to recognize the roles they assign themselves. They seem to be motivated by a mixture of three desires: the desire to be re-elected, the desire to do good, and the desire to be somewhere else.

The common assumption is that members of Congress organize their actions around the desire to be re-elected. The next election is never far away for members of the House of Representatives, and even senators seem well aware of their limited tenure. To the extent that members are preoccupied with their re-election prospects, they will feel obliged to do three things: serve their constituents and key supporters first, take only safe or "popular" positions on legislative issues, and seek publicity at home at every opportunity. It does not usually require a lengthy period of observation to determine whether a member is motivated primarily by a desire to be re-elected.[17]

The second driving force is the desire to do good, and it can predominate in some cases. Someone once said that those who put the national interest ahead of their constituents are known as former Congressmen. There are some exceptions, but it helps to have a stable, one-party state or district from which to run. Those in the Congress who fervently wish to do good are of two sorts, statesmen and true believers, and it is not always easy to tell one from the other. Harry McPherson described Senator William Fulbright as resembling Senator Paul Douglas in that "He sometimes seemed to have a stake in losing, in being isolated and right. Johnson had to urge them both to want to win."[18]

Statesmen are generally recognized by their appeal to high principle, but something more is required to advance broader interests effectively in Congress. Legislation must be managed and brokered; it will not arrange itself. Statesmen in the Congress distinguish themselves by their management of legislation. Those who merely shout to the galleries leave little lasting imprint on the law or on people's lives.

But there is a third breed within the Congress: those who would rather be someplace else. Some are candidates, in their own minds at least, for President, or governor, or for the Senate (in the case of members of the House of Representatives). Others are candidates for retirement or for a different career, probably one with more financial reward and less pressure. These members of the Congress chafe under the burdens of the place and long to be off to their chosen destination. They are surprisingly large in number.[19]

Knowing what motivates members (I have left out the more venal motivations to which a few succumb) does not suffice to know who is worth knowing, if the question is how to get a bill through Congress or how to get help in dealing with an executive agency. Knowing who is powerful in Congress is a constant diversion for Washingtonians. It is easy to know who ought to be powerful: the elected floor leadership and the chairmen of committees, together with the ranking minority members. If a matter is considered by a subcommittee, its chairman and ranking member ought to be important too. But not all chairman are powerful; some are incapable of winning votes even within their own committee or subcommittee.

The best guide in the end may well be word of mouth, because it is reputation in addition to formal position that counts for influence in the Congress. Harry McPherson described the minimum requirements for being a "whale" in the Senate as follows:

> A chairmanship, longevity in the Senate, devotion to the legislative process, command over the giving or withholding of benefits in which large numbers of Senators had an interest—there were other qualities that could not be easily measured. Manliness, perhaps—Big Daddy-ness; the natural assumption of authority; the willingness, in fact the need, to take responsibility; and a tough seriousness about the daily game of making laws. (pp.50-51)

Power is more dispersed and less predictable in the Congress in the 1980's than it was in the 1950's when McPherson observed it, but the qualities to look for in leaders remain the same. There are more independent centers—subcommittees, in particular—with smaller pieces of power. Figuring out who will be important on a given piece of legislation is becoming tougher all the time, but it pays to begin by looking for those members who ought to be powerful with respect to the legislation, by virtue of their formal positions or reputation for interest in, and effective action on, the subject.

GETTING TO KNOW THE RULES OF THE GAME

Law making is the primary function of Congress. To understand how laws are made and how to influence the making of laws, it is necessary to know the written and unwritten rules of the legislative process and the protocol which pertains to participation in the process by outsiders. Mastery of the detailed and complicated procedures of the Senate and the House of Representatives can be very helpful in deciding when and how to intervene. I have known many situations in which a lobbyist or legislative strategist lost out simply by not knowing the steps and timing of the legislative process. Remarkably few Washington representatives know even the rudiments of how a bill becomes a law.

Congress publishes a handy elementary guide entitled "How Our Laws Are Made," which ought to be required reading for anyone working in or with Washington. It is available from the Government Printing Office or, while supplies last, from the offices of members of Congress. The discussion which follows parallels and supplements "How Our Laws Are Made," with the intention of offering some helpful hints not found in official publications.

Introduction of Bills and Referral to Committee

Everything begins, more or less, with the introduction of a bill in the House or Senate by a member of the respective chamber. No one but a member may introduce a bill, and any member may introduce any number of bills on any subject. Anyone who has observed the thousands of bills introduced each year, most of which do not pass, may wonder what prompts members to introduce bills.[20]

A significant number of bills are introduced by members at the request of the administration or an independent federal agency. Such bills are usually introduced by the chairman or ranking minority member (depending upon partisan alignment with the administration) of the committee with jurisdiction over the subject matter covered in the bill. The words "by request" will appear after the introducer's name in the *Congressional Record* and on the face of the printed bill. If a member introduces a bill "by request," he or she may have no personal commitment to its passage. For that reason, members introducing administration bills which they do strongly support will sometimes omit the words "by request" in order to signal their support for the measure. I know of one instance in which a staffer preparing an administration bill for introduction forgot to include the words "by request" and thereby embarrassed his boss, who wanted nothing to do with the bill. In another case, a senator introducing a bill prepared by a trade association deliberately inserted the words "by request." This indicated that he did not support the bill in full but felt it should be available in printed form to the committee when it considered rival proposals. The trade association may well have felt it was damned with faint praise, and so it was.

The administration may find itself in a peculiar and uncomfortable situation when it sends to the Congress a bill opposed by both the floor leadership of the administration's party and the chairman (or ranking minority member) of the relevant committee. Such situations arise only when an administration is rather badly out of line with the members of its party in one or both chambers—for example, when the party in the White House controls neither chamber and wishes to accommodate the majority party in Congress. In such circumstances, the administration may be forced to go shopping for someone to introduce its bill, even turning to the majority party, if necessary. Bills which are opposed by the chairman or ranking minority member of the committee of jurisdiction may also be sent forward by the administration. In such cases, the majority leader or minority leader will normally introduce the bill on the administration's behalf.

One of the purposes for introducing a bill is to attempt to get it enacted into law. Another purpose is to influence the passage or consideration of other legislation. For example, the introduction of an extreme measure may spur passage of a milder measure. By contrast, opponents of a measure under consideration may introduce a rival bill in order to demonstrate their seriousness and to rally opposition to the primary measure.

Another reason for introducing a bill is to influence executive branch rule making or some other executive branch policy activity. Normally, this is done when someone opposes what the executive branch proposes to do or what it has already done and wishes to reverse the decision. Resolutions to disapprove certain executive branch actions are quite common. The struggle between the Reagan Administration and some members of Congress over the sale of AWACS to Saudi Arabia in 1981 took the form of a battle over a resolution of disapproval. Specific procedures for consideration of resolutions of disapproval are provided in the Arms Export Control Act, and are one form of the legislative veto.

Other examples of bills intended to influence executive branch action include bills to cut off funding or to transfer a function from one agency to another. Senator Jake Garn (Republican of Utah) introduced a bill in the Ninety-Sixth Congress to transfer the administration of export controls from the Department of Commerce to an Office of Strategic Trade to be established in the Executive Office of the President. Senator Garn made clear that his bill was stimulated as much by his disagreement with the Commerce Department's licensing of certain exports to communist countries as with inefficiencies in the administration of export licensing. He did not reintroduce his bill in the first session of the Ninety-Seventh Congress because he wished to give the new Republican administration an opportunity to demonstrate that it could administer export controls properly within the Commerce Department.

Sometimes when a policy decision within the administration is bogged down in interagency rivalry, one agency will surreptitiously get a key supporter in Congress to introduce a bill favoring the agency's position. Unless the forces on the other side can make an equal showing of Congressional support (or get the President on their side), they are likely to lose the interagency contest.

Members of Congress regularly introduce bills in order to show support for a particular cause or organization, even if passage of the bill is unlikely and the member has no intention of exerting effort to see that the bill goes any farther. Introduction of a bill is a relatively safe and easy favor a Congressman can bestow on his friends. Misunderstandings can arise, however, if the friends expect the member to do something more than introduce the bill.

If you would like to have a bill introduced in Congress, there are several points to consider. First, who should introduce the bill and who should be invited to be original cosponsors of the bill? Assuming you would like to see the bill pass, the optimal original sponsors are the chairmen of the House and Senate committees and subcommittees to which the bill will be referred. If the bill will require appropriations to achieve its purpose, the support of the chairmen of the relevant House and Senate Appropriations subcommittees would be helpful, perhaps essential. If it is possible to obtain cosponsorship from the ranking minority members of the same committees and subcommittees, the bill will avoid being cast as a partisan measure. But think carefully about whether you want your bill to be bipartisan or partisan. In election years, Presidents and Congressional leaders work harder to secure passage of their party's legislation and spurn bipartisan bills. Normally, however, a bill's chances are greatly improved if it has early bipartisan support. It is very helpful to have cosponsorship from floor leaders of either party in either chamber. It is also helpful to have cosponsorship by any member regarded as influential or otherwise respected. There is one caveat to what has been said, however. If a chairman or ranking minority member is weak or despised by his colleagues, his association with your bill can be the kiss of death.

Obtaining cosponsors is usually done in a series of steps, beginning with the primary sponsor, who can both help and hinder the process of securing cosponsors. The primary sponsor may not want to have the bill cosponsored by members with whom he prefers not to be associated, even if their cosponsorship would help pass the bill. He may have friends among the members whom he would like to include among the original cosponsors but whose cosponsorship would scare away other, more influential members. Bills can quickly become identified with their original cosponsors: "liberals," "internationalists," "protectionists," etc.[21]

Once the bill has been introduced, it is customary for the original sponsor and cosponsors to send a letter to their colleagues inviting them to cosponsor the measure. Once a "Dear Colleague" letter has gone out, cosponsors are added to the bill as they indicate their willingness to cosponsor. Control over the distribution of cosponsorship is often lost at this point, so that the bill may acquire a partisan or special interest image simply because some members are quicker than others to cosponsor it. Therefore, a "Dear Colleague" seeking cosponsorship should not be sent before key cosponsors, also known as "original sponsors," have been lined up. One useful tactic after a "Dear Colleague" has gone out and members begin to inform the original sponsor of their interest is to delay listing the cosponsors in the *Record* until the names can be submitted in groups balanced by partisan or other considerations. This is the responsibility of the staffer for the primary sponsor of the measure.

A second consideration with regard to introducing a bill is what the administration's attitude toward the bill is likely to be. Presumably the reaction will fall somewhere between lukewarm support and bitter hostility; if the administration thought the idea was the greatest thing since sliced bread, it would have offered the bill itself. The decision to have a bill introduced, therefore, is usually a signal to the administration of some degree of dissatisfaction with its program. Any departments or offices within the administration which might be sympathetic to the bill will need to be curried carefully. Often it is possible to work with parts of the executive branch before a bill is introduced to ensure that the bill is framed with an eye to increasing the chances of administration endorsement.

The decision as to how much prior consultation to have with various parts of the administration before introducing a bill depends largely on how valuable technical advice from executive branch specialists would be and how much likelihood there is that the administration can be persuaded to endorse the bill, or at least minimize its opposition. A good rule of thumb is that everything the administration learns about the bill can, and probably will, be used against it. Thus, well-meaning consultation with the administration at too early a point in the process may enable the administration to take effective countermeasures against the bill—for example, warning off potential cosponsors. For this reason, many legislators, especially from the party which does not control the White House, like to keep the administration in the dark as much as possible before a bill is introduced.

The timing of introduction of a bill is another consideration which is too often ignored. Usually the introduction should be timed to maximize publicity for the bill. For example, some legislators prefer to introduce bills on low news days when there is likely to be little competition for press attention. Sometimes a bill can be linked with a national event or special occasion. A civil rights bill, for example, might be introduced on Martin Luther King's birthday or an agriculture bill introduced during a national farmers' convention.

Another consideration is who should draft the bill. Committee staff or personal staff of members may wish to draft the bill; they may obtain assistance from the Office of Legislative Counsel in the Senate or House. Congressional staff may welcome drafting assistance from outsiders, but staff usually like to keep tight control of the process. Developing a good relationship with key Congressional staff at the drafting stage can give an outsider unparalleled access to the process, but this is not always possible. Committee staff are justifiably wary of too-cozy relationships with persons with interests in legislation before the committee. Personal staff take their signals on such relationships from their bosses.

Similar considerations apply to the drafting of introductory statements for the bill's sponsor and the "Dear Colleague" letter to seek additional cosponsors. Interested persons may wish to offer suggestions, even drafts, to Congressional staff, but it is important to avoid seeming to dictate to staffers, who may very well have their egos heavily invested in the project.

A final consideration in introducing bills is the committee and subcommittee to which the bill will be referred in each House. The rule in the Senate is straightforward: referral is based on committee jurisdictions listed in the Senate rules in broad descriptive terms. The bill will be referred to "the committee which has jurisdiction over the subject matter which predominates" in the bill, as determined by the presiding officer as advised by the Senate Parliamentarian.[22] The rule precludes referral to more than one committee, except upon a motion of the majority and minority leaders, a motion which the leaders refuse to offer unless the chairmen and ranking minority members of both committees so request in writing. The purpose of the rule is to streamline Senate consideration of bills by avoiding multiple committee referrals. Multiple referrals, either joint or sequential, are still possible, but they must be carefully negotiated, and the committee to which the bill is initially referred holds most of the cards.

The rules in the House of Representatives work to almost the opposite effect: any committee which has a substantial jurisdictional claim to a significant provision in the bill will receive the bill. There is no limit on the number of committees to which a bill may be referred. The House Parliamentarian takes the initiative in determining the committees to which the bill should be referred and so advises the Speaker of the House, who makes the actual referral.

The sponsors of a legislative proposal give careful thought to the optimal committee referral of the bill they are preparing. In some cases, there is nothing that can be done to alter committee referrals: appropriations measures go to the appropriations committees; tax measures go to the Senate Finance Committee and the House Ways and Means Committee; bills which simply amend existing statutes are referred to the committees which originally reported the statutes. But what if a bill introduced in the Senate amends several statutes which originated in different committees or it contains wholly new statutory language not clearly in the realm of a single committee? In those cases, the Senate Parliamentarian has to make a judgment call or the committees involved must reach an agreement on joint or sequential referrals. Thus the Senate rules leave opportunity for imaginative bill drafters to shape a bill so as to determine which committee has "the subject matter which predominates." Other committees may seek sequential or joint referral, of course, but the point is that they must *seek* joint or sequential referral; referral is not automatically provided. It may therefore prove important to write a bill so it will be referred to the Senate committee where it will receive the best reception.

Examples of this practice abound. The Farm Credit Act Amendments bill in the Ninety-Sixth Congress was referred to the Senate Agriculture Committee. The bill expanded the banking powers of the farm credit system and clearly affected matters within the Banking Committee's jurisdiction, but the Agriculture Committee refused the Banking Committee's request for sequential referral of the bill. Agricultural interests did not wish to see the bill go to the Banking Committee, where banking interests have more friends. If a bill on the same subject had been written by bankers, it would have been constructed so as to be referred to the Banking Committee.

The situation in the House requires a different tactic, if the objective is to bypass a committee which might prove unfriendly to a proposal. In the House, the best approach is to write the bill narrowly and then expand it, if necessary, with amendments in committee. Nongermane amendments are not in order on the House floor; therefore, the scope of a bill can only be expanded by committee action or in conference with the Senate.

Another approach which can be effective in the House is to introduce more than one bill on the same subject, beginning with an omnibus bill which will be referred to several committees and following up with bills containing pieces of the original proposal which can be referred to individual committees. Humpty Dumpty can be reassembled in committee mark-up (executive session) or in conference with the Senate, if the votes are there to do so. It should be said, however, that chairmen of House committees fight vigorously to avoid having their jurisdiction circumvented or eroded, and they usually prevail.

Introducing a bill has as its obvious counterpart efforts to prevent or counter the introduction of bills. The first step, of course, is to "get wind" that someone is planning to introduce a bill. Members of Congress and trade associations are notoriously incapable of keeping secrets. Washington representatives who develop a good network of sources and peruse the newsletters and insider publications in Washington will not be surprised often.

There are several possible responses if you are opposed to a bill that is expected to be introduced. It may be possible to persuade the intended sponsor that the bill is a bad idea and should not be introduced. The administration may be of help in this effort, especially if the member of Congress belongs to the same party as the President and usually supports administration positions. Even if the sponsor cannot be dissuaded, it may be possible to discourage possible cosponsors. The referral of the bill may also be open to some dispute, and a word with the committees to which you would prefer to see the bill referred can be productive.

Introduction of a counterproposal, a bill which takes the opposite tack or is a compromise, can bleed support away from the objectionable bill, but it also tends to draw attention to the issue. In other words, the prior question is whether the bill should be taken seriously or ignored.

Another step is to mobilize administration opposition to the bill. If there is good reason to expect the administration to oppose the bill once its position is formally requested, a sympathetic Congressman can be encouraged to press the administration to state its position. Hearings can be arranged in a friendly subcommittee, either on a counterproposal or hearings of an oversight nature. Speeches and insertions in the *Congressional Record* which argue against the offending bill can also be arranged.

Committee Consideration of Bills

The next phase of the legislative struggle is usually committee consideration of the bill, first in hearings and later in mark-up. It is possible but quite unusual for a bill to be taken up directly on the floor. Those possibilities will be discussed later.

Once a bill is referred to committee the first question is whether it will be referred to a subcommittee or handled at the full committee level. Practice varies by committee: some committees always refer bills to a subcommittee; some keep all legislation at the full committee level; others exercise discretion. Because subcommittee consideration is the first hurdle for most legislation, getting the bill referred to the "right" subcommittee can be very important. Often a bill can easily be referred to more than one subcommittee. Referral is usually decided by the committee chairman, perhaps under the influence of an assertive subcommittee chairman. Where circumstances warrant, it may be advisable to try to persuade the committee or subcommittee chairman to place the bill where it can be expected to get the reception you want.

Because the administration position on a bill is so important to its success, efforts should begin very early to secure as favorable an administration position as possible. In some cases, the best that can be hoped for is muted opposition, or neutrality. The first step is to determine who in the administration will be influential in deciding the administration's position. It is best to try to meet or talk on the telephone with the operating level officials who will be preparing the memoranda on the basis of which a recommendation will be made at a political level, often an Assistant Secretary, and referred to an interagency process for clearance. Offers of information which analyzes the bill and its effects are seldom refused. Information should be prepared as concisely as possible, with an eye to the factors which seem likely to be persuasive with the administration. The presentation should be as balanced as it can be while still reaching the preferred conclusion. Both administration officials and Congressional staff expect to receive an advocacy brief, but, like judges, they resent being deluged with paper which is not directly on point and they react very negatively to submissions carrying errors or obvious misrepresentations. In other words, a bad brief is worse than none at all.

The timing of an administration position is usually within the discretion of the administration. Parties with opposing views will have different timetables, depending on what position they expect the administration to take. An administration which feels it must oppose a bill may nonetheless be willing to delay announcement of a position in order to give supporters of the measure a chance to build support. But one should anticipate that the measure's opponents are pressing equally hard for a prompt administration denunciation of the bill. Finally, many committees have a routine procedure for sending bills referred to the committee to administration agencies for comment. Inquiries of committee staff can determine whether a request has gone forward and, if so, to which agencies. A cautionary note, however: I have known cases in which a lobbyist seeking to determine whether a bill had been referred unintentionally reminded a committee staffer who opposed the lobbyist's position that the referral should be carried out in a manner calculated to shape the outcome in a direction just the opposite of what the lobbyist wanted. For similar reasons, Washingtonians are habitually careful about what they say to persons whose biases and affiliations are not known.

The next step in the legislative process is usually hearings on the bill. Hearings on bills, treaties, or nominations are called "legislative hearings"; hearings not covering legislation but held in order to review administration programs or to receive information on a subject are called "oversight hearings." The bill may be lumped with other similar measures for consideration at a single hearing. Hearings need not be held at all, nor is there any requirement that testimony be taken from the public, from the administration, or from anyone else. If a committee does not wish to hear a particular testimony, it will probably not be heard. Committees seldom refuse to receive testimony from the administration, however, and nongovernment witnesses are usually heard if any committee member requests it. Most committees have rules which permit the minority side of a committee to insist on hearing at least a few witnesses of its choice.

Persons who would like an opportunity to testify at a hearing or simply to attend a hearing often express frustration that there is no foolproof way to receive early notification of planned hearings. Requests to testify should be conveyed to the committee as soon as an individual or organization decides it wishes to testify. There is no need to wait until hearings are planned or announced. As soon as a bill is introduced and referred to committee, a letter requesting a chance to testify can be sent to the chairman of the committee or subcommittee, along with a copy to the ranking minority member. It is a good idea to follow up with phone calls and copies of the correspondence to the majority and minority committee staffers responsible for following the bill, just to make sure they are aware of the interest in testifying. Decisions on which witnesses will be invited are often left to the discretion of committee staff and are usually not made until two or three weeks before a hearing date.

Getting early and reliable notice of when a hearing is scheduled and who is expected to testify usually requires having a friend on the committee professional staff or personal staff of an interested member. The fact that hearings can be called with only a day or two of advance notice makes life in Washington more interesting, but it is a natural peril which cannot be avoided.[23] Some Washington law firms seem to make a habit of calling committee professional staff every few days to see what is scheduled ahead. They waste everyone's time by doing so, and they can build up enough annoyance on the part of staff that the firm's phone messages are left to age on the desk unanswered.

When a Senate committee's clerical staff have definite word on a hearing date, they submit it to the *Congressional Record* where it is printed for the convenience of the public.[24] The House does not have a centralized system for keeping track of hearing announcements, but each committee does make available to the public a list of scheduled hearings. If the professional staff are not ready to release a hearing date to be printed in the *Record* or included in a press release, they are probably not ready to release such information to people who telephone. There are enough exceptions, however, to keep phones ringing incessantly and to keep a great many Washington newsletters in business. The committee professional staffers in charge of a particular set of hearings are the ones who will know the information first. In the end, the only way to get completely reliable, up-to-date information is to ask them, bearing in mind the risk of getting marked down as a pest.

Getting accurate information on the same day that hearings are held or on the day after is quite simple. The *Washington Post* prints a full list of hearings scheduled for the same day, but without complete witness lists. Many committees have telephone recordings which provide a full witness list to anyone who calls. The *Congressional Record*, which is printed overnight, includes in the Daily Digest section an accurate record of hearings held the previous day, together with the names of witnesses who testified.

Finding out which members of a committee are likely to attend a hearing is next to impossible. Normally the chairman and ranking minority member can be expected to attend, although the latter is unlikely to sit through the entire hearing. Other members should usually not be expected to appear unless (a) television cameras are expected to be present or (b) the member has a strong personal or constituency interest in the legislation. Members and their staff are coy about their daily schedules and like to create an impression that they will attend more events than they actually attend. Outsiders should not *expect* members to attend hearings nor should they *expect* to obtain accurate information in advance as to whether a member will attend. Even the committee staff in charge of a hearing generally do not know for certain who will drop in at a hearing; Washington representatives have only the slimmest chance of knowing.

Members can be encouraged to attend hearings by letters or calls from interested persons. Members and their staff usually like to know not just that the hearing is considered important but what points the member might make or what questions the member should ask. Remember that members of Congress are far more interested in what they will *say* at hearings than in what they will *hear*. Providing draft statements and questions to a member is a way to help the member and the staff, while seeing that a particular viewpoint is advanced.[25] If the member does not show up at the hearing or if the questions are not asked, the member may still be willing to submit the questions to the witnesses to be answered for the printed hearing record and to share the answers with you when they are received.

Arranging hearings is largely the prerogative of the committee staff who work for the chairman of the committee or subcommittee involved. They largely determine when hearings are held, who testifies, and the format of the hearings. Getting in touch with the appropriate committee staffer is the best way to keep informed about hearings on a bill in which you are interested. If the relationship is good, you may be able to suggest when hearings could most advantageously be held and who should or should not be invited to testify.

Each committee has its own rules and traditions for the format of hearings and testimony. Often the basic elements are spelled out in a committee handout which can be obtained from committee staff. Anyone who expects to work regularly with Congress should ask each committee for a copy of its rules (which supplement the Senate or House rules) and any other information which is made available to prospective witnesses. In particular, answers to the following questions should be sought: What is the required format and maximum length of written statements? May supplementary materials be submitted for the hearing record? If so, what limitations apply? How many copies must be submitted, and how far in advance of the hearing? How much time will be allowed for an oral presentation to the committee? Does the committee reimburse witnesses for travel expenses?

If you are invited to testify before a Congressional committee, additional points will need to be ascertained. First, will you testify as part of a panel or individually? If you are part of a panel, you may wish to try to coordinate your testimony with that of other witnesses who may hold a similar viewpoint. Repetitive statements quickly bore committee members, so it is to your advantage not to repeat what a previous witness has said. Second, will you testify before or after administration witnesses and who will the other witnesses be? You may wish to shape your testimony to take account of what other witnesses may say, as well as the sequence in which testimony will be heard. Third, what does the committee expect your testimony to cover? Fourth, which members of the committee are likely to attend? Try to ascertain this point, although there can be little certainty about attendance. Fifth, how much time will be allotted for members to question you and what questions are likely to arise?[26] Committee staff will be best able to answer these questions for you, although the answers are likely to be more nebulous than you would prefer.

Normally, hearings are public, and members of Congress have few inhibitions about asking witnesses whatever comes to mind, including questions which can be embarrassing or very sensitive for witnesses to answer. Most committees do not routinely "swear in" witnesses, so statements made to Congressional committees are not regarded as statements made under oath, unless an oath is taken.[27] Consider in advance how you will respond to the most difficult or annoying questions you might be asked. Keep your oral remarks brief and to the point. If you can avoid reading a statement and can instead summarize extemporaneously, you will have better attention from committee members. Most members of Congress have notoriously short attention spans and little tolerance for tedious details, simply because they must grasp the essence of so many complicated subjccts in so little time.

If you would like your testimony to be widely publicized, bring extra copies of your statement for the press, but be sure to check with committee staff for any restrictions on releasing statements prior to the hearing. You may wish to notify the press and others in advance that you will be testifying and what the news interest in your testimony will be.

After hearings on the legislation have been completed ("completion" is determined by the committee; stretching out hearings can be the chairman's device for delaying action on a bill), a "mark-up" (a business meeting of the committee) can be scheduled, if the members of the committee—the chairman, in particular—wish to schedule one. Some committees, especially in the House, mark up legislation first in subcommittee, then report it to the full committee where additional hearings are often held before a full committee mark-up is scheduled. Other committees, especially the smaller Senate committees, normally consider bills directly in full committee mark-up, even if hearings have been held only at the subcommittee level.

Committees normally group legislative items for mark-up sessions, because it is difficult to find convenient dates to mark up legislation and difficult to assemble a quorum of members for the purpose. Some committees have a regular date and time for mark-ups, for example, during 1981 the Senate Foreign Relations Committee held mark-ups on Tuesday mornings. Other committees schedule mark-ups when committee business requires. Mark-up sessions, like hearings, are nearly always open to the public. Closed sessions are held when classified information is received or ethical problems are considered; thus, sessions of the armed services, intelligence, and ethics committees of both houses are frequently closed to the public.[28] Mark-up sessions are usually well attended, so anyone wishing a seat should arrive well before the time scheduled for the mark-up to begin.

The agenda for the mark-up and background material for members of the committee are prepared by the committee staff. Copies are usually made available to the public when the mark-up begins, but supplies are often insufficient to meet demand. Arriving early and sitting near the front or near the press table increases your chances of getting a copy of the agenda.

During mark-up, members of the committee are likely to offer amendments which have not been circulated previously, and copies are unlikely to be passed out to the audience. There is little that can be done during the mark-up, but beforehand you may wish to check with the legislative assistants to find out whether the members are likely to offer amendments. Suggestions for statements, questions, and amendments can be given to members or their staff at the same time. Talking points, which are short explanatory and debating points in outline form, are especially helpful to members who are sympathetic to your viewpoint. Talking points should be written so they provide at a glance the most significant and persuasive information to a member who may be a novice on the subject. Points to rebut all serious counterarguments should be included. Astute drafters even shape talking points to take advantage of the debating style of the member who will use them. Of course, talking points must be politically congenial to the member.

Be sure to check prior to a mark-up session on who may speak or will be invited to speak during the session. Some committees ask the committee staff to lead them through the agenda, explaining each item and answering the member's questions. This procedure obviously leaves considerable responsibility and discretion with the staff. Some committees regularly ask administration representatives to sit at the witness table and comment on each agenda item. Other committees leave administration witnesses to sit in the audience; they are permitted to speak only in response to direct questions. A few committees even permit interested persons in the audience, those who are known to have a large stake in the pending item, to make short statements.

A day or two before a mark-up is the time to check on expected attendance of committee members. If you wish to see a bill reported, encourage members to attend so the committee will have the quorum necessary for transacting business. Committee rules determine what number constitutes a quorum, but committees may bend the rules or enforce them vigorously, depending largely upon the wishes of the chairman and ranking minority member. One Senate committee, for example, counts a senator present for the entire mark-up session if he sticks his head in the door once during the meeting. If a member sympathetic to your views cannot attend, most committees permit a written proxy to be left with another sympathetic member of the committee. Ask the member in advance, and check with staff to be sure the member asked to vote the proxy will vote it correctly. Proxies can be broad, and can usually be cast subject to the instructions of the staff representative of the absent member.

Being acquainted with the personal and committee staff representatives of members can be important when proxies are cast in mark-up sessions. I have seen mark-up situations in which proxies determined the outcome on major issues and those in which proxies appeared to be cast differently than the absentee would have voted. Proxies can seldom be written so tightly as to take account of changes made through amendments adopted in the course of a mark-up session. Thus, the successful use of proxies depends upon placing the proxy in the hands of a member or staff who will cast it as intended. The chairman and ranking minority member routinely try to gather the proxies of members on their respective sides of the committee, but they may have views which do not accord fully with those of the member who will be absent. It is often better not to leave a proxy than to leave one with a member whose views and judgment cannot be fully trusted.

Generally it is not a good idea to try to prevent formation of a quorum by discouraging members from appearing at a mark-up. Since committees have difficulty getting quorums, they resent interference with the process. As a last resort, preventing a quorum may prove necessary, but at best it buys only a few days' time.

Recommending proposals for use in mark-up is an art in itself. Since members like to strike happy compromises, an amendment offered in mark-up which is characterized as a compromise has a better chance of success. Other amendments which fare well in mark-up are "technical" amendments. The word "technical" can be stretched to cover a multitude of substantive changes. The best rule is to be as skeptical of someone else's "technical" changes as they should be of yours.

Your side may not be able to prevail on the bill language you want, but there are often consolation prizes available in the form of "report language" or provisions requiring an executive branch agency to do a report or conduct a study on a particular matter. Members are usually willing to give part of what is requested, especially if they have already decided to give most of the loaf to someone else. Report language (explanatory language to be included in the committee's report on the bill) is more effective as part of the legislative history of the bill if a written version is put before the committee and voted on, instead of being left to staff to draft later. Many members and lobbyists come to mark-ups with "fallback positions" already prepared in multiple copies, including report language.

Written committee reports are prepared on all bills ordered reported from committee, although not on all nominations; lesser posts and noncontroversial nominees do not warrant the staff time to prepare a report. The reports become an important part of the legislative history of bills and are sometimes cited by courts or by the executive branch where legislative intent must be discerned. Committee reports are often the only information used by staff and members to prepare themselves for floor consideration of a bill. Consequently, a report must be carefully drafted from an advocacy standpoint as well as with an eye to ultimate implementation of the statute.

The committee staff draft the reports and may or may not share drafts with the administration and other interested persons outside the committee. The best chance to see the report before it is filed by the committee is either to go through the committee staffers working on the report or the offices of the members of the committee. Each member of the committee receives a copy of the draft report before it is filed, unless the legislation is quite routine. Staff for members usually review the drafts and may welcome help from outsiders in reviewing complex portions.

Committee reports in both Houses are required to contain statements on the budgetary, inflationary, and regulatory impact of the bill reported. The statements are usually routine; the budget estimates are prepared by the Congressional Budget Office and are normally accepted by the committee without comment. The statements can be used to make substantive arguments on legislation, however. A Banking Committee report in the Ninety-Sixth Congress called attention to the increased federal regulatory impact an amendment adopted by the committee would have. The senator who sponsored the amendment (and his staffer) did not notice the "regulatory impact statement" until several days after the report was filed and printed. The alleged regulatory effect of the amendment was later used to modify the amendment in a Senate-House conference committee.

Additional and opposing views can be filed with committee reports and can be effective in rallying opposition to bills on the floor. Friendly committee members can be persuaded to file such views, and their staff will be more receptive to doing so if there is drafting help provided.

Reports are not the final word, of course. Floor debate when a bill is considered can be used to modify or to reinforce statements in the committee report. Colloquies, that is, floor discussions between members who seek to establish a legislative record clarifying the intent of Congress on a particular point in a bill, can be prearranged and even prewritten for this purpose. The legislation adopted in 1981 to extend for four years the operating authority of the Overseas Private Investment Corporation included a broad provision on "additionality" of OPIC insurance which had been added by the Senate Foreign Relations Committee. The committee report filled in the committee's intentions, but after further behind-the-scenes discussions, the chairman of the committee and ranking minority member agreed to include an explanation in the chairman's floor statement during Senate floor debate on the bill. The "explanation" modified the committee's intent as stated earlier in the report. The purpose of the change was to accommodate OPIC officials in order to avoid a floor fight over the amendment; the effect was to alter subtly what the committee had done.

Floor Consideration of Bills

The House has a step prior to floor consideration which the Senate does not have: the House Rules Committee. Controversial bills normally reach the House floor only after a special resolution or "rule" recommended by the Rules Committee has been adopted by the House. The chairman of the committee reporting a bill appears before the Rules Committee to request a resolution providing for the bill's immediate consideration. The rule may waive points of order which would otherwise lie against the bill. If the rule allows unlimited floor amendments, it is called an "open rule." If floor amendments are limited, it is a "closed rule." The rule also specifies the time allowed for debate.

Obtaining a favorable rule from the Rules Committee is important to a bill's success. Supporters of the bill as it is reported from committee seek a rule sharply limiting debate and amendments. Critics of the bill seek an open rule, lengthy debate, or no rule at all. It is unlikely, however, that the Rules Committee will refuse to grant a rule, unless portions of the House leadership oppose a bill. Late in the Ninety-Sixth Congress, supporters of the Export Trading Company Act sought to bring the bill to the floor but were opposed by the chairman of the House Banking Committee, who claimed that his committee needed more time to study the bill, which had originally been referred to four different committees. The House Rules Committee never formally considered the issue but let it be known that they were not ready to grant a rule under the circumstances.

If there is wide support for a reported bill and amendments are not expected, it can be brought up in the House without a rule under a procedure called "suspension of the rules"; in the Senate it can be passed by a unanimous consent procedure. Persons who have objections to minor bills need to watch these two procedures very carefully, or they will suddenly discover the bill they oppose has been enacted. Motions can be made in the House on Mondays or Tuesdays or during the last six days of a session to suspend the rules and pass any reported bill or resolution. If a majority of the members present second the motion, it will be put to a vote after 40 minutes of debate. Amendments are not in order, except for those included in the motion when it is made. Two-thirds of the members voting, a quorum being present, are required to suspend the rules and pass the bill.

Suspension of the rules is more difficult in fact than it would appear. Many members of the House believe the procedure is subject to abuse and ought to be used sparingly. They often rally behind any member who objects to suspension of the rules. Because suspension of the rules cuts off opportunities to amend the bill, members who wish to offer or support an amendment oppose suspension. Trying for suspension of the rules and failing to get it may call attention to the controversial features of a bill and arouse resentment among members who feel the bill managers were trying to slip something through. Thus, failing to get suspension may raise the controversiality of a bill and virtually guarantee that the bill will face a flurry of amendments if subsequently brought to the floor under an open rule.

The Senate has an unofficial unanimous consent procedure which, like suspension of the rules in the House, is used to clear the calendar of noncontroversial measures. The chairman and ranking minority member of the Senate committee which has reported the bill notify the Senate floor leaders of their respective parties that they believe the bill can be adopted by unanimous consent, with or without committee amendments. The floor leaders then make available to every senator a notice that the bill is proposed for unanimous consent adoption. If no senator objects within 24 hours, the floor leaders will move the bill by unanimous consent, probably at the end of the day. No more than two senators, one from each party—usually the floor leaders—need be present. Much time is saved by the procedure, but the risk that a bill will slip through without adequate review is considerable.

Most senators and their personal office and committee staff do not have time to study closely all the legislation under consideration in committees on which they do not serve. They wait until a bill is reported before they give it close scrutiny. Frequently a bill is recommended for unanimous consent consideration only a few days after the committee report on the bill is filed. Because senators do not wish to obstruct the actions of their colleagues needlessly, no senator is likely to object to the unanimous consent procedure unless someone points out something about the bill to which the senator should have serious objections.

Those who oppose a bill or particular provisions in a bill sometimes give up in frustration when a bill is reported unanimously from committee. They neglect the opportunity to gain bargaining leverage by slowing a bill's passage in the Senate. A single senator can prevent use of the unanimous consent procedure, although by objecting the senator incurs a moral obligation to his colleagues to state the basis for his concern and to follow through with a proposal to amend the bill or to try to reach some other agreement with the bill's backers. If the senator is irreconcilably opposed to the bill, he or she is free, of course, to attempt to filibuster the bill or use other parliamentary tactics to prevent the bill's enactment. All the senator's colleagues expect is that the senator have serious legislative concerns and pursue them seriously.

The traditional manner for consideration of bills in the Senate, of course, is under conditions of unlimited debate and with any amendment in order. Senate rules do not require amendments to be germane except for amendments to appropriations bills, budget resolutions, or bills considered following cloture. To expedite Senate business, however, the Senate has developed a practice which is similar to obtaining a rule from the House Rules Committee. Whenever possible, the Senate tries to work out by unanimous consent a "time agreement" for consideration of a bill. Time agreements can take many forms, but they usually limit the time for debate on the bill and on first-degree and second-degree amendments. First-degree amendments amend the bill text as reported from committee. Second-degree amendments amend first-degree amendments. Amendments beyond the second-degree are not in order in the Senate; for example, an amendment to amend an amendment to an amendment to the bill would be ruled out of order.

Time agreements usually include a germaneness rule which further limits amendments to those germane to the bill being considered. To be germane, an amendment must not add new subject matter or amend other legislation or otherwise expand the scope of the bill. "Scope" is a term of art which leaves the Parliamentarian some flexibility to decide whether an amendment is germane or not. Time agreements work to the advantage of supporters of the bill, so agreements are often hard to reach on highly controversial bills.

If a unanimous consent agreement to limit debate cannot be reached in the Senate, cloture can be invoked by three-fifths of the total membership of the Senate. Cloture was rarely used by the Senate before the 1970's, but it has been used frequently in recent years. Because cloture has become relatively common, the mere circulation by the floor leadership of a petition to invoke cloture, which requires the signatures of 16 senators, is often enough to persuade other senators to agree to end debate. The cloture procedure takes at least two days to force debate to a close, even if only a single senator is conducting a filibuster; it takes longer if there is a substantial number of senators engaged in the filibuster. A cloture petition must be submitted 48 hours before it is voted upon. Once cloture has been adopted, each senator may have one hour to debate the bill, which means 100 hours of debate if each senator uses his or her limit. Amendments submitted prior to cloture may be called up for a vote if they are germane and otherwise in order under the rules of the Senate, even if time for debate has been exhausted. Voting on amendments can take many hours if a sufficient number of senators insist on roll call votes. At the close of a session (or just prior to a long recess), the threat by a senator to filibuster or employ other parliamentary delaying tactics becomes a powerful device even though cloture could be adopted.[29]

The Senate also has a tradition which enables individual senators to delay floor consideration of bills by placing a "hold" on them. Senators do so by notifying the majority leader or minority leader, usually by letter, of their desire to be informed before a bill is brought up on the floor. A "hold" is a much more serious step than simply objecting to approval of a bill by unanimous consent. A "hold" implies an intention to filibuster a bill, or at least to offer major, controversial amendments to a bill. Minority holds are less effective because the majority may call up a bill anyway, but they are usually observed for a few days at least. Holds are not usually permitted on appropriations bills or tax bills although a senator can sometimes get even one of these essential measures delayed for a day or two, if he or she has a good reason.

Floor scheduling of bills is much more flexible in the Senate than in the House. The leadership on both sides of the aisle meet almost daily to review the legislative calendar. Bills carrying out the President's program and those that are necessary to meet statutory deadlines for extension or enactment of certain measures are given priority. When the majority party is different from the President's party, there can be tension over scheduling bills requested by the President and those favored by the Senate majority. The President's proposals are usually considered first, if only because the Senate minority can filibuster to prevent the Senate from considering other measures first. The leadership can block floor consideration of nonessential bills, but any senator can find an opportunity to offer the substance of a bill as a nongermane amendment to a pending Senate authorization bill. In scheduling, as in all Senate business, tolerance and comity are the norm, and a determined senator can almost always bring his pet proposal before the full Senate in one form or another.

Floor schedules in the House are more systematic and predictable. The House leadership works closely with the Rules Committee and the chairmen of other House committees to fix the date and time allowed for consideration of each bill. The House schedule is often projected two or three weeks ahead with considerable accuracy. Certain days of the week and month are reserved for consideration of particular kinds of bills, primarily private bills, and noncontroversial measures. Major controversial bills almost always reach the House floor under a rule recommended by the Rules Committee and adopted by the House. The tighter rules and procedures for scheduling bills in the House, together with the rule against nongermane floor amendments, make it very difficult for an individual representative to have his favorite proposal considered by the House unless the majority leadership wants it to be considered.[30] The rules and procedures reinforce the power of House committee chairmen and elected party leadership, thus helping to keep the House more hierarchical than the Senate.

Before a bill is considered on the floor of either House, staff must prepare floor statements for members, amendments, talking points, and fall-back amendments, plus any colloquies which can be prearranged between members. Support must also be organized for or against anticipated amendments and the bill itself. Close coordination at this stage between staff and outside groups with similar viewpoints is often critical. Positions are usually well formulated by this stage, and energy can be concentrated on winning over the uncommitted members or on reaching acceptable compromises between opposing sides. The less left to chance on the floor, the better.

During floor debate and voting on a measure, lobbyists and administration representatives alike have difficulty keeping track of what is happening on the floor and communicating suggestions to the members and staff managing the bill. During roll calls, lobbyists can stand near the elevators to shout cues to members hurrying to the chamber to vote, although this is less effective with the advent of electronic voting in the House. Between votes in the Senate, lobbyists need to know how to make effective use of the public lobby off the Senate floor. Pages carry messages, including letters, efficiently and free of charge to and from members and staff on the floor. Anyone may have a message hand-delivered to his or her senator by giving it to a page in the lobby, *when* the senator is on the floor. The lobby is also the best place to catch staffers hurrying to and from the floor.

Amendments to a Senate or House bill may be formally introduced by any member at any point after the bill is introduced; the bill need not have been reported from committee. The amendment is given a number and printed; it may be obtained from the Senate or House documents rooms, just as bills and reports can be obtained by the public. Members sometimes introduce amendments weeks before a bill is considered on the floor, even when it is still in committee, in order to publicize their position and garner support. Printed or unprinted amendments are sometimes circulated together with "Dear Colleague" letters, and cosponsors are sought, just as is done on behalf of many bills. Printed amendments, however, are just the tip of the iceberg.

Most floor amendments in both the House and Senate are "unprinted," although not necessarily unexpected. Members of either body may wish to surprise the bill's managers and supporters with an amendment which is superficially attractive and cannot be readily discredited in debate. If the bill managers and supporters, which include in most cases the administration, know in advance that an amendment will be offered and see its text, they will prepare counterarguments and substitutes for the amendment. Members planning to offer floor amendments face a dilemma; making an amendment known early forewarns and arms the opposition; offering a surprise amendment leaves little time to gather support and raises suspicions about the motivations and true objectives of those offering the amendment.

A strategy often used is to introduce a printed amendment which, if adopted, would achieve even more than the amendment's sponsors believe is really necessary. This is an amendment which stakes out a bargaining position. If bargaining between the bill's sponsors and the amendment's sponsors does not yield a satisfactory compromise before the bill is considered on the floor, the sponsors of the printed amendment may offer an unprinted amendment which can be described as a compromise offer but which in fact would achieve all the essential objectives originally sought. The bill managers may feel constrained to offer an alternative compromise in order to appear to their colleagues to be reasonable and flexible. The result can be a bargaining process carried out on the floor of the Senate or House in the form of amendments and counteramendments which are often debated at length and revised considerably before a compromise is reached or one side decides to call for a vote.

Anticipating unprinted floor amendments is primarily the responsibility of committee staff who will assist the floor managers of the bill. They welcome clues and assistance from outsiders in divining the intentions of members who may be considering offering floor amendments. Correspondingly, those who plan to offer surprise floor amendments are well-advised to conceal their intentions from the bill managers and the committee staff as much as possible, even though doing so is a mild breach of etiquette. Bill managers try to persuade their colleagues to inform them of probable amendments, but surprises are common and seem to go unpunished, except where a junior member of a committee presents an unpleasant surprise to the committee chairman.

Following floor debate and the amendment process from the public galleries can be entertaining, but it is not especially useful, unless one is listening for possible errors in what members say. Members have a few hours after they speak to correct the transcript which will be printed that night in the *Congressional Record*. If you notice a statement made during floor debate which the member may wish to correct, notify the member or his staffer immediately. Once the *Record* has been printed, mistakes are more difficult to correct. The *Record* contains printer's errors, of course, and there is a procedure for correcting those which can be extended somewhat to correct other errors. The corrections will only appear later in "official" versions of the *Record,* but that is what counts if a court case some day hinges on a word in the *Record.*

Voting in the House and Senate takes three forms: voice vote, show of hands, and recorded vote. Noncontroversial matters are disposed of quickly by voice votes, with the presiding officer judging the preponderance of "yeas" or "nays." If the voice vote seems to have been close or if some member wishes to gauge the views of members present on the floor, a show of hands (called a "division of the House") may be requested by any member and is invariably granted. The presiding officer counts the hands and announces the result. The *Record* shows the number voting each way but not the names of those voting.

Because they are so time-consuming, recorded votes are usually reserved for major issues. Although the House of Representatives now votes by electronic device, both when meeting in the Committee of the Whole[31] and in the House, a recorded vote takes about 30 minutes to complete, as does a roll call vote in the Senate. Both bodies seek to bunch recorded votes back-to-back at times announced in advance (this is especially true of items on the House suspension calendar and treaties and nominations on the Senate executive calendar), but any member can request a roll call or recorded vote. In the Senate one-fifth of those senators present on the floor must concur before the request is approved. When the House is meeting in the Committee of the Whole, as it usually is when legislation is considered, 25 of the members must concur before the request is granted. As a practical matter, both bodies routinely agree to the requests of individual members for record votes, demurring only when a member clearly and repeatedly abuses the privilege in order to obstruct the proceedings of the House or Senate—a rare occurrence.

Deciding whether to seek a record vote on a bill or an amendment is a tactical decision. There is a working assumption that record votes are stronger, clearer assertions of the position held by the majority favoring a proposition. A voice vote carries with it the illusion of unanimity, or near unanimity if opposing voices were actually heard by witnesses. There is also the possibility that the vote was cast by a handful of members on the floor who were indifferent to the result or unrepresentative of how the whole body would have voted if a recorded vote had been held.

Members know they cannot easily be held individually accountable for nonrecorded votes. There is no official record of their presence on the floor during the vote, let alone how they voted. A record vote, on the other hand, appears in black and white for the scrutiny of constituents, interest groups, and political opponents as well as supporters. Scores are kept by all manner of groups on who voted which way and how often.

Proponents of a measure customarily seek recorded votes on issues on which they expect to win handily. They believe the other body will be impressed by the margin of victory, thus smoothing the proponents' way when the other body acts on the measure. On the other hand, I have known senators to bring up an amendment consisting of language expected to be in a House bill but unpopular in the Senate and thereby deliberately lose a roll call vote by so wide a margin as to discourage the House from persisting with the language.

Recorded votes are sometimes avoided in order to conceal the extent of opposition to a measure. Senator Culver decided to avoid a roll call on an amendment in 1978 because he expected 20 to 30 votes to be cast against it. He hoped in conference to persuade the House conferees that the Senate's voice vote on the amendment implied that it was noncontroversial in the Senate. Unfortunately, the record does not show whether the ploy was successful.[32]

Conference Committees

Everyone who has studied American government has been taught that when a bill passes the House and Senate in different versions, a conference committee is appointed to resolve differences between the two versions in an agreed version which must then pass both houses. The fact is that there are ways to obtain an agreed version of a bill without appointing a conference committee.

When one House passes a bill, it is delivered to the other House with a request for concurrence. The leadership must then decide whether to "hold the bill at the desk" or refer it to an appropriate committee. If action on a companion measure (a bill judged to be nearly identical to the one passed by the other chamber) is likely to occur within a few weeks, the bill will probably be held at the desk until action on the companion measure is completed; otherwise, the bill is referred to the committee. Assuming, for example, that the bill at the desk is a House bill, the Senate would complete floor consideration of its own bill; then, in a single amendment to the House bill, the Senate would substitute the *text* of the Senate bill for the *text* of the House bill and send the amended House bill back to the House.

When one chamber returns a bill to the other chamber with amendments, the chamber returning the bill may either request the other chamber's concurrence in the amendments or request a conference on the bill and name its conferees. The chamber receiving the amended bill—the House, in the example above, receiving a House bill amended by the Senate—may accede to the action of the other body, in which case the measure is said to be "cleared" for enrollment and transmission to the White House. Or the chamber receiving the amended bill may further amend it and send it back to the other chamber or agree to a conference and appoint its own conferees.

A bill may be amended twice by each House; for example, a House bill amended by the Senate may be amended by the House, then by the Senate again, and once more by the House. Further amendments by either body would be subject to a point of order in either body. Any of these amendments may range from complete substitutes to technical corrections. In other words, it is possible to bounce a bill back and forth, like a Ping-Pong ball, between the Senate and the House, with each player catching the ball and marking it differently before hitting it back to the other side.

You may well ask why the two bodies would go to the trouble of shuttling a bill back and forth when it seems simpler to appoint a conference committee. The primary reason is that some bills are not worth the trouble of a conference. Using the unanimous consent procedure in the Senate and suspension of the rules in the House, a bill can move quickly from one chamber to the other with a minimum of time invested by members and a maximum of coordination by Senate and House committee staff. A secondary consideration is that shuttling a bill back and forth via the Senate unanimous consent procedure and the House suspension calendar enables the bill managers (the members who managed the bill on the floor of the House, usually the chairman and ranking minority member of the committee from which the bill was reported) to offer amendments while discouraging members from offering minor amendments. As noted above, bills considered under suspension in the House are voted up or down on the basis of a single motion which contains any amendments the bill managers wish to incorporate. A member wishing to amend a bill returned by the Senate must either persuade the bill managers to include the amendment in the motion or try to defeat the motion in the hope of forcing the managers either to call a conference with the other body or to seek a rule for House consideration of the bill. Bills considered by the unanimous consent procedure in the Senate are usually voted up or down without amendment, but sometimes the bill managers propose a single amendment to be approved unanimously. A senator who cannot persuade the bill managers to incorporate his amendment has no recourse except to object to the unanimous consent request, thereby forcing regular consideration of the bill or the calling of a conference. Members of both bodies recognize that their amendments may not prevail within a conference committee or may not be within the scope of a conference. Conferences are limited to consideration of matters falling within one of the two versions of the bill and may not include extraneous matter not adopted by either House nor dollar amounts exceeding the higher figure in the two versions. Therefore, members do not often try to force the bill managers to call for a conference committee.

If a conference is desired, conferees are named by the Speaker of the House and Presiding Officer of the Senate upon the recommendation of the chairmen of the committees reporting the bill in each chamber. Conferees almost always include the chairmen and ranking minority members of the committee and subcommittee which reported the bill, plus a few senior committee members. Lobbyists often miss a bet by not suggesting who should serve as conferees. A relatively junior subcommittee chairman may have brought his bill all the way to conference only to be sold out by a handful of senior members of the full committee who control the conference committee.

A motion to instruct the conferees to insist on certain language may be offered after the Senate (or House) has agreed to a request to join in a conference but before the conferees are appointed. The purpose of a motion to instruct conferees is to bind the hands of the conferees in order to prevent or require specific concessions to the conferees from the other chamber. Instructions to conferees are usually observed although they are not binding; that is, no point of order lies against a conference report which ignores the instructions. If there is good reason to suspect that the conferees will agree to something in conference which a majority of the House (or Senate) strongly opposes, someone in the majority is likely to offer a motion to instruct the conferees. If the motion succeeds, the conferees will have to decide whether to risk bringing back from conference a report inconsistent with the instructions.

The House has a rule which is intended to discourage House conferees from accepting Senate language which is "nongermane" to the version of the bill passed by the House. If a conference report contains provisions which the House Parliamentarian considers to be nongermane, any member of the House may insist that the nongermane provisions be voted upon separately from the rest of the conference report. The House does not relish having nongermane Senate amendments forced upon it; remember that Senate floor amendments are often adopted which have no relevance to the underlying bill. Unless the House conferees make a very strong case to their colleagues, the House is likely to vote down the nongermane Senate amendments. House conferees use the House germaneness rule with some success to try to persuade Senate conferees to drop Senate provisions in conference. The Senate conferees are placed in a bind because they know the House conferees can probably persuade the House Parliamentarian to declare almost any Senate provision nongermane; in that case, the House will probably vote down the provision unless the House conferees fight to save it. Therefore, only those nongermane Senate provisions which are strongly supported by the Senate and House conferees survive in conference reports. Because the Senate has no similar rule, nongermane House provisions (which are rare because the House does not usually permit nongermane floor amendments to House bills) face no unusual obstacles in a conference committee.

Conferees do not necessarily meet in person. Conferences may be conducted by staff, by members talking by telephone, or by a face-to-face meeting of the chairmen of the House conferees and the Senate conferees. Except for very major, divisive issues, it is not worth the trouble to find time for conferees to meet in person.

All conferences, like committee mark-ups, rely heavily on staff to prepare agenda, talking points, compromise proposals, and the conference report. When conferences meet, the House and Senate conferees sit facing each other across a table. A chairman of the conference is elected, usually the chairman of the House or Senate committee which originated the bill. The chairman proceeds through an agenda which lists items where the versions passed by the two Houses differ. The staff from the two committees may have suggested how the differing provisions might be reconciled: the House could recede to the Senate, the Senate could recede to the House, or a compromise provision could be accepted. When items are discussed in a conference committee, staff and administration officials present in the room may be invited to comment, but often only members are allowed to speak. If a consensus does not emerge quickly on an item (conferees are expected to defend the version adopted in their House although their personal views may not accord with that version and the defense is often rather halfhearted), a vote may be taken. A majority of the conferees from each House must agree before an item is approved.

Conferences sometimes become deadlocked over highly controversial differences in the House and Senate versions of bills. The conferees may report back to their respective Houses that they cannot agree and ask that the conference be disbanded, or they may report back agreement on some provisions and disagreement on others. Provisions reported from conference in disagreement must be voted upon separately from the rest of the conference report by each House. Only provisions agreed to by both Houses in identical form can be included in the bill to be sent to the President.

Conferences are usually held in small rooms in the Capitol for the convenience of members who may be called suddenly to vote in the

House or Senate. Although most conferences are open to the public, the small meeting rooms prevent more than a handful of spectators from gaining admission, and they are usually compelled to stand crowded together against a wall for the duration of the meeting. Those who arrive early (admission is first come, first served) may get a place to stand and may even be able to pass handwritten notes to committee staff or members. On the whole, however, persons interested in the outcome of a conference must make their case to members or staff before the conference convenes or during breaks in the conference.

An explanatory statement of managers of the conference is always prepared and printed as part of a conference report. Opportunities for public comment or advice are usually limited to whatever can be communicated via key committee or personal staff. Some conferences on major issues, such as budget resolutions or tax bills, can drag on for weeks, leaving ample opportunities for interested persons to make their views known to conference participants between conference sessions.

Conference reports, together with official signature sheets, are circulated to conferees for review. Few members have time to read the reports, however, so any mistakes must be pointed out to them by someone who has reviewed the reports carefully. Obtaining an advance copy of a conference report depends upon the same informal access to members or staff which is necessary to obtain other committee reports before adoption or publication.

A conference report is usually voted upon first by the House which *agreed* to convene a conference, followed by the House which first asked for a conference. Proponents of a bill sometimes arrange for the conference report to be voted on first in the House likely to be most favorable to the conference report, in the hope that the other House will be persuaded by the margin of support demonstrated in the first vote. Conference reports are privileged business in both Houses; that is, they may be brought up for a vote as soon as the report is completed and often even before it is printed. Amendments to conference reports are not in order in either House. If the conference report is approved in both Houses, the bill goes to the President, after enrollment. If a conference report is rejected, the conferees may meet again to try to produce a more acceptable report, or they may inform the House and Senate that they cannot reach agreement. Most bills which reach the conference stage get adopted in some form before adjournment.[33]

Enrollment and Signing of Bills

Enrollment of a bill passed in identical versions by both Houses consists of very careful preparation of the final version by the enrolling clerk of the House in which the bill originated, printing of the enrolled bill on parchment, and signing by the Speaker of the House and President of the Senate. If an interested person has reason to be concerned that an error may occur in the process of enrollment, he or she may ask the enrolling clerk to allow the enrolled bill to be inspected in the clerk's offices in the Capitol. The Committee on House Administration is responsible for presenting the bill to the President.

The process of enrollment and presentation to the President can be accelerated by using messengers to hand-deliver the bill to each of its destinations and by alerting the enrolling clerk and other officials that the bill is an urgent matter. The process can also be slowed down by the enrolling clerks, the Speaker of the House, the President of the Senate (the Vice President of the United States, who may insist on signing bills personally), and the Committee on House Administration. With the willing or willful efforts of various parties, a bill may reach the White House on the day it passes Congress, or it may not reach the White House for weeks.

The President may sign the bill or he may veto it by returning it unsigned to Congress with his objections. A vetoed bill is usually voted upon immediately; a two-thirds vote of the members present in each body is required to enact a bill despite the President's veto.

Article I, section 7 of the Constitution provides that "If any Bill shall not be returned by the President within ten Days (Sundays excepted) after it shall have been presented to him, the Same shall be a Law, in like Manner as if he had signed it, unless the Congress by their Adjournment prevent its Return, in which Case it shall not be a Law."

The adjournment of Congress enables the President to "pocket veto" bills passed during the preceding 10 days, that is, to prevent a bill from becoming law without stating his objections to it and without running the risk that Congress would override the veto. Because many bills are passed in the final days of a session of Congress, the date of adjournment can become critical. Equally critical is the date on which the bill "shall have been presented" to the President. By custom, the date on which the enrolled and signed parchment copy of the bill is delivered to the White House is the date from which the 10-day period is calculated. Accelerating or delaying the process by which a passed bill reaches the White House can determine the fate of the bill.[34]

Special Rules for Money Matters

What has been said to this point about the legislative process must be modified by the special rules which apply to the consideration of money matters: revenue bills, appropriations, and budget measures. Article I, section 7 of the Constitution provides that "all bills for raising revenue shall originate in the House of Representatives." By tradition, appropriations bills are also considered first by the House, although in 1981 the Senate passed its bill appropriating funds for foreign aid before the House acted.

Revenue bills (taxes) are within the jurisdiction of the House Ways and Means Committee and the Senate Finance Committee. The Joint Committee on Taxation (comprised of members of the Ways and Means and Finance Committees) employs a staff of tax experts who advise the two committees on the meaning and effects of tax provisions and who can recommend language for bills or amendments. Writing tax bills is the specialized province of staff of the three committees, of the Department of Treasury, and of a great host of lawyers outside the government. Major tax bills are not passed often; when they are, the intensity of the struggle is remarkable. Tax specialists tend to have the inside track in shaping tax measures, because tax legislation must be carefully drafted in order to survive Internal Revenue Service interpretations and court rulings with the effect the drafters intended. Tax specialists include both tax economists and tax lawyers, and the only thing the groups agree upon is the incompetence of the other group in setting tax policy.

The Senate has more opportunities to initiate major tax legislation than the Constitution implies. The House periodically sends minor tariff bills and other minor revenue measures to the Senate. The Senate Finance Committee makes a practice of holding a number of the House-passed bills as potential vehicles for more significant tax legislation. By inserting a major Senate tax package as an amendment to a minor House revenue bill, the Senate can initiate tax legislation while technically observing the Constitutional requirement that revenue bills originate in the House. Because successful tax legislation depends upon collaboration between the Senate Finance Committee and the House Ways and Means Committee, the Senate seldom initiates tax measures to which the House Ways and Means Committee is known to be decidedly hostile

Persons seeking minor tariff adjustments or other special tax relief should keep in mind three perils they will face in the tax legislative process. First, a minor tax bill or provision frequently becomes a vehicle, or hostage, or bargaining chip in efforts by the tax-writing committees to enact more significant tax legislation. Second, the tax-writing committees maintain rather strict, limited schedules for considering minor tax measures, and they do not wish to be bothered by such items "out of season." Third, the fate of a minor tax change will turn upon the balance between the strength of advocacy by an interested member or members of the tax-writing committees and the strength of opposition, which is almost always related to the cost (revenue loss) of the tax change. Revenue estimates are prepared by the staff of the Joint Committee on Taxation and the staff of the Department of the Treasury. The estimates frequently differ, with the not-surprising tendency of estimates made by the Joint Committee to come closer to the political preferences of members of the tax-writing committees, while estimates made by Treasury staff closely support the tax proposals and policies preferred by the administration.

The tasks of a tax lobbyist are rather obvious, given the basic structure in which tax legislation is enacted: (a) a tax proposal must be drafted very carefully, (b) a strong champion on the tax-writing committees must be enlisted, (c) a favorable revenue estimate must be obtained, and (d) the proposal must be presented to the tax-writing committees at the appropriate time but should be helped along through the gauntlet without becoming a pawn in larger tax contests. Strong support within the tax-writing committees is essential because their exclusive jurisdiction over tax matters is seldom challenged. Tax measures, like appropriations, do not get attached to other legislation, because members do not wish to offend the tax-writing and appropriations committees, which control legislation of interest to every member, by attempts to bypass their jurisdiction. Floor amendments to tax bills are also usually unsuccessful; in most cases, they are offered to protest the decisions of the tax committees and to force members to record their positions publicly.

Appropriations bills are the exclusive province of the appropriations committees, but the significance of appropriations has eroded somewhat as other committees have authorized federal agencies to guarantee or insure private borrowers and as the Congressional budget process, controlled by the budget committees, has begun to constrain federal spending. In recent years, the appropriations committees have begun to extend their control over federal agencies by including in annual appropriations bills limitations on the amounts federal agencies may lend, guarantee, or insure, even if no appropriation of federal money is required. The Export-Import Bank, which provides loans, guarantees, and insurance to support United States exports, receives no appropriated funds, but since 1975 the appropriations committees have included in annual appropriations bills limits on the amount of loans, guarantees, and insurance the Export-Import Bank can sign each fiscal year.

Appropriations bills are subject to a specific germaneness rule in the Senate.[35] Basically, the rule seeks to exclude "legislation" from appropriations bills, whether in bills reported from committee or in floor amendments. Clever drafting of bill provisions or amendments as limitations on expenditures can usually achieve the intended substantive effect while passing muster with the Senate Parliamentarian. Anyone wishing to place a rider on an appropriations bill, however, should get drafting advice from an expert and have the language checked with the Parliamentarian's office before introducing the amendment.

The relationship between authorization bills and appropriations bills is often misunderstood. Funds can be appropriated for programs which have not been authorized by statute. Appropriations may also exceed levels provided or limitations expressed in authorization statutes. Most of the time, the appropriations committees avoid proposing spending which exceeds limits set in authorization bills, but there are numerous instances in which appropriations have exceeded authorization limits and have even been provided for programs before authorization bills were adopted. Placing limitations in authorization bills warns the appropriations committee that an appropriation bill setting a higher level may face a challenge on the floor; it also allows the authorizing committees to claim credit for limiting expenditures.

The opposite of a limitation contained in an authorization is an "earmarking" of an account which must be spent for specified purposes. Authorization committees try to earmark funds for programs they like but which may be opposed by the appropriations committees or the administration. An appropriations bill can override earmarkings in an authorization bill just as easily as it can override limitations, but the appropriations committees would rather not do so. Persons interested in securing or limiting funds for particular programs usually seek earmarkings or limitations in the authorization process, although they realize the appropriations process must be fought separately. Authorization bills are a warm-up for the main event, as far as funding is concerned.

Floor consideration of appropriations bills falls under special provisions of both House and Senate rules. Appropriations bills in the House, for example, are privileged matters which may be brought up on the floor at any time without a rule from the Rules Committee. A rule is usually obtained, however, in order both to waive points of order which may lie against the appropriations bill and to limit the time for debate. The Senate does not provide for privileged consideration of appropriations bills on the floor, but it does have a rule which limits the kinds of floor amendments which may be offered to appropriations bills. Rule XVI prohibits amendments, for example, which would increase an appropriation above the level in the appropriations bill being considered, unless a higher level were requested by the President or approved in an authorization Act, or unless the amendment were moved by a committee of appropriate jurisdiction.

The most confusing part of the appropriations process is the use of "continuing resolutions" to appropriate funds for the government when one or more of the 13 regular appropriations bills for a current fiscal year (October 1 to September 30) have not been enacted. Continuing resolutions are joint resolutions to continue funding federal programs temporarily while the regular appropriations process is being completed. The basic rule about continuing resolutions is that basically there are no rules about continuing resolutions. They may be enacted for any period of time within a fiscal year. They may continue appropriations at the previous year's level or at a higher or lower level, although the level is usually lower, whether that matches the level of the previous year's appropriation or any current year appropriation bill passed by the House or the Senate. Like regular appropriations, continuing resolutions may provide appropriations for newly authorized programs and even for programs which Congress has never authorized. The House forbids appropriations for items not authorized by law (Clause 2 of House Rule XXI) but does not consider continuing resolutions to be general appropriations bills subject to the ban. The Senate permits the Senate Appropriations Committee to recommend appropriations for unauthorized programs in any appropriations bill, although Senate Rule XVI bars floor amendments for the same purpose.

Continuing resolutions may be proposed at any time, but they are usually brought up just a week or two before the beginning of a new fiscal year (October 1) or before the existing continuing resolution expires. Continuing resolutions are handled at the full committee level by the appropriations committees, which tends to diminish the influence of the appropriations subcommittee chairmen and ranking minority members, who are more influential when regular appropriations bills are considered.

Continuing resolutions have become increasingly common as Congress has found it harder and harder to complete regular appropriations bills before the beginning of the fiscal year. At least one continuing resolution has been enacted each year since 1954; 27 continuing resolutions were enacted between 1972 and 1980. Regular appropriations were never enacted in fiscal year 1973 for foreign assistance or for the Departments of Labor and of Health, Education, and Welfare. Regular appropriations were not adopted for foreign assistance for fiscal years 1980 and 1981. In each case, the programs received funding under continuing resolutions for the entire fiscal year.

President Reagan took the unprecedented action of vetoing a continuing resolution in November 1981 because the spending levels would have exceeded his budget request to the Congress. The failure to enact a continuing resolution left most federal agencies without funding for a few days, a situation which also arose several times during the 1970's when Congress failed to pass a continuing resolution before appropriations expired. The legal situation confronting federal agencies when appropriations expire is not altogether clear. Presumably agencies may continue to expend funds to close down the government in an orderly fashion. Recent interpretations have justified expenditures to carry on essential services necessary to protect life, liberty, and property. If lapses in appropriations occur in the future as frequently as they have in the past, Congress and the executive branch may try to determine in advance which federal government programs are so essential that they must continue even when appropriations expire.

The Congressional budget process is another special phenomenon which requires special attention. The Budget Act of 1974 laid down a timetable for Congressional consideration of budgetary matters, provided for adoption each fiscal year of concurrent resolutions limiting federal spending, and placed the responsibility for recommending budget limits and enforcing the timetables and limits set by the Budget Act in the hands of newly formed budget committees in the House and the Senate. The budget process has become more important as recent Presidents have sought to cut federal spending, and the budget committees have tried to place constraints on authorization and appropriations bills.

Some of the deadlines in the budget timetable are rigorously followed and others are ignored. The first significant deadline is May 15th. By that date authorizing committees are required to report from committee all authorizing bills for a forthcoming fiscal year (October 1 to September 30). For example, authorizations for fiscal year 1986 should be reported by May 15, 1985. The committees strive to meet this deadline by cramming mark-ups into the final two weeks of April and the first two weeks of May. Nearly all authorizing bills are, in fact, reported by May 15th. There is a waiver procedure available for bills reported after May 15th, but the budget committees discourage its use except in unusual circumstances.

Budget resolutions are central to the effort to limit federal expenditures. Soon after May 15th, and before June 15th, the Congress considers and adopts a First Concurrent Budget Resolution, which sets broad spending and revenue targets for the coming fiscal year. Federal programs are lumped into broad budget categories, conforming roughly to the jurisdictions of subcommittees of the appropriations committees. A Second Concurrent Budget Resolution setting more specific but still quite broad targets is supposed to be adopted by September 15th, that is, just before the fiscal year begins. The second resolution is more likely than the first resolution to be delayed, especially if appropriations bills for the impending fiscal year have not been adopted. The Budget Act states that all appropriations bills are to be enacted by the first week of September, but that deadline has yet to be met in any year for all 13 regular appropriations bills, and even authorization bills frequently are not passed until after the fiscal year has begun. A third budget resolution can be passed later in the year, if necessary, in order to adjust the budget to changed circumstances.

The most significant part of the budget process is the effort to compel the authorizing and appropriating committees to keep their bills within the limits set by the budget resolutions, which include projected budget ceilings for the "out years," that is, fiscal years beyond the fiscal year to which the resolution is immediately addressed. Through the "budget reconciliation" process, the budget committees notify the authorizing committees when the programs within their jurisdiction must be cut back in order to meet overall budget limits set in previously adopted budget resolutions. The authorizing committees are then required by the 1974 Budget Act to report to the Senate and House the cuts they will recommend to programs within their committee jurisdiction. A reconciliation measure specifying these reductions is then adopted in a version agreed upon by both bodies and presumably limits the appropriations process as well as the authorization process. The reconciliation process was completed successfully in 1980 and 1981, but it would be foolhardy to predict its future.

Constraints adopted in budget resolutions force authorizing committees and appropriations committees to make unpleasant choices as to which programs within their jurisdiction should bear the brunt of budget cuts and which should enjoy the benefit of whatever increases are possible. Ways to minimize cuts are avidly sought by authorizing and appropriations committees. Some of the devices successfully used are (a) approving budget authority but underestimating or deferring budget *outlays,* which are taken more seriously than budget authority; (b) going off-budget by providing guarantee and insurance authority in place of loans or grants; (c) working the jurisdictional mismatches between authorizing committees to try to increase the room within budget ceilings for funding for favored programs; and (d) taking the higher numbers from each House in conference reports on appropriation bills.

The budget committees have also sought to limit the use of federal credit, that is, the lending, guaranteeing, and insuring activity of federal agencies. These contingent liabilities of the federal government have grown rapidly and are presumed to affect credit markets significantly. The budget committees and appropriations committees continue to look for ways to make sure authorizing committees do not permit such credit activity to grow too rapidly. Many of the programs which use federal "full faith and credit" to back their obligations are not subject to appropriations and are not included in the federal budget presented to Congress by the President. Congress may include these programs in its own estimates of budget outlays and budget authority but seldom chooses to do so.

The budget committees obtain their estimates of revenue and outlays from the Congressional Budget Office and from analyses by committee staff. Disagreements with the administration and with other Congressional committees over estimates can be substantial. The budget committees and their staff seem to have taken on more of a siege mentality as they have become the center of controversy and criticism. Budget cutters seem to evoke the same response among their fellow citizens as do tax collectors.

THE LEGISLATIVE CYCLE

A Congress lasts two years, but the flow of legislative activity is very unevenly distributed within the two-year period. A new Congress convenes in January of odd-numbered years. All members of the House of Representatives having been elected or re-elected the previous November or appointed to fill subsequent vacancies are sworn in and the House adopts its rules and appoints its committees and officers anew. Changes are usually minimal, but since 1970, there have been significant contests for committee chairmenships which previously were filled only on the basis of seniority, that is, the majority member with the longest continuous service on the committee became chairman.

The Senate, which is a continuous body, swears in the one-third or more of its membership which has been newly elected or appointed, elects officers of the Senate, and shuffles committee membership as necessary to accommodate new members and older members who may wish to take advantage of vacancies to switch committee assignments.

Committees in both bodies subsequently meet to adopt rules and form subcommittees. Although many bills will have been introduced on the first day Congress is in session and each day thereafter, committees usually do not begin legislative hearings before February or often March. One reason is that the administration does not present its budget for the next fiscal year until late January and detailed presentations by the administration are often not available until mid-February.

The second factor affecting the spring schedule of all authorizing committees is the requirement in the Budget Act of 1974 that all authorizing legislation for the next fiscal year must be reported from the authorizing committees by May 15th. The authorizing committees schedule their mark-up sessions for late April and early May and try to complete hearings on authorizing legislation by late March or early April. Thus authorizing committees have little time to hold oversight hearings between mid-February and mid-May. Oversight hearings by authorizing committees and subcommittees (as opposed to committees or subcommittees which have solely oversight responsibilities) are usually held in the periods from late May to late July or September through mid-November.

Legislation which does not authorize appropriations or affect federal budget authority or outlays or revenues may be reported from committee at any time, but authorizing committees tend to slow their pace of legislative activity after the authorization bills are reported in May. Because authorization bills usually move on a faster track than nonauthorization bills, proponents of a nonauthorizing measure frequently try to attach it to an authorization bill in order to expedite the measure's passage. Opponents seek to decouple the measures, hoping delay will kill the nonauthorizing portion while the authorization proceeds toward enactment.

Floor consideration of authorization bills usually does not begin until May, because the authorizing committees do not report most authorizations before then. Between late January and early May, both chambers are in the odd position of having ample floor time to consider bills, but few important bills to consider and no pressing deadlines for completing action. Controversial bills may be debated for days in the House and for weeks in the Senate in the spring of each year. Noncontroversial items reported from committee are usually passed promptly.

The second session (year) of a Congress entails a more crowded spring schedule for floor consideration of legislation, because there is a lengthy calendar in each House of bills reported in the first session but not considered on the floor. Unfinished authorization and appropriations bills from the previous year can be considered. The first year of a new Congress, by contrast, has no carry-over of legislation to consider; each bill must be introduced and reported afresh, even if considered by a prior Congress.

Summertime in each session is when priority is given to authorization and appropriations bills. In theory, action should be completed on all such measures within seven days after Labor Day or before September 15 when the Second Concurrent Budget Resolution is supposed to be adopted by both Houses of Congress.[36] The deadlines are seldom met, however, and fiscal year 1982, for example, began on October 1, 1981, with only one appropriation bill having passed Congress. Thus, contrary to the ideal schedule set forth in the Budget Act of 1974, it has become common for authorization and appropriation bills to be considered in September, October, and November, and even in the early months of the second session of a Congress.[37]

The legislative pace accelerates at the end of a session, especially at the end of a Congress (the second session). Legislative logjams get broken under the threat of expiration of key statutes, together with a more liberal procedure for considering bills. The rules of the House of Representatives provide that the rules may be suspended for consideration of bills during the last six days of a session (not just on Monday and Tuesday of each week). In addition, there are usually bills of national importance which must be passed in the closing days of a session. Consequently, opportunities arise to "log-roll" measures into omnibus packages of legislation.

Measures which have languished for months in committee or on the calendar suddenly gain new life. The bad reputation of Congress for passing ill-considered, poorly drafted, special interest legislation is largely due to measures patched together in the final hours of a Congressional session, but many important and useful measures get approved through the same process.[38]

The second year of a Congress is always an election year, which may mean lengthier recesses than in odd years, together with a frantic effort to complete legislative business by the end of September. The effort fails more often than it succeeds, so a "lame duck" session of the Congress after the November elections is customary. Lame duck sessions have a tinge of irresponsibility in the public mind, but they have not differed greatly from other end-of-session legislative melees. One should expect lame duck sessions to pass a considerable amount of legislation, for both good and ill. No one seriously interested in the Congressional process should plan to take a vacation in mid-November or early December of an election year on the assumption that either a lame duck session will not be held or will do nothing of significance.

The two-year legislative cycle should be considered when proposing or opposing legislative action. Major controversial measures are seldom enacted in less than two years. The earlier they are introduced in a new Congress, the better the chances of enactment before the end of the Congress. Proposals which can be incorporated into authorization bills should be advanced early in a session in order to be included in the early May mark-ups. If the proposal is not included in the bills reported in May, floor amendments may be the only viable route to enactment. But if a committee chairman is strongly in favor of a bill, he or she can usually muster a majority to report out the bill at any time. Who supports a measure and who opposes it makes more difference in the end than the timing and skillful use of legislative procedures.

The legislative process is influenced not only by the detailed rules for consideration of bills but also by unwritten rules of appropriate behavior. Those who wish to work successfully with members of

Congress must develop sensitivity to the milieu within which Congress operates. Often the only sure guide is an innate sense of what is appropriate or legitimate in a specific situation, but I would suggest a few simple guidelines.

First, Congress is a collegial body which depends upon elementary concepts of fair play in order to function at all. Members are expected to be persistent and even aggressive in using the formal rules to advance their positions on issues, but obstructionism is not acceptable. Obstructionism is a subjective matter, of course, but most people would consider obstructionist a member of Congress who constantly tried to delay proceedings in committee or on the floor, or who always objected to unanimous consent agreements. Members generally sense the difference between waging a good, clean fight and throwing a monkey wrench into the gearbox. When working with a member of Congress, you do neither the member nor yourself any good by encouraging actions which imply a readiness to ride roughshod over the member's colleagues.

A corollary to fair play is to avoid personalizing legislative politics and never embarrass a member of Congress by the positions you ask him or her to take. Most members strive to bring dignity to the legislative process. At times the facade may seem thin, but they will cling to the facade. They will resent anyone who tries to rip it away.

The second major guideline is to take as little of a member's time as possible—always. Members are terribly busy, but most feel even busier than they are. They would rather see you on six different occasions for ten minutes at a time, than once for sixty minutes. Never insist on a personal visit for business you can transact by telephone. If a matter can be handled with staff, try to do it that way first. Shape what you ask a member to do so as to minimize the amount of his personal time which will be required to do it. If his proxy is all you need at a markup, don't beg for his actual appearance.

Third, be prepared to compromise. The legislative process is fueled by compromise. Members like to reach compromises that at least save face for everyone. Members will seldom wage unyielding fights for a cause, so be ready to help them propose a compromise which is acceptable to you. Otherwise, you may find your position compromised away by your friends.

FOOTNOTES

[1]Since 1789, four senators have been convicted of crimes committed while in office. Since 1940, twenty-four members of the House have been convicted of such crimes. Data is not available on members convicted of, or pleading guilty to, misdemeanors, such as federal or state election law violations or disorderly conduct.

[2]An instructive study of the 1960 and 1964 civil rights bills is Daniel M. Berman, *A Bill Becomes A Law: Congress Enacts Civil Rights Legislation* (2nd ed., New York: The Macmillan Company, 1966).

[3]McCulloch v. Maryland, 17 U.S. (4 Wheat.) 316 (1819).

[4]"HISC Investigates: The Strategy of Exposure, with and without a Legislative Purpose," in Theodore J. Lowi and Randall B. Ripley, eds., *Legislative Politics U.S.A.* (3rd ed., Boston: Little, Brown & Co., 1973), pp. 352-366.

[5]The rationale for the system of separation of powers, but with the comingling implied by checks and balances, is set forth in *The Federalist,* Numbers 47 through 51, by James Madison.

[6]The Founders may not have wished to thwart majority rule, see George W. Carey, "Separation of Powers and the Madisonian Model: A Reply to the Critics," *The American Political Science Review* (Vol. 72, No. 1), March 1978, pp. 151-162.

[7]Barbara Hinckley, "The Seniority System," in Lowi and Ripley, *Legislative Politics U.S.A.*, pp. 122-130, at p. 129.

[8]See James MacGregor Burns, *The Deadlock of Democracy* (Englewood Cliffs, N.J.: Prentice-Hall, 1963) and Richard Bolling, *House Out of Order* (New York: Dutton, 1965).

[9]Joseph S. Clark, ed., *Congressional Reform: Problems and Prospects* (New York: Thomas Y. Crowell Company, 1965), p.vi.

[10]See Leroy N. Rieselbach, *Congressional Reform in the Seventies* (Morristown, N.J.: General Learning Press, 1977). Reform has gone further since Rieselbach's study. Senate Resolution 4, adopted early in 1977, made important changes in Senate rules.

[11]Recent Congresses have passed fewer but lengthier bills. For example, the 80th Congress passed 906 bills with 2,236 pages; the 96th Congress passed 613 bills with 3,583 pages.

[12]The basic study is J. Lieper Freeman, *The Political Process: Executive Bureau–Legislative Committee Relations* (revised ed., New York: Random House, 1965), although Freeman studied only two sides of the triangle.

[13]For additional information see *Studies on the Legislative Veto,* prepared by the Congressional Research Service for the Subcommittee on Rules of the House Committee on Rules, U.S. House of Representatives, February 1980, Committee Print, 96th Congress, 2nd Session.

[14]For the arguments against the Congressional role provided in the War Powers Act, see John G. Tower, "Congress Versus the President: The Formulation and Implementation of American Foreign Policy," *Foreign Affairs,* Vol. 60, No. 2 (Winter 1981/82), pp. 229-246.

[15]The story of Washington's personal appearance before the Senate in 1789 to

discuss negotiating instructions for proposed Indian treaties is retold in George H. Haynes, *The Senate of the United States* (New York: Russell and Russell, 1960), pp. 62-68.

[16]On the Trade Act of 1974 and the negotiation and ratification of the agreements in the Trade Act of 1979, see I.M. Destler, *Making Foreign Economic Policy* (Washington, D.C.: Brookings Institution, 1980).

[17]Numerous studies indicate that elected representatives adopt positions closer to those of their constituents as elections near. See James Kulinski, "Representativeness and Elections: A Policy Analysis," *The American Political Science Review,* Vol. 72, No. 1 (March 1978), pp. 165-177.

[18]Harry McPherson, *A Political Education* (Boston: Little, Brown & Co., 1972), p. 35.

[19]There were 59 members (49 representatives and 10 senators) who chose not to seek re-election in 1979. The number not seeking re-election in 1980 dropped to 39 (34 representatives and 5 senators), a 10-year low in the number of voluntary retirees.

[20]During the 95th Congress (1977-78), 3,800 bills and 714 resolutions were introduced in the Senate, and 15,587 bills and 2,213 resolutions were introduced in the House of Representatives.

[21]On the perils and promises of cosponsorship, see Eric Redman, *The Dance of Legislation* (New York: Simon and Schuster, 1973), pp. 77-100.

[22]See Rule XVII of the Standing Rules of the Senate.

[23]The key hearing on the bill Eric Redman drafted was called with three days' notice; see Redman, *Dance of Legislation,* pp. 110-115.

[24]During the Ninety-Seventh Congress, advance listings of Senate hearings were printed in the *Congressional Record* each Monday and Wednesday.

[25]In the case of the Senate Health Subcommittee hearing on the National Health Service Corps bill, the chairman's statement was prepared by a staffer for another senator, the bill's sponsor; see Redman, *Dance of Legislation,* p. 114.

[26]Questions and answers can sometimes be precooked. See, for example, Redman, *Dance of Legislation,* p. 125.

[27]For guidance on testifying under oath, a common practice in nomination and investigative hearings, I would advise competent, experienced legal counsel.

[28]Open mark-ups are a recent practice. As a legislative assistant to a senator not serving on the committee, Eric Redman could not attend the 1970 mark-up in the Senate Labor and Public Welfare Committee of the bill and report he had written; see Redman, *Dance of Legislation,* pp. 148-152.

[29]The cloture rule is contained in Rule XXII of the Standing Rules of the Senate.

[30]Clause 7 of Rule XVI of the Rules of the House of Representatives provides that "no motion or proposition on a subject different from that under consideration shall be admitted under color of amendment." The House Parliamentarian interprets the germaneness rule very strictly.

[31]The Committee of the Whole is a procedural device which enables the House of Representatives to consider legislation less formally and with a smaller quorum required than when the House itself is deliberating. All members of the House are members of the Committee of the Whole. The House often resolves itself into the

Committee of the Whole for debate and preliminary consideration of a bill, then transforms itself by a stroke of the gavel back into the House in normal session to complete action on the measure.

[32]Elizabeth Drew, *Senator*. (New York: Simon and Schuster, 1979) pp. 63-64.

[33]Over 95 percent of bills sent to conference are enacted by the end of the Congress in which the conference occurs.

[34]For a description of an unsuccessful attempt to accelerate delivery of a bill in order to avoid a veto, see Redman, *Dance of Legislation*, pp. 253-285.

[35]Rule XVI of the Standing Rules of the Senate.

[36]Sections 309 and 310 of the Budget Act of 1974.

[37]Continuing appropriations resolutions have been necessary in every recent Congress.

[38]Note that the National Health Service Corps legislation, whose passage Eric Redman discusses in the *Dance of Legislation*, was passed at the end of a session, despite poor prospects for its passage earlier in the session.

Chapter 7

CORPORATE WASHINGTON REPRESENTATION

DR. FRUZSINA M. HARSANYI*

The date is January 20, 1981. A sunny day in Washington. The most festive and expensive Presidential inauguration in American history has just taken place and the city is teeming with inaugural guests and onlookers. No one can recall when there were so many limousines on the streets of the nation's capital. The owner of a firm renting limousines predicts prosperity for his business on the grounds that Republicans use limousines more than Democrats.

Undoubtedly, many of those limousines are carrying business executives who have come to town for this event. Corporate Washington representatives have been busy for weeks preparing for their arrival; for whether they supported Ronald Reagan or not, the inauguration is an occasion to host dinners and receptions, an excuse to bring together people of influence, an opportunity to see and be seen, to position oneself with the new administration.

No new administration begins with a clean slate, but it does bring with it new people and policies. Candidates from both political parties wait in the wings as the process of filling thousands of positions

---

*Dr. Fruzsina M. Harsanyi is the Director for International Government Affairs for Combustion Engineering, Inc., a diversified international energy systems company. She has worked on domestic and foreign policy issues as a corporation executive, Federal Government official, public interest group lobbyist and university instructor.

in the executive branch begins. Who are these candidates? What are their views? Their qualifications? When will the positions be filled? What happens in the meantime? Who is running the bureaucracy? What policy changes will there be? What are the priority issues for the administration? The Congress?

These are some of the questions that were asked almost as soon as Jimmy Carter conceded to Ronald Reagan on election night. Responsibility for getting the answers rests with the staffs of the government affairs offices of the hundreds of interest groups—among them corporations—that are represented in Washington. Their job is to identify the players, help shape the policies, and communicate both the good and bad news of government decisions to people in "the field" or at "headquarters."

This chapter will explore Washington representation from the corporate perspective. It will examine the ingredients of effective representation by looking at how the corporation organizes itself for the task of communicating its interests to the government. Effective representation depends in part on understanding how Washington works. But equally important, it depends on how an interest—in this case, the corporation—conceptualizes its relationship with the government and how it manages the process of representation.

BUSINESS AND GOVERNMENT: TWO DIFFERENT WORLDS

To begin to understand what makes for effective representation of business interests, it is necessary to understand the social and political environments in which the corporate Washington representative functions. On the one hand, there is the world of which he is a part in Washington; on the other, there is the world of the corporate interests he represents. These two worlds or cultures differ in many respects, and he has to bridge the gap between them.

The difference between the two cultures has an historical source. According to one scholar, it can be traced to the uneven growth of the administrative hierarchies of business and government in the United States.

> Because two sets of administrative hierarchies grew at different periods of time for different reasons to carry out different functions with different objectives, two quite different cultures appeared. The work, attitudes, and perspectives of the business manager and the civil servant became and remained . . . distant and separate . . .[1]

It is Chandler's hypothesis that the adversarial relationship between business and government in the United States goes back to the rise of the large-scale enterprise and its apparent threat to other business. Government responded by legislating restraints on big business through such laws as the Interstate Commerce Act of 1887, the Sherman Antitrust Act in 1890, and the Clayton and Federal Trade Commission Acts of 1914. These laws, and the regulations implementing them, set the tone for a relationship characterized by conflict more often than by cooperation.

Whatever the origins of the adversarial aspect of the relationship, there is plenty to reinforce it. People in business like to describe Washington as not the "real world." Many think that Washington bureaucrats (a catch-all word for just about anybody who works in the government) are insulated from what goes on in the rest of the country and, therefore, have no real sense of how their decisions affect people. They think that bureaucrats cannot understand what the impact of their decisions is on business since, as the expression goes, they have never had to meet a payroll.

Not all business people actually think this way, but this is still the prevalent rhetoric. Washington is a foreign city. It is something to watch on the news, not a place to live in. Everything in Washington is in flux. The players are constantly changing; the product is intangible. Even seasoned Washingtonians admit that sometimes it is difficult not only to see where you are going but to recognize the ground you have covered.

By contrast, the corporation is a structured unit, in which functions are highly differentiated, products are tangible, and objectives are quantifiable. This is not to say that there are no redundancies, ambiguities, and, indeed, politics in a corporation. The difference is one of degree and a question of whether these qualities are essential to accomplishing the primary task of the organization or whether they are incidental.

Because people in business and government operate in different milieus and are organized for the accomplishment of very different tasks, they frequently have difficulty understanding each other's world. Government civil servants who have never been in business (and most have not) act on the basis of their perception of business, and business executives do the same with government. It is worth exploring the most popular of these perceptions (or misperceptions) because they are part of the two worlds in which the corporate Washington rep moves. He must be aware of these perceptions, understand them, and be sensitive to them if he is to develop effective communication between the company he represents and the government.

First, business's views of government. Columnist, William Greider, has described Washington as ". . . a maze of incredible complexity, hundreds of agencies, thousands of bureaus, cubicles within cubicles, impossible webs of interdepartmental task forces. Washington is a marblefront rat's nest of confusion."[2] This description would ring true to many business people. Not understanding the process of government and having difficulty identifying the product, business people cannot figure out "what all those people do." What they see is that government is big—too big—and that it interferes with commerce. They know firsthand of the restrictions on their activities and the costs of compliance resulting from federal regulations. Because business's experience with government is rarely benign, it should not be a surprise that business has been a leading proponent of reducing the size of the federal government and its ever-growing intrusion into the marketplace. The past two Presidential campaigns echoed that theme and found a receptive audience in business as well as the general public.

Business's dislike of the size of the government is reinforced by experiences with its inefficiency. This, of course, also comes in part from not understanding the process by which decisions are made—especially in the executive branch—and not allowing for the magnitude of the tasks assigned to a given department. Instead, business suspects that all too often there is a direct correlation between government inefficiency and incompetence in the bureaucracy. It does not take many experiences to reinforce a stereotype, and most business people can point to at least one useless meeting in the bowels of an executive agency with an uninformed civil servant. They can also cite people who have been appointed to positions of power on the basis of their contribution to a political campaign rather than because of their expertise in a particular subject. This tends to make business cynical about the decision-making process, and many wonder whether their efforts to influence government decisions are worth the candle.

What galls business even more than what it perceives as incompetence or inefficiency is the level of salaries in Washington, not of the political appointees (they are expected to live on psychic income) but of the career government employee. One corporate manager, particularly peeved at seeing government drive up salaries in the job market (he wanted to hire someone who was working for the government), devoted considerable staff time to researching government pay scales and benefits; showing how they are more generous than what is offered in the private sector; and, suggesting that taxpayers should not subsidize this difference. He was not alone in making this case. Whatever its merits, the point here is that business has an impression of overpaid and underworked bureaucrats.

Add to these perceptions the reality of the government's organizational structure where lines of authority are not linear and responsibility is not clear. Under these conditions, policy formulation or conflict resolution of matters that have political implications tends to move at a glacierlike pace. Secretary of State George Schultz, who has traveled in both business and government worlds, describes the government as having

> . . . . a deliberately flat organizational structure, stemming from the concept of checks and balances. The resulting disposition to delay has been compounded in recent years with action-stopping power widely distributed in Congress and in the Executive Branch. Government action is crablike at best, with an overwhelming emphasis on policy formulation as opposed to execution.[3]

By contrast, he notes, business has a pyramidal structure of organization and a very different incentive system from government. To quote Schultz again:

> In government and politics, recognition and, therefore, incentives go to those who formulate policy and maneuver legislative compromise. By sharp contrast, the kudos and incentives in business go to the

> person who can get something done. It is execution that counts. Who can get the plant built, who can bring home the sales contract, who can carry out the financing, and so on.
>
> This contrast between "debating" and "criticizing" organizations, with their dispositions to delay, and "doing" organizations, with their spirit of action, adds to the abrasiveness of the business-government interface. People just have a hard time understanding each other.[4]

The most damning criticism that business has of government—and the one that says more than any other that "they are not like us"—is that government does not know the discipline of the bottom line. No exercise in zero-base budgeting can convince business that anyone in government is held accountable for what is spent and what is gained to justify the expenditure.

The "discipline of the bottom line" is central to business and, therefore, to business's relations with the government. The emphasis on the bottom line explains business's preoccupation with three interrelated subjects: (a) the need to reduce government spending, (b) the cost impact of federal regulations, and (c) the amount of waste in the bureaucracy. The attitude of people in business toward the federal bureaucracy is colored by their experience with and understanding of the staff function in the corporation. Business in general is suspicious, if not disdainful, of the staff function because "staff" does not produce goods. A staff produces decisions, memos, questions, and plans—not products for the marketplace. "Staff" means overhead, and somebody's sales have to pay for it. In this analogy, the United States government is like one big overgrown staff that needs to be watched and periodically trimmed.

The government's stereotype of business is no more charitable and is equally characterized by misperceptions. The first misperception is that business is monolithic. Government, like the public, ascribes a great deal of likemindedness to business, and business itself tends to foster the impression. But this perception of likemindedness confuses the business consensus in support of the free enterprise system with agreement on specific government programs. By and large, a company's stand on specific programs is dictated by what affects its bottom line. That differs from one company to another. In fact, there may be differences even within a company, especially if it is a diversified multinational with several distinct product lines.

Another common misperception is that business is efficient and organized and, therefore, adept at accomplishing any task. But, as one observer noted, "policy is not soap and government is different from Procter & Gamble. You cannot touch policy or clean clothes with it or beautify yourself with it. All you can do is suffer with it. Policy is impalpable."[5] In other words, the organizational skills necessary to make a product and produce a profit are different from the skills needed to affect policy. In fact, corporate organizational structure and the discipline of the bottom line may produce a certain rigidity and shortsightedness in dealing with problems.

What passes for efficiency in one environment may be a constraint in another. Efficiency in producing widgets is not a skill transferrable to the task of defending or promoting one's interests in Washington. And yet, people in government expect business to know what it is doing even in the nonbusiness environment. The dangerous corollary of this view is that if a company does not do what it should (according to government), government assumes that it was the result of a conscious decision by that company. The perception of business as an efficient machine, always in control, does not make sufficient allowance for the human dimension: irrationality, turfism, poor judgment, inadequate information, faulty analysis, hasty action or inaction. These exist in business, as in any organization.

A final perception worth mentioning is government's perception of business as a powerful actor *in the political arena*. The emphasis here is on the political as distinct from the economic or from the political as a by-product of the economic. Focusing on business's power to affect government decisions underestimates the fragmentation of business interests and the variety of resources (human and financial) available to any *one* company. At the same time, it overestimates business's willingness to become involved in public policy processes and to be active on any but the most parochial issues.

The past decade has seen an increase in business activity in the political arena. Chief executive officers have been pressed into action through groups such as the Business Roundtable, and corporate Washington representation has become more visible. In the late 1970's, there were several legislative victories which buoyed business and focused attention on its role as a player in public policy politics. These victories (defeat of labor law and consumer protection legislation among others) not only made business *appear* to be powerful but also boosted business's confidence in its political efficacy.

But business power was limited. What went unnoticed during that time is that for the most part, business lobbying had been a defensive measure. Business's track record of success when it is on the offensive—promoting what it wants instead of opposing what it does not want—is not as clear. In politics, as a general rule, it is easier to get agreement on what you do not want than to agree on positive alternatives. The experience of business confirms this rule and points to the organizational challenges ahead.

ENEMY PARTNERS

During the 1960's and 1970's, the federal government's intervention in society and the economy expanded to the point where almost every aspect of business activity was subject to regulation. According to the General Accounting Office, 116 government agencies and programs now regulate business. As government reached out to redirect business activity toward the pursuit of societally agreed upon goals—or Washington's interpretation of those goals—it placed increasingly greater burdens on business to comply not only with the pursuit of those goals but also with Washington's dictates of how they could be achieved. Washington decided what *and* how. This is important to understand from both the government and business perspectives. Government clearly had to regulate business practices in certain areas, and business recognized that there were societal goals that had to be balanced against its unfettered right to operate as an economic unit. The real issue between government and business was how to achieve those goals, how fast, and at what cost.

The result was that business perceived itself to be operating in a hostile environment, where policy processes were dominated by labor, environmental, and consumer interests. In such an environment, an attack on business was quickly translated into an attack on free enterprise, and business eventually developed a fortress mentality. The less business shared voluntarily with the government, the less vulnerable it felt. As a former EPA official observed, business complied with the law, but only by doing what was required by the letter of the law. Government, knowing this, responded by developing ever more detailed requirements.

This vicious cycle was broken by the convergence of two developments. On the one hand, there was the deteriorating economic situation: inflation, high unemployment, low productivity, and a trade deficit. On the other, there were the gains made in environmental quality, consumer protection, and equal opportunity. The time was ripe for slowing the pace of government regulation through a stricter cost-benefit analysis of its impact. Business interpreted the 1980 election results as a sign that the hostile environment was changing and that, with the inauguration of a probusiness President, it would finally be working with a friendly administration. Read what Ronald Reagan said in the *Wall Street Journal:*

> One can argue validly, . . . that as Washington's influence over our lives increased, the political value of nailing corporate scalps to the wall increased, too. By the early 1970s, some congressional hearings actually seemed to have been designed to make various industry representatives look foolish.
>
> I see as major goals of this decade (the 1980s) the control of inflation, the reestablishment of U.S. competitiveness and the achievement of near independence in energy supplies.
>
> To reach these goals, both business and government will have to learn to lay aside old hostilities and assume a new spirit of cooperation and shared responsibility.[6]

While the promise of a new spirit of cooperation is very attractive to business, it would be unrealistic to expect cooperation to become the norm. For example, the Japanese model of business-government relations, which has become such a popular reference point for anyone criticizing the United States government's behavior toward business, is simply not workable in the American context. The structure of the American political system and the culture of a pluralistic society would militate against an alliance between business and government. Instead of a partnership, a more accurate description of the relationship between business and government is that they are "enemy partners."[7]

The concept of enemy partners has an empirical and a normative dimension: it describes what the relationship is and what it should be. It suggests that the relationship has elements of cooperation and conflict and that effective Washington representation depends on managing both. Effective Washington representation begins with business understanding the fundamental tenets of democratic politics, not in an academic sense, but in terms of what it actually means for corporate behavior in pursuit of its interests in Washington. It means understanding the federal government's societal function and accepting conflict *and* compromise as normal.

Business and government have different missions and responsibilities in society. They have different sources of power and are accountable to different constituencies. Business, after all, is one of many interests, some broader, others narrower, which compete for limited resources. Business's task is to articulate its own demands, make sure they are heard and ultimately granted. Government's role through its various institutions is to represent, aggregate, and balance the competing demands flowing from society's interests as articulated by business and other groups. Conflict is part of this process and compromise of some sort is the product. This implies that the conflict cannot be ideological because ideology by definition cannot admit compromise. It must be pragmatic and based on mutual respect among the protagonists. In other words, the adversarial relationship is only one side of the coin. The other side is that business and government must also be partners. Democratic politics works only if the participants all play by the same rules and believe they have more to gain from dialogue than from combat. In this sense, a partnership exists between business and government. It is not the partnership described by Dwight D. Eisenhower as the military-industrial complex (although that is not excluded) or the partnership embodied in the Japanese model but a partnership based on government's recognition of the essential function of business in the economy and business's faith in the ultimate fairness of the political process—you win some and you lose some, but you are better off playing than sitting out the game.

Whether in conflict or cooperation with government, business has a legitimate role to play in the political process. Acceptance of this proposition is central to an understanding of business-government relations. Moving one step further, if business represents an interest that should be included in public policy deliberations, then business has a responsibility to articulate that interest, and government has a responsibility to make sure it is included.

For the most part, business people *are* beginning to accept this formulation of business-government relations. Despite their rhetoric, business people recognize the historical evolution of government and, although they want to reduce its size and limit its growth, they know they cannot turn the clock back. The alternative is to work with government when that is appropriate, to seek its assistance when it is available, and to maximize corporate objectives consistent with the national interest whenever possible. In this context, lobbying is not a dirty word but an essential part of the political process.

What are the limits of business involvement in the political process? Laying aside the very obvious activities that are either prohibited by law (for example, the Federal Election Campaign Act or the Foreign Corrupt Practices Act) or limited by custom, business is still left with a philosophical and practical question of what the extent of its role should be. The Supreme Court helped define it legally by its ruling in April 1978, in *First National Bank of Boston* vs. *Bellotti*: corporations are entitled to First Amendment protection when they speak out on issues, even when those issues affect them only indirectly. But the practical answer to this question still rests with each company's management, in part on a definition of the interests business represents and in part on a judgment of how vigorously those interests should be pursued.

Are those interests very narrow ones, related directly to the company's ability to function as an economic unit (produce a product, sell it, and make a profit) and permit management to discharge its responsibility to the company's shareholders? Or are those interests broader, reflecting, as some have suggested, big business's quasi-governmental status in society? In between these two definitions of business interest is the one to which most companies active in Washington would subscribe. These companies would distinguish the business interest from the so-called issue interest groups or "special interest" groups such as those pleading for or against abortion, nuclear power, ERA, or the environment. The "business interest," by contrast, can be identified with a cluster of interests relating to products, workers, communities, and the nonbusiness environment. It is a broader interest flowing from business's many social and economic responsibilities. Not all companies concern themselves with all these interests and not all these interests need to be pursued simultaneously. Each company must choose for itself how broadly or narrowly to define what *its* interests are. The Washington representative takes part in this process of definition and identifies the forces that threaten, preserve, or enhance the company's interests. Working with appropriate departments in his company, he seeks to clarify his company's interests and, knowing Washington, to develop a strategy to maximize those interests.

The effective Washington representative can accomplish this task best if he is able to move and communicate between the two cultures of business and government, explaining the one to the other and, where necessary, contributing to changes in the behavior of each.

THE CORPORATION IN POLITICS

In 1981, the Public Affairs Research Group of Boston University's School of Management published the results of a nationwide survey[8] of public affairs units—defined broadly as corporate external (including federal government) relations—in American corporations. The survey of Washington- and non-Washington-based public affairs offices was based on responses from 401 out of 1,000 large and medium-sized firms. Its purpose was to gather data on the organization of the public affairs function and on trends in order to provide a factual baseline for future studies.

The study documents the tremendous growth in this field over the past 10 years as evidenced by the number of companies creating public affairs departments and by the increases in the size of their staffs. Before 1950, 32 of the companies surveyed had a public affairs department. Between 1950 and 1969, the number increased by 117; and between 1970 and 1980, it increased by 212. This means that 60 percent of the public affairs departments were created in the past decade. Looking strictly at Washington-based government relations activity, the survey results indicate that 73 percent of the responding companies maintain a "significant involvement or presence" in Washington. This involvement is achieved through the following kinds of activity, listed in order of significance: trade associations; Washington visits by senior executives; company offices in Washington; Washington law firms; Washington-based government relations counsel; and Washington public relations firms.

The Public Affairs Council, an organization of corporate public affairs executives, estimates that there are well over 400 full-time government affairs offices representing corporations in Washington. The 1980 directory of *Washington Representatives*, which defines representatives as ". . . persons engaged in influencing federal government policies, decisions, and action in behalf of others," lists 1,000 corporate executives.

These figures reflect a quantitative increase in corporate government relations activity, but there has been a qualitative change as well. Corporate Washington offices are more visible not just because there are more of them but also because they function differently than they did in the past.

There are several reasons for these quantitative and qualitative changes. The first and most obvious is the growth of government regulation of business, all business. In fact, many people have made the observation that we can no longer distinguish between regulated and unregulated industries. Instead, we have more or less regulated ones, ever since the establishment of agencies such as the Environmental Protection Agency, the Consumer Product Safety Commission, and others, whose regulatory authority cuts across industry lines.

One corporation, surveying only those agencies and issues having a *significant* impact on its operations, compiled a list of 19 agencies and 30 issues. This is a long list because the company is a large, diversified multinational, but even half the list would be enough to make the point: almost every aspect of business activity is regulated. The government affairs office of this company was charged with the task—at a minimum—of monitoring developments in these agencies as well as in the Congress when decisions there affect the authority of these agencies. The office was also charged with taking action to promote favorable decisions and to resist or turn around unfavorable decisions. And, finally, it was expected to anticipate these decisions in time to have an impact on them.

To carry out these functions, the company's government relations office had to be in tune with how Washington operates. And that brings up the second explanation for the changes in business representation. In the past decade, Washington itself has changed, and the corporate government affairs function has had to change with it. The single most noticeable manifestation of this change has been a decreased emphasis on whom you know and an increased emphasis on what you know.

Today, there is a greater emphasis on information than on contacts, or on information together with contacts. Or—to borrow a title from a book—what you say after you've said hello. Congressional reform is partly responsible for this emphasis on information. It has increased the amount of information available and, at the same time, increased the demand for more information. Congressional reform opened up the legislative process to public scrutiny. By decentralizing power and redistributing it and by rearranging the influence of individuals, committees, and political parties, it rearranged the rules of the game by which outsiders can influence the legislative process.

For the Washington representative, it means that there are more actors involved in every stage of Congressional deliberations. The influx of new members elected on platforms that reflect local, regional, or single-issue interests contributes to the fragmentation of the Congress, the lack of discipline and the independence of the individual member vis-à-vis the Congressional leadership as well as the White House. It is no longer enough to know a few key individuals, such as committee chairmen or "the leadership." It means thinking *strategically* about the entire process and assessing the role of the most junior members.

The result of these changes in how Washington works has been a change in the model Washington representative and in the staffs of government affairs offices. In the days when lobbying was a more personalized function based on contacts and individual relationships, the corporate lobbyist was frequently a person who was hired because of his contacts. A former vice president of ITT gave this devastating description of his company's lobbying in the 1960's:

> The "representatives" exploited contacts and an intimate knowledge of certain military programs for as long as both lasted. The span was usually two to three years. Wild parties, magnificent expense accounts, weekends at game preserves and in the sea yachts. Always

> lots and lots of money. Then, as had to happen, friends retired or were transferred and new program groups formed. The "representative" became ineffective and was gradually removed from the scene to be replaced by a more recent model. He had been milked of his useful information, and his contacts had lost their influence.[9]

Not all corporate lobbying was done in ITT's style, but the model of the influence-peddling lobbyist who traded on his contacts and conducted his business on the golf course was not uncommon.

Today, the trend is toward the professionalization of the Washington representative. He must have a set of skills acquired through training and experience and a knowledge of systematic procedures for organizing and applying resources. According to one consultant, whose clients include the Washington reps of several major multinational companies, this professionalism is manifested in the increased demand for her firm's services. Not only has the demand for information increased but also for analysis. Furthermore, information and analysis are required on a timely basis because the representative must anticipate what action will be required and be able to plan and organize for it.

The third reason for the increase in corporate government relations activity is that the scope of the government representative's function has expanded. Business has come to recognize that legislative activity is only part of the process and that whatever is won on "the Hill" may easily be lost on Pennsylvania Avenue or, for that matter, anywhere else around town where bureaucrats are at work. The executive branch, therefore, needs to be watched not only for what decisions come out of it but for the opportunities that exist to affect those decisions, if a company is willing to learn what the access points are. In addition to working the key stages of "how a bill becomes a law," corporate reps have added the labyrinthine processes of how laws are implemented to their portfolio. The increase, then, in the scope of corporate representation is partly because of this extended coverage and also because of business's apparent willingness to take on government on all fronts.

This focus on the executive as well as the legislative branch, together with the increase in the sheer number of issues, has required Washington offices to give considerable thought to what the distribution of expertise should be among the staff. The result has been that Washington corporate offices now need a staff with a mix of political and substantive skills. More and more, the organization of the corporate government affairs office is dictated by what the company's interests are and not by how the government is organized. For example, the larger Washington offices have people working on specific issues and developing detailed knowledge rather than just covering the Hill.

The fourth reason for the change in corporate representation is the change in how companies themselves view Washington. There is no doubt that during the past decade companies have recognized how much Washington decisions influence business activity and the business environment. One corporate CEO, who has spent a great deal of time in Washington, explained that he did so because he felt that more decisions affecting his company are made in Washington than in the board room. The proportions implied in this statement may be arguable but the point is a good one. Once corporate management realizes the impact that government decisions have on business, it has two choices: one, to become an informed, active participant in the policy process; or, two, to sit out the great debates and accept decisions as they are handed down. The choice taken by the company determines how its government affairs function will be carried out. Many companies believe they can handle their relations with the federal government adequately from corporate headquarters in Stamford, Houston or Los Angeles. Others have found that, to be most effective, they need an on-going corporate presence in Washington.

Companies arrive at the decision to upgrade or establish a Washington office in different ways. For many, it is an evolutionary process. The function grows in response to increased governmental activity. Or the company itself grows; perhaps new businesses are acquired that are regulated by agencies not previously monitored by the company. The company's understanding of how Washington works improves as it becomes more involved and learns to differentiate the many stages of the decision-making process and how it varies from agency to agency.

Another route companies may take to establishing a Washington office is through dealing with a crisis. The crisis could be a phrase in a new law, a surprise ruling, a penalty incurred, or an opportunity lost—in other words, any kind of governmental activity that presents the company with a problem that could have been avoided or minimized if the company had known about it early enough to do something. If the price tag is big enough, the company will take notice.

A third route may be a combination of crisis and evolution or simply a management decision to create or upgrade this function. The accession of a new chief executive officer who wants to speak out on public policy issues or a chief operating officer who recognizes the importance of government relations to his company's business may be the essential catalyst in establishing active Washington representation.

FACTORS SHAPING THE GOVERNMENT AFFAIRS OFFICE

Once the decision is made, deliberately or incrementally, that Washington representation is of value to the company, there are many factors that shape the program and the operation of its government affairs unit. In general, these factors may be divided into four categories: (a) what kind of company it is, (b) how it views business-government relations, (c) how the Washington office relates to the rest of the company organizationally and operationally, and (d) what external forces have an impact on it.

First, the most obvious determinant of the work of a government affairs office is the kind of company it represents—how big it is, what its products are, where its markets lie. Since the work of the government affairs office is to represent the interests of the company, its starting point has to be the company itself. For example, a look at the company's size in itself reveals something about what kinds of issues the government affairs office will focus on and what the minimum level of activity is likely to be. Some companies simply because of their size have to deal with the government, and the government has to deal with them. General Motors, Exxon, and AT&T are such corporate giants. Business-government relations for them is not really a matter of choice; even if they wanted to sit out the great debates, the government or the public would draw them in.

Today, even the top 500 or top 1,000 companies cannot escape being involved in the policy process. The Carter Administration asked them to take a stand in support of the wage-price guidelines;

the Department of Commerce asked if they supported the OECD guidelines on international investments; the Reagan Administration wanted their backing on the budget proposals. Interest groups watch them to see what they do on clean air compliance, equal employment opportunity, and product safety. In a word, big companies operate in a fishbowl. They can be identified and watched; their behavior can be evaluated and judged.

The company's product line also influences the work of the government affairs office. In deciding what issues to follow, what agencies to watch, and what kind of staff expertise to employ, the determining factor is the company's product line. Is the company in a highly regulated industry? Does it have one product that is or may be the target of government action? What is the importance of that product in the total product mix of the company? Is the product import-sensitive? Is it export competitive?

The company's markets are another determining factor. Are they mostly domestic, international, or evenly split? If the markets are international, are they in the developed or developing countries? Is the company trade- or investment-oriented, or both? If it is primarily domestic, where are its markets? Its manufacturing facilities? Are they concentrated in a few states, a few Congressional districts, or are they spread across the map? The answers to these questions will influence how the office is staffed and what kinds of issues will be watched. A company with manufacturing facilities in several states may need the capability to monitor legislation at the state level. A company with subsidiaries in several countries may have to have its staff supplemented with a network of country-specific consultants.

A second category of factors shaping the Washington office is how the company views business-government relations. In its most illusive form, this translates into how the company (read: the essential persons in the company) "feels" toward Washington. Angry? Frustrated? Defensive? Does it understand the political process? Is it basically disdainful of politicians or does it have respect for people who work for the government? If the company's orientation to business-government relations is generally positive, its participation in the political process will tend to be active rather than passive, continuous rather than ad hoc. Its Washington office will be more than a listening post and corporate management will be more than an observer.

The affective orientation of the company toward the government is determined to a great extent by the company's experience with the federal government and by its knowledge of how Washington works. Perhaps the hardest thing for business people to understand is the give and take of politics and the shifting coalitions of people who are on the same side on one issue and on opposite sides on another. For example, multinational corporations and the League of Woman Voters have been allies on international trade legislation but adversaries on many environmental issues.

Everybody is familiar with the expression, "Politics is the art of the possible." What business people forget is that the difference between what is or is not possible is not always a matter of rational negotiation, or at least not rational in the ordinary use of the term though it may be rational within the context of the political game. Armed with facts, corporate lobbyists walk into a Congressman's office to persuade him of the rightness of their cause. The figures demonstrate that one course of action would be preferable to another. The member agrees but says that unfortunately he cannot vote with them because a large group in his district is opposed and his re-election may be jeopardized. The businessmen are astounded, dismayed. They criticize the system and the member for not voting on the merits of the case. They neglect the fact that, for the member, the merits of the case go beyond figures. Part of his calculation is and must be how his vote on an issue will be perceived by his constituents and whether it will cause him to win or lose support.

A third set of factors that affects the work of the Washington office concerns the organizational and operational relationships between it and the rest of the company. The Washington office must be sensitive to these relationships because they are a reflection of the politics within the corporation. Questions which need to be asked include the following: Is the company decentralized or not? If it is, what kind of authority does headquarters have vis-à-vis the subsidiaries (operating groups, units, divisions), and how is that authority exercised? The answers to these questions influence the Washington office's ability to initiate decisions and coordinate actions. In a highly decentralized company, each subsidiary may want its own autonomous representation with only minimal coordination by a corporate staff.

The Washington office is also affected by the distribution of power within the company. Does one unit have disproportionately more clout than the others? If that is the same unit that has the greatest demands on the Washington office, the politics of the situation are fairly obvious. But perhaps one unit that needs more help than the others is not a strong unit in terms of its sales figures or growth potential. How the Washington office apportions its time is thus a political question that must be answered as much in terms of who holds power in the company as who needs assistance.

Another organizational issue is the reporting relationship. To whom does the Washington office report? To the CEO? The chief operating officer? The general counsel? Public affairs? The legitimacy and authority of the Washington office flows, in part, from the executive to whom it reports. The fashionable public affairs formula has been to insist on the importance of the CEO's support for the government relations office. A corollary to this formula has been the importance of access to the CEO. If a Washington office can demonstrate that the CEO is interested, involved, and accessible, it is perceived to be a more effective office than one that cannot. This formula, though widely accepted and ritualistically incanted, is too simplistic to be a guide to successful organization.

Having the backing of the CEO is important, but it is not enough. In fact, Washington offices have found that they are extremely vulnerable if they have concentrated primarily on cultivating their relationship with the CEO and have relied on him for their survival. Sometimes, of course, it is not the Washington office's choice; the CEO himself may be very active in government relations and may preempt all their time. The Washington office must look at who else is important in the company, not just at the corporate level but throughout. Therefore, a key to an effective Washington office—and indeed to its survival—is to institutionalize the government affairs function by demonstrating its usefulness throughout the corporation.

Its substantive program is determined in no small way by where it sits on the organization chart. A Washington office that reports to the corporate general counsel will look at issues differently and even look at different issues than one that reports to a public affairs office. Which reporting relationship is better is not a relevant question. What should be asked is what does the company need and what will work? It can be argued, for example, that the general counsel will look at the legal ramifications of an issue, may be more cautious, and will probably want to restrict the number of players compared with the public affairs officer who will tend to give more weight to political factors and be more willing to open up the process. On the other hand, there is a danger that the public affairs office will be too process-oriented and tend to deal more in form than substance.

Both the general counsel and the public affairs officer have a role to play, and the Washington office must be organized to make that possible. Increasingly, the discipline of the bottom line—which guides the operating units of the company—is also applied to the work of the Washington office. The effective Washington office chooses the issues that are most important to the company and selects the mode of operation that is likely to work. Increasingly, that is becoming an interdisciplinary approach drawing on the legal, public affairs, financial, and technical expertise within the company.

A final category of factors that shapes the work of the Washington office is external to the company. These are factors over which the Washington office has the least control but which, nevertheless, affect what it can do. They include changes in government—how decisions are made and who the incumbents are—as well as in the larger nonbusiness environment. If these changes are major, as they were after the Congressional reforms, the Washington representative may have to change his entire method of operation. Indeed, the company may have to change its representative. With the emphasis less on whom you know and more on what you know, there are fewer reasons to hire a former Congressman or ambassador whose main resource may be his contacts, a diminishing asset in any case. If the changes are more limited, such as the reorganization of a government department or a new policy initiative, the Washington office may respond by adjusting its own work program. The dismantling of a federal agency, such as is being proposed in the Department of Energy, or an increase in budget for one program and the phase-out of another will affect what the Washington office can do.

The political climate also affects the parameters within which companies can pursue their objectives. Some administrations are more friendly to business than others; some times are more hospitable to business activism. When confidence in business is low, the range of issues on which business can act with credibility is narrowed and the individual company has to assess what objectives it can realistically advance. Last but not least, there is the impact of economic conditions. For example, companies interested in undertaking costly and risky synthetic fuels projects were encouraged to do so when oil prices were high. Public anxiety over dependence on imported oil spurred government support for exploring alternatives. When oil prices dropped, the energy crisis seemed more remote and the need for alternate sources less urgent. Companies (and their Washington offices) that had geared up to do synthetic fuels projects during the Carter Administration had to change course when the Reagan Administration came in.

SUPPORT FUNCTIONS OF THE WASHINGTON OFFICE

The main purpose of Washington representation is to defend or promote the company's interests. This section deals with the support functions that are carried out as part of this process.[10]

Information Gathering

Information gathering is the most basic and universal function of a Washington office because information is necessary for survival. Effective Washington representation depends on having timely, accurate information on developments of concern to the company.

Information gathering is a generalized function precedent to "issue identification" but not as focused as "issue monitoring," which will be discussed later. It is a scanning operation whose objective is to know what is going on. Describing information gathering as a generalized function does not mean that it is totally nondirected. There is too much happening in Washington on too many fronts for an office not to be selective. But an effective Washington office must allow itself to be open and sensitive to information about a wide variety of subjects—some not immediately or apparently relevant to the interests of the company—from a multitude of sources.

Most Washington representatives, if they have worked in this city for a while, develop a routinized set of relationships. First and foremost, they are in regular contact with other corporate representatives in their industry. They see each other at trade association meetings, on industry advisory committees, and at social events. The Washington representative's circle of contacts widens when he joins organizations and attends meetings that cut across industries. But even this is too limited to provide him with adequate sources of information. Washington is a small town in many ways, and if a representative does not make an effort to widen his circle, he can easily move from one meeting to the next with many of the same characters.

To break out of this situation, the Washington representative must make an effort to seek fresh contacts and to listen to different points of view. There are numerous "think tanks," university-sponsored workshops or seminars, and conferences where the Washington representative can hear and meet people from labor, academic, and nongovernmental organizations. By selectively participating, he can learn about issues that are new to him or get a new slant on something he is already covering.

Information about people is as important as information about events or ideas. What is simply an interesting news story to someone outside Washington may be essential information to a Washington insider. The replacement of a key Presidential advisor or the resignation of a Cabinet member, for example, could have repercussions that affect various relationships of influence. Cherished sources may be cut off, a knowledgeable or sympathetic figure in a decision-making chain may be reassigned, or a case may be lost in the chaos of transition.

Washington is information rich, so just keeping up with the quantity of available information is enough to keep an office busy. Printed sources of information are voluminous and consultants are legion. The trick is to choose carefully but not too narrowly, to maintain a balance between breadth and depth, and to break away now and then from one's familiar pattern of gathering information.

Issue Identification

One of the most important processes in a Washington office is identifying the issues of interest to the company. The most obvious reason for doing this is to make sure the Washington office is tuned in to the needs of the company and following the issues that will affect the company. This is especially important in a small office where limited staff time has to be targeted more carefully than in a large office.

Issue identification is a difficult process; it is part detective work, part guessing game. It is difficult because issues do not always present themselves full blown in a form that the company can recognize as relating to its interests. Even when they do, the Washington representative may not always anticipate which issues will generate a corporate response. Issue identification may involve projecting what is likely to be on Congress's or the President's agenda and matching it up with the company's interests. Or it may be an ongoing activity, watching developments and picking out what is of concern to the company. In either case, issue identification is like shooting at a moving target: it is always subject to change.

One former corporate executive, when asked to describe how he identifies issues and decides what priority to give them, explained that his guide is the CIA—"Chairman's Index of Affection."[11] With this very descriptive phrase, he was merely reflecting what many Washington representatives know—that issue identification is a process of matching up what is objectively of interest to the company with what is subjectively determined to be of interest. The chairman's judgment is one guide to what is important, a guide that would be disregarded only by the most naive Washington office.

An issue can be any item of public policy, legislative or regulatory, that may affect a company positively or negatively. *How* does a Washington office identify an issue and *when*? The Washington representative of a major company describes the issue identification process this way:

> The landscape of government activity is blurred. To the uninitiated, everything is moving; everything is equally important. My job is to bring this landscape into focus, to sort out the important from the unimportant; the matters needing attention today from the ones needing attention tomorrow; the matters needing *my* attention. What I use to bring it into focus is the knowledge I have about my company. I look at the landscape, as if through a telescope, using my company's interests to guide me.[12]

Easier said than done. The twin poles of effective Washington representation are knowing your company and knowing the government. One of the toughest decisions in setting up a Washington office is to decide who should head it. In making that decision, companies have to consider whether it is more important to have a person who knows the government or one who knows the company, an outsider or an insider. If an outsider, should there be people on his staff who come from the company or should they all be Washington "hands"? If an insider, how will he learn the ropes in Washington? One company's creative solution to this problem was to assign an insider to Washington; but first the company sponsored him for a year in a federal exchange program between private and public sector executives to give him in-depth exposure to the workings of government.

Another company's answer to the insider vs. the outsider question was to hire an outsider who knew Washington but who also had extensive business experience. Still another company hired an outsider but insisted that he conduct government affairs from corporate headquarters rather than from Washington, on the theory that he would be better informed about the company if he were physically part of it. A fourth company assigned its executives to Washington on a rotating basis, recalling them to headquarters or sending them to an operating unit after a few years in Washington.

The outsider who joins a company with the job of representing it in Washington needs a crash course in the company's organization and products. He needs to make field trips, take plant tours, study pamphlets and catalogues, and interview key executives. On balance, however, this approach is more likely to succeed than the one of taking the insider and training him in the ways of Washington. Government relations as a field of activity is too big and too complex and the pace is too fast for that. By comparison, learning one's way around even the most diversified corporation is more manageable.

Depending on the complexity of the issues and the level of familiarity aimed at, this process could take six months or several years. As the new Washington representative moves through this process, he is examining the company and its products from a public policy perspective, always asking the questions "What decision could be made by the federal government that would have an impact on the company (the product)?" and "What decision should the federal government make that would benefit the company?" What he learns about the company in answer to these questions becomes his reference points when he tries to bring the Washington landscape into focus.

His first objectives will be to become familiar enough with his company to recognize when it has an interest in an issue and to assess how significant that interest is. From there, he will consider whether and when government action is likely and what he should do with respect to that action: promote it, attempt to modify it, or resist it.

Because there are so many issues of such varied significance to the company, it is useful to break them down into at least four categories. The first and most important issues are the so-called "bottom line" issues. Governmental action on these issues would affect operations, sales, markets, and profits or profitability. Air quality regulations for General Motors, taxation of Americans working abroad for Bechtel, the windfall profits tax for Exxon, mandatory deposit legislation for American Can, toxic substances regulations for Dupont—these are all bottom line issues. Bottom line issues may affect the corporation as a whole or one of its units. The effect of government action may be directly on the product (carcinogen regulation), on the employees (plant closing legislation), on management (corporate governance legislation), on the workplace (OSHA noise control requirements), or on the business environment (economic policy).

A bottom line issue may be relatively narrow; for example, when it affects only one line of business or one industry. Or it may cut across several industries. Conglomerate merger legislation which proposed to restrict acquisitions by corporations beyond a certain size unless they could demonstrate that it was an economic necessity could potentially have affected any of the Fortune 500. The Business Roundtable's policy committee identified it as an issue to follow in the 96th Congress.

"General business" issues are another category. These usually arise from governmental decisions regarding the economy, the society, or foreign policy. As the name suggests, they affect companies in general, regardless of their line of business. The distinction between bottom line and general business issues is obviously not hard and fast. Wage and price controls, monetary policy, and the federal budget may all have bottom line implications either directly or by their effect on the environment in which business operates.

For example, was the sale of highly sophisticated aircraft (AWACS) to Saudi Arabia an issue from a general business point of view? A company that supplied equipment for these aircraft had a clear interest in the outcome of the Senate deliberations. But what about companies whose interest was in peace in the Middle East, both as a value in itself and because regional stability is good for business? Does that interest make it a business issue? Should companies become involved in foreign policy only when the direct bottom line impact is clear, or should they never become involved in foreign policy debates? These are the kinds of questions companies have to answer in attempting to identify an issue. One criterion to apply in answering these questions is whether the company feels it has anything special to contribute to the debate on the issue; for example, it may have technical expertise or special information about a country with which the United States has no diplomatic relations. If a company can make this kind of contribution, it has a responsibility to speak up.

Issue identification for a company is not an academic process. It is a practical exercise consisting of focusing on the problem (the bill, the decision, the policy), assessing its impact, and determining *whether the company has anything to offer to its solution*. Unless all these elements are present, there is no issue as far as the company is concerned.

A third kind of issue is the good government issue. Like the general business issue, this may also have a bottom line impact, but it is more remote. Issues such as regulatory reform, government reorganization, campaign financing, and lobby reform are good government issues. Business has an interest in them to the extent that its operations are affected by how government decisions are made. But the linkage may not be very obvious, and for companies less experienced in the ways of Washington, the issues may be somewhat esoteric. There is also the problem of time. With limited resources, a staff has to spend its time on the bottom line issues. Working on good government issues is rarely a priority.

A fourth category may be described as emerging issues. Strictly defined, these are not yet issues—they are ideas, trends, and problems. They only become issues when they have been articulated in some form requiring action, and when a company has linked them to its own interests.

The corporate Washington office has a role in identifying an idea or trend that is likely to become an issue. This category is different from the other three. It is proactive, whereas the others are more likely to be reactive in the identification stage. Furthermore, identifying emerging issues calls for different resources and skills than identifying issues that have already crystallized; for example, knowing how to analyze trends and public opinion polls, working closely with the corporate R&D or strategic planning units, and attending risk analysis and forecasting courses.

This function is a fairly recent addition to the work of the Washington office. It developed as a necessary concomitant of increased business activism: the more business wanted to participate in shaping the legislative agenda, the more it had to adopt a long-range perspective for identifying issues. The contribution of the Washington office is to look at emerging issues in a political context, to determine whether broad social or economic developments are likely to become issues requiring government action, and to project a time frame for action.

Several criteria may be applied to determine whether an issue has crystallized to the point where the company has to pay attention to it in an active way, as opposed to just watching it.

1. When another major interest group has an item on its agenda that is likely to affect business; for example, if labor is actively campaigning for legislative action in areas that will affect business, the issue cannot be ignored even if the company rep decides that it is not "ripe" for legislation. Legislative victories have been known to occur simply because nobody was looking.

2. When action is taking place at the state level that may presage broader national interest in an issue. Many corporate government affairs offices focus only on the federal government and ignore state governments both as regulators of business and as testing grounds for national action. Proposition 13 in California and the nationwide tax limitation movement is one example among many.

3. When an issue is raised in several different contexts. The Washington insider's best indicator that an issue is ripening is who is talking about it. The seasoned Washington representative knows who the opinion leaders are. Using his experience and judgment, he sifts through the political rhetoric in public and private statements to identify what may be a program, a policy, or a proposal for new legislation or regulation. He compares what he hears from one source with what he hears from another. He checks to see who is "staffing" the issue (who is preparing papers and drafting proposals) and determines whether or not the issue has captured the attention of people who have the power to make things happen.

In any case, the Washington representative is most effective if he operates in the present with a sense of the past. There is a saying in Washington that what goes around comes around. Civil servants use this expression to describe the policies proposed by the political appointees of a new administration. For the civil servant who has been with an agency through several administrations, new policies are often just new versions of policies that have been tried before. The Washington representative benefits from knowing what has or has not worked and under what conditions a policy was tried.

Issue Monitoring

Issue monitoring differs from information gathering in several respects. First, it is a more focused process. It is keyed to the issues the company has identified and rated. Second, it is more action-oriented; the purpose of monitoring is to be ready to do something. Issue monitoring is not an academic process. It is tracking a bill or a case from one stage to the next, one office to the next. The Washington representative has to calculate when a decision is likely to be made. If action is required, he must take it before it is too late. This means that the accuracy and timeliness of the information become all important. The reliability of sources also becomes more important.

Evaluating the reliability of sources is part science, part art. Just as a good journalist or detective follows a set procedure for checking and cross-checking information, so must the Washington representative. There are public sources such as the "Congressional Record," the "Federal Register," and the Bureau of National Affairs' "Daily Report for Executives." There is information obtained by consultants whose reliability is a matter of reputation. And, finally, there are the personalized sources—the people whom the Washington representative knows and trusts because they have "delivered" for him in the past.

Two important questions to measure reliability in evaluating a source are (a) How close is he to the center of decision making? In other words, is he a participant in making the decision or is he an observer? If the latter, is he a direct observer or is he getting information third- and fourth-hand? (b) What is his competence for evaluating what he sees and hears?

An aspect of the legislative process that depends completely on the reliability of one's source is the head count. This is a process of canvassing members of Congress to ascertain how they will vote on an issue. A typical scene in Washington is a meeting where members of an interest group gather to report on the legislators they have contacted with respect to their position in an upcoming vote. The accuracy of the head count will be directly related to the reliability of the sources questioned and the judgment of the canvasser in evaluating what he heard. For example, a novice lobbyist may report that a Congressman said he would vote "no." The seasoned lobbyist may hear the same response from the member but conclude that the "no" is not to be taken as final. Perhaps the member has to be negative at "this stage of the process," but he will vote "yes" if he is "really needed" because he has "always voted with us" on this issue in the past.

How an office monitors issues depends on many factors, including the size of the staff, the budget for outside consultants, the visibility of the office, and its reputation in Washington. The last two factors in particular affect the kind of information-gathering resources it has. An office with a reputation for being particularly knowledgeable on an issue may be called in for consultation by the government before a decision is made. If an office is known to be an opinion leader in an industry or among other Washington offices, it may be given advance warning of a decision or it may be privy to deliberations that others hear of only later.

Whether the corporate government affairs office is in the mainstream of activity or on the periphery also has a great deal to do with how much and what kind of information it gets. One could postulate that there is a positive correlation between how activist an office is and how well-informed it is. Washington representatives who are passive participants, who are note-takers at meetings, or who rely primarily on printed sources are never as well informed about an issue as those who are "working" on it. On any given issue, the Washington representatives who are actively working on it are always ahead of the information game compared with those who are not. They are making things happen and, therefore, are always a little ahead of the news. If one is not actively working on an issue, the next best thing is to know someone who is and who is willing to share information.

Reporting

The flow of adequate, reliable communication from the company to the government and back again is central to effective Washington representation. Inaccurate information is of no use; information collected but not reported is a waste. The Washington representative must know where to go for the right information and to whom it should be communicated both inside and outside the company. Unless this loop is closed, the Washington representative is in danger of losing his source of information and his point of reference and support, or both.

Who needs to know? Who needs to know first? For every item that needs to be communicated within the company these two questions must be answered. Corporate bureaucracies operate like bureaucracies elsewhere: there are hierarchies of power and built-in functional redundancies. Coordination is as much a function of good management as of organizational structure. When coordination is lacking, people either do not know what is going on or they trip over each other to find out information that their unit already has.

The Washington office, if it is a corporate function, services the entire company and can therefore relate to almost every part of it. It works with staff and line people and across product groups and geographic boundaries. It is, therefore, in a special position to facilitate the exchange of information within the company and to coordinate action.

The effective Washington representative must know the standard operating procedures of his company. This is especially true when deciding whom to call first on what; who should receive information and who should be consulted? Every company has certain procedural rules with which the Washington representative must be familiar—for example, Who is copied routinely on different kinds of communication? What kind of action or communication needs clearance from corporate or subsidiary heads? What needs legal clearance?

He also needs to know as much about the politics of the corporation as about politics in Washington. It might make a difference, for example, to know that two executives, one subordinate to the other, are related to each other by marriage; that two others have been enemies for years; and that two others are competing for the same position. Misplaced information in any of these cases could cause damage and affect the ability of the Washington office to discharge its functions.

The Washington representative does not have total control over "who should know." Company people outside the Washington office may have their own contacts or they may simply learn about something through the media, through professional organizations, or through trade associations. Or, worst of all, they may learn something from a customer or a competitor that they feel they should have heard from their Washington office. If the mistake is serious enough (read: costly enough), the Washington representative loses a great deal of credibility, and maybe his job.

The opposite of providing too little information is blanketing the company with information. This approach is equally ineffective. Too much information or information in the wrong format sent to people who do not need it is just as much an indication of a Washington office that does not know the company as one that does not send enough information.

Developing and Maintaining Access

The most famous or infamous function of the Washington representative is developing and maintaining access. This is a euphemism for knowing the right people in the right places. Although Washington has changed and information has become more important, the Washington representative still has to know who counts so that his information gets to the people closest to a decision. In the vast bureaucracy of the federal government, titles are only rough indicators of power. A deputy assistant secretary in one agency may be the key person to resolve a problem; in another agency an office director could do the same.

Who the "right" people are—that means who the influential people are on any given issue—is not apparent from any organization charts. Knowing them takes homework. When a new administration comes into office, Washington representatives very carefully watch each position as it is filled. They examine the circumstances of the appointment or nomination: Who recommended the person for the job? Who supported or opposed the nomination? What are the person's qualifications? Finally, if the Washington representative does not know the incoming official personally, he looks for acquaintances that they may have in common. That acquaintance may be helpful in providing an introduction or arranging a meeting. Government officials in Washington are remarkably accessible; nevertheless, there are too many demands on their time and too many good secretaries protecting them from frivolous callers and appointment seekers. To get to see them, therefore, an intermediary is useful, perhaps a friend of the official who vouches for the would-be caller.

Another reason to look for common acquaintances is to identify potential allies, should their assistance be needed to influence the official. Like everyone else in Washington, government officials tend to be deluged with information, and they too need guidance in sorting through it. A trusted friend, a former law partner, a recognized authority—these are the kinds of "common acquaintances" the Washington representative seeks.

This line of inquiry, though heightened after an election, is really an on-going activity because personnel changes and reorganizations take place all the time. The State Department, more than any other agency, has to be monitored constantly for personnel changes. The system of rotating foreign service officers ensures that just when a country desk officer has developed some expertise on one country, he is assigned to another.

Knowing who the right people are is only part of the task. Having access to them is the other, more difficult part. This, too, is difficult for business people to understand. When they have a problem, they want to go to the top with it. The democratic political culture has encouraged them to believe that they can have access when they need it; indeed, that it is their right.

"Access" does not just happen. It has to be nurtured, cultivated. Company visibility helps. A company that is known as a leader in its industry or as a spokesman on business issues will have name recognition in government offices. Government officials call on people they know, and they are more likely to make time for people they know. The burden is on the company, specifically on the Washington representative, to be among those people.

The best way to nurture access is to develop a reputation for being a reliable source of information. Since the Washington representative's role is to represent his company's interest, there is a natural bias here. The representative must be careful to back up his position with solid arguments based on an accurate reporting of the facts. If the Washington representative is found to have misrepresented his company's case, his credibility and, therefore, his access to decision makers will be damaged.

No description of the Washington representative's role would be complete without a discussion of the Washington social circuit. To outsiders, this appears to be the easiest part of being in Washington; although frequently enjoyable, however, it is also time-consuming and demanding. It is not unusual for the head of a Washington office to attend a dinner or reception three nights a week and sometimes three events in one evening. The small dinner party that brings together people who do not usually see each other is a particularly nice vehicle for getting to know Washington dignitaries. Since these dignitaries are busy and a dinner in itself is not a special event for them, the Washington representative has to create an occasion, a reason for the get-together, or produce a guest who could draw the others.

Big receptions serve a different purpose. Going to them, the Washington representative shows the "company flag," gets to meet officials informally, and gives support to colleagues. In other words, he circulates. Washington is a superficially gregarious city where people trade on whom they know. For the hundreds of Washington representatives competing for access, receptions provide a convenient forum for mixing with their peers and officials without spending too much time with anyone.

RESOURCES OF THE WASHINGTON OFFICE

The corporate representative has a wide selection of external and internal resources to draw on in performing the functions described above. Representation is no longer a simple one-on-one format of a citizen petitioning his government for a redress of grievances. It is a *process,* requiring organizational skills, planning, and money.

INTERNAL SUPPORT

Before a Washington representative can act effectively on a legislative issue, he has to have the company's internal resources in place and the company prepared for action. He cannot just push a button and expect things to happen. People have to be informed and mobilized. On a companywide basis, this process can take years to accomplish. If the resources are not in place at the time the Washington representative needs them, it is usually too late to develop them.

There are internal resources for analysis and advice. On issues the Washington office monitors, it should communicate regularly with the cognizant functional offices. Not only is it valuable for the Washington representative to get the views of those offices, but it is also a way of keeping them informed and up-to-date on what is happening. What the Washington representative is looking for in consulting with the tax, legal, and other specialists in the company is their analysis of an issue *as it relates to the company.*

One of the strongest trends in recent years has been the growth of companywide public affairs or "grass roots" programs. These programs, which vary with the size of the company and how active it is in business-government relations, have developed in response to changes in Congress. As a result of the Congressional reforms, more members "count" in the legislative process. The Washington representative cannot cover them all by himself and, even if he could, it would not be nearly as effective as reaching a member through his constituents. That is the key to every grass roots program: a cadre of people selected and trained to promote or defend the company's interests by speaking out on issues from their vantage point as company employees *and* voters in a Congressional district and state.

The government affairs office, in Washington or elsewhere, usually has the responsibility for developing the company's grass roots program. Two prime ingredients for a successful program are support from top management and the right people in the program. Without the former, you do not get the latter. But if top management backs the program and encourages qualified people to spend their time on what are traditionally seen as nonbusiness activities, then the program is off to a good start. The number of people in the program varies, but generally the idea is to have a network of people representing each plant or facility.

Picking the right people may be a long process in itself. Some of the criteria that should be applied in making the selection are the person's position, his interest in or awareness of politics, his ability as a communicator, his standing with his peers and subordinates and possibly his standing in the community.

Once selected, basic training is essential. Some companies have elaborate programs to teach new "public affairs representatives" what their function is, how they communicate the company's interests, and what legally they can or cannot do on behalf of the company. Training seminars are a popular practice, a way of teaching the new reps the basics and developing an esprit de corps among them. The training seminars are then followed up with regular communications, information on issues, and other developments of interest.

The guide to how much communication with the field is needed is whatever it takes to maintain the public affairs or grass roots representative in an action-ready state. For people in the field, public affairs is a secondary function; therefore, they need regular reminders of what is happening in Washington that touches on their job. The public affairs communications of many companies have, consequently, become quite sophisticated.

Issue task forces may be constituted to develop arguments for and against an issue and to advise in the preparation of an issue handbook that is distributed to all the company's public affairs representatives. Some companies prepare small reference libraries as part of their education program. "Issue updates," newsletters, special backgrounders, videotapes, and instruction guides are all part of the communications arsenal.

Again, it would be wrong to present a formula here for what works best. Each company has to find the right mix, based on its size, issue coverage, level of activity, and resources. Companies do not, however, have to stumble around in the dark or reinvent the wheel. Many companies are willing to share their experiences directly or through organizations such as the Public Affairs Council, the National Association of Manufacturers, the United States Chamber of Commerce, or the Business Roundtable. Companies can, for example, learn from each other how to "sell" a grass roots program to corporate management, how to solicit contributions to a political action committee, how to conduct a plant tour for visiting government officials, and how to mobilize local resources for legislative action.

How the Washington office organizes its contacts in the field is also important. The public affairs representatives have to be well informed and ready for action, but not everybody needs to be involved in every issue. For example, if a Congressional committee is about to act, perhaps only the company's facilities in the districts with members on that committee need to be contacted. Unless the Washington office has this capability to communicate selectively with the field, it will not be able to respond effectively when the time comes. The complexity of organizing in this manner can be enormous. Some companies have therefore installed elaborate computer systems, word processors, and electronic mail. The objective is to be prepared to act, to allow the company to have its say while there is still time to affect a decision.

One organization common to most corporate public affairs programs is the Political Action Committee (PAC). Much has been written about "the business PAC phenomenon"—why corporate PACs have grown, whether or not their growth in numbers and dollars represents an increase in business's influence in politics, and what their potential impact may be inside and outside the corporation. Briefly, companies can legally participate in elections by forming political action committees to channel voluntary contributions in support of candidates. Although individual and company campaign contributions are regulated by the Federal Election Campaign Act of 1971 as amended in 1974, 1976, and 1979, the significant benchmark for business PACs was 1974. In that year, Congress removed the ban on federal contractors forming PACs. The result, as Michael J. Malbin has pointed out, was dramatic. On December 31, 1974, there were 89 corporate PACs, 201 labor, and 318 "others" (such as trade associations). By the end of 1976, the number of corporate PACs increased to 433 and the amount of money they contributed to candidates tripled the amount they gave in 1974.[13] Today, there are more than 1,000 corporate PACs.

A PAC is a resource for a company's Washington activity in two ways. First, and most obviously, it provides money, which gives the company a voice in the electoral process. Most corporate PACs have a steering or candidate selection committee and a set of criteria for determining which candidates to support. The Washington office is usually represented on these committees; whether it dominates the selection process and the committee ratifies the Washington office's recommendation or whether it has little control over the process varies from one company to another. The important point is that PACs enable companies to participate in an aspect of political life which, from the elected official's point of view, is critical to every other activity.

The role of PAC contributions in providing access to elected officials is often misunderstood. If a company does not participate, even in a token way, in supporting a candidate, it does not mean that the company is "locked out" when the candidate is elected. PAC contributions do not ensure "access." In fact, the figures show that, with very few exceptions, the size of the contributions in relation to the total cost of a campaign is not significant enough to "buy" anything. What PAC contributions do, however, is demonstrate a company's political realism; they say to an official that the company recognizes that without financial support he would not be in Washington.

One corporate lobbyist tells the story of meeting with a senator to gain his support on an issue of vital interest to the company. The senator met with the lobbyist for a few minutes, just long enough for the senator to tell him that he had voted "right" on that issue in the past and yet the company had never supported him. The lobbyist was embarrassed, the senator said he was in a hurry, and the meeting ended after seven minutes. This story illustrates that while a PAC contribution may not get a company access, it does create a measure of good will which is useful in political relations.

Recognizing the importance of financial support, companies are becoming more sophisticated in administering their PAC funds. That means they are becoming less cautious about the candidates they select and how much money they give to each. The safest policy is to give a small amount to many candidates, mostly incumbents. The more risky approach, but the one with the larger impact, is to target the funds—more money to fewer people, including challengers. The Washington representative of a Fortune 500 company describes this as the rifle vs. the shotgun approach. His company's political action committee uses the rifle approach with a remarkable rate of success; at the same time, funds are available for token participation through smaller amounts. The latter enables the company to show the flag at fund-raising events.

Besides allowing companies to participate in the electoral process, PACs also serve another function. They are an instrument for broader political education within the company. Soliciting money may be a first step in generating interest among a company's managers and employees in how government decisions affect their business. Nurtured with information about issues and feedback on how the recipient of PAC funds voted on those issues, employee interest can grow into much more than an annual contribution. It can evolve into a more active participation in politics, and that ultimately is even more important than money. To quote Malbin again, *"just as members do not depend on any one set of groups for significant portions of their campaign funds, neither do the most successful groups rely on contributions as the basis of anything more than a small part of their overall lobbying strategies."* p. 37 (emphasis his).[14]

External Support

Among a company's external resources are Washington's corps of lawyers and consultants, many of whom have served in previous administrations or Congresses, some of whom are waiting to serve in some future one. Most of these lawyers and consultants specialize in an area or have various specialties represented in the firm. Things to look for are not only what they offer but what "baggage" they carry with them. Where do they have access? (Here again that all-important question comes up.) How thoroughly do they do their homework? How creative are they in approaching a problem?

Consultants come in two categories: those who provide information and counsel and those who lobby on behalf of an interest. The reasons for retaining either kind are the same: to supplement staff and to buy information, experience, access, or judgment. The consultant who provides information may be a tremendous asset to the Washington office in obtaining information that perhaps the company could not get or in obtaining a different, possibly more candid, version than the company got. The consultant's analysis of the information may be particularly valuable, and he may be used to shed new light on a subject or to validate another source.

Another role for the consultant-lawyer is to give assistance on problems involving a level of detail or complexity with which the Washington office may have neither the time nor the capability to deal. Consultants who are familiar with the legislative history of a bill or the intricacies of a regulation are better able to tell a company what it can do than people who are not as familiar.

Trade associations are another resource for the company. Most companies belong to the association representing their particular industry as well as one cutting across industries, such as the National Association of Manufacturers and the United States Chamber of Commerce. Trade associations come in all shapes and sizes, some strong and active, others moribund and aimless; the quality of their staff varies as does their style of operation. The good ones can be of great help to the company. They supplement the company's own Washington staff by monitoring issues and gathering and analyzing information. They provide a forum where a company can get a reading on what other companies are doing on issues of common concern. Trade associations can amplify a company's voice by combining it with others to advocate a common position. Companies who are members of a strong trade association have an advantage over ones that are not, both in the kind of information they can get and the kind of clout they have.

A company can use a trade association to advance its particular interest, but only if it can develop support for its position among member companies. This means convincing other members that they have a stake in the outcome of the issue. Typically, an issue raised by one member is referred to a committee or task force which will study it and evaluate how it fits into the program of the association. If an issue is disproportionately important to one company, it may not be able to get the trade association to take up its cause. The government loan guarantee was such an issue for Chrysler. If an issue is particularly divisive, the association may be reluctant to take a position on it. For years, one prominent association had trouble coming to a consensus on international trade issues because its membership included some of the major steel companies, which tended to be protectionist, as well as other companies whose interest was in trade expansion.

Sometimes an association is formed to deal with a specific issue either because existing associations do not cover it adequately or because a new association would cut across existing groupings and pull together only companies—and possibly their nonbusiness allies—interested in that particular issue. Rarely is a legislative battle won by one company acting alone. Rather, it is done by a coalition of companies interested in that issue; or, more broadly, by a coalition that includes diverse interests that happen to come together on an issue. One example was the Tax Fairness Committee, a coalition of companies that lobbied for changes in sections of the tax code dealing with the taxation of foreign earned income. The coalition was formed for this specific objective and its *raison d' ˆetre* ended when the tax bill was passed. Another example is the Coalition for Employment Through Exports (CEE), a coalition to promote a common interest in export financing. This coalition of big and small business *and* labor *and* governors was formed to tell the story of the importance of exports to the United States economy and to generate support for adequate funding of the Export-Import Bank.

Ultimately, an association—whether ad hoc or institutionalized—is only as good as its member companies. The most skillful trade association staffs cannot make up for a weak corporate membership. Nevertheless, the quality of the trade association staff is very important and a measure of how strong the association is. If the staff is on top of issues; if the members provide the member companies with information or, better yet, analysis not readily available from other sources; if they provide some leadership by articulating disparate corporate interests and by coordinating action; and, finally, if they are respected by government decision makers and have access to them—these are all indicators of a strong trade association. The most important resource of the association is what the individual company can draw on internally. The Washington office is responsible for identifying these internal resources, preparing for action, and organizing the effort.

THE PROCESS OF REPRESENTATION

Preparing for Action

Having described some of the key support functions of a government affairs office, the next step is to show how they fit into the whole process of representation. In other words, having gathered the necessary information or having identified an issue, what does the Washington representative do with it? The process of representation is a dynamic, two-way process with the Washington representative in the center. Given a problem, he directs the flow of information, helps define the company's objectives, analyzes the Washington dimension of the problem, and coordinates the company's resources for action.

The objectives are not always obvious or easy to articulate. The problem may be ill-defined or it may only be anticipated. Preventive action may avoid the problem or may bring it on. The first decision of the Washington representative, if he initiated the action or brought the problem to the company's attention, is who should be involved in analyzing it and defining the company's objectives. If it is an issue involving one of the business units, it may not be appropriate to involve corporate headquarters. The level of involvement should be considered carefully. Just as it would be wrong to take a problem too high too soon in Washington, so it would be in a company. Bringing something to corporate's attention, for instance, automatically elevates its importance. If done too soon or without adequate preparation, it can impede the resolution of the problem.

Who participates in a decision is also a matter of judgment by the Washington representative. He may have to trace down who is responsible. If, for example, the problem involves financing a project in a foreign country, here are some of the people who may be included: the regional sales director, the project manager, the financial staff, the proposal development staff, and the marketing director. If it is a problem that might get the attention of the press or if it is likely to escalate, the sales, commercial and financial vice presidents may have to be brought in along with their counterparts at corporate headquarters and the staff concerned with press relations.

During the discussion, notes are compared. The Washington office's information may not be accurate, or it may be accurate but may contradict information from other sources. How the problem may unfold is discussed in terms of various scenarios, each one assessed as to its impact on the company. Questions are asked: What action needs to be taken? Perhaps more or different information is needed? Does old information need to be rechecked, confirmed, or updated? How far is the company willing to go to surmount obstacles to its project? Perhaps it has other, more important interests in the same country and this project would only upset the company's broader strategy. Perhaps this is a test market and the effort can be scrubbed without great cost.

The Washington representative has to know all this before he can develop a strategy for communicating the company's interests to the government. He has to know not only how much of his own or his staff's resources to commit but whom in the government he should approach. How urgent is the question? How much is at stake?

Getting the company's evaluation of a problem helps ensure that the Washington representative focuses on issues the company cares about. Much happens in Washington that is of interest only to people in Washington. Issues tend to develop a momentum of their own and the talk of the town is usually the President's or the Congress's agenda. The Washington representative's job is to select from that agenda the items that have an impact upon the company and to make sure that he takes his direction from the company's priorities, not from Washington's.

Setting priorities within the company is in itself a process involving the Washington representative. Some companies have a very formalized process, others not. Whatever procedure is followed, certain criteria must be met. Among the foremost considerations is that the company's priorities can be developed only in the context of what is realistically judged to be possible. The Washington office makes the political assessment of whether an issue is likely to be on the Congressional agenda, whether the climate is right to initiate action on a controversial subject, whether the company would be alone on an issue or joined by others, whether the administration would be receptive or is preoccupied by too many other concerns.

Setting priorities is not only useful to the company but is essential for the Washington representative. Once he knows what the company's priorities are, he is in a better position to allocate his own resources. He has a guideline for accepting or rejecting new demands placed on him by the company.

In one company with a fairly formalized process for setting priorities, the Washington office asks top management's approval twice a year on issues listed in order of priority according to the following categories: primary, major concern, and general. The Washington office prepares the list based on its knowledge of company interests and the likelihood that there will be government action on these interests. Primary measures are those that are of extreme importance to the company. They are the bottom line issues which, according to the Washington office, are ripe for action on the basis of its assessment of the Washington political scene. Issues of major concern are arbitrarily defined as affecting two or more major organizational divisions of the company. For example, legislation that is product specific may affect only the division producing that product, but a bill that imposes a new tax may affect several divisions. Issues of general interest affect the company but do not warrant an all-out effort. The amount of time spent monitoring, lobbying, attending mark-ups, working with staff, creating coalitions, and testifying depend on the issue and how it is ranked.

In setting priorities, the company has to decide what issues are ripe for action, what issues need work for eventual action, and what issues should be shelved. Timing is everything. The Foreign Corrupt Practices Act was passed in 1977 in the wake of scandals that companies were paying bribes to get business in foreign countries. For several years thereafter, no company would publicly criticize this confused and poorly formulated law for fear that it would be accused of being in favor of bribes. It would have been totally unrealistic for a Washington representative to recommend lobbying for clarification of the Act until there was a change in the political climate and some indication that his company would not be alone.

Waiting for the right time is best combined with quiet behind-the-scenes preparation. Developing a company position is a prerequisite to action in many companies. This too may be a more or less formalized process. In some companies, a nod from the CEO or a caucus with two or three key people is sufficient to establish the company position. In others, it requires an elaborate process of notification, argumentation, and clearance. Company positions are usually very general statements on an issue or a specific piece of legislation. They should be substantive enough to be of real guidance to the Washington office and anyone else in the company who is likely to take action. At the same time, they should be general enough to allow for flexibility in responding to the many changes a bill undergoes as it moves through Congress. If the Washington representative has to go back for clearance for each change, he cannot possibly be responsive fast enough to be effective. Given sufficient flexibility, he then has to determine when legislative developments fall within the company position and when they represent changes of such scope that new guidance is needed from the company.

The thorniest problem that can arise in developing a company position is when two units of the company are diametrically opposed to each other. What should the company position be when one unit favors trade expansion and the other is looking for protection? What if one unit wants to make air quality regulations less restrictive and the other benefits from strict controls because it manufactures pollution control equipment?

When conflicts like this arise, they cannot always be resolved at the Washington office level. They may require a decision by an appropriate corporate committee or the CEO. As troublesome (and time-consuming) as such a conflict may be, if it exists, the Washington office should encourage surfacing and resolving it. If the conflict were to come out after the corporate position had been defined, the company's ability to implement the position would be undermined.

Developing a company position involves research. First, the issue has to be defined: the problem, the proposed remedy, the arguments pro and con. Second, there has to be a determination of what it means to the company. Researching the answer to this question can serve an educational function for both the Washington staff and the company. When the Washington office brings an issue to the company's attention, it may find that there is little awareness within the company of the problem. If identified early enough, before the issue becomes a news item, there is a likelihood that the company has not focused on it. For example, the issue of barriers to trade in services (as opposed to products) has been gaining attention in Washington. The United States Trade Representative's office has compiled a detailed computerized list of such barriers and several senators have introduced bills dealing with the problem. The Washington office of an engineering and construction company brought these developments to the attention of company executives only to find that they had not given much thought to the subject of trade barriers to their business *as a problem for the government to address.* They had lived with these barriers so long that they were almost resigned to them. Moreover, they felt that lowering these barriers was a complex, long-range process and they did not see what meaning their involvement would have at this point.

The role of the Washington office in this case is not only to inform the company about developments in which it may have an interest but also to "sell" the company on the idea of participating in something which is expected to get results in the distant future, if ever. The Washington office may have to take the initiative to generate interest so that it can get staff assigned to gather data, analyze company impact, or do whatever is needed to back up the position.

The Washington representative can never assume that information is available in the form he needs. For example, the data may exist but may not be organized by Congressional district or state. He may find the information recorded according to products, by contracts, or business units. Or data may not exist at all and may need to be generated, as in the case of the company that wanted to measure how many man-hours are spent on paperwork to comply with government regulations.

The Washington representative may want to use certain figures that have to be checked or he may have to get permission for their release. He may need a survey or study by an independent team of experts. He may have good evidence of how a change in a law would help or hurt the company, but the company does not want to call attention to itself by taking a public stand. The Washington representative then has to decide whether he should let the issue go or try to convince the company otherwise. Frequently he is in a position to see ramifications of inaction that the company cannot. Should a company that has been prosecuted for price-fixing take a position on antitrust legislation? It may, in fact, have something very useful to add to the debate but may shy away from trying.

Companies tend to be quite cautious in taking a position, and rightly so. They have been burned by the public and the press enough times that they are reluctant to enter a public debate on an issue until the sides are clearly defined. The company's first responsibility is to its shareholders, and companies are justifiably leery of bringing upon themselves any publicity that may adversely affect the value of the company's stock. While this reluctance to take the offense may be changing, the tendency in most companies is still to wait for an issue to bubble up before they act.

In some cases this tendency works, particularly with legislative issues which, if they have any degree of complexity, are rarely surfaced and resolved in one session of Congress. With executive branch decision making, the time may be more compressed. Here again, the point is that the more complex the issue, the more sophisticated the information requirements and the more a company has to anticipate what it will need so that it can plan accordingly.

A well-known case is the Lilly company's response to the Nader-sponsored Health Research Group's petition to the Secretary of the Department of Health, Education, and Welfare to ban Darvon. Lilly's effort included ". . . an issues task force, an issues working group, matrix management procedures, a survey to measure physician awareness of Darvon's side effects and proper administration techniques, 289 hours of computer time, and an analysis by five systems analysts and statisticians of 455,000 records from the Drug Abuse Warning Network." The Health Research Group's petition was rejected.[15]

Once developed, the company position should be widely distributed in the company. Certainly, all the executives who are likely to be affected by an issue should have it, as should the grass roots representatives and the communication offices. There is no point in having a company position if it is kept a secret.

Communicating Corporate Interests

The purpose of all this preparation is to communicate the company's interests to the Washington decision maker. To paraphrase Harold Lasswell's famous description of politics, the central question that must be asked here is *Who* communicates *what* to *whom?* A subordinate question is *When* and *where* does the communication take place? Juggling these "five W's" is the final mark of the effective Washington representative. It takes all his experience, creativity, and resources to take any one problem and chart the appropriate course for communicating the company's interests.

What are the forces or organizational issues within the company that he must tackle in the process of communicating the company's interests? One issue certainly is to decide when it is appropriate for the Washington representative to perform the communication function and when it should be done by someone from corporate or from the field. As a general rule, most contacts can be made by the Washington representative. After all, that is why he is in Washington. But it is best for the Washington representative to assess each occasion for a contact (or meeting or communication) with a government official by asking the following questions:

1. What is the purpose of the meeting?
2. Who can communicate the company's message most effectively?
3. What is the appropriate level of participation?
4. Should the Washington representative attend the meeting?

These questions address the substantive and procedural concerns involved in arranging meetings with government officials. If these questions are not taken into consideration when the company and the Washington representative are deciding who should meet whom, the result can be embarrassment, wasted time, and a mismanaged problem.

In answering the who/whom question, the place to begin is not with the players but with the purpose of the meeting. The purpose may be to introduce the company to a government official (for example, to a new appointee in an agency with which the company has regular dealings); to discuss a problem (for example, the interpretation of new regulations); to negotiate a contract; to seek assistance or offer it.

Having determined the purpose of the meeting, the next question is who can communicate the company's message most effectively—the CEO, a lawyer, an engineer, a procurement specialist, a contracts officer? The answer depends on the level of expertise required and also on what the appropriate level of participation is. The objective is to get the right combination of skill and rank. If that combination does not reside in one person, a small delegation may be necessary. Taking into consideration the level or position of the participants is important, and not just for reasons of protocol. Rather it is done because of the likelihood that people of comparable rank have something in common in how they approach an issue, such as the degree of specificity they demand, the range of responsibilities they have, and the amount of authority they can bring to bear to produce results.

While it may be appropriate as a general rule to bring together people of comparable rank, that is not always the case. Titles can be misleading and the importance of staff positions varies from agency to agency as well as between the Congress and the executive branch. The CEO who refuses to talk to the chief counsel of a senate committee on the grounds that he will "only" see a senator is making a mistake and possibly alienating an influential person.

Sometimes the most effective person to communicate with an official is not the highest ranking person or the most competent technically. Instead, it may be someone in the company who knows the official personally. The Washington representative should make a point of seeking out such connections within the company and building on them rather than competing with them. He should never make the mistake of assuming that all wisdom flows from him, that because he is in Washington, he is the only one "in the know." As a general rule, the Washington representative should involve people from the field whenever it is appropriate. Not only will the meetings benefit from the specialized knowledge these people bring, but the Washington office can also benefit from exposing them to how the government works.

A few simple guidelines should be considered in communicating company interests to government officials.

1. Do not go to the top before you pave the way at the bottom. The person at the top will invariably turn to his own people first to be briefed on the subject of a proposed meeting. Subordinates, on the other hand, may become irritated if you jump over them and go to a higher authority. If subordinates are caught by surprise and are ill prepared to brief the boss, they will resent you for having embarrassed them. Whether subordinate levels are with you or against you when you go to the top, you are rarely better off by-passing them entirely.
2. Make sure that information is accurate and the presentation thorough. People in government are busy, and they do not

have time to hear the facts of a problem in installments. You should anticipate as many questions as possible and, if necessary, bring with you the people who have the expertise to answer them. Even if the meeting is with policy level officials, you can expect program and technical level people to be present. This means you have to be prepared to discuss your subject in general terms as well as be able to respond to specific questions. A company president may add luster to a meeting, but he may not be the most informed on the details of the problem.

3. Do not go to the top before it is time. In fact, do not have any meeting unless there is an action component. What are you asking for? If you cannot articulate clearly what you expect to come out of the meeting, chances are you are wasting time because you certainly will not be able to measure what you get.
4. Whenever possible, present your problem in the context of programs or functions which come under the responsibility of the official with whom you are meeting. In other words, do not just throw a problem at him. Give him some of the history behind the problem and put it in perspective by relating it to other germane developments.

   Conversely, let him know that you are sensitive to his problems. For example, if you are making a plea for federal funds, you should be aware of the budgetary constraints under which the official may be operating. You should also know who your competition is and develop a rationale for why your project should be supported.
5. After a meeting, leave behind a succinct statement of the problem or facts about the project or request. It is a small way to control information on what you communicated, but the opportunity should not be wasted.
6. Do not enlist one part of the government to bring pressure on another until it is absolutely necessary. For example, try not to bring Congressional pressure on an executive department or request the assistance of one agency against another. This is the most difficult maneuver to control and may backfire when the various players freeze their positions in the face of pressure from each other.

Another aspect of the who/whom question is whether the Washington representative should attend the meeting. He certainly cannot attend all meetings held in Washington with every person who flies in from his company. On the other hand, he must be kept informed about who is meeting with whom. Here again, there are a few guidelines:

1. Pay attention to any subject, and hence any meeting, that has the attention of your CEO or top management.
2. Attend all meetings where the subject to be discussed has policy implications or ramifications for several divisions of the company. This is to assure that one part of the company does not gain something at the expense of another.
3. Attend meetings where your company is presenting a problem either for the first time or for the first time to that particular official. This is a good way to stay abreast of what is happening and to help set the tone for subsequent meetings. It is especially necessary if Washington followup is required.
4. When the meeting is highly technical or part of an ongoing negotiation, your presence may be superfluous from a technical point of view. Nevertheless, you should attend if you perceive a political dimension to the problem that may require your attention. It is not unusual, for example, for technical people to attend a meeting and arrive at a perfectly good technical solution which has no chance of being implemented for political reasons.
5. If you do not attend, insist on being briefed on the meeting. Often the people in the field think they can handle a problem themselves only to discover at the eleventh hour that they need the Washington office's help.
6. Set up a system for coordinating communications between company employees and government officials.

A common problem for all Washington representatives is how to manage their own company people who either should come to Washington but do not want to or those who are ready to come to Washington at the drop of a hat but are not needed. Then there are those good company bureaucrats who stick with a problem, taking it upon themselves to hound an agency into action. They plague the agency with phone calls, usually not targeted very carefully, and act as if theirs is the only problem Washington should be working on. A particularly counterproductive pattern of behavior—and one which damages the company's reputation—is when three or four different people (sometimes in the same division) call the same government official to ask a question or to get a status report on a case. This behavior gives the appearance of an organization in disarray and it uses up the good will of the government official. The Washington representative usually has the job of patching up relations. Less damage is done (although the inquiry is still redundant) if the four people call the Washington representative and he calls the government official. He may in fact already have the answer to their question. Another type of behavior common in large companies is the "every unit for itself" syndrome. With little knowledge of what another unit is doing and possibly some indifference, each unit tries to get what *it* needs out of Washington. While this may work for a time, it too eventually becomes counterproductive. If there is no mechanism in the company for assigning priorities and coordinating contacts with Washington, the task of deciding which request is most important is left to the government bureaucrat. That is unfair, inefficient, and dangerous.

One company found that each of its units was dealing separately with the Commerce Department's export licensing offices. Each unit would insist that its application be given priority consideration or request expedited action for one reason or another. They would all telephone for status reports. They would write letters to the wrong person and, not knowing how decisions are made, expect a response that only another person could give. This company solved the problem by setting up an export license coordinating unit in its Washington office whose function was to log in every application, transmit it to Commerce, and then monitor its progress, taking action when necessary.

No company has a solution for the "eager beavers" or "nervous Nellies" in the company or, perish the thought, those who do not even think of including the Washington office and decide on their own to communicate with official Washington. Some companies do, however, have a formal process for coordinating contacts. If they do not, they need at the very least a clear directive assigning responsibility for coordination to the Washington office.

Besides the who/whom issue and the problem of coordination, there is the question of what form the communication should take. A study was recently conducted to determine which communication tools Congressional staff members considered useful and how they valued information based upon the source from which it was received.[16] The study found that spontaneous individually composed letters from constituents are the most effective way of communicating with Congressional decision makers. The professional lobbyist is rated higher on issues arising from Congressional review of government agencies and programs than on general or local issues.

As to types of communication, the study found that direct communications of all kinds—letters, phone calls, visits, position papers—are preferred to methods involving the press and broadcast media. The study notes that this may suggest a preference for unfiltered information. Furthermore, compared to other forms of information, written information had a much higher visibility rating.

The effective corporate lobbyist has known for a long time what this study confirmed: the importance of constituents who communicate directly with their representatives, preferably through a printed message. This is the rationale behind grass roots programs and behind all corporate position development and fact-gathering efforts that go into preparing for action.

The tactics lobbyists use in dealing with Congress can also be used effectively with the executive branch. Although both political appointees and career civil servants seem to be immune to grass roots pressure, that is never completely the case. The "who listens to whom" rule still applies, and the good lobbyist searches for access points.

COMMERCIAL SUPPORT

One function performed by the Washington office that may involve both legislative and executive branch advocacy deals with projects and products rather than issues. It is called, for want of a better term, "commercial support" and refers to activities undertaken in Washington to assist a unit of the company to define a market, assess risk, sell a product, or win a project.

This activity may be domestically or internationally oriented, but it takes place in Washington because decisions made there can help or hinder a company's commercial efforts on a project. Companies that deal in high-visibility, big-ticket products or projects—a dam, a refinery, an airplane—are in special need of this kind of Washington support. Products or projects in this category are rarely straight commercial deals; they are not won or lost merely on the basis of quality and price. There may be foreign policy considerations which will influence a customer to buy from a company in one country instead of another. Some countries, for example, may want to diversify their source of supply in order to reduce their dependence on a historical trading partner. Others may want to use a major purchase to extract concessions or leverage decisions in areas that have nothing to do with the commercial deal. Finally, United States companies have to contend with competitors whose governments offer heavily subsidized export credits forcing United States companies to seek matching support.

These and other instances of government involvement in commercial transactions mean that no company can afford to conduct business without being sensitive to noncommercial considerations. The role of the Washington office in supporting the company's commercial activity is to enlist the assistance of the United States government, to insulate the commercial activity against the impact of damaging political developments and, to prevent political issues from skewing a commercial decision.

Organizing this support involves a level of coordination every bit as complex as working on an issue. Take a sales effort on a major project in a foreign country as an example, and examine what is involved in providing Washington support for it. (The example could also apply to a domestic project, but the foreign example illustrates a greater variety of organizational issues. In addition, the Washington component of international commercial activity is not as widely known.) First, the Washington office has to *know* about the sales effort. How does the Washington representative find out? When does he find out? By the time a sales effort becomes a "Washington problem," it is usually too late. The Washington representative has to be plugged in early enough to help prevent a problem or to be ready in case a problem arises.

Some companies ask the Washington office to monitor United States government policies toward countries or markets which the company has targeted as being of strategic importance to its business development. To be able to identify the policy changes that may affect the company's plans in a foreign country, the Washington representative should receive regularly updated information on the company's business activity in that country. The crisis in the Falkland Islands had important ramifications for a company planning to establish a manufacturing facility in Argentina. Changes in United States policy toward the Soviet Union and Eastern Europe have strategic implications for a company that had targeted those markets.

If the effort in the foreign country is to land a contract on a major project, it could involve years of work. Given competing priorities, the Washington office probably will not focus on it until it reaches an active stage. Nevertheless, some companies include their Washington office in the strategic planning process by requesting the representative to review the plans of the business units and comment on the assumptions on which the plans are based. Some companies go a step further and outline what policies in the foreign country would have to be changed (not just taken into account) to achieve company plans or to create a more hospitable business climate.

There are at least five functions related to commercial support where the Washington office has a role to play.

1. *Project Introduction.* In the early stages of a project, such as the bidding period, the Washington office briefs appropriate government people about the scope of the project. These are people who either have (or might have) a decision-making role with respect to the project or who may be good sources of information. They are generally very receptive to such briefings because they too need information. Knowing about the project prepares them to deal with problems should they arise either with the project or in the country where the project is being executed. For example, the State Department should be kept informed of business activity in certain high-risk countries, especially if hostilities are likely. The revolution in Iran, the war between Iraq and Iran, and the conflict between the United States and Libya are examples of situations when United

States companies needed to coordinate with State regarding the advisability of continued business activity in those countries.

2. *Monitoring*. The Washington office can be one of the listening posts for monitoring developments that may affect the project, just as it monitors issue-related developments. The developments to be monitored from Washington fall into two categories: first, foreign policies of the United States government that may not have a direct impact on the project but that could have unintended consequences that have an affect. Second, the business environment in the country where the project is planned. Although there are many sources of information about foreign political and economic developments or on policies which may affect United States trade, certainly the Washington information network should not be overlooked. The CIA, the "country desks" at the Departments of State and Commerce, the embassies, the academic institutions, consultants, and think tanks are all sources of information. The Washington representative must be cautioned, however, not to burden these sources. Talking to them should not be a substitute for reading and their time should not be wasted giving information which is available in public documents.

The Washington office can also perform a useful coordinating function when different parts of the company are doing business in the same foreign country and all need Washington assistance. It is not unusual for one part of the company to be ignorant of what another is doing; and as a result, to fail to share information with the other or even get in each other's way. The Washington office may face another complication when two parts of the company require support for conflicting goals and a decision has to be made in favor of one or the other. The company must have its own house in order; it has to be able to resolve these questions so that the Washington representative can clearly communicate the corporate interest. If he gives conflicting signals or misguides government officials, he may set in motion a chain of events that he cannot control.

3. *Early Warning*. This function flows from the monitoring activities. Presumably, if the information between Washington and the rest of the company is adequate and timely, *in both directions*, the company is able to identify potential problems before they get out of hand. "In both directions" is emphasized because information

from the company to the Washington office is as important as information from Washington to the company. If a major change takes place in the project's life cycle—scope, funding, location, performance, or whatever—and the Washington representative does not know about it, he cannot negotiate the project's course through the political waters.

4. *Crisis Response*. This function is performed in the event there is a problem. Again, the rules that apply to dealing with issues apply to projects. There must be an agreed plan of action. Who needs to be contacted by whom? There is a tendency in companies to want to go to the top with their problems. This attitude is born partly of naiveté and partly of arrogance. CEOs who are used to being treated with deference on their own territory expect easy access to a Cabinet official. They are surprised, possibly indignant, when the Washington office cannot arrange for an appointment. This puts the Washington representative in a bind. Wanting to deliver for the boss but understanding the demands on a Cabinet officer's time, he is careful how he uses his chits with both. One thing is certain: if the right people have been kept informed all along, the chances of getting the right people to focus on the company's problem in a time of crisis are measurably increased.

5. *Education*. A final function in communicating project-related interests is an educational one. Letting official Washington know what a company has done in a country—the award of a project, a noteworthy sale, a completed transaction—publicizes the company, builds name recognition, and, one hopes, enhances its reputation.

REPRESENTING WASHINGTON TO THE CORPORATION

This chapter has been about representing the corporate interest in Washington. But a leitmotif throughout has been that the Washington representative also has to lobby the corporation. This process involves more than reporting back to the company on information gathered or action taken. *It means taking steps to create a receptive audience within the company to receive that information*. It means having an audience that is aware of the Washington dimension of the activity and that knows what to ask of the Washington representative.

A leading Washington consultant approached a major firm's Washington office in an effort to market his services. The company should have been, by any standard, a candidate for more information and analysis. Government decisions affected this company's businesses daily and yet it was not sufficiently involved in those decisions. The consultant's services were turned down because, according to the Washington representative, the company's infrastructure was inadequate to handle the additional information load the consultant was proposing to provide. In other words, not enough people in the right places in the company were sufficiently attuned to Washington to know what to do with the additional information.

The Washington representative has to help his company understand how Washington works. He has to understand the attitudinal factors that may make it difficult for corporate people to deal with Washington. They may misinterpret signals from Washington, be unresponsive when they should be cooperative, or be impatient simply because they do not understand the system. The corporate representative is forever interpreting Washington developments to the people in the field.

Here are three frustrating examples:

- A policy review takes several months longer than expected; business decisions may have to be postponed. If the Washington representative did not prepare his company for this delay, he should try to help the company understand the reasons for it. If the reason is simply the slowness of the bureaucracy, it may lead to one kind of action on the part of the company—waiting. If, on the other hand, the reason is that a new set of circumstances had to be factored into the policy review and those circumstances make it likely that the policy review will result in an unfavorable policy, the company may decide to take measures to protect itself. Conversely, if the outcome of the policy review is likely to be positive, the company can position itself to take advantage of the opportunities.
- A regulation is ambiguous. Not wanting to risk being in violation, a company may err on the side of caution. With the right

kind of guidance, however, from the Washington representative, the company can assess more accurately the parameters of permissible behavior. It should be noted that this is not just a legal question. Political considerations may also be important. For example, the same set of regulations may be interpreted differently by two administrations even though there appears to be continuity on the policy level. The role of the Washington representative in this case would be to sort out what is said from what is likely to be done, based on his knowledge of the players and the process.

- A policy decision is about to be made by the government. Business wants to know who will be involved in that decision, and it turns out that no one controls who will participate. In this case, the Washington representative tries to anticipate developments, prepares the appropriate people in the company, and then carries them along as events unfold. As former Treasury Secretary W. Michael Blumenthal remarked, the difference between business and government in the development and implementation of policy is that in a company you can clearly define who is involved. In government, no one has that power. In government, ". . . you have to learn to become one of a large number of players in a floating crap game, rather than the leader of a well-organized casino that you are in charge of."[17]

Corporate Washington representatives have a saying that they spend 50 percent of their time lobbying their own company. This point goes back to the earlier discussion of the two subcultures of the Washington representative and his role in interpreting and explaining the one to the other. The difficulty in being part of two cultures is that the Washington representative is both an insider and an outsider in each.

On balance, however, he must opt in favor of his corporate identity. If he becomes alienated from his company, if he loses touch with it because he has become so much a part of the Washington scene, then he can no longer do his job. If he cannot communicate his company's interests, he eventually loses his usefulness in Washington.

To maintain his corporate identity and continue to be more of an insider than an outsider in his company, the Washington representative's loyalty is repeatedly tested. The company, being fundamentally distrustful of Washington, wants to make sure its representative has not been coopted. In reporting on a development, the Washington representative may be accused of defending it; by explaining a decision, he may be suspected of pardoning it; by predicting it, he may be misunderstood as seeking it. Therefore, how a Washington representative communicates with his company is very important—how he describes events, frames issues, and especially how he relates bad news. The "shoot the messenger" syndrome is popular in the executive suite.

Educating the company on how to deal with Washington is an ongoing activity not only because normal management turnover brings in new people but also because most company people do not routinely think about Washington when they do their work. There is no substitute for building company awareness of the need to involve the Washington office, especially before problems arise. A directive from corporate headquarters telling managers that they must consult with Washington is one way to do it, but it is not the most effective. The company's officers, managers, service personnel, and others involved have to develop an understanding of what the Washington office does and what it can do for them.

Washington representatives who have had sales experience recognize that they have to do a sales job within the company too. Their product has to be promoted, demand identified or generated, and orders filled. One way to educate the company is, of course, through the grass roots program, but there are other ways. Newsletters or memos to selected company constituencies—technical, financial, international, sales, management, strategic planning—keep people informed of developments in their area and remind them to factor Washington into their thinking. Regular briefings for these constituencies either in Washington or in their home offices are helpful. Participating in the work of committees and task forces where the Washington office has something to contribute provides another good vehicle for educating the company and keeping the Washington staff informed.

Finally, the most effective way to encourage people throughout the company to understand and involve the Washington office is by performing well and keeping a log of all requests for assistance. Many small, routine requests add up to a lot of work, but they may go unnoticed. One Washington representative sends a monthly report to his management to make them cognizant of the scope of his activities. News of success travels fast and every person in the company who has received assistance from the Washington office is a potential ambassador for it. As the demands for his services increase, the Washington representative has to assess how much business he can handle and what kinds of expectations he can reasonably fulfill. Conversely, the company has to evaluate his effectiveness.

It is difficult to measure success in the area of business-government relations. Quantitative measurements which business likes to use are particularly rigid but not impossible to apply. Ultimately, a combination of qualitative and quantitative criteria must be used. The effectiveness of the Washington representative should be evaluted according to his performance in these five areas:

1. Anticipating public policy issues of importance to the company;
2. Advising management in a timely and accurate manner, using good judgment as to what is relevant and important in developments of interest to the company, and recommending appropriate courses of action;
3. Coordinating the communication of the company's views and applying resources in accordance with the company's interests;
4. Contributing to the improvement of political and economic conditions affecting company operations;
5. Developing awareness within the company about corporate responsibility outside the business environment.

Some of these qualitative measurements can be translated into numbers. As one corporate executive instructed its Washington office: "Do not use words such as 'enhance,' and 'contribute,' to describe your function. Describe it in terms of what you contribute to the bottom line." Note the value of a project, of a license, of the impact of a law or regulation. But more important than any numbers are the objectives the Washington representative *negotiates* with his management and whether or not he achieves those objectives. If the Washington operation is taken seriously, corporate management will not impose a numbers game on it, but neither will it let the Washington representative write his own rules.

When asked about trends in public affairs in the next decade, the companies responding to the Boston Public Affairs survey cited these four:

(1) Public affairs, and business in general, will be more "proactive." That is, they will be more constructively involved in formulating and implementing public policy.

(2) Public affairs will become more involved in day-to-day company decision-making and in corporate planning.

(3) Public affairs practitioners will be more sophisticated; they will know more about public policy and about their companies.

(4) Public affairs will increasingly involve managers and employees in activities designed to shape public policy and/or convey the company's opinion to government and the public at large.[18]

If these projections are accurate, there will clearly be more occasions when business and government must communicate with each other. Whatever the issue, the level of professionalism and organization that companies bring to the representation of their interests will affect their relationship with the government. And whether that relationship tends toward conflict or cooperation, the corporate Washington representative's role will be to guide his company to participate in the political process in an informed—and possibly enlightened—way.

FOOTNOTES

[1]Chandler, Alfred D., Jr., "The Adversaries," *Harvard Business Review*, November-December 1979, p. 89.

[2]Greider, William, *Washington Post*, January 20, 1981, Section Z, p. 28, col. A.

[3]Schultz, George P., "The Abrasive Interface," *Harvard Business Review, op. cit.*, pp. 94–95.

[4]*Ibid*, p. 95.

[5]Tyrell, R. Emmett, Jr., *Washington Post*, January 12, 1981, p. 15, col. 1.

[6]Reagan, Ronald, "Government and Business in the 80s," *The Wall Street Journal*, January 9, 1981, p. 18, col. 4.

[7]This term is borrowed from French political scientist, Raymond Aron, who 15 years ago applied it to the relationship between the two superpowers, the United States and the Soviet Union. Aron's concept referred to the relationship between two units (states) of the international system which, despite their differences, have more in common with each other than with third parties. Their interest in preserving the thermonuclear duopoly and their fears of total war form the basis of the kinship-hostility relationship which forces them to continue debate even as they carry on combat. (Raymond Aron, *Peace & War*, New York, Frederich A. Praeger, 1966, pp. 536–572.)

[8]"Public Affairs Offices and Their Functions, Summary of Survey Responses," Public Affairs Research Group, Boston University, March 1981.

[9]Burns, Thomas S., "Inside ITT's Washington Office," *Business and Society*, Autumn 1974 #11, pp. 23–25, p. 24.

[10]McGrath, Phyllis, *Redefining Corporate-Federal Relations*. New York: The Conference Board, 1979. This report contains many examples of the government relations practices of major U.S. corporations.

[11]Hughes, Mike, InterMatrix Incorporated.

[12]O'Shea, Timothy J., Westinghouse. Washington Office.

[13]Malbin, Michael, Jr., "Campaign Financing and the 'Special Interests'," *The Public Interest*, #56 Summer 1979, pp. 21–42, p. 25.

[14]*Ibid*, p. 37.

[15]Gruber, William H. and Raymond L. Hoewing, "The New Management in Corporate Public Affairs," *Public Affairs Review*, 1980, pp. 13–23, p. 21.

[16]Institute for Government Public Information Research, The American University, "Communications and Congress," The Marsteller Foundation, 1981.

[17]Nickel, Herman, "Candid Reflections of a Businessman in Washington," *Fortune*, January 29, 1979, pp. 36–49, p. 45.

[18]Public Affairs Research Group, *op. cit.*, p. 36.

Chapter 8

CORPORATE PLANNING IN A CHANGING WASHINGTON ENVIRONMENT: DIVINING AND SHAPING THE FUTURE

ELLIOT L. RICHARDSON*

When after nearly sixteen years in a (some would say excessive) variety of federal and state positions I eventually rejoined the private sector, I brought with me the impression that few corporations do a good job of trying to anticipate and to shape the public policies vital to their long-term interests. It was a notion that I might quickly have put aside as a bit of excess baggage picked up during my government service but for the fact that during the several following weeks I ran into a number of people who could not have been accused of the same bias but who shared the same view. One was a senior executive in a company that performs economic studies for at least half of the Fortune 500, one was a principal in a highly successful policy analysis firm, two were responsible for corporate planning in large corporations, and several others were lawyers with extensive experience in representing corporate clients in their deal-

---

*Elliot L. Richardson is the senior resident partner in the Washington, D.C. office of Milbank, Tweed, Hadley & McCloy. Former Lieutenant Governor and Attorney General of Massachusetts, he served as Under Secretary of State, Secretary of HEW, Secretary of Defense, Attorney General of the United States, Ambassador to Great Britain, Secretary of Commerce, and Ambassador-at-Large for the Law of the Sea Conference. He also currently serves as Chairman of the United Nations Association of the U.S.A.

ings with the federal government. Subsequent inquiries and observations have convinced me not only that my initial impression is valid but that it reflects a situation bad for the business community, bad for the government, and bad for the nation as a whole.

That this state of affairs could have come about in the first place is the consequence of a failure of imagination. That failure has led in turn to deficiencies in the strategic planning process that must be overcome if business is to play a more intelligent and far-sighted role in the shaping of public policy.

Planning is figuring out where you are, where you want to go, and how to get there. Strategic planning takes in a wide contemporary horizon and looks as far into the future as it is possible to see. Tactical planning embraces the practical, immediate steps required to carry out the strategic plan.

Corporate planners have traditionally selected concretely definable objectives, looked for paths toward those objectives that could take maximum advantage of the corporation's strengths, and sought to minimize risks. Basic to the corporate plan is a comprehensive study of the total environment in which the corporation is expected to operate. This involves not only careful assessment of the existing facts but the discernment of current trends and their projection ahead in order to arrive at an assessment of future conditions.

Educated guesses as to the likely direction, velocity, and impact of such large-scale phenomena as demographic trends, pervasive social changes, and economic cycles are obviously important to such an assessment. The same is true of major political events such as the Yom Kippur War, the rise of OPEC, or the fall of the Shah, although their predictability is less a matter of projecting trends than of the imaginative analysis of intelligence. While corporate leaders may not in fact be altogether helpless to influence, as distinguished from hedging against, developments of this magnitude, few chief executives since William Randolph Hearst have regarded them as subject to manipulation. They are reckoned with instead, like the seasons and the weather (which may on occasion be ripe for cloud-seeding), simply as factors to be taken into account.

But not all environmental facts are beyond the reach of corporate influence. The planning process, nevertheless, does not often give high priority to the question of when an effort to modify some environmental circumstance should be made an objective of the plan. In many situations it is obvious that such a modification would—if it could be achieved—be of major benefit to the corporation. For example, public attitudes toward regulation may be susceptible to influence through the political and educational process. In such a case, not to incorporate the objective into the plan would be justified only if the factor in question were found to be so completely resistant to modification that the cost of attempting to modify it would exceed the benefit.

To the extent, of course, that a given social, economic, or political trend is both favorable to the corporation and likely to persist without the intervention of some external influence, there is no need to do anything about it—except to pray for its continuation. To the extent, on the other hand, that such a trend seems likely to lead to an undesirable consequence, the question of how and through whom to counteract it has to be considered. Few such consequences are so small or so localized that they can be dealt with by a single company, however large. Most consequences require affirmative action, either through an industrial association or through a coalition created for the purpose. In some cases voluntary action, if adequate in scope and taken in time, is sufficient to hold off government intervention. An illustration is the voluntary energy conservation program undertaken by industry in response to the 1973 oil embargo and the subsequent increase in petroleum prices. By the close of 1979, the heaviest industrial energy consumers had achieved efficiency savings, per unit of production, of 15 percent in comparison to the 1972 base period. In 1979, five industries—food, petroleum, transportation equipment, chemicals, and machinery (except electrical)—had surpassed their 1980 energy efficiency improvement targets by 3 to 10 percent.[1]

Generally speaking, the larger the problem and the more serious its potentional consequences, the more certain it is that some form of government action will ensue. The proper tasks of the planning process are to discern such problems at the earliest possible stage, to anticipate the forms that public intervention may take, and to seek to bring about a result that efficiently accommodates both the public interest in coping with the problem and the public interest in the freedom of private enterprise. The defect of most corporate attempts to influence government action, however, is that they tend to focus only on the most obvious components of the political process—elective contests at one end of the spectrum and the regulatory free-for-all at the other—but to neglect the in-between process of policy development. And yet policy development is likely to have far more direct relevance for the corporation's long-term interests. It is with respect to policy development, in any case, that creative strategic planning can have its greatest impact. It is here also that the Washington representative can rise to—or neglect—his most important opportunities.

A public policy aims at promoting a result that would not otherwise occur. Every such policy, whether embodied in an act of Congress, an administrative regulation, or a court decision, is an intervention into the flow of events. The occasions for intervention that most concern business are by-products of normal business activity whose downstream consequences affect some broad public interest such as employee health and safety, a clean environment, energy conservation, freedom of competition, or a fair securities market. Even where the resulting regulation cannot in a given case legitimately be challenged on the grounds that government should altogether have stayed its hand, business has long had reason to be concerned that the cumulative effect of separately defensible regulations has been to create a serious drag on growth and productivity. To reduce this drag, future government intervention, where it cannot be avoided, must be designed with an eye to performing its purpose with the maximum of precision and a minimum of unwanted side effects.

In order to help assure that a governmental response to an emerging problem would meet these specifications, policy-oriented planning would seek to discern the early signs of public demand for corrective action and would propose steps that business leaders and their Washington representatives could jointly take. One example of a situation in which this did *not* happen is the consumer movement. Originally, one might have thought that the maxim "the customer is always right" would have prompted corporate managers to seek ways of anticipating consumer complaints and thereby to minimize the necessity for government intervention. Instead, the consumer movement was treated as a hostile force. Its demands were met grudgingly and only under pressure. Regulations requiring automobile safety measures, truth in lending, informative labeling, and drug purity and effectiveness were forced upon industries insistent that no problem existed. Small wonder, therefore, that the outcome was a solution more burdensome and expensive than would have emerged from a cooperative effort to maximize the economy and efficiency of a regulatory result which, in some form, could have been foreseen as inevitable.

Public demands for a cleaner environment, safer working conditions, and safeguards against toxic substances met similar industry resistance and led to similar results. Such defensiveness is shortsighted. Although sound planning could have stimulated collaboration, the consequence instead has been confrontation. Adversarial encounters have displaced joint participation in the design of a balanced approach. The regulators and their constituencies have become combatants when they could have been partners. This antagonism has led in turn to an excess of zeal on the regulators' part that was bound to reinforce the vicious circle. As Robert Reich, former Director of Policy Planning and Evaluation for the Federal Trade Commission, has pointed out, retaliation by the regulatory agencies has taken such forms as threatening massive subpoenas, broadcasting adverse publicity, and installing cumbersome mechanisms of compliance. He adds, "As a result, the process of designing and implementing regulations has become a terribly expensive zero-sum game: if business wins, the proposed regulation is stymied; if government wins, a new and seemingly oppressive regulation is imposed."[2]

Deficient strategic planning, an excessively combative attitude toward the regulatory process, and too much litigation are related but distinguishable phenomena. All have undesirable consequences, all impose excessive costs. Tackling the shortcomings of the planning process should come first, however, because early identification of problems likely to lead to demands for government intervention and early efforts to solve these problems in ways that minimize government intrusion and maximize reliance on private initiative are likely to reduce the occasions for confrontation, to short-circuit the need for adversary proceedings, and thus to head off costly litigation.

How best to avoid the unnecessary costs of confrontation and to shape efficient instruments of public policy are questions uniquely appropriate for strategic planners. The fact that planners are seldom asked to address these questions weakens the process by which the balance is struck between the public interest in encouraging entrepreneurial initiative and the public interest in protecting or promoting some other interest. But responsibility for the nonparticipation of strategic planners in this process cannot fairly be laid at their own door. Part of the blame belongs to the regulatory agencies, which have commonly preferred to keep business at arm's length during the formative stages of their planning lest they be—or seem to be—subject to undue influence by the subjects of their regulation. Conditioned to believe that government and business should never meet except in combat, the regulators have typically avoided opportunities for early consultation with representatives of the regulated industry.

Another part of the blame belongs to the corporate side. The blame is shared between senior managers whose experience has not exposed them to the arena in which public policies are formed and Washington intermediaries who, having spent their lives in that very arena, think of it primarily as a place for the display of their gladiatorial prowess. Reluctant to commit corporate resources to the policy development process as early as the stage when the first stirrings of public concern with an emergent problem have begun to disturb the status quo, the managers are prepared to address the problem only when it has already begun to obtrude itself on the day-to-day demands of the business. The intermediaries, who in most cases have not even been hired until confrontation is imminent, take it for granted that they should report for duty prepared to do battle. And even when called upon early enough so that a remedial solution is still possible, they tend to be no less wary than the regulatory staff of letting their principals become involved at an early stage lest credence thereby be given to the agency's concerns.

Even the legislation creating the regulatory framework can sometimes discourage a problem-solving approach. Take the case of the Clean Air and Clean Water Acts, for example. At a recent conference on environmental disputes held under the auspices of The Center for Public Resources, it was concluded that these statutes are deliberately designed to foster adversarial antagonism. The acts are dogmatically prescriptive and excessively detailed; they discourage innovative techniques; they impose rigid deadlines, thus denying the parties the time needed to build a workable consensus. The result of "Congress's presumption of adversariness among the parties," according to the conference participants, is "an elaborate procedural game—a game whose outcome is win-lose (as opposed to negotiation's win-a-little/win-a-little), and which makes winning a function of how well the adversary game is played."[3]

Corporate planning departments, meanwhile, have been allowed to regard the early manifestations of an emerging public concern as a remote phenomenon—one to be reckoned with rather than influenced, like those other impervious forces mentioned earlier. When impact of the problem does finally create alarm, the reaction is apt to be panicky if not purposeless. This reaction is one that I have often encountered in the course of my government service, and it has always brought to mind a picture of people in a riverside town frantically piling sandbags on the levee after the flood crest has already passed downstream.

Strategic planning on a scale involving positive steps to shape public policy requires creative collaboration between far-sighted business leadership and broad-gauged Washington representatives. To be effective even at the late confrontational stage of a public-policy issue, the Washington representative must be able to draw upon an intimate understanding of an intricate web of personal and institutional relationships. He must know how executive branch agencies work and what objectives motivate them. He must understand "the Hill," its processes and personalities. He must know who will be affected, how, and by what proposed policy. He must know which interests coincide and which diverge.

If the Washington representative is also to play a useful part in strategic planning, he must in addition be able to match the planners at corporate headquarters in the ability to think in long-range terms. He must have a feel for the social, economic, and political forces behind the evolution of public policies and know how to interpret the aims and attitudes of the groups pressing for change. He must be capable of providing sound and resourceful advice about how best to modify or redirect the thrusts emanating from these forces. Above all, he must possess the imagination and creativity to invent ways of reconciling public and private interests—which is to say, reconciling competing public interests. And that means that he must also be resourceful in finding ways to convince the private interests he represents of the necessity for compromise with other private interests.

For lawyers in particular, the formulation and execution of a long-range approach to a strategic goal does not come naturally. Trained as advocates, we tend to be combative. Although we do not lack a capacity for compromise, our usual compromises seek to balance litigating chances rather than to create a charter for an enduring relationship. One reason for this, I believe—apart from our conditioning by the adversary system—is that the case method by which we were taught in law school relies almost entirely on appellate court opinions. These invariably rest on a summary of the facts as they existed at a given moment. The result is that our powers of analysis have been developed by the scrutiny of frozen cross sections rather than by the effort to anticipate the downstream implications of events.

In the real world, of course, no set of facts stands still. Every "statement of a case" is a static abstraction from a dynamic process. Although no intelligent lawyer is unaware of this, his instinctive tendency is to deal with the situation as he finds it—to think in terms of "the facts," "the parties," "the interests at stake," and so on. This tendency leads him at most to be willing to "take the dynamics into account" instead of making them his point of departure.

In my own case, an awareness of this limitation of my legal training was a lesson taught by political and administrative experience, and I suspect that most lawyers who have become effective public policy strategists have benefited from immersion in the legislative, bureaucratic, or political cauldron. Not that there are no other apprenticeships. Indeed, I have often thought that a useful way to offset the habit of static analysis would be to expose lawyers to a postgraduate course in situation management in which the vocabulary was borrowed from a textbook on fluid dynamics.

From the standpoint of the general public interest there is good reason to be concerned about the consequences of a short-range, narrow, and combative approach to conflicts among competing interests. One of these consequences is too much law. In a speech at the Harvard Law School calling for a national effort to stem the legal flood and to eliminate or streamline much of the law that we now have, Judge Henry J. Friendly observed, "No small part of the perilous decline in the productivity of the United States is due to an overdose of law."[4] Judge Friendly is among the most eminent as well as eloquent of those who have viewed this development with dismay, but he is by no means alone. It is clear, in any case, that in referring to "an overdose of law" he meant to include the regulatory process. As to the regulatory process, many even among those who make a living from resistance to regulation would agree with Reich that:

> We can no longer afford the high price of regulatory warfare. It saps the scarce resources of business and government and fails to solve critical public problems. The regulatory process should never become a free-for-all confrontation. It should facilitate compromise and flexibility, not unblinking rigidity. Above all, it should encourage creative problem solving, not tactical gamesmanship.[5]

That creative problem solving benefits the general public interest is scarcely debatable. It is not self-evident, however, where corporate interests are concerned. What saps the resources of government may be a wise investment for the private sector. It is perhaps demonstrable, indeed, that many a battle against regulation has paid for itself through the savings generated by delay, the extraction of an outcome less stringent and therefore less expensive than would otherwise have resulted, or some combination of both.

The paper companies, for example, may be able to show that their fight against pollution controls bought just such a net benefit. Why should it matter, then, that the industry thereby gave itself a public black eye? Since the industry was collectively able to exercise sufficient discipline over its members to preserve a united front, no company could gain a competitive advantage by currying public favor. There was no significant risk, moreover, that public hostility would accelerate the substitution of other materials—plastic or cloth, for instance. Where else could anyone go for paper?

It is arguable, in any case, that corporations have an obligation to their shareholders to resist any proposed government regulation or control that would add to the costs of doing business and thus reduce the bottom line. Indeed, it is possible to conceive of situations in which corporate managers would be exposed to personal liability for voluntarily adopting some costly constraint not required by law. Be that as it may, the belief that regulation should be imposed, not embraced, leads logically to the conclusion that it must be resisted.

Is there, then, no purely prudential case to be made for a de-escalation of regulatory conflict other than the saving of professional fees? Is this the only corporate justification for an approach to public policy issues that recognizes the possible desirability of accepting less than the corporation's maximum demands?

If the answer to these questions had to be "yes," the outlook for the reversal of current trends toward more conflict, more litigation, and more embittered regulatory warfare would be bleak indeed. Recent history, however, points to a different answer. It suggests, even demonstrates, that the reward for inflexible and shortsighted combativeness is a regulatory outcome more burdensome, more cumbersome, more restrictive, and more costly than would result from a more flexible and broad-gauged strategy.

The case of the coal industry is instructive. Early in the 1970's, when the regulatory movement began to gather momentum, industry and advocates of "the public interest" found themselves from the outset thrust into an adversarial mode. Each in consequence staked out harder positions than either would otherwise have been likely to adopt. Heavily outnumbered and outgunned, the industry was forced to seek help even from its perennial adversary, the United Mine Workers. The opposition, meanwhile, was able to enlist the aid of a host of environmental lobbyists. Clean air, mine safety, black-lung disease, the restoration of scarred landscapes—all were causes more appealing to the national editorial pages than marginal cost savings to an industry long regarded as equally callous toward the public and its own employees. Given the circumstances, Congressional support for the environmental side was not long in mobilizing.

As the din of battle rose, the propaganda barrages launched by each side became at once more strident and more simplistic. Time, energy, and resources were preempted by the preparation of blasts and counterblasts to campaign for public support. The tasks of painstaking cost-benefit analysis and careful draftsmanship were pushed aside by tactical maneuvers, infighting, lobbying, and the exertion of pressure, all at the expense of substance.

By the end of the decade, 13 major federal laws affecting coal mining and use had been enacted, including the Federal Coal Mine Health and Safety Act of 1969, the Federal Coal Leasing Amendments Act of 1975 and 1976, the Federal Mine Safety and Health Act of 1977, and the Surface Mining Control and Reclamation Act of 1977. Rushed to final passage in the closing hours of Congressional sessions, many of these statutory provisions are clumsy, crude, and ambiguous. The industry had won some victories, but even these were marred by the necessity for haste. Instead of reflecting a careful balance among valid competing interests, the resulting regulations are excessively cumbersome, voluminous, and conducive to continuing conflict. Looking back, a leading industry spokesman remarked ruefully, "Almost without exception we found ourselves in a reactive mode, scrambling to cope with laws passed and regulations proposed rather than having a meaningful say at the conceptual stage."[6]

Apart from the likelihood that regulatory warfare will lead to a bad result from the corporate as well as the public standpoint, there is a second reason why the problem-solving approach is better for both.

Suppose that the private-sector side, by pulling out every stop, gains an all-out victory. What has it actually won? The very fact that business is perceived to have swept the field creates an inherently unstable situation. Such an outcome virtually guarantees the reopening of the battle as soon as the vanquished proponents of the public side are able to regroup, augment their forces, and launch a counterattack. Any bargain in which one side has been overreached, or is perceived to have overreached, is similarly flawed, especially where the losing side retains the power to get even. And this is a power the general public, through government, always possesses. The more badly, therefore, the public side is beaten, the greater the likelihood that its eventual vindication will bring with it a substantial measure of retribution.

Apart from the consideration that what may at first look like total victory is likely in due course to prove Pyrrhic, it is also well to keep in view the fact that one possible result of an all-or-nothing gamble is a total loss. This outcome carries with it a triple penalty: an unsatisfactory and unworkable regulatory result, a legacy of hostility on the part of the forces holding ultimate power, and an unrewarded investment in a costly undertaking.

One instructive example can be found in the failure of the business community to develop a coherent strategy toward the threat of criminal penalties for improper payments in other countries. In 1975-76 the Securities and Exchange Commission had uncovered a considerable number of such payments, and the situation was rapidly developing into a major scandal. At this point, as Secretary of Commerce, I arranged to meet with the Business Council in order to try to persuade its members to deal with questionable corporate payments abroad through a voluntary code of ethics. Although many individual companies did adopt their own codes, others were reluctant to handicap themselves competitively against their foreign rivals by voluntarily forswearing the use of questionable payments in countries where such payments were a normal business practice. Neither the Business Council nor any of the several other business groups I approached could be convinced to take any action at all. The Congressional reaction, meanwhile, was gathering force. Brushing aside the Administration's argument that a disclosure requirement should be sufficient to alert other countries to the possible violation of their own laws, Congress made it a crime under United States law to pay a bribe in another country. Congress is at present (1982) considering legislation pulling back from this anomaly.

As an antidote to the combative impulse, I venture to offer a practical rule of thumb. It is that a strategy that seeks to benefit a narrow corporate interest at substantial expense to a broad public interest is almost invariably misguided. The strategy, in other words, should never aim at a cost-benefit equation that cannot persuasively be defended as producing a net balance favorable to the public interest.

Lest the merits of the broad-gauged, long-range, problem-solving approach seem to have been overstated, a qualifying comment is in order. It does not follow from this approach that the wider, longer-range considerations should invariably prevail. They could be given their full due and still not justify the subordination of a narrower, shorter-range interest. In this connection, the strategist's task is basically that of identifying the values appropriate to each of the relevant considerations.

Where the other elements of the situation are weak or inconclusive a single dominant factor can be decisive. One such factor might be the predictable force of a negative public reaction. Only some truly extraordinary short-run consideration, for example, would warrant a flat refusal to stop the leakage of radioactive wastes. Another such factor might be the exorbitant cost of compliance. For example, a small marginal risk should not be allowed to compel the installation of sophisticated stack scrubbers at vast expense. In situations where the factors involved are more closely balanced and more numerous, the analysis becomes more complicated, but the problem is no different in kind.

Apart from the external factors creating choices between broad and narrow, long- and short-range objectives, the strategic planner may also be called upon to deal with choices arising out of conflicts internal to the corporation, the industry to which it belongs, or business generally. Many such choices present similar multidimensional aspects. These have to be sorted out, separately assessed, and—so far as reasonably possible—factored into the larger picture. There are inevitable limits to this analytical process, of course. Given the complexities of the issues and the necessity for dealing with them in a limited period of time, it is seldom realistic to insist upon a neatly ordered solution. Nevertheless, as John Gardner, the former head of Common Cause, once remarked, it is in a sense possible to have your cake and eat it too: the trick is to achieve a synthesis that can embrace elements that only *seem* irreconcilable.

The exercise comes full circle when, as is often the case, the internal choices are themselves subject to influence by external factors. An energy company, for example, aware that its oil and gas explorations may not be successful, might plausibly be faced with the question of whether it should hedge against that possibility by investing in oil-shale development or by building a slurry pipeline for the transportation of its coal. Each alternative will have proponents within the company who, in advocating the interests of their own corporate divisions, are likely to stress such purely economic factors as extraction, construction, and operating costs, distribution and marketing requirements, and, not least, the likely trend of oil prices. To this mix of short- and long-term economic factors the company's financial officers can be expected to add the company's cash position, tax situation, borrowing capacity, and so on, and these too will have to be addressed in both short- and long-range terms.

Except in the unusual situation where the combined economic and financial analysis has produced a lopsided result, the probable impact of the applicable public policies will also have to be taken into account. Such an assessment involves three distinct elements:

1. *The prediction of substantive policies.* In the case assumed, prediction would necessitate sorting out the competing public

interests in the cheap transportation of coal, the economic health of the railroad industry, and the conservation of scarce water resources (one major pipeline would require 15,000 to 20,000 acre feet of water per year) in order to assess the prospects for legislation granting the power of eminent domain for rights-of-way over private property.

2. *The identification of procedural obstacles.* What agencies at what levels of government have jurisdiction over what components of the project? Which agencies can in effect exercise veto power over the entire project by refusing to approve a part of it? A depressing case in point is the pipeline proposed by Sohio for the transportation of Alaskan oil from California to the Midwest. Although every indication pointed to the economic feasibility of the project, its sponsors gave up in despair over the practical impossibility of securing timely acquiescence from the multitude of authorities involved. Developers of coal slurry pipelines are confronted by similar problems under bills now pending in the House and Senate which leave control over water and environmental issues to the individual states traversed by the pipeline.

3. *Appraisal of the practical opportunities to influence the substance and cope with the procedure.* In the case of the slurry pipeline, success will depend on demonstrating two propositions: (a) that excessive costs to the public will result from leaving monopoly power over the bulk transportation of coal in the hands of the railroads and (b) that slurry pipelines require less water per ton of coal than such on-site processes as coal gasification or thermal electric generation. In the case of oil-shale, the railroads are not a factor, but water-use problems are, if anything, even more acute, and opposition by environmental groups is formidable. For the planner, the factors of internal choice as well as of external strategy are full of imponderables, and the planners could do worse than urge that the outcome should turn on a cold-eyed calculation of the strength of the political forces that are or could be arrayed on each side of each issue.

At this point, someone will no doubt observe that the discussion has up to now attributed the same weight to a given factor no matter where it fits on the time scale. And it is of course true that, like the bird in hand, a given benefit obtainable now is worth more than the same benefit deferred some years into the future. It may thus be in the corporation's interest to seek a short-term gain—immediate improvement of the bottom line, for instance—where the long-term cost is merely conjectural. But where it is probable not only that the long-term cost will be incurred but that it will more than wipe out the short-term gain, the situation is the same as any other in which an immediate satisfaction has to be weighed against a future benefit. If the indulgence of the former forces the subordination of the latter, what the incumbent managers and the present generation of shareholders gain will have been obtained at the expense of their successors. The public interest is also a long-term loser. And when the next generation wakes up to the realization that its interests have been sacrificed, its resentment could have repercussions damaging to the free enterprise system itself.

In the defense of a bias in favor of birds in the hand as against discounted future values, it can of course be argued that the latter are fiendishly difficult to assess. And certainly the calculation is seldom as easy as it is made to seem by the assumptions stated in the preceding paragraph. To take a harder example, suppose that the question is whether Petroco, an American oil company owning 10 million barrels of oil in the continental United States and another 10 million barrels in a Persian Gulf country, should maximize its lifting of the foreign oil in order to conserve the domestic oil. What are the long-term and short-term interests at stake? Do the company's interests differ from the public interests?

The problem is capable of infinitely elaborate analysis. But it can be approached systematically. To avoid circularity (and the tail wagging the dog), I would address the public interest question first. Its answer depends on such factors as (a) the relative proportion of foreign imports to total domestic consumption, (b) the rate at which new domestic hydrocarbon reserves are being discovered, (c) the adequacy of the national petroleum reserve and the pace of its buildup, (d) the foreseeable development of alternative energy sources, and (e) the rapidity with which we could expand reliance on domestic petroleum reserves in the event of some new curtailment of the Middle Eastern supply. Only if it were possible to base a relatively clear national policy on this analysis could it then be said that a course of action proposed by Petroco's management was or was not consistent with the long-term public interest.

The resulting policy could, of course, be wrong. Hard issues can make bad policy just as hard cases can make bad law. This situation is all the more likely when perceptions, particularly political perceptions, are given precedence over the underlying realities. But the fact that it is necessary to distinguish between perceptions and realities (however the distinction may be drawn) need not vitiate the analysis; the perceptions belong in the equation no less than the realities. Both are relevant to the planning process.

The basic point, in any case, is *not* that sound analysis will always produce the right result, nor that hard cases can be made simple, nor that long-term interests automatically deserve to prevail over short-term interests. The point is, rather, that narrow, short-term interests all too often prevail over long-term interests in situations where any objective analysis would show that such a result is demonstrably wrong. And yet just such distorted judgments are a constant occurrence. These judgments can be accounted for by any of several factors: that senior managers coming close to retirement have only a short time-horizon, that the corporation's planning does not give adequate weight to strategies for dealing with long-term public issues, or that the analysis itself is poor. When to all of these factors is added the tendency to address public-policy issues in an adversarial manner, it is only to be expected that the outcome should so often be clumsy, counterproductive, and wasteful.

The conclusions suggested by anecdotal evidence are corroborated by evidence of quite a different sort. When I came to the Department of Commerce in 1976, one of my first undertakings was to set up an advisory committee whose function was to test the potential for achieving some sort of consensus on issues affecting public confidence in business. The committee comprised a broadly representative, even heterogeneous, group. In addition to chief executive officers from every major field of business, it included such diverse personalities as the well-known environmentalist, Barry Commoner; Jesse Jackson of Operation PUSH; Carol Foreman of the Consumer Federation of America; and Irving Bluestone of the United Automobile Workers.

The advisory committee's first meeting was devoted to the question of corporate responsibility. One might have supposed that individuals of such differing backgrounds could not possibly get together on any definition of such a controversial concept. And yet toward the end of our first meeting there began to emerge agreement, if not on a definition, at least on an approach to a definition that accords remarkably well with the behavior of our best-managed companies. Without calling into question the corporation's primary and inescapable responsibility to shareholders—a responsibility that accepts obligations for the maximization of earnings, the conservation of assets, and the appreciation of shareholders' equity—the definition of corporate responsibility is an approach that addresses these obligations within the framework of wide contemporary horizons and a long-term future. The best interests of the corporation are perceived as inseparably bound up with the well-being both of the smaller communities where its employees work and of the larger community—regional, national, even global—within which it conducts its business. This kind of enlarged vision both of the contemporary world and of the foreseeable future tends automatically to elicit a responsible attitude toward issues of public policy.

One component of this broad-gauged view of corporate responsibility is awareness that business has a stake in earning and keeping public confidence. Such confidence is a resource which serves the same function in the world of business as that served in the conduct of foreign policy by the cultivation of good relations with other countries. Public confidence and good foreign relations are assets that may be needed when push comes to shove in a time of crisis; both ought therefore to be built up and husbanded in normal times. In the case of business, a lack of public confidence diminishes business' ability to win support in any conflict over a policy issue. And when lack of confidence gives way to distrust, the burden of persuasion thereby imposed on business becomes immeasurably heavier.

In light of these considerations, the polling data indicating that public confidence in business has been slipping should be a matter of serious concern. It would be wrong, however, to assume that the blame belongs wholly to the private sector. "We the people" have unwittingly contributed to the erosion of our own confidence in business. We have thoughtlessly been looking to business to provide us with the highest quality product, at the lowest possible price, manufactured under conditions of maximum safety, minimum impact on the environment, and the largest possible conservation of energy, while at the same time earning a rate of return necessary to attract the capital required to provide the plant and equipment needed to employ ever larger numbers of workers at continually increasing wages. We do not seem even to notice the fact that there are necessary tradeoffs among these objectives. If, therefore, business tilts in favor of any one objective at the expense of another, it can expect to be attacked from the quarter of the disappointed expectation.

A dramatic illustration came to hand at about the time I first began to focus on this syndrome. It was the report of a Commerce Department study of the domestic steel industry showing that to fulfill 100 percent of the then-mandated (very high) environmental standards would require 10 percent more energy (a tremendous quantity) than would be needed to achieve 85 percent (still a high level) of those same requirements. Which public interest—energy conservation or environmental protection—should have priority? This, plainly, is a political, not an economic, much less a business, issue.

Business is fairly chargeable, nevertheless, with blurring the responsibility for choice. Why should a corporation commit itself to one side of a contest between competing public goals when it has no stake of its own in the outcome? Instead of seeking simply to make clear what some new regulatory requirement would cost in terms of higher prices or foregone benefits, the typical corporation obeys a reflexive impulse to behave as if it had a vested interest in preventing any cost from being incurred. The automobile industry, for example, fought against stricter exhaust emission standards as if it had a stake coequal with that of the general public in the choice between cleaner air and higher automobile prices, which of course it does not. As recent polling data have made clear, most people regard clean air as an economic good that they are willing to pay for. How much they value it is their business.

Some companies have seen the light. The coal and electric utility industries, for example, are attempting to respond to the public concern about acid rain by encouraging a thorough scientific analysis of the adequacy of the data on which this concern is based and to promote an intelligent assessment of the costs associated with implementation of the policies being advocated. Also in point is the

Cummins Engine Company's approach to the new emissions standards for heavy-duty diesel engines proposed by Environmental Protection Agency (EPA). Although implementation of these more stringent standards would be expensive, Cummins acknowledged at the outset that standard-setting should be health-based. Noting that there would always be varying degrees of uncertainty about the factors relevant to rational standard-setting, it agreed that society has the right as a matter of prudence, despite the inconclusiveness of the evidence, to promulgate standards reasonable in cost and technical achievability. These considerations led Cummins to suggest that EPA establish on a set schedule a repetitive standard-setting process for regulating all emissions from heavy-duty diesel engines, thus ensuring reasonably achievable standards in the short run and promising better information on which to base future standards—stricter if necessary—over the longer run. This would enable the necessary trade-offs to be made as reasonably as possible, avoid "winner-take-all" rule making, and assure to the public steady improvements in public health and air quality. The more typical reaction—taking a hard-line opening position and then digging in—would have precipitated a head-on confrontation with environmental and health-oriented citizens groups and thereby weakened the company's ability to help bring about a sensible outcome.

We are also beginning to see examples of corporate efforts to communicate with groups which, because they were so long ignored, had acquired the habit of pursuing their grievances through regulatory channels. ARCO recently sponsored a two-day conference for its senior managers and representatives of a wide array of environmental groups. The conference was a success because it was held without reference to any immediate problem, because it was agreed that it should be periodically reconvened, and because of its direct and continuous involvement of key corporate decision-makers.

Another example is the National Coal Policy Project which came together because both the coal mining industry and environmental groups "found the existing adversary system more often than not to be time-consuming, expensive, and unpredictable; apparent victories often turned out to be hollow as the confrontation moved from one arena to another." The project's stated aim was to escape the adversary relationship that dominated "the legislative, regulatory, and legal process where the parties at issue were most likely to meet."[7] The project provided instead a setting in which the parties could discuss their differences candidly and openly. The results have been substantial. In addition to formulating more than 200 policy recommendations that have resulted in new laws and simpler regulations, the project has contributed to more enlightened debate on such issues as slurry pipelines, electric power rate-making, and railroad deregulation.[8]

Although less relevant to the strategic planning process, examples of devices for escaping from the other end of the adversary trap are even more numerous. Some of these techniques, particularly mediation, can be as useful in developing the consensus that heads off a dispute as in developing the consensus that resolves a dispute. In each case, the keys to the process are techniques for managing animosity and distrust and for revealing the competing and overlapping values at stake.[9]

Nowhere is the new mood more evident, perhaps, than in the case of new procedures for dealing with consumer-related disputes in the area of product and service warranties, consumer credit, and products liability.[10] These procedures have been found useful in providing consumers with easy means of communicating with the seller, in supplying feedback with regard to new products and product design, and in deflecting litigation. One company has even revived the maxim that the customer is always right.[11]

Better communication with citizen groups and better dispute-settlement procedures, however, can only supplement, but not supplant, the need for better strategic planning. In the case of complex public-policy issues, such planning requires effective coordination among each of the special capabilities required for the plan's formulation and execution. These capabilities include policy analysis; legal, legislative, and lobbying skills; and communications, media, public relations, and advertising. All of them should, of course, draw on the economic and financial information already provided to the corporation for its analysis of the factors antecedent to the public policy issues, supplementing them as necessary.

Awareness of the interrelatedness of these professional capabilities has already led, as Reich has pointed out, to the creation of "integrated 'full service' organizations modeled after the public interest groups that since the mid-1960s have coordinated information, legal representation, administrative tactics, and political pressure within a single, overall strategy."[12] Although Reich is concerned that the trend toward the integration of services may exacerbate the tension between business and government, this danger would be radically diminished if the strategic approach advocated here were to gain broad acceptance. It is one thing to devote an integrated array of resources to a short-range confrontational purpose and quite another to apply it to the goal of a wise accommodation among the relevant claims legitimately entitled to public recognition. Just such accommodations, indeed, are what the political process is all about.

One last ingredient of the role of effective Washington representation in strategic planning remains to be mentioned—that of generalship. If the several components of a sound strategic plan are to make their appropriate contributions to a coherent whole, they must have coordinated direction. The team needs a quarterback. For this role, breadth of experience and a capacity for judgment tested under pressure are indispensable requirements. The successful execution of the strategic plan depends on the degree to which these qualities are brought to bear on the public policy process. They are also, as it happens, the qualities that chiefly distinguish Washington's most respected representatives of private-sector interests.

The tidal wave of regulation that inundated business in the 70's is receding. Constructive steps toward deregulation are under way. But the lessons of the past will have been only partly effective if their teaching is applied solely to the formulation of regulations and not to the shaping of the public policies from which regulations emerge.

The future, like the past, will face its own share of problems calling for some form of government intervention. The current revolution in information processing and communications technology will in due course overturn the present pattern of regulations governing financial-service institutions, and the question of what the new pattern should look like is a prime candidate for broad-gauged, imaginative strategic planning. Biological engineering and the new kinds of relationships between commercial producers of genetic material and institutions of higher education have already given rise to a host of complex and baffling problems whose solution will require much time and thought. The extent to which employers should be made the first line of defense against an ever-increasing flood of illegal immigrants, and the manner in which this should be done, are equally demanding concerns. To cite an even more difficult example, the more efficient management of the by-products of global interdependence in the whole range from technology transfer to transborder data flows is a challenge whose full dimensions are only beginning to emerge.

Business can be either a willing partner in the solution of these and other foreseeable problems or an unwilling victim of solutions imposed by others. This is the fundamental choice that has to be made. If business does not begin to think, to plan, and to act in strategic terms, it will have become a victim by default. And that, surely, would be un-American!

FOOTNOTES

[1]Department of Energy Annual Report, the Industrial Energy Efficiency Improvement Program, at 6 (December 1980). This, of course, was a situation in which voluntary action yielded direct and immediate benefits to the companies' bottom lines. A more persuasive example would be one in which an industry, in order to forestall the higher long-term costs of additional regulation, adopted a voluntary program at additional cost without receiving any immediate payback. I have not found any such example.

[2]R. Reich, *Regulation by Confrontation or Negotiation?*, 59 Harv. Bus. Rev. 82 (1981).

[3]E. Dauer, *Proceedings of the Conference on Environmental Disputes* (April 30-May 1, 1981), in A Manual of Innovative Corporate Strategies for the Avoidance and Resolution of Legal Disputes VII-C.1, C.4 (Supp. 5, 1981) (published by The Center for Public Resources, Inc., 1980).

[4]Speech by Judge Henry J. Friendly, 31 Harv. L. Sch. Bull. 34, 36 (Fall 1979).

[5]R. Reich, *supra* note 2, at 93.

[6]Remarks by G. Jackson, Director of Planning, Peabody Coal Company, at the MMIJ/AIME Joint Meeting in Tokyo 7 (November 4-8, 1980) (discussing the mining industry in a regulated environment).

[7]F. Murray, *The National Coal Policy Project*, in A Manual of Innovative Corporate Strategies for the Avoidance and Resolution of Legal Disputes II-A. 1, A.5 (1980).

[8]*Id.* at II-A. 11.

[9]E. Dauer, *supra* note 3, at VII-C.6.

[10]E. Dauer, *Proceedings of the Consumer Disputes Task Force* (May 1981), in A Manual of Innovative Corporate Strategies for the Avoidance and Resolution of Legal Disputes VII-D.1 (Supp. 5, 1981).

[11]*Id.* at VII-D.5.

[12]R. Reich, *supra* note 2, at 86.